Better Homes and Gardens.

365

vegetarian
meals

inspiring meals for every day of the year

Published by John Wiley & Sons, Inc., Hoboken, New Jersey

Published simultaneously in Canada

For general information on our other products and services or for technical support, please contact our Customer Care Department within the United States at (877) 762–2974, outside the United States at (317) 572–3993 or fax (317) 572–4002.

Wiley also publishes its books in a variety of electronic formats. Some content that appears in print may not be available in electronic books. For more information about Wiley products, visit our web site at www.wiley.com.

Library of Congress Cataloging-in-Publication Data

Better homes & gardens 365 vegetarian meals.

    p. cm. -- (Better homes & gardens cooking ; 48)

Better homes and gardens 365 vegetarian meals

Includes index.

    ISBN 978-0-470-88660-1 (pbk.); 978-0-470-94695-4 (ebk.); 978-0-470-94696-1 (ebk.); 978-0-470-94697-8 (ebk.)

1. Vegetarian cooking. 2. Cookbooks. I. Better homes and gardens.

TX837.B4856 2011

641.5'636--dc22

                 2010042160

Better Homes and Gardens® 365 Vegetarian Meals

Meredith Corporation
Editor: Jan Miller, R.D.
Contributing Editor: Sheena Chihak, R.D.
Recipe Development and Testing:
Better Homes and Gardens® Test Kitchen

John Wiley & Sons, Inc.
Publisher: Natalie Chapman
Executive Editor: Anne Ficklen
Editor: Charleen Barila
Production Editor: Abby Saul
Production Director: Diana Cisek
Interior Design: Jill Budden
Layout: Indianapolis Composition Services
Manufacturing Manager: Tom Hyland

Our seal on the back cover of this book assures you that every recipe in *365 Vegetarian Meals* has been tested in the Better Homes and Gardens® Test Kitchen. This means that each recipe is practical and reliable, and meets our high standards of taste appeal. We guarantee your satisfaction with this book for as long as you own it.

Table of Contents

Vegetarian Basics 4

1 Breakfast 11

2 Slow Cooker 43

3 Short & Simple 73

4 Pasta 111

5 Pizzas & Sandwiches . . . 163

6 Salads 199

7 Grilling 231

8 Casseroles 263

9 Beans, Rice, & Grains . . 319

10 Soups & Stews 369

Metric Information . . 402

Index 403

Vegetarian Basics
Go Veggie!

There are many reasons to choose a vegetarian diet. And there are plenty of delicious and satisfying foods for vegetarians to eat.

VEG OUT FOR YOUR HEALTH

A meatless diet is generally lower in saturated fat and cholesterol. It also tends to be higher in fiber and some vitamins and minerals, such as vitamins A and C, potassium, and magnesium.

Vegetarian diets are linked with lower rates of cancer and a reduced risk of heart disease, high blood pressure, osteoporosis, and type 2 diabetes. Many vegetarians have lower cholesterol and a lower body mass index than nonvegetarians.

IT'S EASIER THAN YOU THINK

Remember when the word "vegetarian" brought to mind tasteless tofu and salads for every meal? Those days are long gone. Today you can choose from a variety of delicious meatless convenience products or whip up a homemade dish using fresh, local, and organic ingredients.

Here are some ideas for making flavorful vegetarian meals.

Go Local. The movement to buy local is bigger than ever. Foods that don't have to be shipped long distances are often fresher and taste better. As an added bonus, less shipping is good for the environment.

Farm It. Food you grow yourself is as local as it gets. Meals made with garden-fresh ingredients are bursting with flavor and considerably less expensive. Plus you can grow them your way—without herbicides or pesticides.

Follow the Season. Enjoy produce at its peak by buying in season. Sure, you can find pears year-round. But you'll get the most flavorful ones in the fall.

Go Whole. Flavors in food diminish the more the food is processed. Choose whole, unprocessed foods without artificial flavors, colors, or preservatives for the best taste and nutrition.

Join a CSA. When you join a CSA (community-supported agriculture group), you pay a farmer to raise your food. During the growing season, you'll receive fresh produce every week. It's a great way to support a local farmer, and it can help you eat a greater variety of veggies, greens, and herbs.

Veg-ify your life in 4 easy steps

Not a vegetarian yet? These simple steps will ease you into the veggie way of living.

1 Start by listing some meatless foods you already enjoy, such as pasta with marinara sauce, cheese pizza, or veggie stir-fry.

2 Next think of the meat-containing foods you currently eat and find ways to make them without meat. For instance, instead of beef tacos, prepare them with beans or soy crumbles.

3 Now head to the grocery store and check out the vegetarian options available in every aisle. Also research what restaurants in your area offer vegetarian options.

4 You will discover that you have lots of foods to choose from. Now it's time to eat! That doesn't mean you have to be a full vegetarian right away. Start by replacing one or two meals a week with a meatless option. Even a few meatless meals each week can contribute to a more healthful lifestyle.

Nutrition: What to Watch For

Despite all the benefits of a vegetarian diet, going veggie can leave you missing out on some important nutrients. As with any diet, you need to plan your meals and snacks so that they include a variety of nutritious foods that will meet your specific needs.

WHAT'S MISSING?

The nutrients that are most likely to be lacking in vegetarian diets include vitamin B_{12}, vitamin D, iron, calcium, zinc, and omega-3 fatty acids. Because these nutrients are typically found in many animal products, it makes sense that these nutrients could be a concern, especially if you're vegan or don't eat a well-rounded vegetarian diet.

The good news is that lots of products are fortified with vitamins and minerals. For instance, soymilk is often fortified with calcium and vitamin D. Hot and cold cereals are fortified with many vitamins and minerals, including B vitamins, iron, calcium, vitamin D, and zinc. And some breads, yogurts, and juices are fortified with omega-3 fatty acids.

If you're concerned that you're not getting enough nutrients in your diet, consult with a registered dietitian (R.D.). An R.D. can help determine what nutrients are lacking in your diet. This is especially important if you're pregnant or breastfeeding. If the youngsters or teens in your home are following a vegetarian diet, an R.D. can help you make sure their diet has enough calories and nutrients for healthy growth.

CONCERNS ABOUT PROTEIN

Many vegetarians are worried about getting enough protein. If you eat dairy products, eggs, or soy, you're probably getting a good amount of protein from those foods alone. In fact, research shows that even vegans, who don't eat any animal products, are meeting or even exceeding their protein needs each day.

In addition to getting enough protein, you may worry about getting the right type of protein. That's because the protein in plants is not the same as the protein in animals. Plant proteins lack certain amino acids that the body needs. That's why vegetarians used to be told to combine different foods, such as beans and corn, in order to make a "complete protein." Research now shows that these foods don't have to be eaten together at the same meal. As long as you eat a variety of foods each day, your body will get the amino acids it needs.

Protein by the Numbers

How much protein do you need? Not that much.

Experts recommend that 10% to 30% of the calories in your diet come from protein. For adult men, the recommended daily allowance (RDA) is 56 grams. For adult women, the RDA is 46 grams or 71 grams if the woman is pregnant or breast-feeding. Divided throughout the day, that's about 19 grams per meal for men or 15 grams per meal for women. Those are general recommendations.

To figure individual needs, try this. Multiply your weight in pounds by 0.36 to get the grams of protein you need each day. That calculation works for most healthy adults (who aren't pregnant or breast-feeding). Because plant proteins are used by the body differently than animal proteins, some experts suggest vegans eat slightly more protein. The calculation for vegans is 0.45 gram of protein per pound of body weight. For athletes, protein needs may be higher depending on the intensity of their training. Athletes, especially endurance athletes, should see a registered dietitian (R.D.) to help determine their individual needs.

THE UNHEALTHY VEGETARIAN

People new to being vegetarian sometimes make the mistake of relying on meat-less versions of their favorite convenience foods, which tend to be high in fat, calories, and sodium. Or they load up on refined carbohydrates, such as white bread and pasta, or add high-fat cheese to everything.

The key to following a healthful vegetarian diet is similar to following any healthy diet—just without the meat. Focus on whole grains, legumes, low-fat dairy (if you eat dairy), fruits, and vegetables. It's OK to have convenience products but eat them only occasionally and focus on whole, unprocessed foods for the majority of meals.

MIX UP YOUR MENU

It's easy to get in a rut of eating the same thing day in and day out. If rice and pasta are your only go-to grains or tofu is your standby protein source, start mixing things up.

Varying the foods you eat helps you have a more nutritious diet, especially if you add lots of colorful fruits and vegetables and high-fiber whole grains. Trade in that bowl of rice for barley or quinoa. Buy a vegetable you've never tried. Check out all the different types of beans available and add some new ones to your meals.

This cookbook includes a wide variety of different grains, veggies, and meatless protein sources combined in delicious, creative ways. Once you get used to buying and cooking with these ingredients, start including them in more meals to keep your diet fresh and flavorful.

What type are you?

Do people ever ask you what type of vegetarian you are? Are you unsure how to answer? Here's a quick guide to the different types of vegetarians.

- **Flexitarian.** Eats a mostly vegetarian diet but occasionally will eat meat.
- **Lacto-ovo vegetarian.** Eats no animal meat but does eat eggs and dairy products.
- **Lacto-vegetarian.** Eats no animal meat or eggs but does eat dairy products.
- **Ovo-vegetarian.** Eats no animal meat or dairy products but does eat eggs.
- **Pesco-vegetarian.** Eats no animal meat except for fish. Also eats eggs and dairy products.
- **Raw food vegan.** Similar diet restriction as a vegan but will not eat foods heated above 115°F.
- **Semi-vegetarian:** Eats no red meat but does eat poultry, fish, eggs, and dairy products.
- **Vegan.** Eats no animal meat, dairy, eggs, animal products, or animal by-products. Look for this icon throughout the book for recipes that meet vegan criteria.

Guide to Grains

Whether you top rice with stir-fried veggies, add barley to soup, or toss cooked quinoa in a salad, grains are a versatile staple in many vegetarian diets.

As you plan your meals, remember to make sure that at least half of the grains you eat are whole grains. All of the grains listed are whole grains except for white, Arborio, and converted rice.

White rice Basic white rice comes in long, medium, and short grain. If you want sticky rice (the kind served in Asian restaurants), choose short grain rice. Its high starch content helps it stick together when cooked. Medium or long grain rice is lighter and fluffier when cooked. To save time, buy instant or quick-cooking rice, which is partially or fully cooked before it's packaged.

Arborio rice High in starch, this Italian short grain rice is most often used for risotto. The starch helps give the dish its signature creaminess.

Converted rice This type of white rice has been parboiled before it goes through the refining process, which helps retains some B vitamins. Brown rice. Unlike white rice, brown rice still has its germ and bran layer intact. This gives it more nutrients and fiber.

Wild rice It's included in the rice family, but wild rice is actually a grass. Although it has a long cooking time, its nutty taste and chewy texture are worth the wait. Wild rice is sold in a bag or box in the rice aisle of most stores.

Quinoa It looks like a tiny grain, so it's treated like one. But quinoa is actually a relative of Swiss chard and spinach. Quinoa is great for vegetarians because of its complete protein. It's also quick and easy to make—ready in about 15 minutes. Many stores carry quinoa in the health food section or the pasta and rice aisle. You'll find it at health food stores as well.

Barley For the most health benefits, seek out hulled or hulless barley, which has more of its fiber-rich bran layer left than pearl barley, which has little to no bran layer. The soluble fiber in barley may help reduce cholesterol and manage blood glucose. But when you're short on time, pearl barley is faster to cook. Pearl barley is sold in bags or boxes in the rice and pasta aisle. For hulled or hulless barley, you'll need to go to a health food store or the health food section of a large supermarket.

Bulgur This versatile grain cooks up fast and has more fiber than both quinoa and oats. Bulgur is made by boiling and drying wheat kernels. A Middle Eastern favorite, bulgur is most known as the main ingredient in tabbouleh. Find it in the pasta and rice aisle of large supermarkets or in the store's health food section. It's also sold in

health food stores and some ethnic grocery stores.

Spelt With its tough outer husk, spelt is a type of wheat used for animal feed. But many people are cooking with it because of its high protein content and nutty, slightly sweet flavor. You can find spelt berries in bulk or bags in the health food section of large supermarkets or at a health food store. These places often carry spelt products such as spelt flour, bread, and pasta.

Buckwheat A relative of rhubarb, buckwheat isn't a grain but looks and tastes like one and is often included in lists of grains. Buckwheat—ln the form of buckwheat flour—is used to make soba, a Japanese noodle. You can also steam buckwheat groats and serve them for breakfast in place of oatmeal or serve as a side dish instead of rice. You'll find buckwheat in bulk or bags at health food stores or the health food section of large supermarkets.

Wheat berries Wheat kernels that are kept whole are called wheat berries. Usually you soak them overnight, then boil them for about an hour to make them tender and chewy. Find them in bags or bulk in health food stores or the health food section of large supermarkets.

Cracked wheat As the name implies, cracked wheat is just wheat kernels that have been broken apart so water can quickly get in the kernels, helping them cook quickly. Many people eat it as a hot cereal, but you can also try adding a little cracked wheat to baked goods and casseroles to add texture and fiber.

Cracked wheat is sold in bulk or bags in health food stores or the health food section of large supermarkets.

Oats Some people think instant oats are too processed to be a whole grain; however, most all oats you buy contain the whole grain. During processing, oats are steamed, then flattened. But the germ and fiber-rich bran layers remain. The more steaming and flattening, the faster they cook, as in the case of instant oats. If the oat kernel is left whole but simply chopped into pieces, the result is steel-cut oats. All oats are high in soluble fiber, which may help lower cholesterol.

Guide to Legumes

High fiber and phytonutrients and low in fat, beans and legumes are essential to a healthy vegetarian diet. These hearty ingredients are inexpensive and can offer texture, flavor, and important vitamins and minerals to your meal.

Beans, lentils, peas, and peanuts are all part of the legume family. Legumes are plants that have pods with edible seeds inside. Most legumes are high in fiber, especially soluble fiber that can help lower cholesterol. They also have protein. Some, such as soybeans and peanuts, have healthy fats as well.

Beans There are lots of different types of beans, making them a useful food ingredient for adding color and flavor to your meals. The most commonly eaten beans in the U.S. are black beans, red kidney beans, Great Northern beans, pinto beans, and navy beans. That's why you'll usually find these beans sold ready to eat in cans.

You can find a wider variety of beans in dried form. Dried beans are often found in bags next to the canned beans or in bulk bins at health food stores. Many people avoid dried beans because they aren't sure how to cook them, but dried beans are actually very easy to cook. They just take more time because they need to be soaked and boiled. And home-cooked beans are much lower in sodium than canned beans.

Soybeans A great substitute for meat, soybeans provide good amounts of complete protein as well as iron and omega-3 fatty acids. Although soy's benefits are still being debated, research indicates that soy may help ease menopausal symptoms, manage blood glucose levels in people with diabetes, lower cholesterol, and even prevent some cancers.

Soy is found in many different forms: tofu, tempeh, edamame, soy flour, soy nuts, and many processed soy products (bars, imitation meat). The form you buy it in will determine where you'll find it in the store.

Lentils When time is short, make lentils for a side dish or to mix into your main dish. Most lentils cook in 30 minutes or less, and red lentils cook even faster. You can mix chilled cooked lentils into a salad, add dried lentils to soups, and use hot cooked lentils to boost the protein in veggie stir-fries.

You'll find bags of brown, green, and red lentils in the bean aisle of large supermarkets. Look for other types of lentils in bulk or bags at health food stores.

Cooking Dry Legumes

Rinse beans, lentils, and split peas. (See special cooking instructions, below, for black-eyed peas, fava beans, lentils, and split peas.) In a large Dutch oven combine 1 pound beans and 8 cups cold water. Bring to boiling; reduce heat and simmer for 2 minutes. Remove from heat. Cover and let stand for 1 hour. (Or omit simmering; soak beans in cold water overnight in a covered Dutch oven.) Drain and rinse. In the same Dutch oven combine beans and 8 cups fresh water. Bring to boiling; reduce heat and simmer, covered, for time listed below or until beans are tender, stirring occasionally.

VARIETY	AMOUNT	COOKING TIME	YIELD
Black beans	1 pound	1 to 1½ hours	6 cups
Black-eyed peas	1 pound	Do not presoak. Simmer, covered, for 45 minutes to 1 hour.	7 cups
Fava beans	1 pound	Bring beans to boiling; simmer, covered, 15 to 30 minutes to soften skins. Let stand 1 hour. Drain and peel. To cook, combine peeled beans and 8 cups fresh water. Bring to boiling; reduce heat. Simmer, covered, 45 to 50 minutes or until tender.	6 cups
Garbanzo beans (chickpeas)	1 pound	1½ to 2 hours	6¼ cups
Great Northern beans	1 pound	1 to 1½ hours	7 cups
Kidney beans, red	1 pound	1 to 1½ hours	6 ⅔ cups
Lentils (brown or French)	1 pound	Do not presoak. Use 5 cups water. Simmer, covered, about 30 minutes.	7 cups
Lima beans, Christmas (calico)	1 pound	45 minutes to 1 hour	6½ cups
Lima beans, large (butter beans)	1 pound	1 to 1¼ hours	6½ cups
Navy or pea beans	1 pound	1 to 1½ hours	6¼ cups
Pinto beans	1 pound	1¼ to 1½ hours	6½ cups
Red beans	1 pound	1 to 1½ hours	6½ cups
Soybeans	1 pound	3 to 3½ hours	7 cups
Split peas	1 pound	Do not presoak. Use 5 cups water. Simmer, covered, about 45 minutes.	5½ cups

Soy Staples

Soy-based products are very popular among vegetarians, particularly for their low calorie count and high protein content. Many of these ingredients are used in recipes throughout the book. Use this guide to learn more about each product and the best way to use them.

SOY TYPE	WHAT IT IS	HOW TO USE	SPECIAL FEATURES	WHERE TO FIND IT
Tofu	Also known as bean curd. Tofu is curdled soymilk.	Marinate or combine with other ingredients because it easily absorbs flavors; add to casseroles and stir-fries	Tofu comes in a range of textures from soft and silken to extra-firm. You can also purchase already flavored tofu.	Usually in the produce or dairy section of the supermarket
Soymilk	Liquid pressed from the soybean	In place of dairy milk	Lactose-free, cholesterol-free, and flavored varieties are available	In the dairy section
Tempeh	Fermented soybean	Marinate, grill, or fry as a meat substitute	Comes in one solid piece, often called a cake. Preseasoned varieties are available	In the refrigerator or freezer case. Store in the refrigerator up to 10 days or in the freezer up to 3 months.
Miso	Paste made from fermented grains and soy	In soups, marinades, dips, and sauces	May aid digestion	In the refrigerated section in Japanese markets and natural food stores
Soy Cheese	Cheese made from tofu or soymilk	In place of dairy cheeses	Loses some nutritional value in processing, but can be a good option if you avoid all animal products	In the produce or dairy section of the supermarket
Edamame	Fresh green soy beans	Boil and lightly salt for a snack; add to soups and noodle and rice dishes	Comes shelled or in pods, frozen or already cooked	In the produce or frozen vegetables section of the supermarket

Breakfast

Start your day right with one of these body- and brain-boosting breakfasts. Whether you have time for a decadent egg-based strata or just a grab-and-go breakfast bar, you'll find a recipe to kick-start your metabolism and your mind for a great day.

Cheddar and Zucchini Frittata

PREP: 20 minutes BAKE: 5 minutes OVEN: 450°F MAKES 4 servings

1 cup refrigerated or frozen egg
   product, thawed, or 4 eggs

½ cup finely shredded reduced-
   fat cheddar cheese (2 ounces)

2 tablespoons snipped fresh
   Italian (flat-leaf) parsley

¼ teaspoon ground black pepper

⅛ teaspoon salt

2 teaspoons olive oil

12 ounces zucchini, halved
    lengthwise and sliced

½ cup sliced green onions (4)

1 Position a rack in the upper third of the oven and preheat oven to 450°F. In a medium bowl whisk together egg, cheese, 1 tablespoon of the parsley, the pepper, and salt; set aside.

2 In a medium oven-going skillet heat oil over medium-high heat. Add zucchini and green onions; cook for 5 to 8 minutes or just until tender, stirring frequently.

3 Carefully pour egg mixture over vegetables in skillet. Cook over medium heat. As mixture sets, run a spatula around edge of skillet, lifting egg mixture so that the uncooked portion flows underneath. Continue cooking and lifting edge until egg mixture is nearly set and surface is just slightly moist.

4 Bake about 5 minutes or until frittata is firm and top is golden brown. Sprinkle with the remaining parsley.

PER SERVING: 115 cal., 5 g total fat (2 g sat. fat), 10 mg chol., 321 mg sodium, 6 g carb., 1 g fiber, 11 g pro.

tip

Add a protein punch to your morning meal with your favorite brand of soy bacon or soy sausage. Choose the microwave method and these products are ready in seconds. The additional protein will help keep you full longer.

Mediterranean Frittata

START TO FINISH: **25 minutes** MAKES **6 servings**

- 3 tablespoons olive oil
- 1 cup chopped onion (1 large)
- 2 cloves garlic, minced
- 8 eggs
- ¼ cup half-and-half, light cream, or milk
- ½ cup crumbled feta cheese (2 ounces)
- ½ cup chopped roasted red sweet peppers
- ½ cup sliced pitted kalamata or ripe olives (optional)
- ¼ cup shredded fresh basil
- ⅛ teaspoon ground black pepper
- ½ cup onion-and-garlic croutons, coarsely crushed
- 2 tablespoons finely shredded Parmesan cheese
- Fresh basil leaves (optional)

1 Preheat broiler. In a large broilerproof skillet heat 2 tablespoons of the oil over medium heat. Add onion and garlic; cook just until onion is tender, stirring occasionally.

2 Meanwhile, in a medium bowl whisk together eggs and half-and-half. Stir in feta cheese, roasted peppers, olives (if desired), shredded basil, and black pepper. Carefully pour egg mixture over onion mixture in skillet. Cook over medium heat. As mixture sets, run a spatula around edge of skillet, lifting egg mixture so that the uncooked portion flows underneath. Continue cooking and lifting edge until egg mixture is nearly set and surface is just slightly moist.

3 In a small bowl combine croutons, Parmesan cheese, and the remaining 1 tablespoon oil; sprinkle croutons over frittata.

4 Broil 4 to 5 inches from the heat for 1 to 2 minutes or until top is set and croutons are golden brown. Cut into wedges. If desired, garnish with basil leaves.

PER SERVING: *246 cal., 19 g total fat (5 g sat. fat), 295 mg chol., 383 mg sodium, 8 g carb., 1 g fiber, 11 g pro.*

Herbed Frittata with Edamame

START TO FINISH: 25 minutes MAKES 4 servings

8 eggs
⅓ cup water
¼ cup finely chopped green onions (2)
¼ cup snipped fresh cilantro
¼ teaspoon salt
¼ teaspoon ground black pepper
1 tablespoon olive oil
1 cup shredded Italian cheese blend (4 ounces)
1 cup frozen shelled sweet soybeans (edamame), thawed
1 medium carrot, shredded or cut into ribbons
  Fresh cilantro sprigs
  Shaved Parmesan cheese (optional)

1 Preheat broiler. In a medium bowl whisk together eggs, the water, green onions, snipped cilantro, salt, and pepper; set aside.

2 In a large broilerproof skillet with flared sides heat oil over medium heat. Pour in egg mixture. Cook over medium heat. As mixture sets, run a spatula around edge of skillet, lifting egg mixture so that the uncooked portion flows underneath. Continue cooking and lifting edge until egg mixture is nearly set and surface is just slightly moist.

3 Sprinkle with cheese. Broil 3 to 4 inches from the heat about 1 minute or until cheese is melted. Cut into wedges. Stack wedges; top with edamame, carrot, and cilantro sprigs. If desired, sprinkle with Parmesan shavings.

PER SERVING: *306 cal., 22 g total fat (8 g sat. fat), 443 mg chol., 482 mg sodium, 6 g carb., 2 g fiber, 23 g pro.*

tip

If you're likely to forget to budget time for the edamame to thaw, try a precooked refrigerated product such as Melissa's Organic Edamame. Look for it in the produce department.

Tomato-Broccoli Frittata

PREP: 20 minutes   BROIL: 5 minutes   STAND: 5 minutes   MAKES 4 servings

3 eggs

6 egg whites

¼ teaspoon salt

¼ teaspoon ground black pepper

¼ cup crumbled reduced-fat or regular feta cheese (1 ounce)

2 cups small broccoli florets

2 tablespoons finely chopped shallot (1 medium)

1 teaspoon olive oil

1¼ cups cherry tomatoes, quartered

1 Preheat broiler. In a medium bowl whisk together eggs, egg whites, salt, and pepper. Stir in cheese; set aside.

2 In a large broilerproof skillet cook broccoli and shallot in hot oil over medium heat for 8 to 10 minutes or just until tender, stirring occasionally. Carefully pour egg mixture over broccoli mixture in skillet. Cook over medium-low heat. As mixture sets, run a spatula around edge of skillet, lifting egg mixture so that the uncooked portion flows underneath. Continue cooking and lifting edge until egg mixture is nearly set and surface is just slightly moist.

3 Top frittata with tomatoes. Broil 4 to 5 inches from the heat about 5 minutes or until center is set. Let stand for 5 minutes before serving.

PER SERVING: *134 cal., 6 g total fat (2 g sat. fat), 161 mg chol., 416 mg sodium, 7 g carb., 2 g fiber, 14 g pro.*

Mushroom-Olive Frittata

PREP: 25 minutes STAND: 5 minutes MAKES 4 servings

- 1 cup sliced fresh cremini mushrooms
- 1 tablespoon olive oil
- 2 cups coarsely shredded Swiss chard or fresh spinach
- 1 large shallot, thinly sliced
- 4 eggs*
- 2 egg whites*
- 2 teaspoons snipped fresh rosemary or $\frac{1}{2}$ teaspoon dried rosemary, crushed
- $\frac{1}{4}$ teaspoon ground black pepper
- $\frac{1}{8}$ teaspoon salt
- $\frac{1}{4}$ cup thinly sliced pitted kalamata olives
- $\frac{1}{3}$ cup shredded Parmesan cheese

1 Preheat broiler. In a medium broilerproof nonstick skillet cook mushrooms in hot oil over medium heat for 3 minutes, stirring occasionally. Add chard and shallot. Cook about 5 minutes or until mushrooms and chard are tender, stirring occasionally.

2 Meanwhile, in a medium bowl whisk together eggs, egg whites, rosemary, pepper, and salt. Pour egg mixture over vegetables in skillet. Cook over medium heat. As mixture sets, run a spatula around edge of skillet, lifting egg mixture so that the uncooked portion flows underneath. Continue cooking and lifting edge until egg mixture is nearly set and surface is just slightly moist.

3 Top frittata with olives; sprinkle with cheese. Broil about 4 inches from the heat about 2 minutes or until top is light brown and center is set. Let stand for 5 minutes before serving.

PER SERVING: *165 cal., 11 g total fat (3 g sat. fat), 216 mg chol., 416 mg sodium, 4 g carb., 1 g fiber, 12 g pro.*

*tip

If desired, substitute 1¼ cups refrigerated or frozen egg product, thawed, for the 4 eggs and 2 egg whites.

Oven Omelets with Artichokes and Spinach

START TO FINISH: **25 minutes** OVEN: **400°F** MAKES **6 servings**

10   eggs
¼   cup water
½   teaspoon salt
¼   teaspoon ground black pepper
2   6-ounce jars marinated artichoke hearts, drained and chopped
4   cups chopped fresh spinach leaves
¾   cup shredded Swiss or provolone cheese (3 ounces)

1 Preheat oven to 400°F. Grease a 15×10×1-inch baking pan; set aside.

2 In a medium bowl whisk together eggs, the water, salt, and pepper until combined but not frothy. Place the prepared pan on an oven rack. Carefully pour egg mixture into pan. Bake about 7 minutes or until egg mixture is set but still glossy.

3 Meanwhile, for filling, in a large skillet cook artichoke hearts over medium heat until heated through, stirring occasionally. Add spinach; cook and stir until spinach is wilted.

4 Cut the baked egg mixture into six 5-inch-square omelets. Using a large spatula, remove omelet squares from pan and invert onto warm serving plates.

5 Spoon filling onto half of each omelet square. Sprinkle with cheese. Fold the other omelet half over the filled half, forming a triangle or rectangle.

PER SERVING: *225 cal., 16 g total fat (5 g sat. fat), 367 mg chol., 342 mg sodium, 7 g carb., 2 g fiber, 16 g pro.*

tip

Need a quick side for eggs? Make diner-style breakfast potatoes by tossing chopped boiled potatoes with a little chili powder, then browning in a skillet with a little oil and onions.

Breakfast

Mock Cheese Soufflé

PREP: 15 minutes CHILL: 2 to 24 hours BAKE: 45 minutes OVEN: 350°F MAKES 6 servings

6 cups white bread cubes

1½ cups shredded sharp cheddar cheese or Monterey Jack cheese with jalapeño peppers (6 ounces)

4 eggs, lightly beaten

1½ cups milk

2 teaspoons Worcestershire sauce

½ teaspoon salt

1 Place half of the bread cubes in an ungreased 1½-quart soufflé dish. Sprinkle with half of the cheese. Repeat layers; press lightly.

2 In a medium bowl combine eggs, milk, Worcestershire sauce, and salt. Pour mixture evenly over layers in soufflé dish. Cover and chill for 2 to 24 hours.

3 Preheat oven to 350°F. Bake for 45 to 50 minutes or until a knife inserted near center comes out clean. Serve immediately.

PER SERVING: *284 cal., 15 g total fat (8 g sat. fat), 176 mg chol., 639 mg sodium, 21 g carb., 1 g fiber, 16 g pro.*

tip

Boost the fiber and nutrients in this recipe by using whole wheat bread instead of white bread. Cut the fat by using reduced-fat cheese and milk.

Mushroom, Asparagus, and Tofu Quiches

PREP: 25 minutes BAKE: 20 minutes OVEN: 350°F MAKES 6 servings

1 12.3-ounce package light firm silken-style tofu (fresh bean curd)

½ cup refrigerated or frozen egg product, thawed, or 2 eggs

¾ cup finely shredded cheddar-flavor soy cheese (3 ounces)

2 tablespoons snipped fresh basil

¼ teaspoon ground black pepper

⅛ teaspoon salt

2 teaspoons olive oil

12 ounces fresh asparagus, trimmed and cut into 1-inch pieces

1½ cups sliced fresh mushrooms (such as cremini, stemmed shiitake, morel, and/or button)

¼ cup finely chopped shallots (2 medium)

1 Preheat oven to 350°F. In a blender or food processor combine tofu and eggs. Cover and blend or process just until combined. Transfer to a large bowl; stir in cheese, 1 tablespoon of the basil, the pepper, and salt. Set aside.

2 In a large skillet heat oil over medium-high heat. Add asparagus, mushrooms, and shallots. Cook and stir for 5 to 8 minutes or just until vegetables are tender; cool slightly. Stir vegetables into tofu mixture.

3 Divide tofu mixture among six 6-ounce au gratin dishes or ramekins. Place dishes in a 15×10×1-inch baking pan.

4 Bake about 20 minutes or until filling is set and edges are bubbly. Sprinkle with the remaining 1 tablespoon basil. Serve warm.

PER SERVING: *108 cal., 6 g total fat (1 g sat. fat), 0 mg chol., 319 mg sodium, 5 g carb., 1 g fiber, 10 g pro.*

Fennel and Asparagus Pie

PREP: 25 minutes BAKE: 42 minutes STAND: 10 minutes OVEN: 425°F/375°F MAKES 6 servings

- ½ of a 15-ounce package (1 crust) rolled refrigerated unbaked piecrust
- 1 medium fennel bulb
- 1 pound fresh asparagus, trimmed and cut into 1-inch pieces (about 2½ cups)
- ½ cup chopped onion (1 medium)
- ¾ cup fat-free milk
- 2 tablespoons all-purpose flour
- 3 eggs
- 1 tablespoon snipped fresh basil or 1 teaspoon dried basil, crushed
- ½ teaspoon salt
- ⅛ teaspoon ground black pepper
- 1 cup shredded mozzarella cheese (4 ounces)
- Fresh basil leaves (optional)

1 Preheat oven to 425°F. Let piecrust stand according to package directions. Line a 9-inch pie plate with pastry. Trim pastry to ½ inch beyond edge of pie plate. Fold under extra pastry even with edge of plate. Crimp edge as desired. Do not prick pastry. Line pastry with a double thickness of foil. Bake for 8 minutes. Remove foil. Bake for 4 to 5 minutes more or until pastry is set and dry. Remove from oven. Reduce oven temperature to 375°F.

2 Meanwhile, trim fennel bulb, reserving some of the feathery leaves for garnish. Thinly slice fennel. In a covered medium saucepan cook fennel, asparagus, and onion in a small amount of boiling water for 4 to 6 minutes or just until vegetables are tender. Drain.

3 In a medium bowl whisk together milk and flour until smooth. Whisk in eggs, snipped or dried basil, salt, and pepper.

4 Spoon fennel mixture into baked pastry shell. Sprinkle with cheese. Slowly pour egg mixture over mixture in pastry shell.

5 Bake for 30 to 35 minutes or until filling is set in center. If necessary, cover edge of pie with foil during the last 5 to 10 minutes of baking to prevent overbrowning. Let stand for 10 minutes before serving. Garnish with the reserved fennel leaves and, if desired, basil leaves.

PER SERVING: *290 cal., 15 g total fat (6 g sat. fat), 122 mg chol., 524 mg sodium, 28 g carb., 3 g fiber, 12 g pro.*

Tomato, Spinach, and Feta Strata

PREP: 30 minutes CHILL: 4 to 24 hours BAKE: 70 minutes STAND: 10 minutes OVEN: 325°F MAKES 6 servings

4   cups whole grain bread cubes

1   pound fresh asparagus, trimmed and cut into 1-inch pieces (about 2½ cups)

1   cup chopped onion (1 large)

2   cups fresh baby spinach

6   eggs

1   cup fat-free milk

⅛   teaspoon sea salt or kosher salt

⅛   teaspoon freshly ground black pepper

2   roma tomatoes, thinly sliced

½   cup reduced-fat or regular feta cheese (2 ounces)

¼   cup snipped fresh basil

1 Grease a 2-quart rectangular baking dish. Arrange half of the bread cubes in the prepared dish.

2 In a covered medium saucepan cook asparagus and onion in a small amount of boiling water for 2 to 3 minutes or just until tender; stir in spinach. Immediately drain well. Spoon half of the asparagus mixture over bread in baking dish. Top with the remaining bread cubes and the remaining asparagus mixture.

3 In a large bowl whisk together eggs, milk, salt, and pepper. Pour evenly over mixture in baking dish. Using the back of a large spoon, press lightly. Top with tomato slices, cheese, and basil. Cover with foil and chill for 4 to 24 hours.

4 Preheat oven to 325°F. Bake, covered, for 30 minutes. Bake, uncovered, about 40 minutes more or until temperature in center registers 180°F on an instant-read thermometer (there will be some liquid left in center that will be absorbed during standing). Let stand for 10 minutes before serving.

PER SERVING: *247 cal., 9 g total fat (3 g sat. fat), 216 mg chol., 419 mg sodium, 27 g carb., 7 g fiber, 18 g pro.*

Huevos Rancheros

START TO FINISH: **40 minutes** MAKES **4 servings**

3 tablespoons olive oil or vegetable oil

5 6-inch corn tortillas

1/2 cup chopped onion (1 medium)

2 cloves garlic, minced

1 14.5-ounce can tomatoes, drained and cut up

1 to 2 chipotle peppers in adobo sauce, chopped,* or half of a 4-ounce can diced green chile peppers, drained

2 tablespoons snipped fresh cilantro

1/4 teaspoon ground cumin

8 eggs

1 tablespoon water

1/2 cup shredded Monterey Jack cheese or crumbled queso fresco (2 ounces)

Fresh cilantro or parsley sprigs (optional)

1 In an extra-large skillet heat 2 tablespoons of the oil over medium-high heat. Dip tortillas, one at a time, into the oil just until hot. Drain on paper towels (do not stack), reserving oil in skillet. Keep 4 of the tortillas warm on a baking sheet in a 300°F oven. Reserve the remaining tortilla.

2 For salsa, cook onion and garlic in the reserved hot oil over medium heat for 2 to 3 minutes or until tender. Stir in drained tomatoes, chipotle peppers, snipped cilantro, and cumin. Bring to boiling; reduce heat. Simmer, uncovered, for 5 minutes. Transfer mixture to a blender or food processor. Tear the reserved tortilla into pieces; add to blender or processor. Cover and blend or process until a coarse puree forms. Cover and keep warm.

3 In the same skillet heat the remaining 1 tablespoon oil over medium heat. Carefully break eggs into skillet. When whites are set and edges turn white, add the water. Cover skillet and cook eggs to desired doneness (3 to 4 minutes for soft-set yolks or 4 to 5 minutes for firm-set yolks).

4 To serve, place a warm tortilla on each dinner plate. Top each with 2 fried eggs. Spoon warm salsa over eggs; sprinkle with cheese. If desired, garnish with cilantro sprigs.

PER SERVING: *413 cal., 26 g total fat (7 g sat. fat), 437 mg chol., 397 mg sodium, 27 g carb., 3 g fiber, 20 g pro.*

*tip

Because chile peppers contain volatile oils that can burn your skin and eyes, avoid direct contact with them as much as possible. When working with chile peppers, wear plastic or rubber gloves. If your bare hands do touch the peppers, wash your hands and nails well with soap and warm water.

Huevos Rancheros Breakfast Nachos

START TO FINISH: **30 minutes** MAKES **4 servings**

4½ cups baked tortilla chips (3 ounces)

¼ teaspoon cumin seeds

½ cup canned black beans, rinsed and drained

½ cup salsa

2 eggs

3 egg whites

3 tablespoons fat-free milk

⅛ teaspoon ground black pepper

Nonstick cooking spray

½ cup shredded reduced-fat Mexican cheese blend (2 ounces)

1 Divide chips among serving plates, spreading into single layers; set aside. In a small dry saucepan heat cumin seeds over medium heat about 1 minute or until toasted, stirring frequently. Stir in black beans and salsa. Cook for 1 to 2 minutes or until heated through, stirring occasionally. Remove from heat; cover and keep warm.

2 In a medium bowl whisk together eggs, egg whites, milk, and pepper. Coat a medium nonstick skillet with cooking spray; heat skillet over medium heat. Pour in egg mixture. Cook over medium heat, without stirring, until mixture starts to set on the bottom and around edge. Using a spatula or large spoon, lift and fold the partially cooked egg mixture so that the uncooked portion flows underneath. Continue cooking for 2 to 3 minutes or until egg mixture is cooked through but still glossy and moist. Remove from heat immediately.

3 Break up cooked eggs and spoon onto tortilla chips. Top with salsa mixture and cheese. Serve immediately.

PER SERVING: *207 cal., 6 g total fat (3 g sat. fat), 113 mg chol., 503 mg sodium, 26 g carb., 4 g fiber, 14 g pro.*

Mushroom and Herb Pizza

PREP: 35 minutes   BAKE: 12 minutes   OVEN: 425°F   MAKES 8 servings

Nonstick cooking spray

1 **16-ounce loaf frozen honey-wheat bread dough, thawed**

6 **eggs**

1/3 **cup fat-free milk**

1 **tablespoon olive oil**

3 **cups sliced fresh mushrooms (such as stemmed shiitake, cremini, and/or button)**

1/3 **cup snipped fresh basil and/or parsley or 2 teaspoons dried Italian seasoning, crushed**

1 **tablespoon snipped fresh oregano (optional)**

3 **cloves garlic, minced**

1/4 **teaspoon salt**

1 **cup shredded mozzarella cheese (4 ounces)**

1/4 **cup finely shredded Parmesan cheese (1 ounce)**

Freshly ground black pepper (optional)

1 Preheat oven to 425°F. Lightly coat a 15×10×1-inch baking pan with cooking spray; set aside. On a lightly floured surface roll bread dough into a 15×10-inch rectangle.* Transfer dough to the prepared baking pan. Prick dough generously with a fork. Let stand for 5 minutes. Bake about 10 minutes or until light brown. Cool for 5 minutes.

2 Meanwhile, in a medium bowl whisk together eggs and milk. Coat a large nonstick skillet with cooking spray; heat skillet over medium heat. Pour in egg mixture. Cook over medium heat, without stirring, until mixture starts to set on the bottom and around edge. Using a spatula or large spoon, lift and fold the partially cooked egg mixture so that the uncooked portion flows underneath. Continue cooking for 2 to 3 minutes or until egg mixture is cooked through but still glossy and moist. Transfer to a medium bowl; set aside.

3 In the same skillet heat oil over medium heat. Add mushrooms, basil, oregano (if desired), garlic, and salt. Cook for 5 to 7 minutes or just until mushrooms are tender, stirring occasionally. Fold cooked eggs into mushroom mixture.

4 Sprinkle mozzarella cheese over partially baked crust. Top with egg mixture and Parmesan cheese. Bake for 12 to 15 minutes or until toppings are heated through and crust is golden brown. If desired, sprinkle with pepper.

PER SERVING: *274 cal., 11 g total fat (3 g sat. fat), 170 mg chol., 575 mg sodium, 30 g carb., 3 g fiber, 17 g pro.*

*tip
If the dough is difficult to roll out, let it rest for a few minutes, then try rolling again.

Super Breakfast Burritos

START TO FINISH: **30 minutes** MAKES **6 servings**

2 teaspoons olive oil

2 medium fresh poblano chile peppers, seeded and chopped*

¾ cup canned black beans, rinsed and drained

¾ cup frozen corn, thawed

⅓ cup tomato salsa or green salsa

½ teaspoon ground cumin

½ teaspoon chili powder

6 eggs

Dash salt

Dash ground black pepper

6 8-inch whole grain tortillas, warmed

¾ cup crumbled queso fresco or shredded reduced-fat Monterey Jack cheese (3 ounces)

¼ cup snipped fresh cilantro

½ cup tomato salsa or green salsa (optional)

1 In a large skillet heat 1 teaspoon of the oil over medium heat. Add chile peppers; cook about 3 minutes or just until tender, stirring occasionally. Stir in drained beans, corn, ⅓ cup salsa, cumin, and chili powder. Cook and stir about 2 minutes or until heated through. Remove vegetable mixture from skillet.

2 In a medium bowl whisk together eggs, salt, and black pepper. In the same skillet heat the remaining 1 teaspoon oil over medium heat. Pour in egg mixture. Cook over medium heat, without stirring, until mixture starts to set on the bottom and around edge. Using a spatula or large spoon, lift and fold the partially cooked egg mixture so that the uncooked portion flows underneath. Continue cooking for 2 to 3 minutes or until egg mixture is cooked through but still glossy and moist. Remove from heat immediately. Gently fold in vegetable mixture.

3 Spoon about ⅔ cup of the egg mixture down the center of each warm tortilla. Top with cheese and cilantro. Fold in opposite sides; roll up tortillas. To serve, cut burritos in half diagonally and, if desired, serve with ½ cup salsa.

PER SERVING: *297 cal., 12 g total fat (4 g sat. fat), 216 mg chol., 602 mg sodium, 29 g carb., 12 g fiber, 20 g pro.*

*tip
Because chile peppers contain volatile oils that can burn your skin and eyes, avoid direct contact with them as much as possible. When working with chile peppers, wear plastic or rubber gloves. If your bare hands do touch the peppers, wash your hands and nails well with soap and warm water.

Basic Crepes

PREP: 15 minutes STAND: 30 minutes COOK: 3 minutes per crepe MAKES 8 crepes

2   eggs
⅔   cup water
½   cup light or fat-free milk
1   tablespoon olive oil
1½   teaspoons snipped fresh
     parsley, basil, and/or thyme
¼   teaspoon kosher salt
⅛   teaspoon freshly ground black
     pepper
1   cup whole wheat flour
     Nonstick cooking spray

1 In a blender combine eggs, the water, milk, oil, herb(s), salt, and pepper. Add flour. Cover and blend on low speed until combined. Blend on high speed for 1 minute. Pour into a medium bowl; cover lightly and let stand at room temperature for 30 minutes. (The batter should be the consistency of whipping cream. If too thick, thin with a little water or milk.)

2 To make crepes, lightly coat a medium nonstick skillet with flared sides with cooking spray; heat skillet over medium-low heat until a drop of water sizzles. Spoon in about ¼ cup batter; lift and tilt skillet to spread batter. Cook for 2 to 3 minutes or until bottom is browned and top looks dry. Carefully turn crepe; cook about 1 minute more or until bottom is light brown but crepe is still pliable. Carefully invert onto waxed paper. Repeat with the remaining batter.

PER CREPE: *91 cal., 3 g total fat (1 g sat. fat), 54 mg chol., 86 mg sodium, 12 g carb., 2 g fiber, 4 g pro.*

Make-Ahead Directions: Prepare as directed; cool completely. Layer crepes between waxed paper, using two sheets between each crepe, in an airtight container; cover. Freeze for up to 3 months. To serve, thaw crepes at room temperature for 1 hour.

🌿 Poblano-Tofu Scramble

START TO FINISH: **35 minutes** MAKES **4 servings**

1 **16- to 18-ounce package extra-firm tub-style tofu (fresh bean curd)**

1 **tablespoon olive oil**

1 **to 2 fresh poblano chile peppers, seeded and chopped***

½ **cup chopped onion (1 medium)**

2 **cloves garlic, minced**

1 **teaspoon chili powder**

½ **teaspoon ground cumin**

½ **teaspoon dried oregano, crushed**

¼ **teaspoon salt**

1 **cup seeded and chopped roma tomatoes (3 medium)**

1 **tablespoon lime juice**

Fresh cilantro sprigs (optional)

1 Drain tofu. Cut tofu in half horizontally; pat dry with paper towels. Crumble tofu into a medium bowl; set aside.

2 In a large nonstick skillet heat oil over medium-high heat. Add chopped chile pepper(s), onion, and garlic; cook and stir for 4 minutes. Add chili powder, cumin, oregano, and salt; cook and stir for 30 seconds more.

3 Add crumbled tofu to chile pepper mixture; reduce heat. Cook for 5 minutes, gently stirring occasionally. Before serving, gently stir in tomatoes and lime juice. If desired, garnish with cilantro.

PER SERVING: *182 cal., 10 g total fat (1 g sat. fat), 0 mg chol., 158 mg sodium, 11 g carb., 3 g fiber, 13 g pro.*

*tip

Because chile peppers contain volatile oils that can burn your skin and eyes, avoid direct contact with them as much as possible. When working with chile peppers, wear plastic or rubber gloves. If your bare hands do touch the peppers, wash your hands and nails well with soap and warm water.

Breakfast Pita Pizza

PREP: 20 minutes BAKE: 8 minutes OVEN: 375°F MAKES 2 servings

½ cup sliced fresh mushrooms

½ cup chopped red or green sweet pepper (1 small)

1 teaspoon olive oil

3 ounces firm tub-style tofu (fresh bean curd), drained and crumbled (about ½ cup)

2 tablespoons thinly sliced green onion (1)

1 clove garlic, minced

⅛ teaspoon ground black pepper

1 whole wheat pita bread round, split in half horizontally

½ cup shredded reduced-fat cheddar cheese (2 ounces)

1 Preheat oven to 375°F. In a medium skillet cook mushrooms and sweet pepper in hot oil over medium heat for 5 to 8 minutes or until tender, stirring occasionally. Stir in tofu, green onion, garlic, and black pepper.

2 Place pita halves, cut sides down, on an ungreased baking sheet. Sprinkle with ¼ cup of the cheese. Top with mushroom mixture; sprinkle with the remaining ¼ cup cheese.

3 Bake for 8 to 10 minutes or until heated through and cheese is melted.

PER SERVING: *256 cal., 11 g total fat (5 g sat. fat), 20 mg chol., 417 mg sodium, 24 g carb., 4 g fiber, 15 g pro.*

♦ make it vegan

Substitute soy cheese for the cheddar cheese.

Pear-Ginger Pancakes

START TO FINISH: **30 minutes** MAKES **4 servings**

½ cup all-purpose flour
½ cup whole wheat flour
1 tablespoon packed brown sugar
2 teaspoons baking powder
¼ teaspoon ground ginger
⅛ teaspoon salt
¾ cup fat-free milk
¼ cup refrigerated or frozen egg product, thawed, or 1 egg
2 tablespoons canola oil
½ of a medium pear, cored and finely chopped (½ cup)
1 recipe Apricot-Pear Syrup

1 In a medium bowl stir together all-purpose flour, whole wheat flour, brown sugar, baking powder, ginger, and salt. Make a well in center of flour mixture. In a small bowl whisk together milk, egg, and oil; stir in chopped pear. Add egg mixture all at once to flour mixture; stir just until moistened.

2 For each pancake, pour ¼ cup of the batter onto a hot, lightly greased griddle or heavy skillet, spreading batter into an even layer if necessary. Cook over medium heat for 2 to 4 minutes or until pancakes are golden brown, turning to second sides when pancakes have bubbly surfaces and edges are slightly dry. Keep pancakes warm in a 300°F oven while cooking the remaining pancakes.

3 Serve pancakes with warm Apricot-Pear Syrup.

PER SERVING: *242 cal., 7 g total fat (1 g sat. fat), 1 mg chol., 243 mg sodium, 39 g carb., 4 g fiber, 7 g pro.*

Apricot-Pear Syrup

In a small saucepan combine half of a medium pear, cored and finely chopped (½ cup), and 1 tablespoon lemon juice. Stir in 2 tablespoons low-sugar apricot preserves, 1 tablespoon water, and ⅛ teaspoon ground ginger. Heat over low heat until preserves are melted and mixture is warm, stirring occasionally.
MAKES about ½ cup

Breakfast

Fluffy Oat Bran Pancakes

START TO FINISH: 30 minutes MAKES 4 servings

2/3 cup all-purpose flour

1/3 cup oat bran

1 tablespoon packed brown sugar

2 teaspoons baking powder

1/8 teaspoon salt

1 cup fat-free milk

1 tablespoon vegetable oil

2 egg whites

1/2 cup sugar-free pancake syrup

1 teaspoon finely shredded orange peel

Orange wedges (optional)

1 In a medium bowl stir together flour, oat bran, brown sugar, baking powder, and salt. Stir in milk and oil just until combined.

2 In a small bowl beat egg whites with an electric mixer on medium speed until stiff peaks form (tips stand straight). Fold beaten egg whites into batter (small mounds of egg white will remain).

3 For each pancake, spoon 1/4 cup of the batter onto a hot, lightly greased griddle or heavy skillet, spreading batter to a 4-inch circle if necessary. Cook over medium heat about 4 minutes or until pancakes are golden brown, turning to second sides when pancakes have bubbly surfaces and edges are slightly dry. Keep pancakes warm in a 300°F oven while cooking the remaining pancakes.

4 Meanwhile, in a small saucepan heat syrup until warm. Stir in orange peel. Serve pancakes with syrup and, if desired, orange wedges.

PER SERVING: *180 cal., 4 g total fat (1 g sat. fat), 1 mg chol., 299 mg sodium, 32 g carb., 2 g fiber, 7 g pro.*

Blueberry-Oat Bran Pancakes:

Prepare as directed, except after spooning batter onto the hot griddle, sprinkle pancakes with 1/2 cup fresh blueberries. Continue as directed.

Double Pumpkin Bars

PREP: 15 minutes BAKE: 20 minutes OVEN: 350°F MAKES 8 bars

1 cup rolled oats

½ cup whole wheat pastry flour or white whole wheat flour

½ teaspoon baking soda

½ teaspoon ground cinnamon

½ teaspoon ground allspice

¼ teaspoon salt

1 egg

½ cup canned pumpkin

¼ cup sugar

¼ cup canola oil

1 teaspoon vanilla

½ cup chopped pitted dates

¼ cup pumpkin seeds (pepitas) or chopped walnuts

1 Preheat oven to 350°F. Lightly grease an 8×8×2-inch baking pan or 2-quart square baking dish; set aside.

2 In a medium bowl stir together oats, flour, baking soda, cinnamon, allspice, and salt. In a small bowl whisk together egg, pumpkin, sugar, oil, and vanilla. Add pumpkin mixture to flour mixture; stir just until combined. Stir in dates and pumpkin seeds. Spread mixture evenly in the prepared baking pan.

3 Bake about 20 minutes or until top is firm and a toothpick inserted near center comes out clean. Cool in pan on a wire rack. Cut into bars.

PER BAR: *264 cal., 12 g total fat (2 g sat. fat), 27 mg chol., 163 mg sodium, 34 g carb., 4 g fiber, 8 g pro.*

Make-Ahead Directions: Prepare and cool as directed. Wrap bars individually in plastic wrap and store in the refrigerator for up to 1 week.

Everything Breakfast Bars

PREP: 20 minutes BAKE: 15 minutes OVEN: 350°F MAKES 24 bars

Nonstick cooking spray

2 eggs, lightly beaten

¼ cup vegetable oil

3 tablespoons water

1 14-ounce package fat-free banana muffin mix

2 cups round toasted oat cereal

1 cup crisp rice cereal

1 cup low-fat granola

1 cup semisweet chocolate pieces

½ cup sliced almonds

½ cup dried cranberries

1 Preheat oven to 350°F. Line a 13×9×2-inch baking pan with foil, extending the foil over edges of pan. Lightly coat foil with cooking spray; set pan aside.

2 In a large bowl combine eggs, oil, and the water. Stir in muffin mix, oat cereal, rice cereal, granola, chocolate, almonds, and dried cranberries. Transfer mixture to the prepared baking pan. Using the back of a large spoon, press mixture evenly onto bottom of pan.

3 Bake for 15 to 18 minutes or until edges start to brown. Cool in pan on a wire rack. Using the edges of the foil, lift baked mixture out of pan. Cut into bars.

PER BAR: *168 cal., 6 g total fat (2 g sat. fat), 18 mg chol., 181 mg sodium, 27 g carb., 2 g fiber, 3 g pro.*

Peanut Butter Breakfast Bars

PREP: 20 minutes BAKE: 28 minutes OVEN: 325°F MAKES 16 bars

Nonstick cooking spray

4 cups sweetened oat cereal flakes with raisins

¾ cup quick-cooking rolled oats

½ cup all-purpose flour

½ cup snipped dried apples

2 eggs, lightly beaten

½ cup honey

½ cup chunky peanut butter

⅓ cup butter, melted

1 Preheat oven to 325°F. Line a 9×9×2-inch baking pan with foil, extending the foil over edges of pan. Lightly coat foil with cooking spray; set pan aside.

2 In a large bowl combine cereal, oats, flour, and dried apples. In a small bowl combine eggs, honey, peanut butter, and melted butter. Pour egg mixture over cereal mixture; stir to combine.

3 Transfer mixture to the prepared pan. Using the back of a large spoon, press mixture evenly onto bottom of pan. Bake for 28 to 30 minutes or until edges are brown. Cool in pan on a wire rack. Cut into bars.

PER BAR: *208 cal., 9 g total fat (3 g sat. fat), 37 mg chol., 131 mg sodium, 29 g carb., 2 g fiber, 5 g pro.*

Make-Ahead Directions: Prepare and cool as directed. Wrap bars individually in plastic wrap and store in the refrigerator for up to 3 days or freeze for up to 3 months. To serve, thaw in the refrigerator overnight if frozen.

tip

Some purchased breakfast bars are high in sugar and artificial colors and flavors. Make your own bars that use less sugar and ingredients you can pronounce. You'll save money too.

Banana-Oat Breakfast Cookies

PREP: 20 minutes BAKE: 14 minutes per batch OVEN: 350°F MAKES 12 breakfast cookies

½ cup mashed banana
½ cup low-salt and low-sugar chunky peanut butter or regular chunky peanut butter
½ cup honey
1 teaspoon vanilla
1 cup rolled oats
½ cup whole wheat flour
¼ cup nonfat dry milk powder
2 teaspoons ground cinnamon
¼ teaspoon baking soda
1 cup dried cranberries or raisins

1 Preheat oven to 350°F. Lightly grease a large cookie sheet; set aside. In a large bowl combine banana, peanut butter, honey, and vanilla. In a small bowl stir together oats, flour, milk powder, cinnamon, and baking soda. Stir oat mixture into banana mixture until combined. Stir in dried cranberries.

2 Using a ¼-cup measure, drop mounds of dough 3 inches apart onto the prepared cookie sheet. Using a narrow metal spatula dipped in water, flatten and spread each mound of dough to a 2¾-inch circle.

3 Bake for 14 to 16 minutes or until browned. Transfer to a wire rack; cool.

PER COOKIE: *227 cal., 6 g total fat (1 g sat. fat), 0 mg chol., 77 mg sodium, 37 g carb., 4 g fiber, 6 g pro.*

To Store: Layer cookies between sheets of waxed paper in an airtight container; cover. Store at room temperature for up to 3 days or freeze for up to 2 months.

Blueberry-Oat Scones with Flaxseeds

PREP: 20 minutes BAKE: 16 minutes OVEN: 400°F MAKES 12 scones

- 2 tablespoons flaxseeds, toasted*
- 1½ cups all-purpose flour
- ½ cup rolled oats
- ¼ cup sugar
- 2 teaspoons baking powder
- ¼ teaspoon salt
- ¼ cup butter
- 1 egg white
- ⅔ cup plain fat-free or low-fat yogurt
- 1¼ cups fresh blueberries
- Fat-free milk
- Rolled oats and/or flaxseeds (optional)

1 Preheat oven to 400°F. Line a baking sheet with parchment paper or foil; set aside. Place toasted flaxseeds in a spice grinder; cover and pulse until ground to a fine powder.

2 In a medium bowl combine ground flaxseeds, flour, ½ cup oats, sugar, baking powder, and salt. Using a pastry blender, cut in butter until mixture resembles coarse crumbs. Make a well in center of flour mixture; set aside.

3 In a medium bowl combine egg white and yogurt. Gently fold in blueberries. Add yogurt mixture all at once to flour mixture. Using a fork, stir just until moistened.

4 Turn dough out onto a lightly floured surface. Knead dough by folding and gently pressing it for 10 to 12 strokes or until nearly smooth. Pat or lightly roll dough into a 10-inch circle. Cut into 12 wedges.

5 Place wedges 1 inch apart on the prepared baking sheet. Brush wedges with milk and, if desired, sprinkle lightly with additional oats and/or flaxseeds. Bake for 16 to 18 minutes or until golden brown. Serve warm.

PER SCONE: *148 cal., 5 g total fat (3 g sat. fat), 11 mg chol., 133 mg sodium, 22 g carb., 2 g fiber, 4 g pro.*

*tip

To toast flaxseeds, place in a small dry skillet over medium heat. Cook and stir until the seeds are fragrant and start to pop.

tip

To get the most nutrients out of flaxseeds, you need to grind them. If you eat whole flaxseeds, most will pass through your body undigested. Grinding is easy if you have a coffee grinder or spice grinder.

Grilled Peanut Butter, Banana, and Berry Sandwiches

START TO FINISH: 20 minutes   MAKES 4 sandwiches

¼   cup peanut butter

8   slices whole grain cinnamon-raisin bread

1   medium banana, cut into 16 slices

4   fresh strawberries, each cut into 4 slices (16 slices total)

4   teaspoons grated bittersweet or semisweet chocolate

1   tablespoon butter

1 Spread peanut butter evenly onto 1 side of each bread slice. Divide banana slices and strawberry slices among 4 of the bread slices; sprinkle with grated chocolate. Top with the remaining 4 bread slices, peanut butter sides down.

2 In an extra-large skillet* or large griddle heat butter over medium heat. Add sandwiches; cook about 4 minutes or until crisp and golden brown, turning once halfway through cooking.

PER SANDWICH: *375 cal., 16 g total fat (5 g sat. fat), 8 mg chol., 374 mg sodium, 49 g carb., 8 g fiber, 13 g pro.*

*tip
If all of the sandwiches will not fit in the pan at once, cook in two batches, adding half of the butter with each batch.

Peanut Butter–Pear Sandwiches

START TO FINISH: 25 minutes   MAKES 4 sandwiches

1½   cups granola with oats and honey, coarsely crushed

4   eggs, lightly beaten

2   tablespoons milk

½   teaspoon ground cinnamon

¼   teaspoon ground nutmeg

8   slices crusty country bread

⅓   to ½ cup smooth peanut butter

1   medium pear or apple, thinly sliced

2   to 3 tablespoons honey

2   tablespoons butter or canola oil

1 Place granola in a shallow dish. In another shallow dish combine eggs, milk, cinnamon, and nutmeg. Set aside.

2 Spread 4 of the bread slices with peanut butter. Layer pear slices on top of peanut butter; drizzle with honey. Top with the remaining 4 bread slices; press lightly. Dip sandwiches in egg mixture, then in crushed granola to coat.

3 In an extra-large skillet or large griddle heat butter over medium heat. Add sandwiches; cook for 4 to 6 minutes or until crisp and golden brown, turning once halfway through cooking.

PER SANDWICH: *633 cal., 29 g total fat (11 g sat. fat), 228 mg chol., 572 mg sodium, 84 g carb., 11 g fiber, 22 g pro.*

tip
Granola may seem like a health food, but some varieties are very high in fat and calories. Check labels and look for a lower-calorie, lower-fat version. Or make your own.

Tortillas Filled with Mushrooms, Spinach, and Fresh Mozzarella

START TO FINISH: **30 minutes** MAKES **4 servings**

1½ pounds sliced fresh mushrooms (such as stemmed shiitake, oyster, cremini, and/or button)

1 tablespoon olive oil

Kosher salt

Freshly ground black pepper

6 cloves garlic, minced

2 tablespoons balsamic vinegar

2 cups fresh baby spinach

2 ounces fresh mozzarella cheese, cut into ½-inch pieces, or ½ cup shredded mozzarella cheese (2 ounces)

2 tablespoons snipped fresh basil

8 8-inch whole wheat tortillas

¼ cup finely shredded Parmesan cheese (1 ounce)

1 In an extra-large skillet cook mushrooms in hot oil over medium-high heat for 8 to 10 minutes or until golden brown, stirring occasionally. Sprinkle with salt and pepper. Add garlic; cook and stir for 1 minute. Add vinegar; cook and stir for 1 minute. Add spinach, mozzarella cheese, and basil; cook and stir for 1 to 2 minutes more or just until spinach is wilted.

2 Preheat broiler. Spread about ¼ cup of the mushroom mixture over the bottom half of each tortilla. Starting from the bottom edge, roll up tortilla. Place in a 13×9×2-inch broilerproof baking pan. Sprinkle tortilla rolls with Parmesan cheese.

3 Broil 3 to 4 inches from the heat for 1 to 2 minutes or until heated through and cheese starts to brown.

PER SERVING: *381 cal., 15 g total fat (5 g sat. fat), 122 mg chol., 485 mg sodium, 51 g carb., 8 g fiber, 17 g pro.*

make it vegan 🍃
Substitute mozzarella-flavor soy cheese for the mozzarella cheese and substitute desired soy cheese for the Parmesan cheese.

Breakfast

Oatmeal with Fruit and Nuts

START TO FINISH: 20 minutes   MAKES 4 servings

3 cups water
½ teaspoon ground cinnamon
¼ teaspoon salt
1⅓ cups regular rolled oats
1 small apple or pear, chopped
¼ cup snipped pitted whole dates (optional)
2 tablespoons sliced almonds, toasted
1 tablespoon packed brown sugar
Fat-free milk, warmed (optional)

1 In a medium saucepan combine the water, cinnamon, and salt. Bring to boiling; stir in oats. Cook for 5 minutes, stirring occasionally. Cover and let stand until oatmeal reaches desired consistency.

2 Divide oatmeal among cereal bowls. Top with apple, dates (if desired), almonds, and brown sugar. If desired, serve with warm milk.

PER SERVING: *148 cal., 3 g total fat (0 g sat. fat), 0 mg chol., 152 mg sodium, 27 g carb., 4 g fiber, 4 g pro.*

make it vegan
Do not use optional milk, or substitute soymilk for dairy milk.

Pumpkin-Apple Quick Oatmeal

START TO FINISH: **15 minutes** MAKES **4 servings**

1⅓   cups water
⅔   cup apple juice
½   cup canned pumpkin
⅓   cup snipped dried apples
1¼   cups quick-cooking rolled oats
1   tablespoon packed brown sugar
1   teaspoon ground cinnamon
¼   teaspoon ground nutmeg
½   cup vanilla fat-free yogurt
      Ground cinnamon or stick cinnamon (optional)

1 In a medium saucepan combine the water, apple juice, pumpkin, and dried apples. Bring to boiling. In a small bowl combine oats, brown sugar, 1 teaspoon cinnamon, and nutmeg. Stir oat mixture into boiling juice mixture. Cook for 1 minute, stirring occasionally.

2 Divide hot oatmeal among cereal bowls. Top with yogurt and, if desired, garnish with additional cinnamon.

PER SERVING: *168 cal., 2 g total fat (0 g sat. fat), 1 mg chol., 30 mg sodium, 35 g carb., 4 g fiber, 5 g pro.*

make it vegan
Substitute soy yogurt for the dairy yogurt.

Breakfast

Mixed-Grain Muesli

PREP: 30 minutes CHILL: 12 hours MAKES 4 (¾-cup) servings

1¼ **cups water**

3 **tablespoons steel-cut oats**

3 **tablespoons quick-cooking barley**

3 **tablespoons cracked wheat**

⅔ **cup plain low-fat yogurt**

½ **cup fat-free milk**

1 **tablespoon honey**

¼ **teaspoon apple pie spice or pumpkin pie spice**

⅛ **teaspoon salt**

1 **small red-skin apple, chopped**

3 **tablespoons assorted dried fruit (such as cranberries, blueberries, snipped apricots, snipped plums [prunes], and/ or dried fruit bits)**

¼ **cup coarsely chopped almonds, pecans, or walnuts, toasted**

1 In a 2-quart saucepan combine the water, oats, barley, and cracked wheat. Bring to boiling; reduce heat. Simmer, uncovered, for 8 minutes (grains will not be tender). Transfer to a medium bowl; cool for 5 minutes. Stir in yogurt, milk, honey, apple pie spice, and salt. Cover and chill for at least 12 hours or up to 3 days.

2 To serve, transfer cereal to a medium saucepan.* Cook and stir over low heat until heated through. Stir in apple and dried fruit. Sprinkle with almonds.

PER SERVING: *203 cal., 4 g total fat (1 g sat. fat), 3 mg chol., 120 mg sodium, 36 g carb., 5 g fiber, 7 g pro.*

*tip

You may serve the cereal without heating. Just let it stand at room temperature for 15 minutes before serving.

✿ make it vegan

Substitute soy yogurt for the dairy yogurt and soymilk for the dairy milk.

Spiced Irish Oatmeal

PREP: 10 minutes   COOK: 25 minutes   MAKES 4 servings

3   cups water
1   cup steel-cut oats
1   tablespoon packed brown sugar
¼   teaspoon ground cinnamon
⅛   teaspoon salt
⅛   teaspoon ground allspice
     Dash ground cloves or nutmeg
     Fat-free milk (optional)

1 In a medium saucepan combine the water, oats, brown sugar, cinnamon, salt, allspice, and cloves. Bring to boiling; reduce heat. Simmer, uncovered, for 25 to 30 minutes or until oats are desired doneness, stirring occasionally. If desired, serve with milk.

PER SERVING: *174 cal., 3 g total fat (0 g sat. fat), 0 mg chol., 79 mg sodium, 31 g carb., 4 g fiber, 7 g protein.*

make it vegan

Do not use optional milk, or substitute soymilk for dairy milk.

tip

Cook breakfast while you sleep. Make oatmeal in your slow cooker using hearty, old-fashioned oats cooked overnight on low for 7 to 9 hours. You'll wake up to a tasty, no-fuss breakfast.

Berry-Peach Breakfast Smoothies

START TO FINISH: 10 minutes   MAKES 2 (about ¾-cup) servings

1   cup frozen unsweetened peach slices*
⅔   cup plain soy yogurt
½   cup frozen mixed berries or frozen unsweetened whole strawberries, raspberries, or blueberries
⅓   cup orange juice
1   teaspoon sugar

1 In a blender combine peach slices, yogurt, berries, orange juice, and sugar. Cover and blend until mixture is smooth. Serve immediately.

PER SERVING: *157 cal., 1 g total fat (0 g sat. fat), 0 mg chol., 12 mg sodium, 26 g carb., 3 g fiber, 3 g pro.*

*tip

For a smoother drink, let the frozen peach slices stand at room temperature for 20 to 30 minutes before adding to blender.

Peanut Butter–Berry Smoothies

START TO FINISH: 10 minutes   MAKES 4 (about 8-ounce) servings

2   cups plain fat-free yogurt

2   cups sliced fresh strawberries
    or frozen unsweetened whole
    strawberries

2   medium ripe bananas, cut
    into chunks

2   tablespoons honey

2   tablespoons peanut butter

    Halved fresh strawberries
    (optional)

1 In a blender combine yogurt, 2 cups strawberries, bananas, honey, and peanut butter. Cover and blend until smooth. Serve immediately. If desired, garnish with additional fresh strawberries threaded onto skewers.

PER SERVING: *223 cal., 5 g total fat (1 g sat. fat), 2 mg chol., 133 mg sodium, 39 g carb., 3 g fiber, 10 g pro.*

make it vegan
Substitute soy yogurt for the dairy yogurt.

tip
Skip the fruit juices and opt for the whole fruit instead. You'll get more fiber and a lot less sugar.

Power Smoothies

START TO FINISH: 10 minutes   MAKES 2 (about 11-ounce) servings

1   cup fresh blueberries

1   cup fresh blackberries

²⁄₃   cup blueberry fat-free yogurt

½   cup pomegranate juice

1   tablespoon honey

    Fresh blueberries and/or
    blackberries (optional)

1 In a blender combine 1 cup blueberries, 1 cup blackberries, yogurt, pomegranate juice, and honey. Cover and blend until nearly smooth. If desired, press mixture through a fine-mesh sieve to remove blackberry seeds.

2 Serve immediately. If desired, garnish with additional blueberries and/or blackberries.

PER SERVING: *190 cal., 1 g total fat (0 g sat. fat), 2 mg chol., 54 mg sodium, 43 g carb., 6 g fiber, 5 g pro.*

2

Slow Cooker

The ultimate appliance for ease and convenience is not just for soups and stews. Expand your slow cooker repertoire with pasta, casseroles, soups, and even burritos that are ready to eat when you are.

Greek Beans and Barley

PREP: 20 minutes COOK: 6 to 8 hours (low) or 3 to 4 hours (high) STAND: 10 minutes MAKES 6 to 8 servings

Nonstick cooking spray

1 28-ounce can diced tomatoes, undrained

2 medium zucchini, halved lengthwise and cut into 1-inch pieces

2 medium yellow summer squash, halved lengthwise and cut into 1-inch pieces

1⅔ cups regular barley

2 tablespoons tomato paste

3 cloves garlic, minced

1 teaspoon dried oregano, crushed

½ teaspoon coarsely ground black pepper

1 cup chicken-flavor vegetable broth

1½ cups frozen Italian green beans

¼ cup crumbled feta cheese (1 ounce)

1 Lightly coat the inside of a 3½- or 4-quart slow cooker with cooking spray. In the prepared cooker combine undrained tomatoes, zucchini, yellow squash, barley, tomato paste, garlic, oregano, and pepper. Pour broth over mixture in cooker.

2 Cover and cook on low-heat setting for 6 to 8 hours or on high-heat setting for 3 to 4 hours. Stir in frozen beans. Cover and let stand for 10 minutes. Sprinkle each serving with cheese.

PER SERVING: *264 cal., 3 g total fat (1 g sat. fat), 6 mg chol., 502 mg sodium, 52 g carb., 14 g fiber, 11 g pro.*

make it vegan

Substitute feta-flavor soy cheese for the feta cheese.

tip

Don't let your veggies get soggy. Add vegetables that cook quickly, such as tomatoes and zucchini, during the last 45 minutes of cooking.

Vegetarian Feijoada Brazilian Rice and Black Beans

PREP: 25 minutes COOK: 5 to 6 hours (low) or 2½ to 3 hours (high) STAND: 10 minutes MAKES 6 servings

4 cups chopped fresh kale leaves (6 ounces)

2 15-ounce cans black beans, rinsed and drained

1 14.5-ounce can diced tomatoes, undrained

1 8-ounce package smoked tempeh or tempeh bacon, crumbled*

1 cup chopped onion (1 large)

¾ cup chopped red sweet pepper (1 medium)

1 medium fresh poblano chile pepper, seeded and chopped**

3 cloves garlic, minced

1 teaspoon ground cumin

½ teaspoon salt

½ teaspoon dried oregano, crushed

½ teaspoon crushed red pepper

1 14-ounce can vegetable broth

1 8.8-ounce pouch cooked long grain rice

1 In a 4- to 5-quart slow cooker combine kale, drained beans, undrained tomatoes, tempeh, onion, sweet pepper, poblano pepper, garlic, cumin, salt, oregano, and crushed red pepper. Pour broth over mixture in cooker.

2 Cover and cook on low-heat setting for 5 to 6 hours or on high-heat setting for 2½ to 3 hours. Stir in cooked rice. Cover and let stand for 10 minutes.

PER SERVING: *328 cal., 6 g total fat (1 g sat. fat), 0 mg chol., 1,187 mg sodium, 56 g carb., 12 g fiber, 24 g pro.*

*tip

If you prefer, use regular tempeh (fermented soybean cake) and add ½ teaspoon liquid smoke.

**tip

Because chile peppers contain volatile oils that can burn your skin and eyes, avoid direct contact with them as much as possible. When working with chile peppers, wear plastic or rubber gloves. If your bare hands do touch the chile peppers, wash your hands well with soap and warm water.

Slow Cooker

Sweet Potato Tamale Pie

PREP: 25 minutes COOK: 7 to 8 hours (low) or 3½ to 4 hours (high) STAND: 5 minutes MAKES 6 servings

- 1 **pound sweet potatoes (2 to 3 medium), cut into 1-inch pieces**
- 1 **15.5-ounce can hominy, rinsed and drained**
- 1 **15-ounce can pinto beans, rinsed and drained**
- 1 **14.5-ounce can diced tomatoes and green chiles, undrained**
- 1½ **cups shredded Monterey Jack cheese (6 ounces)**
- ⅔ **cup vegetable broth**
- ½ **cup chopped onion (1 medium)**
- 1 **teaspoon ground cumin**
- 1 **16-ounce tube refrigerated cooked polenta, cut into ¼-inch slices**
- **Snipped fresh cilantro and/or sour cream**

1 In a large bowl combine sweet potatoes, drained hominy, drained beans, undrained tomatoes, 1 cup of the cheese, the broth, onion, and cumin.

2 Transfer half of the sweet potato mixture to a 3½- or 4-quart slow cooker. Top with half of the polenta slices. Add the remaining sweet potato mixture and the remaining polenta slices.

3 Cover and cook on low-heat setting for 7 to 8 hours or on high-heat setting or 3½ to 4 hours.

4 Sprinkle with the remaining ½ cup cheese. Let stand, uncovered, about 5 minutes or until cheese is melted. Top each serving with cilantro and/or sour cream.

PER SERVING: *338 cal., 11 g total fat (7 g sat. fat), 30 mg chol., 991 mg sodium, 45 g carb., 9 g fiber, 16 g pro.*

make it vegan

Substitute desired soy cheese for the Monterey Jack cheese and tofu sour cream for the dairy sour cream.

Mexican Burritos or Tacos

PREP: 20 minutes COOK: 4 to 6 hours (low) MAKES 10 servings

1 12-ounce package refrigerated or frozen cooked and crumbled ground meat substitute (soy protein), thawed

1 15-ounce can pinto beans, rinsed and drained

1 14.5-ounce can diced tomatoes and green chiles, undrained

1 cup salsa

½ cup chopped onion (1 medium)

2 cloves garlic, minced

10 6- to 8-inch flour tortillas

⅔ cup shredded Monterey Jack cheese

Shredded lettuce

Sour cream (optional)

1 In a 3½- or 4-quart slow cooker combine ground meat substitute, drained beans, undrained tomatoes, salsa, onion, and garlic. Cover and cook on low-heat setting for 4 to 6 hours.

2 Divide bean mixture among tortillas. Top with cheese, lettuce, and, if desired, sour cream. For burritos, fold up bottom edge of each tortilla. Fold in opposite sides; roll up from the bottom. For tacos, fold tortillas in half.

PER SERVING: *245 cal., 8 g total fat (1 g sat. fat), 6 mg chol., 602 mg sodium, 27 g carb., 5 g fiber, 14 g pro.*

tip

Always fill a slow cooker at least half full but not more than two-thirds full. If you use a slow cooker often, invest in one that converts to multiple sizes so there's no need to adjust recipes for a different capacity.

Taco-Style Black Beans and Hominy

PREP: 15 minutes COOK: 7 to 8 hours (low) or 3½ to 4 hours (high) MAKES 9 servings

Nonstick cooking spray

2 15.5-ounce cans golden hominy, drained

2 15-ounce cans black beans, rinsed and drained

1¼ cups water

1 10.75-ounce can condensed cream of mushroom soup

½ of a 1.25-ounce envelope (1½ tablespoons) taco seasoning mix

18 taco shells

Sliced green onions, chopped tomatoes, and/or shredded lettuce (optional)

1 Coat the inside of a 3½- or 4-quart slow cooker with cooking spray. In the prepared cooker combine drained hominy, drained beans, the water, soup, and taco seasoning mix.

2 Cover and cook on low-heat setting for 7 to 8 hours or on high-heat setting for 3½ to 4 hours.

3 To serve, spoon bean mixture into taco shells. If desired, sprinkle with green onions, tomatoes, and/or lettuce.

PER SERVING: *317 cal., 10 g total fat (2 g sat. fat), 0 mg chol., 1,001 mg sodium, 52 g carb., 11 g fiber, 12 g pro.*

Chili Beans and Potatoes

PREP: 15 minutes COOK: 8 to 9 hours (low) or 4 to 4½ hours (high) MAKES 6 servings

2 pounds round red or russet potatoes, cut into 1-inch pieces

2 15-ounce cans vegetarian baked beans, undrained

1 10-ounce package frozen whole kernel corn

½ cup vegetable broth

1 tablespoon chili powder

½ teaspoon unsweetened cocoa powder

½ cup shredded cheddar cheese (2 ounces)

½ cup sour cream

1 In a 4- to 5-quart slow cooker combine potatoes, undrained beans, corn, broth, chili powder, and cocoa powder.

2 Cover and cook on low-heat setting for 8 to 9 hours or on high-heat setting for 4 to 4½ hours. Top each serving with cheese and sour cream.

PER SERVING: *357 cal., 8 g total fat (4 g sat. fat), 20 mg chol., 629 mg sodium, 60 g carb., 10 g fiber, 15 g pro.*

tip
Don't peek into the cooker to stir or taste food. Taking the lid off can extend the cooking time by up to 30 minutes.

Red Beans Creole

PREP: 25 minutes COOK: 11 to 13 hours (low) or 5½ to 6½ hours (high) + 30 minutes (high) STAND: 1 hour

MAKES 4 or 5 servings

3½   cups dried red beans
     (1½ pounds)

5   cups water

3   cups chopped onions (3 large)

2   4-ounce cans (drained weight)
     sliced mushrooms, drained

2   tablespoons Creole seasoning

6   cloves garlic, minced

2   cups uncooked instant brown
     rice

2   cups green sweet pepper
     strips (2 medium)

1   14.5-ounce can diced tomatoes
     with basil, garlic, and
     oregano, undrained

     Bottled hot pepper sauce
     (optional)

1 Rinse beans. In a large saucepan combine beans and enough water to cover beans by 2 inches. Bring to boiling; reduce heat. Simmer, uncovered, for 10 minutes. Remove from heat. Cover and let stand for 1 hour. Drain and rinse beans.

2 Transfer beans to a 3½- or 4-quart slow cooker. Stir in the 5 cups water, onions, drained mushrooms, Creole seasoning, and garlic.

3 Cover and cook on low-heat setting for 11 to 13 hours or on high-heat setting for 5½ to 6½ hours.

4 If using low-heat setting, turn to high-heat setting. Stir in uncooked rice, sweet pepper strips, and undrained tomatoes. Cover and cook for 30 minutes more. If desired, serve with hot pepper sauce.

PER SERVING: *415 cal., 2 g total fat (0 g sat. fat), 0 mg chol., 541 mg sodium, 81 g carb., 16 g fiber, 23 g pro.*

White Beans with Dried Tomatoes

PREP: 15 minutes COOK: 6 to 8 hours (low) or 3½ to 4 hours (high) + 15 minutes (high) MAKES 6 servings

3 15- to 19-ounce cans cannellini beans (white kidney beans), rinsed and drained

1 14-ounce can vegetable broth

3 cloves garlic, minced

1 7-ounce jar oil-packed dried tomatoes, drained and chopped

1 cup shaved Asiago or Parmesan cheese (4 ounces)

⅓ cup pine nuts, toasted (optional)

1 In a 3½- or 4-quart slow cooker combine drained beans, broth, and garlic.

2 Cover and cook on low-heat setting for 6 to 8 hours or on high-heat setting for 3½ to 4 hours.

3 If using low-heat setting, turn to high-heat setting. Stir in dried tomatoes. Cover and cook for 15 minutes more. Top each serving with cheese and, if desired, pine nuts.

PER SERVING: *283 cal., 12 g total fat (5 g sat. fat), 20 mg chol., 884 mg sodium, 38 g carb., 12 g fiber, 18 g pro.*

🌿 make it vegan

Substitute desired soy cheese for the Asiago cheese.

tip

Dried tomatoes are loaded with flavor. Chop them up and use in salads, sandwiches, and pasta dishes. Or mix into cream cheese for a quick snack spread to use on crackers or veggies.

Vegetarian Gumbo 🌿

PREP: 10 minutes COOK: 6 to 8 hours (low) or 3 to 4 hours (high) MAKES 6 servings

2 15-ounce cans black beans, rinsed and drained

1 28-ounce can diced tomatoes, undrained

1 16-ounce package frozen sweet pepper and onion stir-fry vegetables

2 cups frozen cut okra

2 to 3 teaspoons Cajun seasoning

3 cups hot cooked white or brown rice

Chopped green onions (optional)

1 In a 3½- to 4½-quart slow cooker combine drained beans, undrained tomatoes, frozen stir-fry vegetables, frozen okra, and Cajun seasoning.

2 Cover and cook on low-heat setting for 6 to 8 hours or on high-heat setting for 3 to 4 hours. Serve over hot cooked rice and, if desired, sprinkle with green onions.

PER SERVING: *250 cal., 1 g total fat (0 g sat. fat), 0 mg chol., 695 mg sodium, 53 g carb., 12 g fiber, 14 g protein.*

Vegetable Casserole

2 19-ounce cans cannellini beans (white kidney beans), rinsed and drained

1 19-ounce can garbanzo beans (chickpeas) or fava beans, rinsed and drained

½ cup chopped onion (1 medium)

¼ cup basil pesto

4 cloves garlic, minced

1½ teaspoons dried Italian seasoning, crushed

1 16-ounce tube refrigerated cooked polenta, cut into ½-inch slices

2 cups finely shredded Italian cheese blend (8 ounces)

1 large tomato, thinly sliced

2 cups fresh spinach leaves

1 cup torn radicchio

1 tablespoon water

1 In a large bowl combine drained cannellini beans, drained garbanzo beans, onion, 2 tablespoons of the pesto, the garlic, and Italian seasoning.

2 In a 4- to 5-quart slow cooker layer half of the bean mixture, half of the polenta, and half of the cheese. Add the remaining bean mixture and the remaining polenta. Cover and cook on low-heat setting for 4 to 6 hours or on high-heat setting for 2 to 2½ hours.

3 Add tomato slices and the remaining cheese; top with spinach and radicchio. In a small bowl combine the remaining 2 tablespoons pesto and the water; drizzle over greens. Let stand, uncovered, for 5 minutes.

PER SERVING: *360 cal., 12 g total fat (6 g sat. fat), 26 mg chol., 926 mg sodium, 46 g carb., 10 g fiber, 21 g pro.*

Chili Bean-Stuffed Peppers

PREP: 20 minutes COOK: 6 to 6½ hours (low) or 3 to 3½ hours (high) MAKES 4 servings

- 4 **small to medium green, red, or yellow sweet peppers**
- 1 **15-ounce can vegetarian baked beans, undrained**
- 1 **cup cooked converted rice**
- 1 **15-ounce can no-salt-added tomato sauce**
- ⅓ **cup finely chopped onion (1 small)**
- ¾ **cup shredded Monterey Jack cheese (3 ounces)**
-    **Chili powder (optional)**

1 Remove tops, seeds, and membranes from sweet peppers. Chop enough tops to make ⅓ cup; set aside. If necessary, cut a thin slice from the bottom of each pepper so it sits flat.

2 In a medium bowl stir together undrained beans and cooked rice; spoon into peppers. Pour tomato sauce into the bottom of a 4½- to 6-quart slow cooker; stir in onion and the reserved ⅓ cup chopped pepper. Place filled peppers, filling sides up, in cooker.

3 Cover and cook on low-heat setting for 6 to 6½ hours or on high-heat setting for 3 to 3½ hours.

4 To serve, transfer peppers to dinner plates and, if desired, cut in half. Spoon tomato mixture over peppers. Sprinkle with cheese and, if desired, chili powder.

PER SERVING: *314 cal., 7 g total fat (4 g sat. fat), 19 mg chol., 522 mg sodium, 47 g carb., 9 g fiber, 13 g pro.*

🌿 Sweet-and-Sour Cabbage Rolls

PREP: 45 minutes COOK: 7 to 9 hours (low) or 3½ to 4½ hours (high) MAKES 4 servings

1   large head green cabbage

1   15-ounce can black beans or red kidney beans, rinsed and drained

1   cup cooked brown rice

½   cup chopped onion (1 medium)

½   cup chopped celery (1 stalk)

½   cup chopped carrot (1 medium)

1   clove garlic, minced

3½   cups marinara sauce or meatless spaghetti sauce

⅓   cup raisins

3   tablespoons lemon juice

1   tablespoon packed brown sugar

1 Remove 8 large outer leaves from cabbage. In a large Dutch oven cook cabbage leaves in boiling water for 4 to 5 minutes or just until leaves are limp; drain. Trim the heavy vein off back of each leaf even with rest of leaf; set trimmed leaves aside. Shred 4 cups of the remaining cabbage. Place shredded cabbage in a 3½- to 6-quart slow cooker.

2 In a medium bowl combine drained beans, cooked rice, onion, celery, carrot, and garlic. Stir in ½ cup of the marinara sauce. Place about ⅓ cup of the bean mixture on each cabbage leaf. Fold in sides. Starting at an unfolded edge, carefully roll up each leaf.

3 In another medium bowl combine the remaining 3 cups marinara sauce, raisins, lemon juice, and brown sugar. Pour about half of the sauce mixture over shredded cabbage, stirring to combine. Add cabbage rolls. Top with the remaining sauce mixture.

4 Cover and cook on low-heat setting for 7 to 9 hours or on high-heat setting for 3½ to 4½ hours. Carefully remove cooked cabbage rolls and serve with shredded cabbage mixture.

PER SERVING: *406 cal., 12 g total fat (3 g sat. fat), 0 mg chol., 69 g carb., 15 g fiber, 14 g pro.*

Mushroom-Barley Soup

PREP: 20 minutes COOK: 8 to 10 hours (low) or 4 to 5 hours (high) MAKES 6 servings

8 ounces fresh portobello mushrooms, cut into thirds and sliced

8 ounces fresh button mushrooms, sliced

1 14.5-ounce can diced tomatoes, undrained

1 cup sliced carrots (2 medium)

1 cup chopped onion (1 large)

½ cup regular barley

2 tablespoons tomato paste

1 tablespoon balsamic vinegar

3 cloves garlic, minced

1 teaspoon dried marjoram, crushed

½ teaspoon salt

½ teaspoon paprika

3 14-ounce cans vegetable broth

Finely shredded Pecorino Romano cheese and/or snipped fresh Italian (flat-leaf) parsley

1 In a 4- to 5-quart slow cooker combine mushrooms, undrained tomatoes, carrots, onion, barley, tomato paste, vinegar, garlic, marjoram, salt, and paprika. Pour broth over mixture in cooker.

2 Cover and cook on low-heat setting for 8 to 10 hours or on high-heat setting for 4 to 5 hours. Garnish each serving with cheese and/or parsley.

PER SERVING: *135 cal., 1 g total fat (0 g sat. fat), 2 mg chol., 1,192 mg sodium, 28 g carb., 6 g fiber, 6 g pro.*

 **make it vegan**
Substitute desired soy cheese for the Pecorino Romano cheese.

Gingered Carrot Soup

PREP: **20 minutes** COOK: **10 to 11 hours (low) or 5 to 5½ hours (high)** MAKES **6 servings**

4 cups coarsely chopped carrots
   (8 medium)

1¼ cups coarsely chopped russet
    potato (1 medium)

1 cup coarsely chopped
   parsnips (2 medium)

½ cup chopped onion
   (1 medium)

1 tablespoon grated fresh
   ginger

2 cloves garlic, minced

1 teaspoon ground cumin

½ teaspoon salt

¼ teaspoon ground black pepper

3 14-ounce cans vegetable broth

½ cup sour cream

½ teaspoon finely shredded
   lemon peel

1 In a 3½- or 4-quart slow cooker combine carrots, potato, parsnips, onion, ginger, garlic, cumin, salt, and pepper. Pour broth over vegetables.

2 Cover and cook on low-heat setting for 10 to 11 hours on high-heat setting for 5 to 5½ hours.

3 Using an immersion blender, blend vegetable mixture until smooth. Or transfer mixture, in batches, to a blender or food processor; cover and blend or process until smooth.

4 In a small bowl combine sour cream and lemon peel. Top each serving with sour cream mixture.

PER SERVING: *121 cal., 4 g total fat (2 g sat. fat), 8 mg chol., 1,045 mg sodium, 21 g carb., 4 g fiber, 2 g pro.*

make it vegan

Substitute tofu sour cream for the dairy sour cream.

Savory Bean and Kale Soup

PREP: 20 minutes COOK: 5 to 7 hours (low) or 2½ to 3½ hours (high) MAKES 6 servings

- 3 14-ounce cans vegetable broth
- 1 15-ounce can tomato puree
- 1 15-ounce can small white beans or Great Northern beans, rinsed and drained
- ½ cup uncooked converted rice
- ½ cup finely chopped onion (1 medium)
- 2 cloves garlic, minced
- 1 teaspoon dried basil, crushed
- ¼ teaspoon salt
- ¼ teaspoon ground black pepper
- 8 cups coarsely chopped fresh kale leaves (12 ounces)

  Finely shredded Parmesan cheese (optional)

1 In a 3½- or 4-quart slow cooker combine broth, tomato puree, drained beans, uncooked rice, onion, garlic, basil, salt, and pepper.

2 Cover and cook on low-heat setting for 5 to 7 hours or on high-heat setting for 2½ to 3½ hours.

3 Before serving stir in kale. If desired, sprinkle each serving with cheese.

PER SERVING: *188 cal., 1 g total fat (0 g sat. fat), 0 mg chol., 1,306 mg sodium, 42 g carb., 7 g fiber, 10 g pro.*

make it vegan

If using, substitute desired soy cheese for the Parmesan cheese.

tip

Kale, like other dark, leafy greens, is particularly beneficial for vegetarians because of its high calcium and iron content.

Curried Lentil Soup

PREP: 20 minutes COOK: 8 to 10 hours (low) or 4 to 5 hours (high) MAKES 4 to 6 servings

- 1 pound sweet potatoes (2 to 3 medium), peeled and coarsely chopped
- 1 cup brown or yellow lentils, rinsed and drained
- ½ cup chopped onion (1 medium)
- 1 medium fresh jalapeño chile pepper, seeded and finely chopped*
- 3 cloves garlic, minced
- 3 14-ounce cans vegetable broth
- 1 14.5-ounce can diced tomatoes, undrained
- 1 tablespoon curry powder
- 1 teaspoon grated fresh ginger
- Plain yogurt or sour cream (optional)
- Sliced fresh jalapeño chile pepper* and/or crushed red pepper (optional)

1 In a 4- to 5-quart slow cooker combine sweet potatoes, lentils, onion, finely chopped jalapeño pepper, and garlic. Stir in broth, undrained tomatoes, curry powder, and ginger.

2 Cover and cook on low-heat setting for 8 to 10 hours or on high-heat setting for 4 to 5 hours. If desired, top each serving with yogurt and garnish with sliced jalapeño pepper and/or crushed red pepper.

PER SERVING: *316 cal., 2 g total fat (0 g sat. fat), 0 mg chol., 1,425 mg sodium, 60 g carb., 18 g fiber, 18 g protein.*

*tip
Because chile peppers contain volatile oils that can burn your skin and eyes, avoid direct contact with them as much as possible. When working with chile peppers, wear plastic or rubber gloves. If your bare hands do touch the peppers, wash your hands and nails well with soap and warm water.

make it vegan
Substitute soy yogurt or tofu sour cream for the dairy yogurt or sour cream.

Spicy Winter Squash Stew 🌿

PREP: 20 minutes   COOK: 5 to 6 hours (low) or 2½ to 3 hours (high)   MAKES 6 servings

1   **pound butternut or acorn squash, peeled and chopped**

1   **15-ounce can garbanzo beans (chickpeas), rinsed and drained**

1   **14.5-ounce can diced tomatoes, undrained**

½   **cup uncooked quinoa, rinsed and drained**

½   **cup finely chopped onion (1 medium)**

¼   **cup golden raisins**

2   **cloves garlic, minced**

½   **teaspoon salt**

½   **teaspoon ground ginger**

½   **teaspoon ground coriander**

¼   **teaspoon ground cinnamon**

¼   **teaspoon cayenne pepper**

1   **14-ounce can vegetable broth**

1 In a 3½- or 4-quart slow cooker combine squash, drained garbanzo beans, undrained tomatoes, quinoa, onion, raisins, garlic, salt, ginger, coriander, cinnamon, and cayenne pepper. Pour broth over mixture in cooker.

2 Cover and cook on low-heat setting for 5 to 6 hours or on high-heat setting for 2½ to 3 hours.

PER SERVING: *213 cal., 2 g total fat (0 g sat. fat), 0 mg chol., 806 mg sodium, 44 g carb., 7 g fiber, 7 g protein.*

Cha-Cha Corn Chowder

PREP: 15 minutes COOK: 6 to 8 hours (low) or 3 to 4 hours (high) MAKES 6 servings

1 pound round red potatoes (3 medium), chopped

2 14.75-ounce cans cream-style corn

1¾ cups chicken-flavor vegetable broth

1 11-ounce can whole kernel corn with sweet peppers, drained

1 4-ounce can diced green chile peppers, undrained

1½ teaspoons bottled minced roasted garlic

¼ teaspoon ground black pepper

Cracked black pepper (optional)

Saltine crackers (optional)

1 In a 3½- or 4-quart slow cooker combine potatoes, cream-style corn, broth, drained whole kernel corn, undrained chile peppers, roasted garlic, and ground black pepper.

2 Cover and cook on low-heat setting for 6 to 8 hours or on high-heat setting for 3 to 4 hours.

3 If desired, top each serving with cracked black pepper and serve with crackers.

PER SERVING: *202 cal., 1 g total fat (0 g sat. fat), 0 mg chol., 832 mg sodium, 48 g carb., 5 g fiber, 5 g protein.*

tip
Root veggies such as potatoes should be cut before being added to the slow cooker. Left whole, potatoes, carrots, turnips, and other firm whole vegetables will take too long to cook in a slow cooker.

Southwestern Corn Spoonbread

PREP: 15 minutes COOK: 3¼ to 3¾ hours (low) COOL: 45 minutes MAKES 6 to 8 servings

Nonstick cooking spray

4 eggs, lightly beaten

2 8.5-ounce packages corn muffin mix

1 14.75-ounce can cream-style corn

1 cup fresh corn kernels (2 ears) or frozen whole kernel corn, thawed

¾ cup milk

1 medium fresh poblano chile pepper, seeded and chopped*

½ cup chopped sweet onion (such as Vidalia or Walla Walla) (1 medium)

1 teaspoon ground cumin

½ cup shredded Monterey Jack cheese with jalapeño peppers (2 ounces)

1 Lightly coat a 3½- or 4-quart slow cooker with cooking spray; set aside.

2 In a large bowl combine eggs, corn muffin mix, cream-style corn, corn kernels, milk, poblano pepper, onion, and cumin. Spoon mixture into the prepared cooker.

3 Cover and cook on low-heat setting for 3¼ to 3¾ hours or until a wooden skewer inserted near center comes out clean.

4 Remove liner from cooker, if possible, or turn off cooker. Sprinkle top of spoonbread with cheese. Cool, uncovered, about 45 minutes before serving. Serve warm.

PER SERVING: *511 cal., 16 g total fat (4 g sat. fat), 153 mg chol., 888 mg sodium, 79 g carb., 2 g fiber, 16 g pro.*

*tip

Because chile peppers contain volatile oils that can burn your skin and eyes, avoid direct contact with them as much as possible. When working with chile peppers, wear plastic or rubber gloves. If your bare hands do touch the chile peppers, wash your hands and nails well with soap and warm water.

Corn and Grain Gratin

PREP: 20 minutes COOK: 5 to 5½ hours (low) or 2½ to 3 hours (high) MAKES 6 servings

- 1 cup regular barley
- ⅔ cup wheat berries
- 2 14-ounce cans vegetable broth
- 1 cup frozen whole kernel corn
- 1 4-ounce can (drained weight) sliced mushrooms, drained
- ½ cup thinly sliced carrot (1 medium)
- ½ cup finely chopped onion (1 medium)
- ½ cup chopped roasted red sweet peppers
- ½ cup dry white wine or vegetable broth
- ½ cup water
- 2 cloves garlic, minced
- ¼ teaspoon ground black pepper
- ¼ cup finely shredded Parmesan cheese (1 ounce)

1 Rinse and drain barley and wheat berries. In a 3½- or 4-quart slow cooker combine barley, wheat berries, broth, corn, drained mushrooms, carrot, onion, roasted peppers, wine, the water, garlic, and black pepper.

2 Cover and cook on low-heat setting for 5 to 5½ hours or on high-heat setting for 2½ to 3 hours. Stir before serving. Sprinkle each serving with cheese.

PER SERVING: *259 cal., 2 g total fat (1 g sat. fat), 2 mg chol., 659 mg sodium, 50 g carb., 9 g fiber, 9 g pro.*

make it vegan

Substitute desired soy cheese for the Parmesan cheese.

tip

You may have heard that frozen foods shouldn't be added to a slow cooker, but that rule is mainly for meat, poultry, fish, and other foods that could pose a food safety hazard. Frozen vegetables are fine to add to the slow cooker.

Lentil "Moussaka"

PREP: 20 minutes COOK: 6 hours (low) or 3 hours (high) + 30 minutes (high) MAKES 6 servings

- 2 cups cubed potatoes (2 medium)
- 1 cup vegetable broth
- ¾ cup brown or yellow lentils, rinsed and drained
- 2 cloves garlic, minced
- ½ teaspoon salt
- ¼ teaspoon ground cinnamon
- ¼ teaspoon ground black pepper
- 5 cups cubed eggplant (1 medium)
- 1½ cups thinly sliced carrots (3 medium)
- 1 14.5-ounce can diced tomatoes with basil, garlic, and oregano, undrained
- 2 eggs, lightly beaten
- 1 8-ounce package cream cheese, softened

1 In a 3½- or 4-quart slow cooker combine potatoes, broth, lentils, garlic, salt, cinnamon, and pepper. Top with eggplant and carrots.

2 Cover and cook on low-heat setting for 6 hours or on high-heat setting for 3 hours. Stir in undrained tomatoes. If using low-heat setting, turn to high-heat setting.

3 In a medium bowl combine eggs and cream cheese. Beat with an electric mixer on low speed until smooth. Spoon cream cheese mixture over lentil mixture. Cover and cook for 30 minutes more.

PER SERVING: *333 cal., 15 g total fat (9 g sat. fat), 112 mg chol., 868 mg sodium, 36 g carb., 11 g fiber, 15 g pro.*

Ratatouille with Lentils

PREP: 25 minutes COOK: 8 to 9 hours (low) or 4 to 4½ hours (high) MAKES 6 servings

1 **12-ounce eggplant (1 small), peeled and cubed**

2 **14.5-ounce cans diced tomatoes with basil, garlic, and oregano, undrained**

2 **medium yellow summer squash and/or zucchini, halved lengthwise and cut into ½-inch pieces (2½ cups)**

2 **cups coarsely chopped onions (2 large)**

1 **cup brown or yellow lentils, rinsed and drained**

¾ **cup chopped red sweet pepper (1 medium)**

½ **cup water**

¼ **to ½ teaspoon ground black pepper**

1 In a 3½- or 4-quart slow cooker combine eggplant, undrained tomatoes, squash, onions, lentils, sweet pepper, the water, and black pepper.

2 Cover and cook on low-heat setting for 8 to 9 hours or on high-heat setting for 4 to 4½ hours.

PER SERVING: *215 cal., 1 g total fat (0 g sat. fat), 0 mg chol., 713 mg sodium, 42 g carb., 14 g fiber, 12 g pro.*

Thai-Style Vegetable Rice 🌿

PREP: 20 minutes   COOK: 4½ to 5 hours (low) or 2 to 2½ hours (high) + 10 minutes (high)   MAKES 6 servings

- 4 cups vegetable broth
- 3 cups frozen shelled sweet soybeans (edamame)
- 2 medium sweet potatoes, peeled and cut into 1-inch pieces (3 cups)
- 1½ cups thinly sliced carrots (3 medium)
- 3 cloves garlic, minced
- 1½ teaspoons curry powder
- ½ teaspoon ground cumin
- ½ teaspoon ground ginger
- 3 cups uncooked instant brown rice
- ¾ cup unsweetened light coconut milk
- 3 tablespoons snipped fresh cilantro
- ⅓ cup chopped cashews

1 In a 3½- or 4-quart slow cooker combine broth, edamame, sweet potatoes, carrots, garlic, curry powder, cumin, and ginger.

2 Cover and cook on low-heat setting for 4½ to 5 hours or on high-heat setting for 2 to 2½ hours.

3 If using low-heat setting, turn to high-heat setting. Stir in uncooked rice. Cover and cook for 10 to 15 minutes more or until rice is tender and most of the liquid is absorbed. Stir in coconut milk and cilantro. Sprinkle each serving with cashews.

PER SERVING: *364 cal., 11 g total fat (2 g sat. fat), 0 mg chol., 697 mg sodium, 53 g carb., 9 g fiber, 15 g pro.*

tip

Fresh herbs don't hold up well in the slow cooker. Add them at the end of cooking or right before serving. Most dried herbs and spices will be fine in a slow cooker. As a general rule you can swap 1 teaspoon of dried herbs for 1 tablespoon of fresh.

Curried Couscous with Vegetables

PREP: 15 minutes   COOK: 4 to 6 hours (low) or 2 to 3 hours (high)   STAND: 5 minutes   MAKES 8 servings

2   14.5-ounce cans petite diced tomatoes with jalapeños, undrained

2   cups coarsely chopped yellow summer squash and/or zucchini (2 small)

2   cups water

1   large onion, cut into thin wedges

2   5.7-ounce packages curry-flavor couscous mix

1   cup chopped toasted slivered almonds

⅓   cup raisins (optional)

Fresh cilantro sprigs (optional)

1 In a 3½- or 4-quart slow cooker combine undrained tomatoes, squash, the water, onion, and seasoning packets from couscous mixes.

2 Cover and cook on low-heat setting for 4 to 6 hours or on high-heat setting for 2 to 3 hours. Stir in couscous. Turn off cooker. Cover and let stand for 5 minutes. Fluff couscous mixture with a fork.

3 Sprinkle each serving with almonds and, if desired, raisins. If desired, garnish with cilantro.

PER SERVING: *280 cal., 9 g total fat (1 g sat. fat), 0 mg chol., 842 mg sodium, 43 g carb., 6 g fiber, 10 g protein.*

tip

Quick-cooking couscous is available plain or in flavored mixes. You'll find the popular side dish in the rice and pasta aisle of your supermarket.

Slow Cooker

Slow Cooker Risotto

PREP: 40 minutes COOK: 4 hours (low) STAND: 15 minutes MAKES 6 servings

½ cup wheat berries

1½ cups water

Nonstick cooking spray

1¼ pounds fresh mushrooms (cremini, button, and/or shiitake), sliced

3 14-ounce cans vegetable broth

1⅔ cups uncooked converted rice

½ cup chopped shallots (4 medium)

3 cloves garlic, minced

1 teaspoon dried oregano, crushed

¼ teaspoon salt

¼ teaspoon ground black pepper

1 cup finely shredded Asiago or Parmesan cheese (4 ounces)

3 tablespoons butter, cut up

1 cup sliced fresh mushrooms

½ cup chopped yellow sweet pepper (1 small)

Snipped fresh Italian (flat-leaf) parsley

1 Rinse and drain wheat berries. In a small saucepan combine wheat berries and the water. Bring to boiling; reduce heat. Simmer, covered, for 30 minutes; drain.

2 Lightly coat the inside of a 4- to 5-quart slow cooker with cooking spray. In the prepared cooker combine cooked wheat berries, 1¼ pounds mushrooms, broth, uncooked rice, shallots, garlic, oregano, salt, and black pepper. Cover and cook on low-heat setting about 4 hours or until rice is tender.

3 Stir cheese and butter into rice mixture. Turn off cooker. Cover and let stand for 15 minutes. If risotto is too dry, stir in enough additional broth to moisten.

4 Meanwhile, lightly coat a small skillet with cooking spray; heat skillet over medium heat. Add 1 cup sliced mushrooms; cook until tender, stirring occasionally.

5 To serve, top risotto with cooked mushrooms, sweet pepper, and parsley.

PER SERVING: 427 cal., 14 g total fat (8 g sat. fat), 35 mg chol., 1,102 mg sodium, 64 g carb., 3 g fiber, 15 g pro.

Multigrain Pilaf

PREP: 15 minutes COOK: 6 to 8 hours (low) or 3 to 4 hours (high) MAKES 6 servings

- ²⁄₃ cup wheat berries
- ½ cup regular barley
- ½ cup uncooked wild rice
- 2 14-ounce cans vegetable broth
- 2 cups frozen shelled sweet soybeans (edamame) or baby lima beans
- ¾ cup chopped red sweet pepper (1 medium)
- ½ cup finely chopped onion (1 medium)
- 1 tablespoon butter
- 4 cloves garlic, minced
- ¾ teaspoon dried sage, crushed
- ½ teaspoon salt
- ¼ teaspoon coarse ground black pepper
- Grated Parmesan cheese (optional)

1 Rinse and drain wheat berries, barley, and wild rice. In a 3½- or 4-quart slow cooker combine wheat berries, barley, wild rice, broth, edamame, sweet pepper, onion, butter, garlic, sage, salt, and black pepper.

2 Cover and cook on low-heat setting for 6 to 8 hours or on high-heat setting for 3 to 4 hours. Stir before serving. If desired, sprinkle each serving with cheese.

PER SERVING: *342 cal., 9 g total fat (2 g sat. fat), 5 mg chol., 814 mg sodium, 50 g carb., 10 g fiber, 20 g pro.*

make it vegan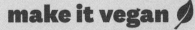

Substitute olive oil for the butter and, if using, substitute desired soy cheese for the Parmesan cheese.

Garlic-Artichoke Pasta

PREP: 15 minutes COOK: 6 to 8 hours (low) or 3 to 4 hours (high) STAND: 5 minutes MAKES: 6 servings

Nonstick cooking spray

3   14.5-ounce cans diced tomatoes with basil, garlic, and oregano, undrained

2   14-ounce cans artichoke hearts, drained and quartered

6   cloves garlic, minced

½   cup whipping cream

12 ounces dried linguine, fettuccine, or other pasta

Sliced pimiento-stuffed green olives and/or pitted ripe olives (optional)

Crumbled feta cheese or finely shredded Parmesan cheese (optional)

1 Coat the inside of a 3½- or 4-quart slow cooker with cooking spray. Drain 2 of the cans of tomatoes (do not drain the remaining can). In the prepared cooker combine drained and undrained tomatoes, artichoke hearts, and garlic.

2 Cover and cook on low-heat setting for 6 to 8 hours or on high-heat setting for 3 to 4 hours. Stir in cream. Cover and let stand about 5 minutes or until heated through.

3 Meanwhile, cook pasta according to package directions; drain. Serve tomato mixture over hot cooked pasta. If desired, top with olives and cheese.

PER SERVING: *403 cal., 8 g total fat (5 g sat. fat), 27 mg chol., 1,513 mg sodium, 68 g carb., 7 g fiber, 13 g protein.*

tip
Dairy products such as milk or cream can break down in the slow cooker if added too early. That's why it's best to add dairy ingredients during the last 15 to 30 minutes of cooking.

Pesto Beans and Pasta

PREP: 20 minutes COOK: 7 to 9 hours (low) or 3½ to 4½ hours (high) MAKES 6 to 8 servings

- 2   19-ounce cans cannellini beans (white kidney beans), rinsed and drained
- 1   14.5-ounce can Italian-style stewed tomatoes, undrained
- 1½   cups chopped green and/or red sweet peppers (2 medium)
- 1   medium onion, cut into thin wedges
- 4   cloves garlic, minced
- 2   teaspoons dried Italian seasoning, crushed
- ½   teaspoon cracked black pepper
- ½   cup vegetable broth
- ½   cup dry white wine or vegetable broth
- 1   7.5-ounce jar basil pesto
- 12   ounces dried penne pasta
- ½   cup finely shredded Parmesan or Romano cheese (2 ounces)

1 In a 3½- or 4-quart slow cooker combine drained beans, undrained tomatoes, sweet peppers, onion, garlic, Italian seasoning, and black pepper. Pour broth and wine over mixture in cooker.

2 Cover and cook on low-heat setting for 7 to 9 hours or on high-heat setting for 3½ to 4½ hours. Using a slotted spoon, transfer bean mixture to an extra-large serving bowl, reserving cooking liquid. Stir pesto into bean mixture.

3 Meanwhile, cook pasta according to package directions; drain. Add cooked pasta to bean mixture, stirring to combine. Stir in enough of the reserved cooking liquid to reach desired consistency. Sprinkle each serving with cheese.

PER SERVING: *580 cal., 20 g total fat (2 g sat. fat), 10 mg chol., 843 mg sodium, 80 g carb., 11 g fiber, 25 g pro.*

tip

Pasta should be cooked before it goes into the slow cooker.
Add it during the last 30 minutes of cooking.

Pasta with Lentil Sauce

PREP: 15 minutes COOK: 12 to 14 hours (low) or 6 to 7 hours (high) MAKES 8 servings

1 **26- to 28-ounce jar meatless tomato-base pasta sauce**
1 **14-ounce can vegetable broth**
½ **cup water**
1 **cup brown or yellow lentils, rinsed and drained**
1 **cup chopped carrots (2 medium)**
1 **cup chopped celery (2 stalks)**
1 **cup chopped onion (1 large)**
¼ **teaspoon crushed red pepper**
4 **cups hot cooked penne pasta**
   Finely shredded Parmesan cheese (optional)

1 In a 4½- or 5-quart slow cooker combine pasta sauce, broth, and the water. Stir in lentils, carrots, celery, onion, and crushed red pepper.

2 Cover and cook on low-heat setting for 12 to 14 hours or on high-heat setting for 6 to 7 hours.

3 Serve lentil mixture over hot cooked pasta. If desired, sprinkle with cheese.

PER SERVING: *404 cal., 4 g total fat (1 g sat. fat), 0 mg chol., 667 mg sodium, 75 g carb., 12 g fiber, 16 g pro.*

🌿 **make it vegan**
If using, substitute desired soy cheese for the Parmesan cheese.

Cheesy Multigrain Spaghetti with Tofu

PREP: 20 minutes COOK: 7 to 8 hours (low) or 3½ to 4 hours (high) MAKES 8 servings

2 14.5-ounce cans no-salt-added diced tomatoes, undrained

1 10.75-ounce can reduced-fat and reduced-sodium condensed cream of mushroom soup

2 cups sliced carrots (4 medium)

1½ cups sliced celery (3 stalks)

1½ cups chopped onions (3 medium)

4 cloves garlic, minced

2 teaspoons dried Italian seasoning, crushed

½ teaspoon salt

¼ teaspoon ground black pepper

8 ounces dried multigrain spaghetti, broken

1 16- to 18-ounce package extra-firm tub-style tofu (fresh bean curd), drained and cubed

½ cup shredded reduced-fat cheddar cheese (2 ounces)

1 In a 3½- or 4-quart slow cooker combine undrained tomatoes and soup. Stir in carrots, celery, onions, garlic, Italian seasoning, salt, and pepper.

2 Cover and cook on low-heat setting for 7 to 8 hours or on high-heat setting for 3½ to 4 hours.

3 Before serving cook spaghetti according to package directions; drain. Gently stir tofu into cooked spaghetti. Serve tomato mixture over hot cooked spaghetti mixture. Sprinkle with cheese.

PER SERVING: *212 cal., 4 g total fat (1 g sat. fat), 5 mg chol., 464 mg sodium, 32 g carb., 5 g fiber, 13 g pro.*

Chili-Style Vegetable Pasta

PREP: 20 minutes COOK: 5 to 6 hours (low) or 2½ to 3 hours (high) MAKES 6 servings

- 2 14.5-ounce cans no-salt-added diced tomatoes, undrained
- 1 15-ounce can garbanzo beans (chickpeas), rinsed and drained
- 1 15-ounce can red kidney beans, rinsed and drained
- 1 8-ounce can tomato sauce
- 1 cup finely chopped onion (1 large)
- 1 cup chopped green or yellow sweet pepper
- 2 to 3 teaspoons chili powder
- 2 cloves garlic, minced
- ½ teaspoon dried oregano, crushed
- ⅛ teaspoon cayenne pepper
- 8 ounces dried whole wheat and/or vegetable wagon wheel pasta
- ½ cup shredded reduced-fat cheddar cheese (2 ounces)

 In a 3½- or 4-quart slow cooker combine undrained tomatoes, drained garbanzo beans, drained kidney beans, tomato sauce, onion, sweet pepper, chili powder, garlic, oregano, and cayenne pepper.

2 Cover and cook on low-heat setting for 5 to 6 hours or on high-heat setting for 2½ to 3 hours.

3 Before serving cook pasta according to package directions; drain. Serve bean mixture over hot cooked pasta. Sprinkle with cheese.

PER SERVING: *327 cal., 4 g total fat (1 g sat. fat), 7 mg chol., 693 mg sodium, 63 g carb., 12 g fiber, 18 g pro.*

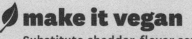

make it vegan

Substitute cheddar-flavor soy cheese for the cheddar cheese.

Short &
Simple

Keep your grocery list short with these easy entrées

that use 8 ingredients or fewer. Many are ready

in less than 30 minutes, making them great

weeknight meals.

Italian Beans with Pesto

PREP: 15 minutes CHILL: 4 hours COOK: 15 minutes MAKES 4 servings

1   14-ounce can vegetable broth
¾   cup bulgur
¾   cup chopped red sweet pepper (1 medium)
⅓   cup basil pesto
¼   cup thinly sliced green onions (2)
2   tablespoons balsamic vinegar
2   cups cooked* or canned red kidney beans, pinto beans, Christmas lima beans, and/or other white beans
    Ground black pepper
    Whole wheat flour tortillas or salad greens (optional)

1 In a large saucepan combine broth and bulgur. Bring to boiling; reduce heat. Simmer, covered, about 15 minutes or until bulgur is tender. Remove from heat. Stir in sweet pepper, pesto, green onions, and vinegar. Stir in beans. Season to taste with black pepper.

2 Transfer bean mixture to a serving bowl. Cover and chill for at least 4 hours. If desired, serve bean mixture rolled up in tortillas or spooned over salad greens.

PER SERVING: *331 cal., 10 g total fat (2 g sat. fat), 7 mg chol., 578 mg sodium, 48 g carb., 12 g fiber, 14 g pro.*

*tip

To cook beans, rinse ¾ cup dried beans. In a large saucepan combine beans and 5 cups water. Bring to boiling; reduce heat. Simmer, uncovered, for 2 minutes. Remove from heat. Cover and let stand for 1 hour. Drain and rinse beans. Return beans to saucepan. Stir in 5 cups fresh water. Bring to boiling; reduce heat. Simmer, covered, for 1¼ to 1½ hours or until beans are tender; drain.

tip

Save money and slash sodium from recipes by cooking your own dried beans rather than using canned. You can save time later by cooking a large batch and refrigerating or freezing leftovers for another use.

Vegetable Curry

START TO FINISH: **20 minutes** MAKES **4 servings**

1   16-ounce package frozen baby
    lima beans

½   cup water

1   15-ounce can tomato sauce
    with garlic and onion

1½ teaspoons curry powder

2   8.8-ounce pouches cooked
    Spanish-style rice
    Olive oil (optional)

¼   cup sliced green onions (2) or
    snipped fresh cilantro

1 In a medium saucepan combine lima beans and the water. Bring to boiling; reduce heat. Simmer, covered, for 5 minutes. Stir in tomato sauce and curry powder. Return to boiling; reduce heat. Simmer, covered, for 3 minutes more.

2 Meanwhile, heat rice according to package directions. Serve bean mixture with warm rice. If desired, drizzle with oil. Sprinkle with green onions.

PER SERVING: *385 cal., 3 g total fat (0 g sat. fat), 0 mg chol., 939 mg sodium, 72 g carb., 9 g fiber, 14 g pro.*

tip

When prepping vegetables, always wash and cut up extra. Not only will you save time, you're also more likely to use vegetables if they're already prepped.

Cashew-Vegetable Stir-Fry

START TO FINISH: **20 minutes** MAKES **4 servings**

1   tablespoon vegetable oil

1   16-ounce package frozen
    stir-fry vegetables (any
    combination)

⅓   cup stir-fry sauce (any flavor)

3   cups hot cooked rice

¾   cup dry-roasted cashews

1 In a large skillet heat oil over medium-high heat. Add vegetables; cook and stir about 3 minutes or until crisp-tender. Add sauce; cook and stir for 1 to 2 minutes more or until heated through.

2 Serve vegetable mixture over hot cooked rice. Sprinkle with cashews.

PER SERVING: *393 cal., 16 g total fat (3 g sat. fat), 0 mg chol., 720 mg sodium, 54 g carb., 4 g fiber, 9 g pro.*

tip

Cook large batches of rice, pasta, and other grains on the weekend so you have them ready to heat and eat during the week for snappy lunches and dinners.

Rice and Sweet Pepper Bowl

START TO FINISH: 30 minutes MAKES 4 servings

- 4   medium green and/or red sweet peppers
- 2   tablespoons water
- 1   8.8-ounce pouch cooked Spanish-style rice
- 1   14.5-ounce can stewed tomatoes, undrained
- 4   slices Monterey Jack cheese with jalapeño peppers (4 ounces)
- 1   tablespoon olive oil
- ¼   cup shaved Parmesan cheese (1 ounce)
-     Fresh oregano sprigs (optional)

1 Quarter sweet peppers; remove stems, seeds, and membranes. Place peppers in a 2-quart square microwave-safe baking dish. Add the water; cover with parchment paper. Microwave on 100 percent power (high) about 4 minutes or until crisp-tender, turning dish once. Remove peppers from dish; drain and set aside.

2 Heat rice in the microwave oven according to package directions. Drain tomatoes, reserving 2 tablespoons liquid.

3 In the same baking dish layer half of the peppers (cut sides up), the rice, drained tomatoes, Monterey Jack cheese, and the remaining peppers (cut sides down). Drizzle with the reserved tomato liquid. Cover with parchment paper. Microwave on high for 5 to 6 minutes or until heated through, turning dish once.

4 Let stand for 5 minutes before serving. Drizzle with oil. Sprinkle with Parmesan cheese and garnish with oregano.

PER SERVING: *319 cal., 16 g total fat (8 g sat. fat), 36 mg chol., 733 mg sodium, 31 g carb., 3 g fiber, 14 g pro.*

tip

Mix frozen vegetable blends with pasta or rice for a quick meal. Avoid ones that are packaged in sauces. Although they add flavor, these sauces are often very high in calories, salt, and fat.

🌱 Stuffed Peppers

START TO FINISH: **25 minutes** MAKES **4 servings**

- 4 large yellow sweet peppers
- 3 tablespoons water
- 1 15.25-ounce can no-salt-added whole kernel corn, drained
- 1 15-ounce can no-salt-added black beans, rinsed and drained
- 1 14.5-ounce can diced tomatoes, undrained
- ½ cup salsa
- ½ teaspoon ground cumin or chili powder
- 1 8.8-ounce pouch cooked brown rice

1 Cut off and discard the tops of sweet peppers; remove seeds and membranes from peppers. Place peppers, cut sides up, in a 2-quart square microwave-safe baking dish. Add the water. Microwave on 100 percent power (high) about 8 minutes or just until peppers start to soften.

2 Meanwhile, in a medium bowl stir together drained corn, drained beans, undrained tomatoes, salsa, and cumin. Heat rice in the microwave according to package directions. Stir rice into bean mixture.

3 Spoon bean mixture into peppers. Microwave on high about 4 minutes more or until peppers are tender and filling is heated through.

PER SERVING: *362 cal., 3 g total fat (0 g sat. fat), 0 mg chol., 327 mg sodium, 76 g carb., 12 g fiber, 13 g pro.*

77

tip

If you're not a stuffed pepper fan, make the corn and bean filling to serve with a hearty whole grain bread or warmed tortillas. Or use the filling for taco salad served on mixed greens with spicy ranch dressing.

Couscous-Stuffed Peppers

PREP: 20 minutes   BAKE: 25 minutes   OVEN: 350°F   MAKES 4 servings

1   **6-ounce package toasted pine nut-flavor couscous mix**

½   **cup shredded carrot (1 medium)**

2   **large or 4 small red, yellow, green, and/or orange sweet peppers**

½   **cup shredded Italian cheese blend (2 ounces)**

1½   **cups mushroom-olive or tomato-basil pasta sauce**

1 Preheat oven to 350°F. Prepare couscous mix according to package directions, omitting oil and adding shredded carrot with the couscous.

2 Meanwhile, cut large peppers in half lengthwise (for small peppers, cut off and reserve tops). Remove seeds and membranes from peppers. In a large saucepan cook peppers (and tops, if using) in a large amount of boiling water for 5 minutes. Drain on paper towels. Place peppers, cut sides up, in an ungreased 2-quart rectangular baking dish. Spoon couscous mixture into peppers.

3 Bake, covered, for 20 to 25 minutes or until peppers are tender and filling is heated through. Sprinkle with cheese. Bake, uncovered, about 5 minutes more or until cheese is melted.

4 Meanwhile, in a small saucepan heat pasta sauce. Serve stuffed peppers with sauce. (For small peppers, place pepper tops on top of couscous filling.)

PER SERVING: *259 cal., 6 g total fat (3 g sat. fat), 10 mg chol., 801 mg sodium, 42 g carb., 7 g fiber, 11 g pro.*

◢ make it vegan

Substitute desired soy cheese for the Italian cheese blend.

Tortilla Lasagna

PREP: 15 minutes BAKE: 35 minutes STAND: 10 minutes OVEN: 400°F MAKES 8 servings

1 6.75-ounce package Spanish rice mix

1 11-ounce can whole kernel corn with sweet peppers, undrained

2 15-ounce cans black beans, undrained

10 6-inch corn tortillas

2 cups shredded Monterey Jack cheese with jalapeño peppers (8 ounces)

1 Preheat oven to 400°F. Grease a 3-quart rectangular baking dish; set aside. Prepare rice mix according to package directions, except substitute undrained corn for $\frac{1}{2}$ cup of the liquid. Place undrained beans in a medium bowl; mash slightly.

2 To assemble, place 5 of the tortillas in the bottom of the prepared baking dish, overlapping and placing slightly up sides of dish (cut tortillas as necessary to fit). Spoon beans evenly over tortillas in dish. Sprinkle with 1 cup of the cheese. Top with the remaining 5 tortillas. Spoon cooked rice evenly over tortillas.

3 Bake, covered, about 30 minutes or until heated through. Sprinkle with the remaining 1 cup cheese. Bake, uncovered, about 5 minutes more or until cheese is melted. Let stand for 10 minutes before serving.

PER SERVING: *406 cal., 12 g total fat (7 g sat. fat), 34 mg chol., 1,101 mg sodium, 60 g carb., fiber, 20 g pro.*

tip

Most restaurants will accommodate vegetarian modifications to their menus. You can make many substitutions that will provide a satisfying meal. Ask for tofu instead of meat or to omit the meat and increase the veggies.

Chipotle-Bean Enchiladas

PREP: 20 minutes BAKE: 30 minutes OVEN: 350°F MAKES 5 servings

10 **6-inch corn tortillas**

2 **10-ounce cans enchilada sauce**

1 **15-ounce can pinto beans or black beans, rinsed and drained**

1 **tablespoon chopped chipotle pepper in adobo sauce***

2 **cups shredded Mexican cheese blend (8 ounces)**

1 Preheat oven to 350°F. Grease a 2-quart rectangular baking dish; set aside. Stack tortillas and wrap tightly in foil. Bake about 10 minutes or until warm.

2 Meanwhile, for filling, in a medium bowl combine ½ cup of the enchilada sauce, the drained beans, and chipotle pepper. Stir in 1 cup of the cheese. Spoon about ¼ cup of the filling onto one edge of each tortilla. Starting from the filled edge, roll up tortilla. Place rolls, seam sides down, in the prepared baking dish. Top tortilla rolls with the remaining enchilada sauce.

3 Bake, covered, about 25 minutes or until heated through. Sprinkle with the remaining 1 cup cheese. Bake, uncovered, about 5 minutes more or until cheese is melted.

PER SERVING: *487 cal., 19 g total fat (8 g sat. fat), 40 mg chol., 1,091 mg sodium, 63 g carb., 14 g fiber, 23 g pro.*

*tip

Because chile peppers contain volatile oils that can burn your skin and eyes, avoid direct contact with them as much as possible. When working with chile peppers, wear plastic or rubber gloves. If your bare hands do touch the chile peppers, wash your hands and nails well with soap and warm water.

Bean and Cheese Burritos

PREP: **20 minutes**   BAKE: **10 minutes**   OVEN: **350°F**   MAKES **4 servings**

- 8   **7- or 8-inch flour tortillas**
- 1   **cup chopped onion (1 large)**
- 1   **tablespoon vegetable oil**
- 1   **16-ounce can refried beans**
- 1   **cup shredded cheddar cheese (4 ounces)**
- 1   **cup shredded lettuce**
- ⅓   **cup salsa**
-       **Sour cream and/or guacamole (optional)**

1 Preheat oven to 350°F. Stack tortillas and wrap tightly in foil. Bake about 10 minutes or until softened.

2 Meanwhile, for filling, in a large skillet cook onion in hot oil over medium heat until tender, stirring occasionally. Add refried beans; cook and stir until heated through.

3 Spread about ¼ cup of the filling over the bottom half of each tortilla; sprinkle each with 2 tablespoons cheese. Fold up bottom edge of tortilla. Fold in opposite sides; roll up from the bottom. Place tortilla rolls in an ungreased 3-quart rectangular baking dish.

4 Bake about 10 minutes or until heated through. Serve with lettuce and salsa. If desired, top with sour cream and/or guacamole.

PER SERVING: *453 cal., 19 g total fat (8 g sat. fat), 39 mg chol., 886 mg sodium, 53 g carb., 8 g fiber, 18 g pro.*

make it vegan 🌿

Substitute soy cheese for the cheddar cheese and do not serve with sour cream.

tip

Foods that typically contain meat, such as pizza, burritos, and lasagna, are often easily altered for a vegetarian diet. Make up for the meat nutrients by adding other sources of protein, iron, and calcium such as beans, whole grains, and soy.

Spicy Bean Tostadas

PREP: 15 minutes BAKE: 10 minutes OVEN: 425°F MAKES 4 servings

4   8-inch whole wheat flour tortillas

Olive oil nonstick cooking spray

1½ cups fat-free spicy refried beans, warmed

1½ cups shredded leaf lettuce

¾   cup fresh deli salsa, drained

½   cup shredded reduced-fat Mexican cheese blend (2 ounces)

1 Preheat oven to 425°F. Lightly coat both sides of tortillas with cooking spray. Place tortillas on an ungreased extra-large baking sheet. Bake for 10 to 12 minutes or until lightly browned and crisp, turning once. Cool tortillas on a wire rack.

2 Spread tortillas with warm refried beans. Top with lettuce, salsa, and cheese.

PER SERVING: *255 cal., 6 g total fat (3 g sat. fat), 5 mg chol., 1,252 mg sodium, 32 g carb., 15 g fiber, 17 g pro.*

Black Bean and Corn Quesadillas

START TO FINISH: 20 minutes MAKES 4 servings

8   8-inch whole wheat or plain flour tortillas

2   cups shredded four-cheese Mexican cheese blend (8 ounces)

1½ cups black bean and corn salsa

1   medium avocado, seeded, peeled, and sliced

Sour cream

1 Sprinkle half of each tortilla with cheese. Spoon 1 tablespoon of the salsa onto each tortilla; top with avocado. Fold tortillas in half over filling, pressing lightly.

2 Heat a large skillet over medium-high heat for 2 minutes; reduce heat to medium. Cook quesadillas, 2 at a time, in hot skillet for 2 to 3 minutes or until light brown and cheese is melted, turning once. Transfer to a baking sheet and keep warm in a 300°F oven while cooking the remaining quesadillas.

3 To serve, cut quesadillas into wedges. Serve with the remaining salsa and sour cream.

PER SERVING: *647 cal., 35 g total fat (16 g sat. fat), 61 mg chol., 1,405 mg sodium, 48 g carb., 23 g fiber, 31 g pro.*

🌱 make it vegan

Substitute soy cheese for the Mexican cheese blend and serve with tofu sour cream instead of dairy sour cream.

Summary Fresh Quesadillas

START TO FINISH: 20 minutes **MAKES 4 servings**

- 4 9- to 10-inch flour tortillas
- 1 tablespoon vegetable oil
- 2 large roma tomatoes, thinly sliced
- 8 ounces fresh thin asparagus spears, trimmed and cut into 1-inch pieces
- ½ cup shredded fresh basil
- 1½ cups shredded mozzarella cheese (6 ounces)
  Fruit salsa or marinara sauce (optional)

1 Brush 1 side of tortillas with oil. Place tortillas, oiled sides down, on an ungreased baking sheet. Top half of each tortilla with tomatoes, asparagus, and basil; sprinkle with cheese. Fold tortillas in half over filling, pressing lightly.

2 For a charcoal grill, grill quesadillas on the rack of an uncovered grill directly over medium coals about 2 minutes or until cheese starts to melt and tortillas start to brown, turning once halfway through grilling. (For a gas grill, preheat grill. Reduce heat to medium. Place quesadillas on grill rack over heat. Cover and grill as above.)

3 To serve, cut quesadillas into wedges and, if desired, serve with salsa.

PER SERVING: *289 cal., 14 g total fat (6 g sat. fat), 27 mg chol., 446 mg sodium, 27 g carb., 2 g fiber, 15 g pro.*

make it vegan
Substitute mozzarella-flavor soy cheese for the Mozzarella cheese.

Savory Stuffed Portobellos

PREP: **35 minutes** BAKE: **15 minutes** OVEN: **350°F** MAKES **6 servings**

Nonstick cooking spray

1/2 cup chopped onion (1 medium)

4 cloves garlic, minced

1 6.75- to 8-ounce package rice pilaf and lentil mix

1 6-ounce jar marinated artichoke hearts, undrained

6 medium fresh portobello mushrooms (about 4 inches in diameter)

1/4 cup finely shredded Parmesan cheese (1 ounce) (optional)

1 Preheat oven to 350°F. Coat a medium saucepan with cooking spray; heat saucepan over medium-high heat. Add onion and garlic; cook and stir until onion is tender. In the same saucepan with the onion and garlic, prepare rice pilaf mix according to package directions.

2 Meanwhile, drain artichoke hearts, reserving marinade. Coarsely chop artichokes; set aside. Cut off mushroom stems even with caps; discard stems. If desired, remove gills from undersides of caps. Brush mushrooms with some of the reserved artichoke marinade; discard any remaining marinade. Place mushroom caps, stemmed sides up, in an ungreased shallow baking pan.

3 Bake for 15 to 20 minutes or until mushrooms are tender. Transfer to a serving platter. Stir artichokes and, if desired, cheese into hot pilaf mixture. Spoon pilaf mixture into mushroom caps.

PER SERVING: *288 cal., 14 g total fat (5 g sat. fat), 16 mg chol., 817 mg sodium, 31 g carb., 4 g fiber, 20 g pro.*

Butternut Squash Phyllo Strudel

PREP: **1 hour** BAKE: **15 minutes** OVEN: **400°F** MAKES **4 servings**

- 2 **pounds butternut squash, peeled, seeded, and cut into ¾-inch pieces**
- 2 **medium cooking apples, peeled, cored, and cut into ¾-inch pieces**
- 1 **cup coarsely chopped red onion**
- 1 **tablespoon vegetable oil**
- ½ **teaspoon salt**
- ¼ **teaspoon ground black pepper**
- ½ **cup crumbled blue cheese or shredded white cheddar cheese (2 ounces)**
- 2 **tablespoons snipped fresh sage or 2 teaspoons dried sage, crushed**
- 12 **sheets frozen phyllo dough (14×9-inch rectangles), thawed**
- **Nonstick cooking spray**
- ½ **cup finely chopped walnuts, toasted**

1 Preheat oven to 400°F. For squash filling, in a 15×10×1-inch baking pan combine squash, apples, and onion. Drizzle with oil and sprinkle with salt and pepper; toss gently to coat. Bake about 35 minutes or until vegetables are tender and light brown. Stir in cheese and sage; set aside.

2 Line a baking sheet with parchment paper or foil; grease foil (if using). Set baking sheet aside. Unfold phyllo dough.

3 For each phyllo roll, place 1 sheet of phyllo dough on a work surface. (While you work, keep the remaining phyllo covered with plastic wrap to keep it from drying out.) Coat phyllo sheet with cooking spray. Using half of the walnuts, sprinkle some of the walnuts over phyllo sheet. Repeat with 5 more phyllo sheets, cooking spray, and walnuts. Spread half of the squash filling along 1 short side of phyllo stack to within ½ inch of the edges. Starting from the filled edge, roll up phyllo.

4 Lightly coat each phyllo roll with cooking spray. Using a serrated knife, gently cut each roll into 4 portions. Place portions, standing upright, on the prepared baking sheet. Bake about 15 minutes or until golden brown.

PER SERVING: *488 cal., 21 g total fat (5 g sat. fat), 11 mg chol., 774 mg sodium, 69 g carb., 8 g fiber, 12 g pro.*

Cheddar-Apple Bundles

PREP: 45 minutes BAKE: 20 minutes COOL: 20 minutes OVEN: 400°F MAKES 8 servings

½ cup packed brown sugar

½ cup chopped pecans

2 cups all-purpose flour

2 cups shredded white cheddar cheese (8 ounces)

1 tablespoon granulated sugar

¼ teaspoon salt

½ cup butter, cut up

6 to 8 tablespoons cold water

2 cups peeled and chopped Granny Smith or Jonathan apples

3 tablespoons fig jam or apricot preserves

1 Preheat oven to 400°F. Line a baking sheet with parchment paper. In a small bowl combine brown sugar and pecans. Set aside.

2 In a food processor combine flour, ½ cup of the cheese, the granulated sugar, and salt. Cover and process with one on/off pulse. Add butter. Cover and process with several on/off pulses until pieces are pea size. With processor running, slowly add enough of the 6 to 8 tablespoons water through feed tube just until dough forms a ball. On a lightly floured surface gently knead dough until smooth. Divide into 8 pieces.

3 For each bundle, roll 1 piece of dough into an 8-inch circle. Place 3 tablespoons of the remaining cheese in center of dough. Top with ¼ cup of the apples and 1 tablespoon of the pecan mixture. Lightly brush edge of dough with water. Bring up dough edge, pleating and pressing together to seal. Place bundles, sealed sides up, on the prepared baking sheet.

4 Bake for 20 to 25 minutes or until pastry is golden brown. Spoon jam over pastry bundles. Cool on baking sheet for 20 minutes. Serve warm.

PER SERVING: *474 cal., 26 g total fat (14 g sat. fat), 60 mg chol., 340 mg sodium, 50 g carb., 2 g fiber, 9 g pro.*

All-Wrapped-Up Salad

START TO FINISH: 20 minutes   MAKES 2 servings

- **2** 8-inch multigrain, whole wheat, or plain flour tortillas
- **¾** cup shredded romaine lettuce and/or fresh spinach leaves
- **½** of an avocado, seeded, peeled, and sliced
- **¼** of a cucumber, halved lengthwise, seeded, and thinly sliced
- **¼** cup shredded Monterey Jack cheese with jalapeño peppers (1 ounce)
- Salsa (optional)

1 On each tortilla, layer lettuce and/or spinach, avocado, cucumber, and cheese. Roll up tightly. If desired, wrap each tortilla roll in plastic wrap and chill for up to 6 hours. If desired, serve with salsa.

PER SERVING: *248 cal., 13 g total fat (4 g sat. fat), 13 mg chol., 401 mg sodium, 20 g carb., 12 g fiber, 13 g pro*

make it vegan 🌿
Substitute soy cheese for the Monterey Jack cheese with jalapeño peppers.

Gardener's Pie

PREP: 15 minutes   BAKE: 45 minutes   OVEN: 350°F   MAKES 4 servings

- **1** 16-ounce package frozen mixed vegetables (any combination), thawed
- **1** 11-ounce can condensed cheddar cheese soup
- **½** teaspoon dried thyme, crushed
- **1** 16-ounce package refrigerated mashed potatoes
- **1** cup shredded smoked cheddar cheese (4 ounces)

1 Preheat oven to 350°F. In an ungreased 1½-quart casserole combine vegetables, soup, and thyme. Stir mashed potatoes to soften. Carefully spread mashed potatoes over vegetable mixture to cover surface.

2 Bake, covered, for 30 minutes. Bake, uncovered, about 15 minutes more or until heated through, topping with cheese during the last 5 minutes of baking. Serve in shallow bowls.

PER SERVING: *308 cal., 17 g total fat (8 g sat. fat), 38 mg chol., 872 mg sodium, 31 g carb., 3 g fiber, 14 g pro.*

tip
Prepackaged convenience foods can be high in added sugars, salt, and fat. Always check labels and compare brands. Products can vary within the same brand as well.

Roasted Vegetables with Polenta

PREP: 20 minutes   ROAST: 15 minutes   OVEN: 425°F   MAKES 6 servings

6   cups assorted cut-up
    vegetables (such as
    asparagus, thickly sliced
    red sweet peppers, sliced
    zucchini or red onions, and/or
    quartered mushrooms)

¼   cup olive oil

¼   teaspoon salt

1   recipe Polenta or one 16-ounce
    tube refrigerated cooked
    polenta

    Shredded Parmesan cheese

1 Preheat oven to 425°F. In a shallow roasting pan combine vegetables, oil, and salt; toss gently to coat. Roast for 15 to 20 minutes or just until vegetables are tender, stirring once.

2 Meanwhile, prepare Polenta. Or slice refrigerated polenta and heat in a skillet according to package directions.

3 To serve, spoon or arrange Polenta in a shallow bowl. Top with roasted vegetables and sprinkle with cheese.

PER SERVING: *222 cal., 11 g total fat (2 g sat. fat), 4 mg chol., 560 mg sodium, 25 g carb., 4 g fiber, 6 g pro.*

Polenta

In a medium saucepan bring 2¾ cups water to boiling. Meanwhile, in a medium bowl combine 1 cup cornmeal, 1 cup cold water, and ½ teaspoon salt. Slowly add cornmeal mixture to boiling water, stirring constantly. Cook and stir until mixture returns to boiling; reduce heat to low. Cook for 10 to 15 minutes or until mixture is very thick, stirring frequently.

make it vegan

Substitute desired soy cheese for the Parmesan cheese.

Spinach and Feta Casserole

PREP: 15 minutes   BAKE: 45 minutes   OVEN: 350°F   MAKES 4 servings

3 eggs, lightly beaten

2 cups cream-style cottage cheese

1 10-ounce package frozen chopped spinach, thawed and well drained

⅓ cup crumbled feta cheese

¼ cup butter, melted

3 tablespoons all-purpose flour

2 teaspoons dried minced onion

Dash ground nutmeg

1 Preheat oven to 350°F. Grease a 1½-quart casserole; set aside.

2 In a large bowl combine eggs, cottage cheese, spinach, feta cheese, melted butter, flour, dried onion, and nutmeg. Transfer mixture to the prepared casserole.

3 Bake, uncovered, about 45 minutes or until center is nearly set (160°F).

PER SERVING: *344 cal., 24 g total fat (14 g sat. fat), 218 mg chol., 784 mg sodium, 12 g carb., 2 g fiber, 22 g pro.*

Bruschetta Burgers

START TO FINISH: **25 minutes** MAKES **4 servings**

Nonstick cooking spray

4 **frozen tomato, basil, and cheese meatless burger patties**

4 **slices mozzarella cheese (3 ounces)**

2 **thin multigrain sandwich rounds, split, or 4 slices whole wheat bread**

8 **to 12 fresh basil leaves**

4 **slices tomato**

Shredded fresh basil (optional)

1 Preheat broiler. Coat a large nonstick skillet with cooking spray; heat skillet over medium heat. Add frozen patties; cook for 8 to 10 minutes or until heated through, turning occasionally.

2 Arrange patties on 1 side of a large baking sheet; top with cheese. Place sandwich rounds, cut sides up, on the other side of the baking sheet.

3 Broil 4 to 5 inches from the heat for 1 to 2 minutes or until cheese is melted and sandwich rounds are toasted. Remove from broiler.

4 Divide basil leaves among sandwich rounds. Top with patties, tomato slices, and, if desired, shredded basil.

PER SERVING: *178 cal., 5 g total fat (3 g sat. fat), 16 mg chol., 538 mg sodium, 21 g carb., 6 g fiber, 17 g pro.*

Double Mushroom Burgers with Onion Spread

START TO FINISH: 25 minutes MAKES 4 servings

- 2 ounces reduced-fat cream cheese (Neufchâtel), softened
- 1 teaspoon onion herb or garlic herb seasoning blend
- Nonstick cooking spray
- 4 frozen mushroom or mushroom-cheese meatless burger patties
- 3 cups sliced fresh mushrooms (8 ounces)
- 2 teaspoons canola oil
- 4 whole wheat hamburger buns, split and toasted
- Butterhead (Boston or Bibb) lettuce leaves and/or tomato slices (optional)

1 In a small bowl stir together cream cheese and seasoning blend; set aside.

2 Coat a large nonstick skillet with cooking spray; heat skillet over medium heat. Add frozen patties; cook for 8 to 10 minutes or until heated through, turning occasionally. In another large skillet cook mushrooms in hot oil over medium heat for 5 to 7 minutes or until tender, stirring occasionally.

3 To serve, spread cut sides of buns with cream cheese mixture. Fill buns with patties, mushrooms, and, if desired, lettuce and/or tomato.

PER SERVING: *298 cal., 14 g total fat (4 g sat. fat), 10 mg chol., 490 mg sodium, 32 g carb., 1 g fiber, 14 g pro.*

tip

Some purchased seasoning blends are loaded with salt. This recipe calls for a salt-free blend. If you can't find it in your grocery store, look for a similar blend that is low in sodium.

You Choose Veggie Burgers

START TO FINISH: **20 minutes** MAKES **6 servings**

- **6 refrigerated or frozen desired meatless burger patties**
- **6 whole wheat hamburger buns, split and toasted**
- **1 recipe Ultra Ketchup Topper, Smoky Berry Topper, or Double Pepper Topper**

1 Heat patties according to package directions. Fill buns with patties and Ultra Ketchup Topper, Smoky Berry Topper, or Double Pepper Topper.

PER SERVING *with Ultra Ketchup Topper: 220 cal., 3 g total fat (0 g sat. fat), 0 mg chol., 798 mg sodium, 36 g carb., 7 g fiber, 18 g pro.*

Ultra Ketchup Topper

In a small bowl combine ½ cup ketchup, 3 tablespoons chopped oil-packed dried tomato, 2 teaspoons packed brown sugar, 2 teaspoons red wine vinegar, dash salt, and dash ground black pepper. Try with roasted onion patties and top with sliced tomatoes.

MAKES about ¾ cup

Smoky Berry Topper

In a small bowl mash ¾ cup fresh blueberries and/or raspberries with a potato masher or fork. Stir in 2 tablespoons bacon-flavor vegetable protein bits and 2 tablespoons cider vinegar. Try with roasted garlic patties and top with watercress.

MAKES about ¾ cup

PER SERVING *with Smoky Berry Topper: 203 cal., 2 g total fat (0 g sat. fat), 0 mg chol., 534 mg sodium, 30 g carb., 7 g fiber, 18 g pro.*

Double Pepper Topper

In a small bowl combine ¾ cup chopped roasted red sweet peppers, 1 tablespoon adobo sauce from canned chipotle peppers in adobo sauce, 1 tablespoon sherry vinegar, and 1 teaspoon sugar. Try with grilled vegetable patties and top with shredded yellow summer squash.

MAKES about ¾ cup

PER SERVING *with Double Pepper Topper: 194 cal., 2 g total fat (0 g sat. fat), 0 mg chol., 503 mg sodium, 30 g carb., 7 g fiber, 17 g pro.*

Ramen Noodles with Vegetables

START TO FINISH: **15 minutes** MAKES **2 to 3 servings**

1 **3-ounce package ramen noodles (any flavor)**

1 **tablespoon vegetable oil**

6 **ounces fresh asparagus, trimmed and cut into 1-inch pieces (1 cup)**

$\frac{1}{2}$ **cup shredded carrot (1 medium)**

$\frac{1}{4}$ **cup light teriyaki sauce**

1 Cook noodles according to package directions (discard seasoning packet); drain. Return noodles to hot pan; cover and keep warm.

2 Meanwhile, in a large skillet heat oil over medium-high heat. Add asparagus and carrot. Cook and stir for 3 to 5 minutes or until asparagus is crisp-tender. Stir in teriyaki sauce and cooked noodles; toss gently to coat.

PER SERVING: *291 cal., 14 g total fat (4 g sat. fat), 0 mg chol., 1,396 mg sodium, 36 g carb., 3 g fiber, 7 g pro.*

Asian Noodle Bowl

START TO FINISH: 25 minutes   MAKES 4 servings

94

8 ounces dried soba
   (buckwheat noodles), udon
   (broad, white noodles), or
   vermicelli

2 cups vegetable broth

½ cup peanut sauce

2 cups frozen stir-fry
   vegetables (any combination)

½ cup dry-roasted peanuts,
   chopped

1 Cook noodles according to package directions; drain in a colander, but do not rinse. Set aside.

2 In the same pan combine broth and peanut sauce. Bring to boiling. Stir in frozen vegetables and cooked noodles. Return to boiling; reduce heat. Simmer for 2 to 3 minutes or until vegetables are heated through.

3 Divide noodles and broth mixture among soup bowls. Sprinkle with peanuts.

PER SERVING: *403 cal., 15 g total fat (2 g sat. fat), 0 mg chol., 1,326 mg sodium, 59 g carb., 4 g fiber, 15 g pro.*

tip

Make extra soba noodles and use them for another meal in place of spaghetti. Made from buckwheat flour, soba noodles have a brownish-gray color and nutty flavor. Find them in Asian grocery stores, health food stores, and in the Asian food section of some large supermarkets.

Tortellini and Peas

START TO FINISH: **20 minutes** MAKES **4 servings**

1 9-ounce package refrigerated cheese tortellini or ravioli

1 cup frozen peas

2 tablespoons all-purpose flour

$\frac{1}{8}$ teaspoon ground black pepper

1 cup half-and-half, light cream, or milk

1 14.5-ounce can diced tomatoes with basil, garlic, and oregano, undrained

Salt and ground black pepper

2 tablespoons finely shredded Parmesan cheese

1 Cook tortellini according to package directions, adding peas during the last 1 minute of cooking; drain. Return tortellini mixture to hot pan.

2 Meanwhile, for sauce, in a medium saucepan stir together flour and pepper. Gradually stir in half-and-half. Cook and stir over medium heat until thickened and bubbly. Cook and stir for 1 minute more. Gradually stir in undrained tomatoes. Season to taste with salt and additional pepper.

3 Pour sauce over cooked tortellini mixture; toss gently to coat. Sprinkle each serving with cheese.

PER SERVING: *410 cal., 13 g total fat (7 g sat. fat), 54 mg chol., 998 mg sodium, 57 g carb., 4 g fiber, 18 g pro.*

Spinach Tortellini with Beans and Feta

START TO FINISH: **20 minutes** MAKES **4 servings**

1   **9-ounce package refrigerated cheese-filled spinach tortellini**

1   **15-ounce can cannellini beans (white kidney beans), rinsed and drained**

¾   **cup crumbled feta cheese with garlic and herbs (3 ounces)**

2   **tablespoons olive oil**

1   **large tomato, chopped**
    Ground black pepper

4   **cups fresh baby spinach**

1 Cook tortellini according to package directions; drain. Return tortellini to hot pan. Gently stir in drained beans, cheese, and oil.

2 Cook over medium heat until beans are heated through and cheese starts to melt, gently stirring occasionally. Stir in tomato; cook for 1 minute more. Sprinkle with pepper.

3 To serve, divide spinach among dinner plates or shallow salad bowls. Top with tortellini mixture.

PER SERVING: *448 cal., 18 g total fat (7 g sat. fat), 61 mg chol., 858 mg sodium, 55 g carb., 9 g fiber, 24 g pro.*

Tortellini Alfredo with Roasted Peppers

START TO FINISH: **20 minutes**   MAKES **2 or 3 servings**

1   **9-ounce package refrigerated cheese tortellini**

½   **cup roasted red sweet peppers, drained and cut into ½-inch strips**

⅓   **cup refrigerated light Alfredo pasta sauce**

½   **cup shredded fresh basil**
    Coarse ground black pepper

1 Cook tortellini according to package directions; drain. Return tortellini to hot pan. Stir in roasted peppers and Alfredo sauce. Cook and stir over medium-low heat until heated through.

2 Stir half of the basil into tortellini mixture. Sprinkle with the remaining basil and black pepper.

PER SERVING: *383 cal., 12 g total fat (8 g sat. fat), 56 mg chol., 775 mg sodium, 51 g carb., 2 g fiber, 17 g pro.*

Linguine with Gorgonzola Sauce

START TO FINISH: 25 minutes MAKES 4 servings

- 1 **9-ounce package refrigerated whole wheat linguine**
- 1 **pound fresh asparagus, trimmed and cut into 2-inch pieces**
- 1 **cup evaporated fat-free milk**
- 2 **ounces reduced-fat cream cheese (Neufchâtel), cubed**
- ½ **cup crumbled Gorgonzola or other blue cheese (2 ounces)**
- ¼ **teaspoon salt**
- 2 **tablespoons chopped walnuts, toasted**

1 Cook linguine and asparagus according to the package directions for linguine; drain. Return linguine mixture to hot pan; cover and keep warm.

2 Meanwhile, for sauce, in a medium saucepan combine evaporated milk, cream cheese, half of the Gorgonzola cheese, and the salt. Bring to boiling over medium heat, whisking constantly; reduce heat. Simmer, uncovered, for 2 minutes, whisking frequently (sauce may appear slightly curdled).

3 Pour sauce over cooked linguine mixture; toss gently to coat. Divide linguine mixture among shallow bowls. Sprinkle with the remaining Gorgonzola cheese and walnuts. Serve immediately (sauce will thicken upon standing).

PER SERVING: *361 cal., 13 g total fat (6 g sat. fat), 42 mg chol., 476 mg sodium, 44 g carb., 7 g fiber, 19 g pro.*

Pasta with Pepper-Cheese Sauce

START TO FINISH: **25 minutes** MAKES **4 to 6 servings**

8 ounces dried medium shell, mostaccioli, or cut ziti pasta

1 0.9- to 1.25-ounce envelope hollandaise sauce mix

1 cup roasted red sweet peppers, drained and chopped

½ cup shredded Monterey Jack cheese with jalapeño peppers (2 ounces)

1 Cook pasta according to package directions; drain. Return pasta to hot pan.

2 Meanwhile, for sauce, prepare hollandaise sauce mix according to package directions, except use only 2 tablespoons butter. Stir in roasted peppers. Remove pan from heat.

3 Slowly add cheese to sauce, stirring until cheese is melted. Pour sauce over cooked pasta; toss gently to coat.

PER SERVING: *384 cal., 13 g total fat (8 g sat. fat), 36 mg chol., 407 mg sodium, 53 g carb., 2 g fiber, 13 g pro.*

tip

Stock up on nonperishable convenience foods when they're on sale. Beans, pasta sauce, rice, boxed vegetable stock, and other basic pantry items have lengthy shelf lives, so if you have the storage space, load up and keep your cupboards well stocked.

Sweet Beans and Pasta

START TO FINISH: **25 minutes** MAKES **4 servings**

8   **ounces dried linguine**

1½ **cups frozen shelled sweet soybeans (edamame)**

1   **cup shredded carrots (2 medium)**

1   **10-ounce container refrigerated Alfredo pasta sauce**

2   **teaspoons snipped fresh rosemary**

1 Cook linguine according to package directions, adding soybeans and carrots during the last 10 minutes of cooking; drain. Return linguine mixture to hot pan.

2 Stir Alfredo sauce and rosemary into cooked linguine mixture; heat through.

PER SERVING: *544 cal., 27 g total fat (1 g sat. fat), 35 mg chol., 280 mg sodium, 57 g carb., 5 g fiber, 20 g pro.*

Two-Cheese Macaroni Bake

PREP: 20 minutes BAKE: 45 minutes STAND: 10 minutes OVEN: 375°F MAKES 8 servings

- 8 ounces dried elbow macaroni (2 cups)
- 4 eggs, lightly beaten
- 2½ cups milk
- 2 cups crumbled feta cheese with basil and tomato or plain feta cheese (8 ounces)
- ¾ cup cream-style cottage cheese
- ½ teaspoon salt

1 Preheat oven to 375°F. Grease a 2-quart square baking dish; set aside. Cook macaroni according to package directions; drain. Transfer macaroni to the prepared baking dish.

2 In a medium bowl combine eggs, milk, feta cheese, cottage cheese, and salt. Pour evenly over cooked macaroni.

3 Bake, uncovered, for 45 minutes. Let stand for 10 minutes before serving.

PER SERVING: *267 cal., 11 g total fat (6 g sat. fat), 136 mg chol., 609 mg sodium, 26 g carb., 1 g fiber, 17 g pro.*

Spicy Pasta and Broccoli 🌿

START TO FINISH: **25 minutes** MAKES **4 servings**

12 ounces orecchiette or medium shell pasta (about 4 cups)

2 tablespoons olive oil

3 cups chopped Broccolini or broccoli florets

1 cup vegetable broth

1/2 teaspoon dried Italian seasoning, crushed

1/4 to 1/2 teaspoon crushed red pepper

1 Cook pasta according to package directions; drain. Return pasta to hot pan. Drizzle with 1 tablespoon of the oil; toss gently to coat. Cover and keep warm.

2 Meanwhile, in a large skillet heat the remaining 1 tablespoon oil over medium-high heat. Add Broccolini; cook and stir for 3 minutes. Add broth, Italian seasoning, and crushed red pepper.

3 Bring to boiling; reduce heat. Simmer, covered, for 2 to 3 minutes or until Broccolini is crisp-tender. Add Broccolini mixture to cooked pasta; toss gently to combine.

PER SERVING: *404 cal., 9 g total fat (1 g sat. fat), 0 mg chol., 214 mg sodium, 67 g carb., 4 g fiber, 14 g pro.*

Saucy Mushroom Borscht

START TO FINISH: **40 minutes**   MAKES **4 servings**

8   ounces baby or small red beets, peeled and cut in half

3   cups dried medium noodles (6 ounces)

2   tablespoons butter or margarine

6   cups sliced fresh mushrooms (about 1 pound)

1   cup chopped roma tomatoes (3 medium)

$2\frac{1}{2}$ cups beef-flavor vegetable broth

2   tablespoons cornstarch

$\frac{1}{4}$ teaspoon ground black pepper

Sour cream (optional)

1 Place beets in a steamer basket. Place basket in a saucepan over 1 inch of boiling water. Steam, covered, for 15 to 20 minutes or until beets are tender. Remove beets from steamer basket; let stand until cool enough to handle. Coarsely chop beets.

2 Meanwhile, cook noodles in boiling, lightly salted water according to package directions; drain. Return noodles to hot pan; cover and keep warm.

3 In an extra-large skillet melt butter over medium heat. Add mushrooms; cook and stir until tender. Add steamed beets and tomatoes; cook and stir for 2 minutes.

4 In a small bowl whisk together $\frac{1}{2}$ cup of the broth, the cornstarch, and pepper. Add the remaining 2 cups broth to the skillet. Stir cornstarch mixture into vegetable mixture in skillet. Cook and stir until thickened and bubbly. Cook and stir for 2 minutes more.

5 Serve borscht over hot cooked noodles. If desired, top with sour cream.

PER SERVING: *297 cal., 8 g total fat (4 g sat. fat), 51 mg chol., 522 mg sodium, 47 g carb., 5 g fiber, 12 g pro.*

Short & Simple

Pasta with Broccoli and Asiago

START TO FINISH: **25 minutes** MAKES **2 servings**

4   **ounces dried spaghetti, linguine, fettuccine, or angel hair pasta or one 9-ounce package desired refrigerated pasta**

1   **cup chopped broccoli**

½   **of a 5.2-ounce container semisoft cheese with garlic and herbs**

¼   **cup milk**

   Finely shredded Asiago or Parmesan cheese

1 Cook pasta according to package directions, adding broccoli during the last 4 minutes of cooking; drain. Return pasta mixture to hot pan.

2 Meanwhile, for sauce, in a small saucepan combine semisoft cheese and milk. Cook and stir over medium heat until smooth.

3 Pour sauce over cooked pasta mixture; toss gently to coat. Sprinkle each serving with Asiago cheese.

PER SERVING: *411 cal., 20 g total fat (13 g sat. fat), 11 mg chol., 316 mg sodium, 47 g carb., 3 g fiber, 14 g pro.*

Noodle Big Bowls with Spinach and Tofu

START TO FINISH: **25 minutes** MAKES **6 servings**

Nonstick cooking spray

1 **16-ounce package extra-firm or firm tofu (fresh bean curd), drained**

⅔ **cup hoisin sauce**

4 **14-ounce cans vegetable broth**

1 **tablespoon bottled minced roasted garlic**

12 **ounces dried udon (broad, white noodles) or linguine, broken**

2 **6-ounce packages fresh baby spinach**

1 Preheat broiler. Lightly coat the unheated rack of a broiler pan with cooking spray. Cut tofu crosswise into 6 slices; pat dry with paper towels. Arrange in a single layer on the prepared broiler rack. Brush tops of tofu with 3 tablespoons of the hoisin sauce. Broil 4 to 6 inches from the heat, without turning, for 8 to 10 minutes or until hoisin sauce is bubbly.

2 Meanwhile, in a 4- to 6-quart Dutch oven combine broth, garlic, and the remaining hoisin sauce. Bring to boiling. Add noodles and cook according to package directions, adding spinach during the last 2 minutes of cooking.

3 To serve, divide noodle mixture among large, deep soup bowls. Cut tofu into cubes or strips; place on top of noodle mixture.

PER SERVING: *337 cal., 6 g total fat (1 g sat. fat), 0 mg chol., 1,561 mg sodium, 56 g carb., 4 g fiber, 15 g pro.*

Ravioli in Browned Butter Sauce

START TO FINISH: **20 minutes** MAKES **4 servings**

- **2** **9-ounce packages refrigerated four-cheese ravioli**
- **8** **ounces fresh green beans, trimmed and cut into 2-inch pieces (2 cups)**
- **¼** **cup butter**
- **1** **tablespoon snipped fresh sage**
- **½** **cup crumbled Gorgonzola or other blue cheese (2 ounces)**
- **½** **cup whipping cream**
- **½** **cup milk**
- **Salt**
- **Ground black pepper**
- **Fresh sage leaves**

1 Cook ravioli and green beans according to the package directions for ravioli; drain. Return ravioli mixture to hot pan.

2 Meanwhile, for sauce, in a large skillet heat butter until melted. Add snipped sage; cook and stir until butter is lightly browned. Stir in cheese and cream. Bring to boiling; reduce heat. Simmer, uncovered, about 2 minutes or until mixture is thickened and cheese is melted, stirring frequently. Whisk in milk. Cook about 2 minutes more or until mixture is slightly thickened, whisking frequently.

3 Stir cooked ravioli mixture into sauce. Season to taste with salt and pepper. Garnish each serving with sage leaves.

PER SERVING: *623 cal., 33 g total fat (21 g sat. fat), 137 mg chol., 1,014 mg sodium, 60 g carb., 5 g fiber, 23 g pro.*

Ravioli with Spinach Pesto

START TO FINISH: **20 minutes**   MAKES **4 servings**

1   9-ounce package refrigerated four-cheese ravioli or tortellini

12 ounces baby pattypan squash, halved, or yellow summer squash, halved lengthwise and cut into $\frac{1}{2}$-inch pieces

$3\frac{1}{2}$ cups fresh baby spinach

$\frac{1}{2}$ cup torn fresh basil

$\frac{1}{4}$ cup bottled Caesar vinaigrette salad dressing with Parmesan cheese

2   tablespoons water

Shredded Parmesan cheese (optional)

1 Cook ravioli according to package directions, adding squash during the last 2 minutes of cooking; drain. Return ravioli mixture to hot pan.

2 Meanwhile, for pesto, in a blender combine spinach, basil, salad dressing, and the water. Cover and blend until smooth, stopping to scrape down blender as needed.

3 Pour pesto over cooked ravioli mixture; toss gently to coat. Sprinkle each serving with cheese.

PER SERVING: *218 cal., 6 g total fat (2 g sat. fat), 27 mg chol., 525 mg sodium, 31 g carb., 3 g fiber, 11 g pro.*

Ravioli Skillet

START TO FINISH: **20 minutes** MAKES **4 servings**

- 1 **14.5-ounce can Italian-style stewed tomatoes, undrained**
- ½ **cup water**
- 2 **medium zucchini and/or yellow summer squash, halved lengthwise and cut into ½-inch pieces (about 2½ cups)**
- 1 **9-ounce package refrigerated whole wheat four-cheese ravioli**
- 1 **15-ounce can cannellini beans (white kidney beans) or navy beans, rinsed and drained**
- 2 **tablespoons finely shredded or grated Parmesan cheese**
- 2 **tablespoons snipped fresh basil or parsley**

1 In an extra-large skillet combine undrained tomatoes and the water. Bring to boiling. Stir in zucchini and/or yellow squash and ravioli. Return to boiling; reduce heat. Boil gently, covered, for 6 to 7 minutes or until ravioli is tender, stirring gently once or twice.

2 Stir drained beans into ravioli mixture; heat through. Sprinkle each serving with cheese and basil.

PER SERVING: *305 cal., 8 g total fat (4 g sat. fat), 44 mg chol., 986 mg sodium, 49 g carb., 11 g fiber, 18 g pro.*

Tomato and Cheese Ravioli

START TO FINISH: **20 minutes** MAKES **4 servings**

1 **9-ounce package refrigerated light four-cheese ravioli or whole wheat four-cheese ravioli**

4 **cups grape or cherry tomatoes, halved**

3 **cups sliced fresh mushrooms (8 ounces)**

1 **tablespoon olive oil**

¼ **cup refrigerated reduced-fat basil pesto**

¼ **cup shredded fresh basil**

1 Cook ravioli according to package directions, omitting oil and salt; drain. Return ravioli to hot pan.

2 Meanwhile, in a large skillet cook tomatoes and mushrooms in hot oil over medium heat for 5 to 7 minutes or just until mushrooms are tender and tomatoes are softened, stirring occasionally.

3 Add pesto to cooked ravioli; toss gently to coat. Stir in tomato mixture and basil.

PER SERVING: *314 cal., 12 g total fat (3 g sat. fat), 35 mg chol., 463 mg sodium, 39 g carb., 5 g fiber, 14 g pro.*

Hot Tossed Vegetable Ravioli

START TO FINISH: **20 minutes** MAKES **4 servings**

1 **9-ounce package refrigerated whole wheat four-cheese ravioli**

1 **16-ounce package frozen broccoli stir-fry vegetables**

¾ **cup roasted red sweet peppers, drained**

⅓ **cup bottled reduced-calorie ranch salad dressing**

¼ **cup packed fresh basil leaves**

1 In a 4-quart Dutch oven cook ravioli according to package directions, adding vegetables during the last 5 minutes of cooking; drain. Return ravioli mixture to hot Dutch oven.

2 Meanwhile, for sauce, in a blender or food processor combine roasted peppers, salad dressing, and basil. Cover and blend or process until smooth. Pour sauce over cooked ravioli mixture; toss gently to coat.

PER SERVING: *278 cal., 11 g total fat (4 g sat. fat), 49 mg chol., 673 mg sodium, 34 g carb., 6 g fiber, 12 g pro.*

4

Pasta

From bubbly lasagnas to classic spaghetti with marinara, pasta is the most versatile ingredient out there. These tasty forkfuls incorporate different veggies, herbs, pastas, and sauces to provide a flavorful fix-up for everyone.

Spaghetti with Fresh Marinara

START TO FINISH: **50 minutes** MAKES **6 servings**

3   **tablespoons olive oil**

1   **cup chopped onion (1 large)**

1   **cup chopped red sweet pepper (1 medium)**

2   **tablespoons minced garlic (12 cloves)**

6   **cups chopped roma tomatoes (about 2½ pounds) or four 14.5-ounce cans diced tomatoes, undrained**

¼   **cup tomato paste**

10   **ounces dried whole grain spaghetti or whole wheat spaghetti**

3   **tablespoons snipped fresh basil**

2   **tablespoons snipped fresh oregano**

1   **tablespoon snipped fresh thyme**

½   **teaspoon kosher salt**

¼   **teaspoon freshly ground black pepper**

½   **cup finely shredded Parmesan cheese (2 ounces)**

1 For sauce, in a large saucepan heat oil over medium heat. Add onion, sweet pepper, and garlic. Cook for 5 minutes, stirring occasionally. Stir in tomatoes and tomato paste. Bring to boiling; reduce heat. Simmer, uncovered, for 20 minutes.

2 Meanwhile, cook pasta in boiling, lightly salted water according to package directions; drain. Return pasta to hot pan; cover and keep warm.

3 Stir basil, oregano, thyme, kosher salt, and black pepper into tomato mixture. Remove from heat. Cool slightly. Carefully transfer half of the tomato mixture to a blender or food processor. Cover and blend or process until nearly smooth. Repeat with remaining tomato mixture.

4 Return all of the blended sauce to the same saucepan. Heat through. Serve sauce over cooked pasta; toss to combine. Sprinkle servings with Parmesan cheese.

PER SERVING: *324 cal., 10 g total fat (2 g sat. fat), 5 mg chol., 393 mg sodium, 48 g carb., 7 g fiber, 14 g pro.*

◖ make it vegan

Substitute desired soy cheese for the Parmesan cheese.

Spaghetti with Fresh Pesto

START TO FINISH: **30 minutes**   MAKES **6 to 8 servings**

12 ounces fresh green beans, trimmed

1 14- to 16-ounce package dried multigrain, whole wheat, or regular spaghetti

1 tablespoon salt

½ cup chopped onion (1 medium)

2 cloves garlic, minced

1 tablespoon olive oil

1 cup packed fresh spinach

¾ cup packed fresh basil

½ cup almonds, toasted

½ cup grated Parmesan cheese

1 teaspoon lemon-pepper seasoning

½ cup olive oil

   Salt

   Ground black pepper

3 hard-cooked eggs, chopped

   Sliced green onions

   Lemon juice

   Toasted baguette slices (optional)

1 Cut one-third of the green beans into 2-inch pieces; set aside.

2 Cook pasta in boiling water with 1 tablespoon salt according to package directions, adding cut beans to water with pasta during the last 5 minutes of cooking. Using a ladle, remove 1½ cups of the pasta cooking water; set aside. Drain pasta and beans. Return pasta mixture to hot pan; cover and keep warm.

3 For pesto, in a medium skillet cook onion and garlic in the 1 tablespoon hot oil until onion is tender. Add whole beans. Cook, covered, for 5 to 7 minutes or until beans are tender, stirring occasionally.

4 In a food processor add bean mixture, spinach, basil, almonds, cheese, and lemon-pepper seasoning. Cover and process with on/off turns until coarsely chopped. With food processor running, add the ½ cup olive oil in thin stream until nearly smooth. Season to taste with salt and pepper.

5 Stir pesto and enough of the reserved 1½ cups pasta cooking water to moisten pasta mixture to desired consistency. Sprinkle with chopped eggs and green onions. Drizzle with lemon juice. If desired, serve with baguette slices.

PER SERVING: *555 cal., 30 g total fat (5 g sat. fat), 112 mg chol., 419 mg sodium, 54 g carb., 8 g fiber, 21 g pro.*

Spaghetti with Two-Tomato Toss

START TO FINISH: **35 minutes** MAKES **8 servings**

- ½ of a 7- to 8-ounce jar oil-packed dried tomatoes
- 4 cloves garlic, minced
- 4½ cups red and/or yellow cherry or grape tomatoes
- 1 teaspoon cracked black pepper or ½ to 1 teaspoon crushed red pepper
- ½ teaspoon salt
- 1 14- to 16-ounce package dried cornmeal, multigrain, whole wheat, or regular spaghetti
- 1 tablespoon salt
- 4 ounces bite-size fresh mozzarella cheese balls (bocconcini), halved
- ½ cup chopped Italian (flat-leaf) parsley or fresh basil

1 For sauce, drain dried tomatoes, reserving 1 tablespoon oil. Halve large tomatoes. In an extra-large skillet cook garlic in oil from tomatoes over medium heat for 1 minute or until tender. Add cherry and oil-packed tomatoes; cook and stir for 8 to 10 minutes or until fresh tomato skins blister. Stir in pepper and ½ teaspoon salt. Set aside.

2 Meanwhile, cook pasta in boiling water with 1 tablespoon salt according to package directions. Using a ladle, remove 1 cup of the pasta cooking water; set aside. Drain pasta. Transfer to skillet with sauce.

3 Add enough of the reserved 1 cup cooking water to thin sauce to desired consistency; toss gently to combine. Top with mozzarella balls and parsley.

PER SERVING: *264 cal., 6 g total fat (2 g sat. fat), 10 mg chol., 229 mg sodium, 47 g carb., 7 g fiber, 8 g pro.*

114

make it vegan

Substitute shredded mozzarella-flavor soy cheese for the mozzarella cheese.

Winter Garden Pasta

START TO FINISH: **30 minutes** MAKES **6 servings**

8   ounces dried whole grain spaghetti

3   cups broccoli florets

1   14.5-ounce can no-salt-added diced tomatoes, drained

1   15-ounce can white kidney beans (cannellini beans), rinsed and drained

2   tablespoons no-salt-added tomato paste

2   cloves garlic, minced

¼   teaspoon salt

¼   teaspoon ground black pepper

2   tablespoons snipped fresh Italian (flat-leaf) parsley

¼   cup grated Parmesan cheese

1 Cook pasta in boiling water according to package directions, except omit the salt, adding broccoli to water with pasta during the last 3 minutes of cooking; drain. Return pasta mixture to hot pan.

2 Add tomatoes, drained beans, tomato paste, garlic, salt, and pepper; stir to combine. Heat through. Stir in parsley. Sprinkle servings with cheese.

PER 1 CUP: *207 cal., 1 g total fat (0 g sat. fat), 1 mg chol., 460 mg sodium, 44 g carb., 5 g fiber, 11 g pro.*

115

make it vegan

Substitute desired soy cheese for the Parmesan cheese.

tip

After cooking pasta, drain it but don't rinse it. The starchy coating that remains on the pasta helps sauces stick to it.

Penne with Walnuts and Peppers

START TO FINISH: **30 minutes** MAKES **4 servings**

6 ounces dried whole wheat or multigrain penne or rotelle pasta

1 tablespoon olive oil

¼ cup walnuts, coarsely chopped

4 large cloves garlic, thinly sliced

2 medium green, red and/or yellow sweet peppers, seeded and cut lengthwise into bite-size strips

1 small red onion, cut into thin wedges

1 cup red or yellow cherry or grape tomatoes, halved

¼ cup snipped fresh parsley

2 teaspoons snipped fresh rosemary or ½ teaspoon dried rosemary, crushed

¼ teaspoon coarsely ground black pepper

2 tablespoons grated Parmesan cheese (optional)

1 Cook pasta in boiling, lightly salted water according to package directions; drain. Return pasta to hot pan; cover and keep warm.

2 Meanwhile, in a large skillet heat oil over medium heat. Add walnuts and garlic. Cook about 2 minutes or until light brown, stirring frequently. Add sweet peppers and red onion. Cook for 5 to 7 minutes or until vegetables are crisp tender, stirring frequently. Add tomatoes; cook and stir until heated through. Stir in parsley, rosemary, and black pepper.

3 In a large shallow bowl place cooked pasta. Top with walnut-pepper mixture; toss gently to combine. If desired, sprinkle with Parmesan cheese.

PER SERVING: *268 cal., 10 g total fat (1 g sat. fat), 0 mg chol., 7 mg sodium, 40 g carb., 5 g fiber, 9 g pro.*

make it vegan

If using cheese, substitute desired soy cheese for the Parmesan cheese.

tip

Walnuts contain omega-3 fatty acids, which research suggests may fight inflammation and protect the heart. Omega-3 fats are mainly found in fish, so walnuts provide a good alternative source of these fats for vegetarians.

Pasta with Green Beans and Dried Tomatoes

START TO FINISH: **35 minutes** MAKES **4 servings**

4   quarts water

1   tablespoon kosher salt

8   ounces dried whole grain penne

12 ounces fresh green beans or 3 cups frozen whole green beans

1   tablespoon olive oil

3   large red and/or yellow sweet peppers, seeded and cut into bite-size strips

1   tablespoon minced garlic

¼   cup oil-packed dried tomatoes, drained and cut into ¼-inch slices

2   tablespoons snipped fresh basil, Italian (flat-leaf) parsley, and/or oregano

3   tablespoons balsamic vinegar
    Kosher salt
    Freshly ground black pepper

2   ounces fresh mozzarella cheese, cut into cubes
    Fresh basil leaves (optional)

1 Cook pasta and, if using, fresh beans in boiling water with the 1 tablespoon kosher salt according to package directions. Or add frozen green beans (if using) to water with pasta during the last 5 minutes of cooking. Using a ladle, remove 1 cup of the pasta cooking water; set aside. Drain pasta and beans. Return pasta mixture to hot pan; cover and keep warm.

2 Meanwhile, in a large skillet heat olive oil over medium-high heat. Add pepper strips; cook for 5 minutes, stirring occasionally. Add the garlic; cook for 30 seconds more. Add the dried tomatoes, basil, and drained pasta mixture. Cook, stirring frequently, until heated through. Stir in balsamic vinegar and enough of the reserved 1 cup pasta cooking water to moisten pasta mixture to desired consistency. Season to taste with additional kosher salt and black pepper.

3 To serve, top with cheese cubes. If desired, garnish with additional fresh basil.

PER SERVING: *348 cal., 9 g total fat (3 g sat. fat), 11 mg chol., 501 mg sodium, 54 g carb., 9 g fiber, 16 g pro.*

make it vegan 🌿

Substitute mozzarella-flavor soy cheese for the mozzarella cheese.

tip

Save on cleanup time by cooking vegetables in the same pot as the pasta. This works best for quick-cooking vegetables, such as green beans and pea pods. Add them to the cooking water the last few minutes of cooking the pasta.

Broccoli Rabe and Penne

START TO FINISH: 25 minutes MAKES 6 servings

1 pound broccoli rabe

8 ounces dried multigrain penne pasta

2 tablespoons olive oil

1 tablespoon minced garlic (6 cloves)

¼ to ½ teaspoon crushed red pepper

¼ cup grated Parmesan cheese

1 tablespoon lemon juice

Kosher salt

Freshly ground black pepper

⅓ cup shredded Parmesan cheese

1 Trim tough stems from broccoli rabe; discard stems. Coarsely chop the broccoli rabe leaves. In a Dutch oven cook broccoli rabe in a large amount of boiling salted water for 5 to 7 minutes or until tender. Drain; plunge broccoli rabe into a large bowl of ice water to cool quickly. When cool, drain well.

2 Meanwhile, cook pasta in boiling, lightly salted water according to package directions. Using a ladle, remove ¾ cup of the pasta cooking water; set aside. Drain pasta. Return pasta to hot pan; cover and keep warm.

3 In a large skillet heat olive oil over medium heat. Add garlic and crushed red pepper. Cook and stir for 1 minute. Add drained broccoli rabe; toss to coat with oil. Add the drained pasta, the ¾ cup reserved pasta cooking water, grated Parmesan cheese, and lemon juice. Cook and stir until heated through. Season to taste with kosher salt and pepper. Sprinkle servings with shredded Parmesan cheese.

PER SERVING: *238 cal., 7 g total fat (2 g sat. fat), 6 mg chol., 263 mg sodium, 30 g carb., 5 g fiber, 12 g pro.*

Tricolor Tomato Ravioli

START TO FINISH: **35 minutes** MAKES **4 servings**

- 1 **24- to 25-ounce package frozen cheese-filled ravioli**
- 4 **large tomatoes (such as Green Zebra, yellow, and/or red), cut into thin wedges and seeded (about 4 cups)**
- ¾ **cup small fresh basil leaves**
- ¼ **cup capers, drained**
- ½ **teaspoon ground black pepper**
- ¼ **teaspoon salt**
- 2 **tablespoons butter**
- 6 **cloves garlic, minced**
- 2 **cups fresh baby spinach**
- ½ **cup shredded Parmesan cheese**

1 Cook pasta in boiling, lightly salted water according to package directions; drain. Return pasta to hot pan; cover and keep warm.

2 Meanwhile, in a large bowl combine tomatoes, basil, capers, pepper, and salt; set aside.

3 For sauce, in a large skillet melt butter over medium heat. Add garlic and cook for 30 seconds. Add tomato mixture; cook just until heated through. Remove from heat; gently stir in spinach.

4 To serve, place cooked ravioli on a large serving platter. Spoon sauce over ravioli. Sprinkle with Parmesan cheese.

PER SERVING: *480 cal., 18 g total fat (11 g sat. fat), 93 mg chol., 914 mg sodium, 57 g carb., 5 g fiber, 22 g pro.*

tip

Whip up a meal in no time with the leftover cooked pasta in your fridge. Mix cold pasta into salads, stir-fries, or chilled, grilled vegetables for a tasty meal in mere minutes.

Ravioli with Sweet Peppers

START TO FINISH: **25 minutes** MAKES **4 servings**

1 **9-ounce package refrigerated whole wheat four-cheese ravioli**

1 **tablespoon olive oil**

2 **medium red and/or green sweet peppers, seeded and cut into thin strips**

2 **medium carrots, thinly sliced**

1 **medium onion, chopped**

2 **cloves garlic, minced**

1 **14.5-ounce can diced tomatoes, undrained**

3 **tablespoons snipped fresh basil or 2 teaspoons dried basil, crushed**

Ground black pepper

Snipped fresh basil and/or small basil leaves (optional)

1 Cook pasta in boiling water according to package directions, except omit any oil or salt; drain. Return pasta to hot saucepan; cover and keep warm.

2 Meanwhile, in a large nonstick skillet heat oil over medium-high heat. Add sweet peppers, carrots, onion, and garlic; cook and stir about 5 minutes or until vegetables are tender. Stir in undrained tomatoes and the 3 tablespoons snipped basil. Cook and stir about 2 minutes more or until heated through. Season to taste with black pepper.

3 Add vegetable mixture to the cooked pasta; toss gently to combine. If desired, sprinkle with additional snipped basil and/or small basil leaves.

PER SERVING: *287 cal., 10 g total fat (4 g sat. fat), 43 mg chol., 617 mg sodium, 38 g carb., 6 g fiber, 11 g pro.*

Linguine in Fresh Tomato Sauce with Garlic-Basil Toast

START TO FINISH: 25 minutes MAKES 4 servings

- 10 ounces dried linguine
- 3 tablespoons olive oil
- 1 tablespoon minced garlic (6 cloves)
- 2 English muffins, split
- ¾ cup snipped fresh basil
- 2¼ cups cherry tomatoes, halved
- 1 teaspoon sugar
- Salt
- Ground black pepper
- ½ cup pitted kalamata olives, halved
- Grated Parmesan cheese (optional)
- Snipped fresh basil (optional)

1 Preheat broiler. Cook pasta in boiling, lightly salted water according to package directions. Using a ladle remove ½ cup of cooking water; set aside. Drain pasta. Return pasta to hot pan; cover and keep warm.

2 Meanwhile, in a small bowl combine 1 tablespoon of the oil and about 1 teaspoon of the minced garlic. Brush on cut sides of muffins. Place muffins on a baking sheet. Broil 3 to 4 inches from heat for 2 to 3 minutes or until golden and toasted. Sprinkle with 1 tablespoon of the snipped basil; set aside.

3 For sauce, in large saucepan heat the remaining 2 tablespoons oil over medium-high heat. Add the remaining 2 teaspoons garlic, the remaining basil, and the tomatoes. Cook for 2 minutes; add the reserved ½ cup broth and sugar. Cook for 3 to 4 minutes more or until tomatoes have softened. Season to taste with salt and pepper. Add pasta and olives to sauce; stir to combine and heat through.

4 If desired, sprinkle with Parmesan cheese and top with basil. Serve with toasted muffins.

PER SERVING: *448 cal., 12 g total fat (2 g sat. fat), 0 mg chol., 429 mg sodium, 72 g carb., 3 g fiber, 12 g pro.*

make it vegan

If serving with cheese, substitute desired soy cheese for the Parmesan cheese.

Smoky Mushroom Stroganoff

START TO FINISH: 25 minutes   MAKES 4 servings

- 1   8.8-ounce package dried pappardelle (wide egg noodles)
- 1   24-ounce package sliced fresh mushrooms (such as button, cremini, and/or shiitake)
- 2   cloves garlic, minced
- 1   tablespoon olive oil
- 1   8-ounce carton light sour cream
- 2   tablespoons all-purpose flour
- 1½   teaspoons smoked paprika
- ¼   teaspoon ground black pepper
- 1   cup vegetable broth
      Snipped fresh Italian (flat-leaf) parsley (optional)

1 Cook noodles in boiling, lightly salted water according to package directions; drain. Return noodles to hot pan; cover and keep warm.

2 In an extra-large skillet cook mushrooms and garlic in hot oil over medium-high heat for 5 to 8 minutes or until tender, stirring occasionally. (Reduce heat if mushrooms brown too quickly.) Remove mushrooms with slotted spoon; transfer to a medium bowl; cover to keep warm.

3 For sauce, in another medium bowl combine sour cream, flour, paprika, and pepper. Add broth, stirring until smooth. Add sour cream mixture to skillet. Cook and stir until thickened and bubbly; cook and stir for 1 minute more. Serve mushroom mixture and sauce over cooked noodles. If desired, sprinkle with parsley.

PER SERVING: *407 cal., 13 g total fat (5 g sat. fat), 72 mg chol., 443 mg sodium, 59 g carb., 4 g fiber, 17 g pro.*

 **make it vegan**

Substitute tofu sour cream for the sour cream.

Fettuccine Alfredo

START TO FINISH: **35 minutes** MAKES **4 servings**

8 ounces dried fettuccine

2 tablespoons butter

1 cup whipping cream

½ teaspoon salt

⅛ teaspoon freshly ground black pepper

½ cup freshly grated Parmesan cheese

Grated or finely shredded Parmesan cheese (optional)

1 Cook pasta in boiling, lightly salted water according to package directions; drain. Return pasta to hot pan; cover and keep warm.

2 Meanwhile, in a large saucepan melt butter. Add whipping cream, salt, and pepper. Bring to boiling; reduce heat. Simmer, uncovered, for 3 to 5 minutes or until mixture begins to thicken. Remove from heat. Stir in the ½ cup grated Parmesan cheese.

3 Stir in cooked pasta; toss gently to combine. If desired, sprinkle with additional Parmesan cheese.

PER SERVING: *515 cal., 32 g total fat (19 g sat. fat), 107 mg chol., 512 mg sodium, 45 g carb., 1 g fiber, 12 g pro.*

Farfalle with Mushrooms and Spinach

START TO FINISH: 25 minutes MAKES 2 servings

- 6 ounces dried farfalle (bow tie pasta)
- 1 tablespoon olive oil
- 1 cup sliced portobello or other fresh mushrooms
- ¾ cup chopped onion
- 2 cloves garlic, minced
- 4 cups thinly sliced fresh spinach
- 1 teaspoon snipped fresh thyme
- ⅛ teaspoon ground black pepper
- 2 tablespoons shredded Parmesan cheese

1 Cook pasta in boiling, lightly salted water according to package directions; drain. Return pasta to hot pan; cover and keep warm.

2 Meanwhile, in a large skillet heat oil over medium heat. Add mushrooms, onion, and garlic. Cook and stir for 2 to 3 minutes or until mushrooms are nearly tender. Stir in spinach, thyme, and pepper; cook 1 minute or until heated through and spinach is slightly wilted.

3 Stir in cooked pasta; toss gently to combine. Sprinkle servings with cheese.

PER SERVING: *438 cal., 10 g total fat (2 g sat. fat), 4 mg chol., 172 mg sodium, 70 g carb., 8 g fiber, 18 g pro.*

make it vegan

Substitute desired soy cheese for the Parmesan cheese.

tip

When in doubt, go whole! Use whole wheat pasta instead of white pasta to gain more fiber and nutrients as well as a chewier texture. If you don't like the taste of whole wheat pasta, try multigrain pasta, which has a milder flavor.

Fusilli with Garlic Pesto and Pecorino Romano

START TO FINISH: **35 minutes** MAKES **6 to 8 servings**

15 cloves garlic, peeled

⅓ cup lightly packed fresh basil leaves

1 16-ounce package dried fusilli, gemelli, or tagliatelle pasta

½ cup olive oil

⅓ cup pine nuts, toasted

2 tablespoons finely shredded Pecorino Romano cheese (½ ounce)

¾ teaspoon sea salt

⅛ teaspoon ground black pepper

1 cup small fresh basil leaves

¼ cup finely shredded Pecorino Romano cheese (1 ounce)

1 In a large saucepan cook garlic cloves in a large amount of boiling, lightly salted water for 8 minutes. Using a slotted spoon, remove garlic and transfer to a blender or food processor. Add the ⅓ cup basil leaves to the boiling water and cook for 5 seconds. Using a slotted spoon, remove basil and drain well on paper towels. (Do not drain boiling water.) Add basil to blender or food processor.

2 Cook pasta in the reserved boiling water according to package directions. Using a ladle, remove ½ cup of cooking water; set aside. Drain pasta. Return pasta to hot pan; cover and keep warm.

3 Meanwhile, for pesto, add oil, 2 tablespoons of the pine nuts, the 2 tablespoons cheese, the salt, and pepper to blender or food processor. Cover and blend or process until nearly smooth (pesto will be thin).

4 Add pesto to cooked pasta; toss gently to coat. If necessary, add enough of the reserved ½ cup cooking water to help coat the pasta evenly with pesto. Transfer pasta mixture to a large serving bowl. Sprinkle with the 1 cup basil leaves, the ¼ cup cheese, and the remaining pine nuts.

PER SERVING: *518 cal., 25 g total fat (4 g sat. fat), 5 mg chol., 264 mg sodium, 61 g carb., 3 g fiber, 14 g pro.*

125

Asparagus Pesto Pasta

START TO FINISH: **25 minutes** MAKES **6 servings**

1   **pound asparagus spears**

1   **cup frozen peas, thawed**

¼   **cup finely shredded Parmesan cheese (1 ounce)**

2   **tablespoons pine nuts, toasted**

1   **teaspoon finely shredded lemon peel**

2   **cloves garlic, quartered**

¼   **teaspoon salt**

¼   **teaspoon ground black pepper**

3   **tablespoons olive oil**

10   **ounces dried fettuccine**

1 Snap off and discard woody bases from asparagus; rinse. Cut asparagus into 2-inch pieces. In a covered large saucepan cook asparagus and peas in a small amount of boiling, lightly salted water for 3 to 5 minutes or until tender; drain.

2 For pesto, in a blender or food processor combine half of the asparagus and peas, the cheese, half of the nuts, the lemon peel, garlic, salt, and pepper. Cover and blend or process with several on/off turns until a paste forms, stopping the machine several times and scraping the sides.

3 With the machine running slowly, gradually add oil and blend or process to the consistency of soft butter. Set aside.

4 Cook pasta in boiling, lightly salted water according to package directions; drain. Return pasta to hot pan; toss pasta with pesto.

5 To serve, top pasta mixture with the remaining cooked asparagus and peas. Sprinkle with the remaining pine nuts.

PER SERVING: *301 cal., 11 g total fat (2 g sat. fat), 3 mg chol., 203 mg sodium, 41 g carb., 4 g fiber, 10 g pro.*

Asparagus-Mushroom Primavera

PREP: 15 minutes   COOK: 5 minutes   MAKES 4 servings

1 pound asparagus spears

8 ounces dried multigrain linguine

1 tablespoon olive oil

4 cloves garlic, minced

¼ teaspoon freshly ground black pepper

1 8-ounce package fresh button mushrooms, halved

¼ cup dry white wine

¼ teaspoon salt

1 tablespoon butter

¼ cup shredded fresh basil

¼ teaspoon crushed red pepper

1 Snap off and discard woody bases from asparagus; rinse. Bias-slice asparagus into 1½-inch pieces; set aside.

2 Cook pasta in boiling, lightly salted water according to package directions; drain. Return pasta to hot pan; cover and keep warm.

3 Meanwhile, in a large skillet heat oil over medium heat. Add garlic and black pepper; cook and stir for 30 seconds.

4 Add asparagus, mushrooms, wine, and salt to skillet. Bring to boiling; reduce heat. Cook, uncovered, about 4 minutes or until asparagus is crisp-tender, stirring occasionally. Remove from heat; stir in butter.

5 Add cooked pasta to vegetables in skillet; toss gently to combine. Top with basil and crushed red pepper.

PER SERVING: 304 cal., 8 g total fat (2 g sat. fat), 8 mg chol., 205 mg sodium, 43 g carb., 6 g fiber, 14 g pro.

make it vegan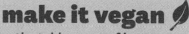

Substitute another tablespoon of olive oil for the tablespoon of butter.

tip

Take this dish from weekday to company-special by using exotic mushrooms, such as shiitake, cremini, and/or oyster.

Garden-Special Primavera

START TO FINISH: 45 minutes MAKES 6 servings

- 6   ounces fresh wax or green beans, trimmed and cut into 2-inch pieces (2 cups)
- 1/2   cup bias-sliced carrot (1 medium)
- 6   ounces asparagus spears, trimmed and cut into 2-inch pieces (1 1/2 cups)
- 1   cup broccoli or cauliflower florets
- 12   ounces dried fettuccine, linguine, vermicelli, or spaghetti
- 1   small red or yellow sweet pepper, cut into thin bite-size strips
- 1   small zucchini or yellow summer squash, halved lengthwise and sliced (1 cup)
- 2   tablespoons butter or margarine
- 1   small onion, cut into thin wedges
- 2   cloves garlic, minced
- 3/4   cup vegetable broth
- 3/4   cup whipping cream
- 2   tablespoons all-purpose flour
- 1/2   cup finely shredded Parmesan cheese (2 ounces)
- 1/4   cup thinly sliced green onions (2)
- 2   tablespoons snipped fresh basil or 2 teaspoons dried basil, crushed
- Finely shredded Parmesan cheese (optional)

1 In a covered large saucepan cook beans and carrot in a small amount of boiling, lightly salted water for 10 minutes. Add asparagus and broccoli. Return to boiling; reduce heat. Cook, covered, about 5 minutes more or until vegetables are crisp-tender; drain. Set aside.

2 Meanwhile, cook pasta according to package directions, adding sweet pepper and zucchini to water with pasta during the last 3 minutes of cooking (vegetables should be crisp-tender); drain. Return pasta mixture to the hot pan. Add the bean mixture to the pasta mixture; cover and keep warm.

3 For sauce, in a medium saucepan melt butter over medium heat. Add onion wedges and garlic. Cook for 5 to 8 minutes or until tender, stirring occasionally. Add broth. Bring to boiling; reduce heat. In a small bowl stir together whipping cream and flour. Add cream mixture to broth mixture in saucepan. Cook and stir until thickened and bubbly. Stir in the 1/2 cup Parmesan cheese, the green onions, and basil. Cook and stir for 1 minute more. Pour sauce over pasta and vegetables; toss gently to combine.

4 On a large serving platter arrange pasta mixture. If desired, sprinkle with additional Parmesan cheese.

PER SERVING: *421 cal., 18 g total fat (11 g sat. fat), 56 mg chol., 288 mg sodium, 53 g carb., 4 g fiber, 13 g pro.*

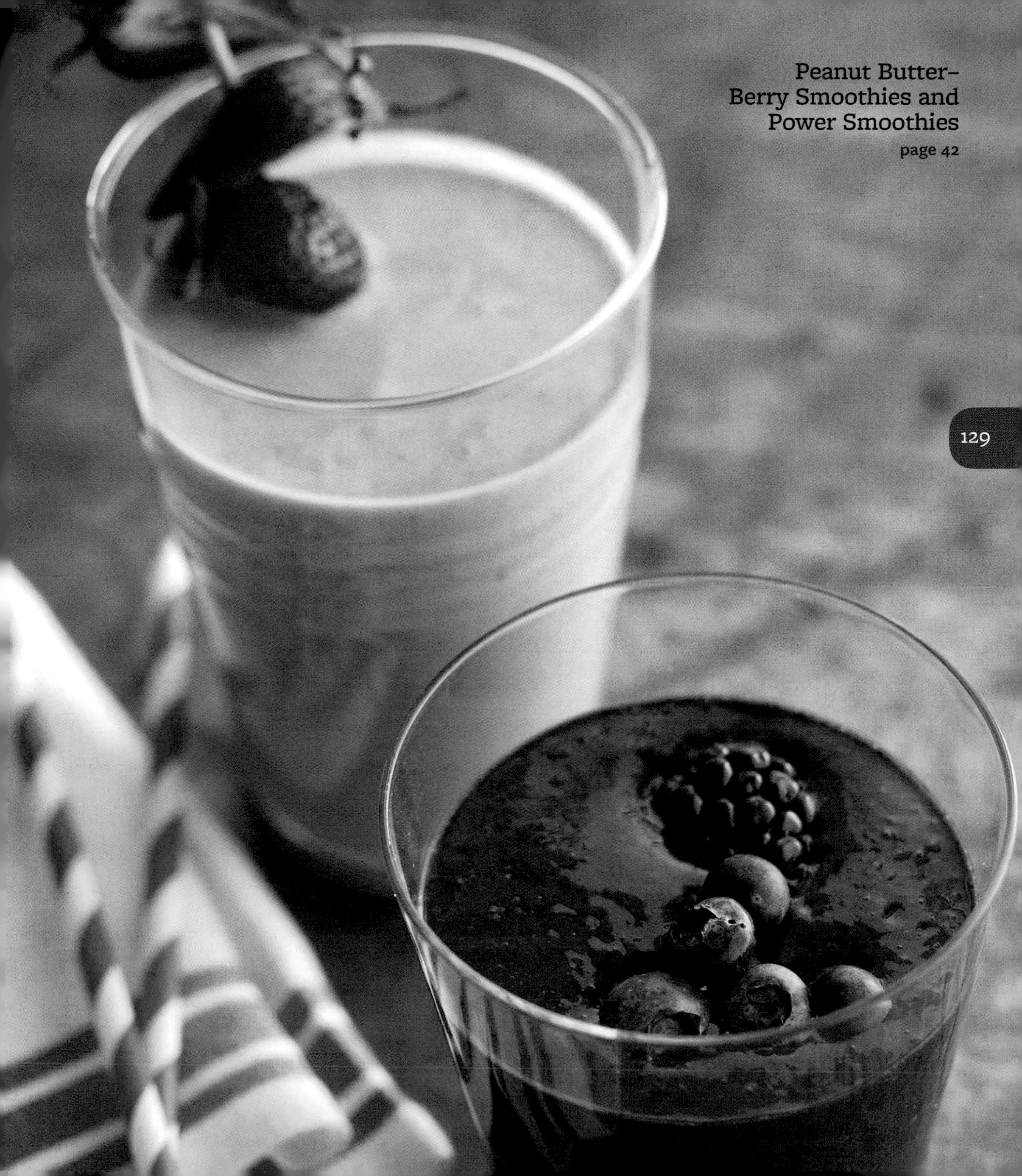

Peanut Butter–Berry Smoothies and Power Smoothies

page 42

Oatmeal with Fruit
and Nuts
page 38

Blueberry-Oat
Scones with
Flaxseeds
page 35

132

Mushroom and Herb Pizza page 24

Mushroom, Asparagus, and Tofu Quiches page 19

133

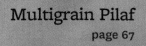
Multigrain Pilaf
page 67

134

Pasta with
Lentil Sauce
page 70

137

Butternut Squash Phyllo Strudel page 85

Black Bean and Corn Quesadillas page 82

You Choose
Veggie Burgers
page 92

Fusilli with Garlic
Pesto and Pecorino
Romano
page 125

Spinach Tortellini with Beans and Feta page 96

140

Saucepan Macaroni and Cheese page 149

Spinach and Feta Casserole page 89

Ravioli with Sweet
Peppers
page 120

Asparagus-Mushroom Primavera

page 127

Butternut Squash
Lasagna
page 155

143

Olive and Arugula
Flatbread Pizza
page 175

144

Fresh-Herb Pasta Primavera

START TO FINISH: **35 minutes** MAKES **6 servings**

8 ounces dried multigrain or whole grain penne or mostaccioli

3 cups assorted fresh vegetables (such as red sweet pepper strips, trimmed sugar snap peas, 2-inch asparagus pieces, and/or quartered-lengthwise packaged peeled baby carrots)

1 cup halved cherry tomatoes

½ cup vegetable broth

3 tablespoons all-purpose flour

½ teaspoon salt

1¼ cups low-fat milk

¼ cup dry sherry or reduced-sodium vegetable broth

3 ounces Parmesan or Asiago cheese, finely shredded (¾ cup)

½ cup lightly packed fresh basil, coarsely chopped

4 teaspoons snipped fresh thyme or oregano

⅓ cup sliced green onions (2 or 3) (optional)

1 Cook pasta in boiling, lightly salted water according to package directions, adding 3 cups assorted vegetables to water with pasta during the last 2 minutes of cooking; drain. Return pasta mixture to hot pan. Add cherry tomatoes; cover and keep warm.

2 For sauce, in a medium saucepan whisk together broth, flour, and salt until smooth. Stir in milk and sherry. Cook and stir until thickened and bubbly; cook and stir for 2 minutes more. Remove from heat; stir in finely shredded Parmesan cheese, basil, and thyme.

3 Serve sauce over pasta mixture; toss gently to combine. If desired, sprinkle with green onions.

PER SERVING: *252 cal., 5 g total fat (3 g sat. fat), 12 mg chol., 527 mg sodium, 40 g carb., 6 g fiber, 13 g pro.*

145

tip

Match your pasta to your sauce. A thin angel hair pasta goes well with a light, thin sauce. A thicker pasta, such as fettuccine, goes well with a heavy sauce.

Pasta with Swiss Chard

START TO FINISH: **35 minutes** MAKES **2 servings**

- 4 ounces dried whole grain bow tie or mostaccioli pasta
- 6 ounces fresh Swiss chard or spinach
- 1½ teaspoons olive oil
- 2 cloves garlic, minced
- ⅓ cup light ricotta cheese
- 2 tablespoons fat-free milk
- 2 tablespoons snipped fresh basil or 1 teaspoon dried basil, crushed
- ⅛ teaspoon salt
- ⅛ teaspoon ground black pepper
  Dash ground nutmeg
- 1 medium tomato, seeded and chopped
- 2 tablespoons shredded Parmesan cheese

1 Cook pasta in boiling water according to package directions, except omit any oil or salt; drain. Return pasta to hot saucepan; cover and keep warm.

2 Meanwhile, cut out and discard center ribs from Swiss chard or remove stems from spinach. Coarsely chop greens; set aside.

3 In a large nonstick skillet heat oil over medium heat. Add garlic; cook for 15 seconds. Add Swiss chard. Cook over medium-low heat about 3 minutes or until greens are wilted and tender, stirring frequently. Stir in ricotta cheese, milk, basil, salt, pepper, and nutmeg. Cook and stir for 3 to 5 minutes more or until heated through.

4 Add the ricotta mixture and tomato to cooked pasta; toss gently to combine. Sprinkle servings with Parmesan cheese.

PER SERVING: *307 cal., 8 g total fat (2 g sat. fat), 14 mg chol., 435 mg sodium, 51 g carb., 8 g fiber, 14 g pro.*

tip
Swiss chard, like kale, is a slightly bitter-tasting green. It's loaded with vitamins, especially vitamins K, A, and C. Both the stems and leaves are edible (the stems do take longer to cook).

Soba-Vegetable Toss

START TO FINISH: **35 minutes** MAKES **4 servings**

6 ounces dried soba (buckwheat noodles) or multigrain spaghetti

1 tablespoon toasted sesame oil

5 cups broccoli florets

3 medium yellow and/or red sweet peppers, seeded and cut into thin strips

6 medium green onions, bias-sliced into 1-inch pieces

¼ cup plum sauce

1 tablespoon rice vinegar

1 tablespoon soy sauce

½ teaspoon crushed red pepper

2 tablespoons sliced almonds, toasted

Bias-sliced green onions (optional)

1 Cook soba according to package directions; drain. Return soba to hot pan; cover and keep warm.

2 Meanwhile, pour oil into a wok or very large skillet. Preheat over medium-high heat. Add broccoli and sweet peppers. Cook and stir for 3 minutes. Add the 6 bias-sliced green onions. Cook and stir for 1 to 2 minutes more or until vegetables are crisp-tender. Add plum sauce, rice vinegar, soy sauce, and crushed red pepper; stir to coat vegetables. Heat through.

3 Serve immediately with soba. Sprinkle with almonds. If desired, top with additional sliced green onions.

PER SERVING: *313 cal., 6 g total fat (1 g sat. fat), 0 mg chol., 737 mg sodium, 59 g carb., 7 g fiber, 12 g pro.*

147

Udon with Tofu 🌿

START TO FINISH: 25 minutes MAKES 6 servings

8 ounces dried udon or whole wheat linguine

2 6- to 8-ounce packages smoked teriyaki-flavor or plain firm tofu (fresh bean curd), cut into ½-inch pieces

1½ cups chopped cucumber

1 large carrot, cut into bite-size pieces

½ cup sliced green onions (8)

1 recipe Ginger-Soy Sauce

1 Cook pasta in boiling, lightly salted water according to package directions; drain. Return pasta to hot pan; cover and keep warm.

2 Meanwhile, in a large bowl combine tofu, cucumber, carrot, and green onions. Add cooked pasta; toss to combine. Drizzle with Ginger-Soy Sauce; toss gently to combine.

PER SERVING: *231 cal., 4 g total fat (0 g sat. fat), 0 mg chol., 571 mg sodium, 39 g carb., 3 g fiber, 7 g pro.*

Ginger-Soy Sauce

In a small bowl whisk together 2 tablespoons rice vinegar or cider vinegar; 1 tablespoon toasted sesame oil; 2 teaspoons reduced-sodium soy sauce; 4 cloves garlic, minced; 1 teaspoon grated fresh ginger; and ¼ teaspoon crushed red pepper.

Saucepan Macaroni and Cheese

START TO FINISH: **30 minutes** MAKES **5 servings**

- 8 **ounces dried multigrain elbow or penne pasta**
- 1 **cup frozen broccoli florets or mixed vegetables**
- 1 **12-ounce can evaporated fat-free milk**
- 2 **tablespoons all-purpose flour**
- $\frac{1}{8}$ **teaspoon ground black pepper**
- 1$\frac{1}{4}$ **cups shredded reduced-fat cheddar cheese (5 ounces)**
- $\frac{1}{4}$ **cup shredded American cheese**

  Ground black pepper (optional)

1 Cook pasta in boiling, lightly salted water according to package directions, adding the broccoli to water with pasta during the last 2 minutes of cooking; drain. Return pasta mixture to hot pan; cover and keep warm.

2 Meanwhile, for sauce, in a medium saucepan whisk together the evaporated milk, flour, and the $\frac{1}{8}$ teaspoon pepper. Cook and stir over medium heat until thickened and bubbly. Add cheddar and American cheeses; cook and stir until cheese melts.

3 Pour sauce over pasta mixture; stir to combine. Heat through. If desired, sprinkle servings with additional pepper.

PER SERVING: *344 cal., 9 g total fat (5 g sat. fat), 28 mg chol., 436 mg sodium, 46 g carb., 4 g fiber, 23 g pro.*

149

Veggie-Stuffed Pasta Shells

START TO FINISH: **40 minutes**   MAKES **4 servings**

- 12   packaged dried jumbo shell macaroni
- 1½   cups coarsely shredded fresh carrots
- 1⅓   cups shredded zucchini (1 medium)
- ½   cup finely chopped onion (1 small)
- 2   tablespoons olive oil
- 1   10-ounce package frozen chopped spinach, thawed and squeezed dry
- ½   of a 15-ounce carton ricotta cheese
- 1½   cups shredded Italian cheese blend (6 ounces)
- ¼   teaspoon salt
- ⅛   teaspoon cayenne pepper
- 1   14- to 16-ounce jar pasta sauce

1 Cook pasta in boiling, lightly salted water according to package directions; drain in colander. Rinse with cold water; drain again.

2 Meanwhile, in a large skillet cook carrots, zucchini, and onion in hot oil over medium-high heat for 3 to 5 minutes or until tender. Stir in spinach; cook and stir for 1 minute. Transfer spinach mixture to a large bowl.

3 Stir ricotta cheese, 1 cup of the Italian cheese blend, salt, and cayenne pepper into vegetable mixture. Spoon a rounded 2 tablespoons cheese mixture into each pasta shell. Pour pasta sauce into skillet; place filled shells in sauce.

4 Cook shells and sauce, covered, over medium heat about 10 minutes or until heated through. Sprinkle with remaining cheese.

PER SERVING: *538 cal., 26 g total fat (11 g sat. fat), 57 mg chol., 891 mg sodium, 52 g carb., 6 g fiber, 27 g pro.*

Eggplant and Caper Tomato Sauce

PREP: 30 minutes BAKE: 18 minutes COOK: 25 minutes OVEN: 375°F MAKES 8 servings

1 medium eggplant, peeled and cut into 1-inch cubes (about 1 pound)

¼ cup olive oil

1 large onion, chopped

1 tablespoon minced garlic (6 cloves)

3 pounds tomatoes, cored and chopped, or four 14.5-ounce cans diced tomatoes, undrained

½ cup capers, rinsed and drained

½ cup pitted kalamata olives, coarsely chopped

2 tablespoons snipped fresh basil

1 tablespoon snipped fresh oregano

1 tablespoon snipped fresh thyme

Kosher salt

Freshly ground black pepper

12 ounces dried multigrain spaghetti

¼ cup finely shredded Parmesan cheese (2 ounces)

1 Preheat oven to 375°F. Place eggplant cubes in a 15×10×1-inch baking pan. Drizzle eggplant with 2 tablespoons of the olive oil; toss to coat. Bake, uncovered, for 18 to 20 minutes or until eggplant is tender but still holding its shape.

2 Meanwhile, for sauce, in a large saucepan heat the remaining 2 tablespoons olive oil over medium heat. Add onion; cook for 5 minutes, stirring occasionally. Add eggplant and garlic; cook about 5 minutes more or until eggplant is very soft and starting to break apart, stirring occasionally.

3 Add tomatoes, capers, and olives to eggplant mixture. Bring to boiling; reduce heat. Simmer, covered, for 10 minutes, stirring occasionally. Uncover and simmer for 15 to 20 minutes more or until desired consistency, stirring occasionally. Stir in basil, oregano, and thyme. Season to taste with kosher salt and pepper.

4 Meanwhile, cook pasta in boiling, lightly salted water according to package directions; drain.

5 Serve sauce over cooked pasta; toss gently to combine. Sprinkle with cheese.

PER SERVING: *311 cal., 11 g total fat (2 g sat. fat), 5 mg chol., 559 mg sodium, 43 g carb., 8 g fiber, 13 g pro.*

151

make it vegan

Substitute desired soy cheese for the Parmesan cheese.

Spaghetti with Roasted Tomatoes and Pine Nuts

PREP: 20 minutes   BAKE: 10 minutes   OVEN: 400°F   MAKES 4 servings

- 6 ounces dried multigrain spaghetti
- 2 cups cherry tomatoes, halved
- ¼ cup olive oil
- ¼ teaspoon kosher salt
- ⅛ teaspoon freshly ground black pepper
- 3 cloves garlic, minced
- ¼ to ½ teaspoon crushed red pepper
- 1 15-ounce can cannellini beans (white kidney beans), rinsed and drained
- 6 cups fresh baby spinach leaves
- 1 cup snipped fresh basil
- 1 teaspoon lemon juice
- ¼ cup pine nuts, toasted
- ¼ cup shredded Parmesan cheese (1 ounce)

1 Preheat oven to 400°F. Cook pasta in boiling, lightly salted water according to package directions; drain. Return pasta to hot pan; cover and keep warm.

2 Meanwhile, place tomatoes in a 15×10×1-inch baking pan. Drizzle tomatoes with 2 tablespoons of the olive oil. Sprinkle with the kosher salt and pepper; toss gently to coat. Bake about 10 minutes or until tender.

3 In a medium skillet heat the remaining 2 tablespoons olive oil over medium heat. Add garlic and crushed red pepper; cook and stir for 30 seconds. Stir in drained cannellini beans; heat through.

4 In a large serving bowl combine tomatoes, spinach, basil, lemon juice, bean mixture. Add cooked pasta; toss to combine. Top servings with pine nuts and Parmesan cheese.

PER SERVING: *435 cal., 21 g total fat (4 g sat. fat), 4 mg chol., 430 mg sodium, 51 g carb., 10 g fiber, 20 g pro.*

make it vegan

Substitute desired soy cheese for the Parmesan cheese.

tip

Pine nuts are actually seeds that come from a specific pine tree. The seeds are harvested from the pinecones. Pine nuts are often used to make pesto but are also delicious on their own.

Mac and Cheese Spaghetti

PREP: 30 minutes BAKE: 5 minutes OVEN: 425°F MAKES 6 to 8 servings

1½ cups coarse white bread crumbs

2 tablespoons grated Parmesan cheese

1 tablespoon butter, melted

1 14- to 16-ounce package dried multigrain, whole wheat, or regular spaghetti

1 tablespoon salt

2 cups fresh broccoli florets or one 10-ounce package frozen peas

2 tablespoons butter

1 teaspoon Dijon-style mustard

8 ounces sharp cheddar cheese, finely shredded (2 cups)

4 ounces American cheese, shredded (1 cup)

1 Preheat oven to 425°F. In a 15×10×1-inch baking pan combine crumbs, Parmesan cheese, and the 1 tablespoon butter. Bake for 5 minutes. Remove from oven; stir. Set aside.

2 Cook pasta in boiling water with the 1 tablespoon salt according to package directions, adding broccoli to water with pasta during the last 3 minutes of cooking. Using a ladle, remove 2 cups of the pasta cooking water; set aside. Drain pasta and broccoli. Return pasta mixture to hot pan; cover and keep warm.

3 In a large saucepan bring 1 cup of the reserved pasta water to boiling. Add the 2 tablespoons butter and mustard. Add cheeses, a handful at a time, continuously stirring after each addition until cheese melts. Stir in more pasta water if needed. Add pasta mixture; toss gently to combine. Sprinkle servings with crumb mixture.

153

PER SERVING: *456 cal., 20 g total fat (12 g sat. fat), 56 mg chol., 561 mg sodium, 47 g carb., 6 g fiber, 23 g pro.*

Mile-High Meatless Lasagna Pie

PREP: 50 minutes BAKE: 60 minutes STAND: 15 minutes OVEN: 375°F MAKES 10 servings

14 dried lasagna noodles

2 tablespoons olive oil

1½ cups finely chopped carrots
(3 medium)

2 cups finely chopped zucchini
(1 medium)

4 cloves garlic, minced

3 cups sliced fresh mushrooms
(8 ounces)

2 6-ounce packages prewashed
baby spinach

2 tablespoons snipped fresh
basil

1 egg, lightly beaten

1 15-ounce carton ricotta
cheese

⅓ cup finely shredded Parmesan
cheese

½ teaspoon salt

¼ teaspoon ground black pepper

1 26-ounce jar tomato-and-basil
pasta sauce (2½ cups)

2 cups shredded Italian fontina
or mozzarella cheese
(8 ounces)

Rosemary sprigs (optional)

1 Preheat oven to 375°F. Cook pasta according to package directions; drain in colander. Rinse with cold water; drain again. Place noodles in a single layer on a sheet of foil; set aside.

2 Meanwhile, in a large skillet heat 1 tablespoon of the olive oil over medium-high heat. Add carrots, zucchini, and half of the garlic. Cook and stir about 5 minutes or until vegetables are crisp-tender. Transfer vegetable mixture to a bowl. Add the remaining 1 tablespoon oil to the same skillet and heat over medium-high heat. Add mushrooms and remaining garlic. Cook and stir about 5 minutes or until tender. Gradually add spinach. Cook and stir for 1 to 2 minutes or until spinach is wilted. Using a slotted spoon, transfer spinach-mushroom mixture from skillet to a bowl. Stir basil into spinach-mushroom mixture; set aside.

3 In a small bowl stir together egg, ricotta cheese, Parmesan cheese, salt, and pepper. Set aside.

4 To assemble pie, in the bottom of a 9×3-inch springform pan spread ½ cup of the pasta sauce. Arrange 3 to 4 of the cooked noodles over the sauce, trimming and overlapping as necessary to cover sauce with one layer. Top with half of the spinach-mushroom mixture. Spoon half of the ricotta cheese mixture over spinach mixture. Top with another layer of noodles. Spread with half of the remaining pasta sauce. Top with all of the vegetable mixture. Sprinkle with half the fontina cheese. Top with another layer of noodles. Layer with remaining spinach-mushroom mixture and remaining ricotta cheese mixture. Top with another layer of noodles (may have extra noodles) and remaining sauce. Gently press down pie with the back of a spatula.

5 Place springform pan on a foil-lined baking sheet. Bake, uncovered, for 45 minutes. Sprinkle with remaining fontina cheese; bake about 15 minutes more or until heated through. Cover and let stand on a wire rack for 15 minutes before serving. Carefully remove sides of pan. To serve, cut into wedges. If desired, garnish with rosemary sprigs.

PER SERVING: *450 cal., 23 g total fat (12 g sat. fat), 82 mg chol., 966 mg sodium, 37 g carb., 6 g fiber, 26 g pro.*

Butternut Squash Lasagna

PREP: 45 minutes BAKE: 50 minutes STAND: 10 minutes OVEN: 425°F/375°F MAKES 8 to 10 servings

1   3-pound butternut squash

3   tablespoons olive oil

½   teaspoon salt

¼   cup butter

1   tablespoon minced garlic (6 cloves)

¼   cup all-purpose flour

½   teaspoon salt

4   cups milk

1   tablespoon snipped fresh rosemary

9   no-boil lasagna noodles

1⅓ cups finely shredded Parmesan cheese

1   cup whipping cream

1 Preheat oven to 425°F. Lightly grease a 15×10×1-inch baking pan; set aside. Halve squash lengthwise; seed and peel squash. Cut crosswise into ¼- to ½-inch slices. Place squash in the prepared baking pan. Add oil and ½ teaspoon salt; toss gently to coat. Spread in an even layer. Bake, uncovered, for 25 to 30 minutes or until squash is tender, stirring once halfway through baking. Remove from oven. Reduce oven temperature to 375°F.

2 Meanwhile, for sauce, in a large saucepan heat butter over medium heat. Add garlic and cook and stir for 1 minute. Stir in flour and ½ teaspoon salt. Gradually stir in milk. Cook and stir until thickened and bubbly. Stir in squash and rosemary.

3 Lightly grease a 3-quart rectangular baking dish. Spread about 1 cup of the sauce in the bottom of the prepared baking dish. Layer one-third of the lasagna noodles in dish. Spread with one-third of the remaining sauce; sprinkle with ⅓ cup of the Parmesan cheese. Repeat layers twice. Pour whipping cream evenly over layers in dish. Sprinkle with the remaining ⅓ cup Parmesan cheese.

4 Bake, covered, for 40 minutes. Bake, uncovered, about 10 minutes more or until edges are bubbly and top is lightly brown. Let stand for 10 minutes before serving.

PER SERVING: *525 cal., 29 g total fat (15 g sat. fat), 76 mg chol., 628 mg sodium, 53 g carb., 4 g fiber, 17 g pro.*

Make-Ahead Directions: Prepare as directed through Step 3. Cover with foil and chill for 2 to 24 hours. To serve, bake, covered, in a 375°F oven for 45 minutes. Bake, uncovered, for 10 to 15 minutes more or until edges are bubbly and top is light brown. Let stand for 10 minutes before serving.

Broccoli Lasagna

PREP: 30 minutes BAKE: 35 minutes STAND: 15 minutes OVEN: 350°F MAKES 8 servings

9   **dried lasagna noodles**

3½ **cups milk**

½   **cup all-purpose flour**

1   **teaspoon salt**

½   **teaspoon dry mustard**

¼   **teaspoon ground black pepper**

¼   **teaspoon bottled hot pepper sauce**

¼   **cup grated Parmesan cheese**

1   **16-ounce package frozen cut broccoli, thawed and drained**

1   **cup shredded carrots (2 medium)**

2   **cups shredded cheddar cheese (8 ounces)**

1 Preheat oven to 350°F. Lightly grease a 3-quart rectangular baking dish; set aside. Cook pasta according to package directions; drain in colander. Rinse with cold water; drain again. Place noodles in a single layer on a sheet of foil; set aside.

2 Meanwhile, for sauce, in a medium saucepan whisk together 1 cup of the milk and the flour until smooth. Stir in the remaining 2½ cups milk, salt, dry mustard, pepper, and hot pepper sauce. Cook and stir over medium heat until thickened and bubbly. Remove from heat; stir in Parmesan cheese.

3 Arrange one-third of the cooked lasagna noodles in the bottom of the prepared baking dish. Top with half of the broccoli, half of the carrots, ¾ cup of the cheddar cheese, and 1 cup of the sauce. Repeat layers of noodles, remaining broccoli, remaining carrots, cheese, and sauce. Top with the remaining noodles, sauce, and cheese.

4 Bake, uncovered, for 35 to 40 minutes or until heated through. Let stand for 15 minutes before serving.

PER SERVING: *325 cal., 13 g total fat (8 g sat. fat), 41 mg chol., 574 mg sodium, 35 g carb., 3 g fiber, 17 g pro.*

Black Bean Lasagna

PREP: 45 minutes   BAKE: 35 minutes   STAND: 10 minutes   OVEN: 350°F   MAKES 8 servings

- 9 **dried lasagna noodles**
- 1 **egg, lightly beaten**
- 1½ **cups shredded Monterey Jack cheese (6 ounces)**
- 1 **12-ounce carton cream-style cottage cheese**
- 1 **8-ounce package cream cheese, softened and cut up**
- 2 **15-ounce cans black beans, rinsed and drained**
- 1 **cup chopped onion (1 large)**
- ¾ **cup chopped green sweet pepper (1 medium)**
- 2 **cloves garlic, minced**
- 1 **tablespoon vegetable oil**
- 1 **15-ounce can Italian-style tomato sauce**
- 4 **teaspoons dried cilantro, crushed**
- 1 **teaspoon ground cumin**
- **Coarsely chopped tomato**
- **Snipped fresh cilantro (optional)**

1 Preheat oven to 350°F. Lightly grease a 3-quart rectangular baking dish; set aside. Cook pasta in boiling, lightly salted water according to package directions; drain. Rinse with cold water; drain again. Place noodles in a single layer on a sheet of foil; set aside.

2 Meanwhile, in a medium bowl combine egg, 1 cup of the Monterey Jack cheese, the cottage cheese, and cream cheese; set aside.

3 In a small bowl mash 1 can of the drained beans with a potato masher or fork; set aside.

4 In a large skillet cook onion, sweet pepper, and garlic in hot oil over medium-high heat until tender. Stir in mashed beans, the remaining can of whole beans, tomato sauce, dried cilantro, and cumin; heat through.

5 Arrange one-third of the cooked lasagna noodles in the bottom of the prepared baking dish. Spread with one-third of the bean mixture, then half of the cheese mixture. Repeat layers. Top with the remaining noodles and the remaining bean mixture.

6 Bake, covered, for 35 to 40 minutes or until heated through. Sprinkle with the remaining ½ cup Monterey Jack cheese. Let stand for 10 minutes before serving. Sprinkle with tomato and, if desired, fresh cilantro.

PER SERVING: *456 cal., 22 g total fat (12 g sat. fat), 83 mg chol., 857 mg sodium, 46 g carb., 8 g fiber, 25 g pro.*

157

Vegetable Lasagna

PREP: 45 minutes BAKE: 50 minutes STAND: 10 minutes OVEN: 350°F MAKES 12 servings

158

9 dried whole grain lasagna noodles

Nonstick cooking spray

½ cup chopped leek (1 medium)

3 medium zucchini, thinly sliced

2 cups sliced mushrooms

¾ cup roasted red peppers, drained and cut into bite-size strips

¼ cup snipped fresh basil

1 24-ounce carton fat-free cottage cheese (scant 3 cups)

2 eggs

2 cloves garlic, minced

1 10-ounce package frozen chopped spinach, thawed and squeezed dry

1 cup shredded low-fat mozzarella cheese (about 4 ounces)

¼ teaspoon ground black pepper

Shredded fresh spinach (optional)

1 Preheat oven to 350°F. Cook pasta according to package directions; drain in colander. Rinse with cold water; drain again. Place noodles in a single layer on a sheet of foil; set aside.

2 Lightly coat a 3-quart rectangular baking dish with cooking spray; set aside.

3 Lightly coat a large skillet with cooking spray. Cook leek over medium heat about 4 minutes or until just tender. Stir in zucchini, mushrooms, and roasted red peppers. Cook and stir for 8 to 10 minutes or until vegetables are tender. Remove from heat; stir in basil.

4 Meanwhile, in a food processor or blender combine cottage cheese, eggs, and garlic. Cover and process or blend until smooth. Stir in thawed spinach.

5 Layer 3 lasagna noodles in bottom of the prepared baking dish and top with half of the zucchini mixture. Spread one-third of the cottage cheese mixture on top. Repeat, ending with a layer of noodles. Spread remaining cottage cheese mixture on top. Sprinkle with mozzarella cheese. Spray a piece of cooking foil with cooking spray and place over the cheese.

6 Bake, covered, for 45 minutes. Uncover and bake for 5 minutes more. Let stand 10 minutes before serving. Sprinkle with black pepper. If desired, garnish with shredded fresh spinach.

PER SERVING: *163 cal., 3 g total fat (1 g sat. fat), 43 mg chol., 292 mg sodium, 21 g carb., 4 g fiber, 14 g pro.*

Garden Vegetables Lasagna

PREP: 45 minutes BAKE: 45 minutes STAND: 10 minutes OVEN: 375°F MAKES 8 servings

Nonstick cooking spray

9 dried white or whole grain lasagna noodles

3 cups broccoli florets

1 red sweet pepper, seeded and cut into bite-size strips

1 medium zucchini, sliced (1¼ cups)

1 medium yellow summer squash, sliced (about 1¼ cups)

2 15-ounce cartons light ricotta cheese

½ cup snipped fresh basil or 1 tablespoon dried basil, crushed

1 tablespoon snipped fresh thyme or 1 teaspoon dried thyme, crushed

3 cloves garlic, minced

½ teaspoon salt

¼ teaspoon ground black pepper

¼ teaspoon bottled hot pepper sauce

2 cups shredded part-skim mozzarella cheese (8 ounces)

1 Preheat oven to 375°F. Lightly coat a 3-quart rectangular baking dish with cooking spray; set aside.

2 Cook pasta according to package directions; drain in colander. Rinse with cold water; drain again. Place noodles in a single layer on a sheet of foil; set aside.

3 In a 4-quart Dutch oven place a steamer basket. Add water to just below the bottom of the steamer basket. Bring to boiling. Add broccoli, sweet pepper, zucchini, and yellow summer squash. Reduce heat. Steam, covered, for 6 to 8 minutes or until vegetables are crisp-tender. Remove from heat.

4 In a large bowl combine ricotta cheese, basil, thyme, garlic, salt, black pepper, and hot pepper sauce.

5 Layer one-third of the cooked noodles in the prepared baking dish. Spread with one-third of the ricotta cheese mixture. Top with one-third of the vegetable mixture and ⅔ cup of the mozzarella cheese. Repeat layers twice.

6 Bake, covered, for 45 to 55 minutes or until heated through and top is lightly brown. Let stand for 10 minutes before serving.

PER SERVING: *293 cal., 9 g total fat (6 g sat. fat), 44 mg chol., 428 mg sodium, 30 g carb., 3 g fiber, 20 g pro.*

159

tip

Although it's easier to buy a vegetable lasagna in the freezer case than to prepare one from scratch, the frozen kind often comes up short on veggies and over the top on high-fat cheese. Make your own lasagna to reduce fat and add all the veggies you want!

Artichoke-Basil Lasagna

PREP: 45 minutes BAKE: 40 minutes STAND: 15 minutes OVEN: 350°F MAKES 8 servings

9 dried whole grain lasagna noodles

1 tablespoon olive oil

2 8- or 9-ounce packages frozen artichoke hearts, thawed and well drained

¼ cup pine nuts

4 cloves garlic, minced

1 15-ounce carton light ricotta cheese

1½ cups reduced-fat shredded Italian cheese blend or part-skim mozzarella cheese (6 ounces)

1 cup snipped fresh basil or 4 teaspoons dried basil, crushed

1 egg

¼ teaspoon salt

1 cup chicken-flavored vegetable broth

¼ cup all-purpose flour

2 cups fat-free milk

Chopped fresh tomato (optional)

Snipped fresh parsley (optional)

1 Preheat oven to 350°F. Cook pasta according to package directions; drain in colander. Rinse with cold water; drain again. Place noodles in a single layer on a sheet of foil; set aside.

2 In a large skillet heat oil over medium heat. Add artichokes, pine nuts, and garlic; cook about 5 minutes or until artichokes, nuts, and garlic start to brown, stirring frequently. Transfer to a large bowl.

3 Add ricotta cheese, ½ cup of the Italian cheese blend, ½ cup of the fresh basil or 1 tablespoon of the dried basil, the egg, and salt; stir to combine.

4 For sauce, in a medium saucepan whisk together broth and flour until smooth. Stir in milk. Cook and stir over medium heat until sauce is slightly thickened and bubbly. Remove from heat. Stir in the remaining ½ cup fresh basil or 1 teaspoon dried basil.

5 Spread 1 cup of the sauce in the bottom of a 3-quart rectangular baking dish. Top with one-third of the cooked lasagna noodles. Spread with one-third of the ricotta mixture, then one-third of the remaining sauce. Sprinkle with ⅓ cup of the remaining Italian blend cheese. Repeat layers twice, beginning with the lasagna noodles and ending with the Italian blend cheese.

6 Bake, uncovered, about 40 minutes or until heated through and top is lightly brown. Let stand for 15 minutes before serving. If desired, top with tomato and parsley.

PER SERVING: *329 cal., 12 g total fat (5 g sat. fat), 52 mg chol., 443 mg sodium, 35 g carb., 7 g fiber, 21 g pro.*

Red Bean Lasagna

PREP: 45 minutes   BAKE: 45 minutes   STAND: 10 minutes   OVEN: 375°F   MAKES 8 servings

- 1 tablespoon cooking oil
- 1 cup chopped onion (1 large)
- ½ cup chopped carrot (1 medium)
- 1 clove garlic, minced
- 1 15- to 16-ounce can red beans, rinsed and drained
- 1 14.5-ounce can diced tomatoes, undrained
- ¼ cup snipped fresh parsley
- 1 tablespoon snipped fresh basil or 1½ teaspoons dried basil, crushed
- 2 teaspoons snipped fresh oregano or 1 teaspoon dried oregano, crushed
- 6 dried whole wheat or regular lasagna noodles
- 2 cups sliced fresh mushrooms
- 1 12-ounce carton low-fat cottage cheese, drained
- 1 cup shredded part-skim mozzarella cheese (4 ounces)
- ¼ cup refrigerated or frozen egg product, thawed, or 1 egg, lightly beaten
- ¼ cup grated Parmesan cheese
- 3 cups coarsely chopped fresh spinach
- 2 tablespoons coarsely snipped fresh parsley, basil, and/or oregano (optional)

1 In a large skillet in heat oil over medium heat. Add onion, carrot, and garlic. Cook about 5 minutes or until just tender, stirring occasionally. Add drained beans, undrained tomatoes, the ¼ cup parsley, the 1 tablespoon basil, and the 2 teaspoons oregano. Bring to boiling; reduce heat. Simmer, covered, for 15 minutes.

2 Cook pasta according to package directions; drain in colander. Rinse with cold water; drain again. Place noodles in a single layer on a sheet of foil; set aside.

3 Preheat oven to 375°F. In skillet mash beans slightly using a potato masher or fork. Add mushrooms to skillet. Simmer, uncovered, for 15 minutes more, stirring occasionally.

4 Meanwhile, in a medium bowl combine cottage cheese, ½ cup of the mozzarella cheese, the egg, and Parmesan cheese; set aside.

5 Spread ½ cup of the bean mixture in the bottom of a 2-quart rectangular baking dish. Arrange 2 noodles in a single layer on top of the bean mixture. Spread with one-third of the cheese mixture. Top evenly with one-third of the remaining bean mixture. Top with half of the spinach. Repeat layers twice, starting with noodles and ending with bean mixture.

6 Bake, covered, about 40 minutes or until heated through. Top with remaining ½ cup mozzarella cheese. Bake, uncovered, 5 minutes more or until cheese melts. Let stand for 10 minutes before serving. If desired, garnish with the 2 tablespoons fresh parsley.

PER SERVING: *243 cal., 6 g total fat (2 g sat. fat), 13 mg chol., 631 mg sodium, 29 g carb., 6 g fiber, 18 g pro.*

Cheese Manicotti with Roasted Pepper Sauce

PREP: 30 minutes   BAKE: 25 minutes   STAND: 10 minutes   OVEN: 350°F   MAKES 4 servings

8   dried manicotti shells
    Nonstick cooking spray
1   cup chopped fresh
    mushrooms
¾   cup shredded carrot
3   or 4 cloves garlic, minced
1   cup light ricotta cheese or
    low-fat cream-style cottage
    cheese
¾   cup shredded reduced-fat
    mozzarella cheese (3 ounces)
2   eggs, lightly beaten
¼   cup grated Parmesan cheese
2   teaspoons dried Italian
    seasoning, crushed
1   14.5-ounce can diced tomatoes
    with basil, garlic, and
    oregano, undrained
1   cup roasted red sweet
    peppers, drained and chopped

1 Preheat oven to 350°F. Cook pasta according to package directions; drain in colander. Rinse with cold water and drain again. Place shells in a single layer on a sheet of foil; set aside.

2 Meanwhile, for filling, coat an unheated large nonstick skillet with cooking spray. Preheat over medium heat. Add mushrooms, carrot, and garlic to hot skillet. Cook for 3 to 5 minutes or just until vegetables are tender, stirring occasionally. Remove from heat; cool slightly. Stir in ricotta cheese, ½ cup of the mozzarella cheese, the eggs, Parmesan cheese, and Italian seasoning. Spoon filling into cooked manicotti shells.

3 For sauce, place undrained tomatoes in a blender or food processor. Cover and blend or process until smooth. Stir in roasted red peppers. Spread about ⅓ cup of the sauce into the bottom of four 12- to 16-ounce ungreased individual baking dishes or a 2-quart rectangular baking dish. Arrange stuffed manicotti shells in individual baking dishes or large baking dish, overlapping shells slightly if necessary. Pour remaining sauce over manicotti.

4 Bake, covered, for 20 to 25 minutes for individual baking dishes, 35 to 40 minutes for large baking dish, or until heated through. Uncover and sprinkle with the remaining ¼ cup mozzarella cheese. Bake for 5 minutes more. Let stand for 10 minutes before serving.

PER SERVING: *378 cal., 13 g total fat (7 g sat. fat), 141 mg chol., 860 mg sodium, 43 g carb., 3 g fiber, 22 g pro.*

Pizzas & Sandwiches

5

These handheld favorites are loaded with fresh herbs, veggies, beans, and grains, offering you a hearty and balanced meal—no fork required!

Herbed Cheese Pizza

PREP: 20 minutes GRILL: 10 minutes MAKES 4 servings

1½ **cups chopped tomato (3 medium)**

½ **cup snipped fresh basil**

1 **tablespoon olive oil**

1 **clove garlic, minced**

1 **16-ounce loaf frozen bread dough, thawed**

   Cornmeal

1 **cup shredded Asiago or Parmesan cheese (4 ounces)**

1 **cup shredded mozzarella cheese (4 ounces)**

1 In a medium bowl combine tomato, basil, oil, and garlic. Set aside.

2 On a lightly floured surface roll dough into a 12-inch circle. Lightly sprinkle both sides with cornmeal. Place on a large baking sheet dusted with cornmeal.

3 For a charcoal grill, transfer dough circle to the rack of an uncovered grill directly over medium coals. Cover and grill about 3 minutes or until top is puffed and bottom is crisp. Turn crust over with a large spatula. Cover and grill for 2 minutes more. Remove from grill.

4 Top pizza crust with tomato mixture, Asiago cheese, and mozzarella cheese. Cover and grill about 5 minutes more or until crust is golden brown and cheeses are melted. (For a gas grill, preheat grill. Reduce heat to medium. Transfer dough circle to grill rack over heat. Cover and grill as above.)

PER SERVING: *483 cal., 24 g total fat (11 g sat. fat), 46 mg chol., 808 mg sodium, 46 g carb., 3 g fiber, 21 g pro.*

Smoked Provolone Pizza:

Prepare as directed, except substitute 2 teaspoons snipped fresh rosemary for the basil and use 1½ cups shredded smoked provolone or Gouda cheese (6 ounces) instead of the Asiago and mozzarella cheeses.

PER SERVING: *468 cal., 15 g total fat (8 g sat. fat), 29 mg chol., 374 mg sodium, 54 g carb., 9 g fiber, 20 g pro.*

make it vegan

Substitute desired soy cheese for the Asiago cheese and mozzarella-flavor soy cheese for the mozzarella cheese.

Mixed-Mushroom Pizza

PREP: 30 minutes BAKE: 25 minutes COOL: 5 minutes OVEN: 375°F MAKES 12 servings

Nonstick cooking spray

1 13.8-ounce package refrigerated pizza dough

8 ounces fontina, provolone, or mozzarella cheese, thinly sliced

3 tablespoons olive oil

2 large sweet onions (such as Vidalia or Walla Walla), halved and thinly sliced (about 4 cups)

3 cups assorted sliced fresh mushrooms (such as stemmed shiitake, oyster, cremini, chanterelle, morel, and/or button)

2 teaspoons snipped fresh rosemary

2 cloves garlic, minced

Snipped fresh parsley

1 Preheat oven to 375°F. Coat a 15×10×1-inch baking pan with cooking spray. Press pizza dough evenly into the prepared pan, building up edges slightly. Arrange cheese slices on top of dough.

2 In a large skillet heat 2 tablespoons of the oil over medium-low heat. Add onions. Cook, covered, for 13 to 15 minutes or until tender, stirring occasionally. Cook, uncovered, over medium-high heat for 5 to 8 minutes or until golden brown, stirring frequently. Remove onions from skillet.

3 In the same skillet heat the remaining 1 tablespoon oil over medium heat. Add mushrooms, rosemary, and garlic; cook until mushrooms are tender, stirring occasionally. Drain well. Spoon mushroom mixture over cheese slices. Top with onions.

4 Bake for 25 to 30 minutes or until bottom of crust is slightly crisp and brown. Cool in pan on a wire rack for 5 minutes. Sprinkle with parsley.

PER SERVING: *201 cal., 11 g total fat (4 g sat. fat), 22 mg chol., 263 mg sodium, 19 g carb., 2 g fiber, 8 g pro.*

Fresh Tomato Pizzas with Three Cheeses

PREP: 20 minutes GRILL: 10 minutes per batch MAKES 6 servings

- 4 **roma tomatoes, thinly sliced**
- 2 **tablespoons snipped fresh Italian (flat-leaf) parsley**
- 2 **cloves garlic, minced**
- 1/2 **teaspoon salt**
- 1/2 **teaspoon freshly ground black pepper**
- 1 **13.8-ounce package refrigerated pizza dough**
- 2 **tablespoons olive oil**
  Cornmeal
- 4 **ounces fresh mozzarella cheese, thinly sliced**
- 1/2 **cup crumbled Gorgonzola or other blue cheese (2 ounces)**
- 1/4 **cup freshly grated Parmesan cheese**
- 1/4 **cup shredded fresh Italian (flat-leaf) parsley or basil**

1 In a medium bowl combine tomato, snipped parsley, garlic, salt, and pepper; set aside.

2 Divide dough in half. On a lightly floured surface pat or roll each portion into a 12-inch circle. Brush tops of dough circles with oil. Stack dough circles on a baking sheet, separating them with a sheet of waxed paper or parchment paper sprinkled with cornmeal.

3 For a charcoal grill, carefully transfer 1 dough circle, oiled side down, to the lightly greased rack of an uncovered grill directly over low coals. Grill about 6 minutes or until light brown (top will be dry but soft). Remove from grill.

4 Turn pizza crust over; top with half of the tomato mixture and half of the cheeses. Cover and grill for 4 to 6 minutes more or until crust is crisp and cheeses are melted, moving pizza around to brown evenly. Repeat with the remaining dough circle and the remaining toppings. (For a gas grill, preheat grill. Reduce heat to low. Transfer 1 dough circle to grill rack over heat. Cover and grill as above.) Sprinkle with shredded parsley.

PER SERVING: *307 cal., 16 g total fat (6 g sat. fat), 25 mg chol., 672 mg sodium, 30 g carb., 2 g fiber, 11 g pro.*

Grilled Vegetable Pizzas

PREP: 20 minutes FREEZE: 10 minutes GRILL: 15 minutes MAKES 6 to 8 servings

1 pound frozen pizza dough, thawed

1/3 cup olive oil

6 cloves garlic, minced

3 medium Japanese eggplants, cut lengthwise into 1/4-inch slices

Salt

Ground black pepper

8 ounces fresh mozzarella cheese, thinly sliced

3 medium red and/or yellow tomatoes, sliced

1 cup fresh basil leaves

Balsamic vinegar

1 Divide pizza dough in half. On a lightly floured surface roll each portion into a 13×10-inch oval. Stack dough ovals on a baking sheet, separating them with a sheet of waxed paper or parchment paper. Freeze about 10 minutes or until dough is firm.

2 Meanwhile, in a small saucepan heat 1/4 cup of the oil over medium heat. Add garlic; cook and stir for 30 seconds. Set aside. Brush both sides of eggplant slices with the remaining oil.

3 For a charcoal grill, grill eggplant slices on the lightly greased rack of an uncovered grill directly over medium-hot coals about 8 minutes or until tender and golden brown, turning once halfway through grilling. Remove from grill.

4 Brush tops of dough ovals with some of the garlic oil; sprinkle with salt and pepper. Carefully place dough ovals, oiled sides down, on grill rack. Grill about 4 minutes or until golden brown. Remove from grill.

5 Brush pizza crusts with garlic oil; turn crusts over and brush grilled sides with garlic oil. Top with mozzarella cheese. Add grilled eggplant and tomato slices; sprinkle with additional salt and pepper. Cover and grill about 3 minutes more or until cheese starts to melt. (For a gas grill, preheat grill. Reduce heat to medium-high. Place eggplant, then pizza crusts, on lightly greased grill rack over heat. Cover and grill as above.) Sprinkle with basil and drizzle with vinegar.

PER SERVING: 670 cal., 17 g total fat (6 g sat. fat), 104 mg chol., 144 mg sodium, 93 g carb., 1 g fiber, 34 g pro.

167

make it vegan

Substitute mozzarella-flavor soy cheese for the mozzarella cheese.

tip

If you want to grill your pizza, make sure to use a pizza stone specially made for a grill. Stones meant for ovens may not hold up to the high heat of a grill.

Thai-Style Veggie Pizza

PREP: 20 minutes BAKE: 6 minutes OVEN: 450°F MAKES 4 servings

1 12-inch whole wheat Italian bread shell (such as Boboli brand)
   Nonstick cooking spray
1 cup sliced fresh shiitake or button mushrooms
⅔ cup fresh pea pods cut into thin strips
¼ cup coarsely shredded carrot
¼ cup sliced green onions (2)
¼ to ⅓ cup peanut sauce
2 tablespoons chopped peanuts
2 tablespoons fresh cilantro leaves

1 Preheat oven to 450°F. Place bread shell on an ungreased baking sheet. Bake for 6 to 8 minutes or until light brown and crisp.

2 Meanwhile, lightly coat a large nonstick skillet with cooking spray; heat skillet over medium heat. Add mushrooms, pea pods, and carrot; cook about 2 minutes or just until tender, stirring occasionally. Stir in green onions. Remove from heat.

3 Spread hot bread shell with peanut sauce. Top with hot vegetable mixture; sprinkle with peanuts and cilantro.

PER SERVING: *286 cal., 8 g total fat (2 g sat. fat), 0 mg chol., 598 mg sodium, 46 g carb., 8 g fiber, 12 g pro.*

168

tip
Do double duty. When grilling vegetables for dinner, make a large batch for leftovers later in the week. Use them hot or cold in sandwiches or as toppers for a quick-fix pizza.

Greek-Style Pizza

PREP: 30 minutes RISE: 30 minutes BAKE: 13 minutes OVEN: 425°F MAKES 6 to 8 servings

1 recipe Pizza Dough

1 tablespoon olive oil

1 tablespoon snipped fresh oregano or 1 teaspoon dried oregano, crushed

2 medium roma tomatoes, thinly sliced

¾ cup roasted red sweet peppers, drained and coarsely chopped

¼ cup pitted kalamata olives, chopped, or sliced pitted ripe olives

¼ cup crumbled reduced-fat feta cheese (1 ounce)

¼ cup finely shredded Parmesan cheese (1 ounce)

   Snipped fresh oregano (optional)

   Cracked black pepper (optional)

1 Prepare Pizza Dough. Preheat oven to 425°F. Grease a large baking sheet; set aside. On a lightly floured surface roll dough into a 14-inch oblong shape. Transfer to the baking sheet. Prick dough all over with a fork. Bake for 8 to 10 minutes or until lightly browned.

2 Brush partially baked crust with oil and sprinkle with 1 tablespoon snipped oregano or 1 teaspoon dried oregano. Top with tomato, roasted peppers, olives, feta cheese, and Parmesan cheese. Bake for 5 to 10 minutes more or until cheeses are melted.

3 If desired, sprinkle with additional snipped oregano and black pepper.

PER SERVING: *236 cal., 8 g total fat (2 g sat. fat), 5 mg chol., 322 mg sodium, 36 g carb., 3 g fiber, 8 g protein.*

169

Pizza Dough

1. In a small bowl combine ⅔ cup warm water (105°F to 115°F) and 1 package active dry yeast, stirring to dissolve yeast. Let stand for 5 minutes. Stir in 1 tablespoon honey and 1 tablespoon olive oil.

2. Meanwhile, in a medium bowl combine ¾ cup white whole wheat flour, ¼ cup cornmeal, and ¼ teaspoon salt. Stir in yeast mixture. Stir in as much of the ¾ to 1 cup all-purpose flour as you can with a wooden spoon.

3. Turn dough out onto a lightly floured surface. Knead in enough of any remaining all-purpose flour to make a moderately stiff dough that is smooth and elastic (6 to 8 minutes total). Shape dough into a ball. Place in a lightly greased bowl, turning once to grease surface. Cover and let rise in a warm place until nearly double in size (30 to 45 minutes). Punch dough down. Turn out onto a lightly floured surface. Cover and let rest for 10 minutes.

make it vegan

Substitute crumbled feta-flavor soy cheese for the feta cheese and desired soy cheese for the Parmesan cheese.

Pizzas & Sandwiches

Mediterranean Pepper and Artichoke Pizza

PREP: 20 minutes BAKE: 20 minutes OVEN: 425°F MAKES 8 servings

1   6- to 6.5-ounce package pizza crust mix

1   teaspoon dried oregano or basil, crushed

½   cup pizza sauce

1   cup roasted red and/or yellow sweet peppers, cut into strips

1   6-ounce jar marinated artichoke hearts, drained and coarsely chopped

¼   cup sliced green onions (2) and/or chopped red onion

1   cup crumbled semisoft goat cheese (chèvre) (4 ounces)

½   cup shredded mozzarella cheese (2 ounces)

Freshly ground black pepper (optional)

1 Preheat oven to 425°F. Grease a large baking sheet; set aside. Prepare pizza crust according to package directions, stirring oregano into dry mixture. Transfer dough to the prepared baking sheet. Using floured hands, press dough evenly into a 15×10-inch rectangle, building up edges slightly (crust will be thin). Bake for 7 minutes.

2 Spread pizza sauce evenly over crust. Top with roasted peppers, artichokes, and green and/or red onions. Sprinkle with goat cheese and mozzarella cheese.

3 Bake for 13 to 15 minutes or until crust is golden brown and cheeses are melted. If desired, sprinkle with black pepper.

PER SERVING: *170 cal., 7 g total fat (4 g sat. fat), 15 mg chol., 419 mg sodium, 19 g carb., 2 g fiber, 7 g pro.*

Southwest Black Bean Pizza

PREP: 20 minutes BAKE: 12 minutes OVEN: 425°F MAKES 4 servings

- 1 portion Whole Grain Pizza Crust (see recipe, page 176)
- 2 teaspoons olive oil
- ¾ cup salsa
- 1 cup canned no-salt-added black beans, rinsed and drained
- ¾ cup red and/or green sweet pepper strips
- 1 fresh jalapeño chile pepper, seeded and cut into thin strips* (optional)
- 1 cup shredded reduced-fat Mexican cheese blend (4 ounces)

1 Preheat oven to 425°F. Grease a 14-inch round baking stone, 12-inch pizza pan, or large baking sheet; set aside. On a lightly floured surface roll Whole Grain Pizza Crust dough into a 12-inch circle. Transfer to the prepared baking stone. Prick dough all over with a fork. Bake for 6 to 8 minutes or until crust is light brown.

2 Lightly brush 1 inch of the edge of hot crust with oil. Spread salsa over crust to within 1 inch of the edge. Top with drained beans, sweet peppers, and, if desired, jalapeño pepper; sprinkle with cheese.

3 Bake for 6 to 8 minutes more or until toppings are heated through and cheese is melted.

PER SERVING (including crust): 319 cal., 10 g total fat (4 g sat. fat), 15 mg chol., 591 mg sodium, 41 g carb., 8 g fiber, 16 g pro.

171

*tip
Because chile peppers contain volatile oils that can burn your skin and eyes, avoid direct contact with them as much as possible. When working with chile peppers, wear plastic or rubber gloves. If your bare hands do touch the peppers, wash your hands and nails well with soap and warm water.

make it vegan 🌿
Substitute desired soy cheese for the Mexican cheese blend.

Salsa, Bean, and Cheese Pizza

START TO FINISH: 20 minutes OVEN: 425°F MAKES 4 servings

- 4 6-inch corn tortillas*
- 4 teaspoons olive oil
- ½ cup chopped onion
     (1 medium)
- 1 fresh jalapeño chile pepper,
     seeded and finely chopped**
- 1 clove garlic, minced
- 1 cup canned black beans,
     rinsed and drained
- 1 cup seeded and chopped
     tomato (2 medium)
- 1 cup shredded Monterey Jack,
     cheddar, or mozzarella cheese
     (4 ounces)
- 2 tablespoons snipped fresh
     cilantro

1 Preheat oven to 425°F. Lightly brush both sides of tortillas with 1 teaspoon of the oil. Place tortillas on an ungreased baking sheet. Bake about 6 minutes or until light brown and crisp, turning once.

2 Meanwhile, in a large skillet heat the remaining 1 tablespoon oil over medium-high heat. Add onion, chile pepper, and garlic; cook until onion is tender, stirring occasionally. Stir in drained black beans and tomato; heat through.

3 Sprinkle tortillas with ½ cup of the cheese. Spoon bean mixture onto tortillas; sprinkle with the remaining ½ cup cheese. Bake about 4 minutes or until cheese is melted. Sprinkle with cilantro.

PER SERVING: *231 cal., 11 g total fat (4 g sat. fat), 20 mg chol., 496 mg sodium, 25 g carb., 6 g fiber, 12 g pro.*

172

*tip
If you prefer, substitute tostada shells for the corn tortillas. Reduce the amount of oil to 1 tablespoon and omit Step 1.

**tip
Because chile peppers contain volatile oils that can burn your skin and eyes, avoid direct contact with them as much as possible. When working with chile peppers, wear plastic or rubber gloves. If your bare hands do touch the peppers, wash your hands and nails well with soap and warm water.

🌱 make it vegan
Substitute desired soy cheese for the Monterey Jack, Cheddar, or mozzarella cheese.

Cheesy Red Pepper Pizza

PREP: **15 minutes** BAKE: **15 minutes** OVEN: **425°F** MAKES **8 servings**

Nonstick cooking spray
1 **13.8-ounce package refrigerated pizza dough**
1 **tablespoon olive oil**
2 **medium roma tomatoes, thinly sliced**
½ **cup sliced roasted red and/or yellow sweet pepper**
2 **tablespoons shredded fresh spinach leaves (optional)**
1 **cup shredded mozzarella cheese (4 ounces)**
¼ **teaspoon coarsely ground black pepper**
2 **tablespoons snipped fresh basil**

1 Preheat oven to 425°F. Coat a 12-inch pizza pan with cooking spray. Press pizza dough into the prepared pan, building up edge slightly. Brush with oil. Bake for 10 minutes. Remove from oven.

2 Arrange tomato, roasted pepper, and, if desired, spinach on top of crust. Sprinkle with cheese and black pepper.

3 Bake for 5 to 10 minutes more or until toppings are heated through and cheese is bubbly. Sprinkle with basil.

PER SERVING: *182 cal., 6 g total fat (2 g sat. fat), 9 mg chol., 359 mg sodium, 25 g carb., 1 g fiber, 8 g pro.*

make it vegan 🌿
Substitute mozzarella-flavor soy cheese for the mozzarella cheese.

173

Camembert Pizzas with Focaccia Crusts

START TO FINISH: **20 minutes** MAKES **4 servings**

4 **6-inch individual Italian flatbreads (focaccia)**
2 **large tomatoes, sliced**
Salt
Ground black pepper
1 **8-ounce round Camembert cheese, chilled**
⅓ **cup chopped walnuts**
2 **tablespoons snipped fresh chives**

1 Preheat broiler. Place flatbreads on the unheated rack of a broiler pan. Top with tomato slices; sprinkle with salt and pepper. Cut cheese into thin slices. Place cheese slices on top of tomato slices.

2 Broil 4 to 5 inches from the heat about 2 minutes or until cheese starts to melt. Sprinkle with walnuts. Broil for 1 minute more. Sprinkle with chives.

PER SERVING: *449 cal., 24 g total fat (11 g sat. fat), 41 mg chol., 1,027 mg sodium, 41 g carb., 6 g fiber, 21 g pro.*

tip
Camembert is a soft, buttery French cheese similar to Brie. You can find it in gourmet food stores or delis as well as supermarkets that have a large cheese selection. When served at room temperature, it makes a delicious spread to serve with crackers and fruit.

Vegetable Flatbreads with Goat Cheese

PREP: 25 minutes   BROIL: 4 minutes   MAKES 4 servings

- ⅓ cup olive oil
- 1 medium yellow summer squash, quartered lengthwise and sliced (about 1¼ cups)
- ½ cup chopped carrot (1 medium)
- ½ cup chopped green sweet pepper (1 small)
- ½ cup chopped red sweet pepper (1 small)
- ½ cup broccoli florets
- ½ of a small red onion, sliced
- 4 cloves garlic, minced
- ⅔ cup chopped roma tomatoes (2 medium)
- 12 pimiento-stuffed green olives, halved
- 1 tablespoon olive liquid from jar
- 4 6- to 7½-inch individual Italian flatbreads (focaccia)
- 2 cups crumbled goat cheese (chèvre) (8 ounces)
  Sea salt
  Freshly ground black pepper

1 Preheat broiler. In an extra-large skillet heat 2 tablespoons of the oil over medium-high heat. Add squash, carrot, sweet peppers, broccoli, red onion, and garlic. Cook and stir for 3 minutes. Add tomatoes, olives, and olive liquid. Cook about 2 minutes more or until vegetables are tender, stirring occasionally.

2 Lightly brush both sides of flatbreads with some of the remaining oil. Place on an ungreased extra-large baking sheet.* Broil about 4 inches from the heat for 2 to 4 minutes or until lightly browned, turning once halfway through broiling. Remove from broiler.

3 Using a slotted spoon, divide vegetable mixture among flatbreads; sprinkle with cheese. Broil about 2 minutes more or until cheese is softened. Drizzle with any remaining oil and sprinkle with salt and black pepper.

PER SERVING: *611 cal., 40 g total fat (15 g sat. fat), 45 mg chol., 894 mg sodium, 45 g carb., 5 g fiber, 20 g pro.*

*tip
If necessary, divide flatbreads between 2 ungreased baking sheets and broil in batches.

🌿 make it vegan
Substitute desired soy cheese for the goat cheese.

Olive and Arugula Flatbread Pizza Salad

START TO FINISH: **25 minutes** MAKES **4 servings**

2   **to 3 tablespoons olive oil**

1   **teaspoon lemon juice**

1   **teaspoon red wine vinegar**

¼   **teaspoon salt**

⅛   **teaspoon cracked black pepper**

2   **cups baby arugula leaves**

1   **14×12-inch Italian flatbread (focaccia) or one 12-inch thin Italian bread shell**

2   **teaspoons olive oil**

¼   **cup olive pesto or tapenade**

6   **pimiento-stuffed green olives, sliced**

¼   **cup shaved Parmesan cheese (1 ounce)***

1 For dressing, in a screw-top jar combine 2 to 3 tablespoons oil, lemon juice, vinegar, salt, and pepper. Cover and shake well. Place arugula in a medium bowl. Shake dressing again; drizzle over arugula, tossing gently to coat.

2 Brush flatbread with 2 teaspoons oil. For a charcoal grill, grill flatbread on the rack of an uncovered grill directly over medium coals for 1 to 2 minutes or just until golden brown, turning once halfway through grilling. (For a gas grill, preheat grill. Reduce heat to medium. Place flatbread on grill rack over heat. Cover and grill as above.)

3 Spread flatbread with pesto. Top with dressed arugula, olives, and cheese.

PER SERVING: *504 cal., 27 g total fat (4 g sat. fat), 14 mg chol., 1,369 mg sodium, 51 g carb., 1 g fiber, 16 g pro.*

175

***tip**
To shave the cheese, use a vegetable peeler or a grater with large holes.

Thin Pizza Crust 🌿

PREP: 25 minutes   CHILL: 2 to 24 hours   STAND: 1 hour   MAKES 1 crust (6 servings)

1	package active dry yeast
1	teaspoon sugar
¼	teaspoon salt
¾	cup warm water (100°F to 105°F)
1	tablespoon olive oil
2	cups bread flour

1 In a large bowl combine yeast, sugar, and salt; stir in the water and oil. Using a wooden spoon, stir in as much of the flour as you can. Using wet hands, work in any remaining flour but do not knead dough. Cover bowl with a towel and let stand at room temperature until nearly double in size (40 to 50 minutes). Chill, covered, for 2 to 24 hours.

2 Turn dough out onto a well-floured surface. Shape into a ball. Cover and let stand for 20 minutes. Use to prepare your favorite pizza.*

PER SERVING (crust only): 191 cal., 3 g total fat (0 g sat. fat), 0 mg chol., 99 mg sodium, 34 g carb., 1 g fiber, 6 g pro.

*tip

To prepare your favorite pizza: Preheat oven to 475°F. Coat a 12- to 14-inch pizza pan or a large baking sheet with nonstick cooking spray. Roll Thin Pizza Crust dough into a 12- to 14-inch circle or a 12×8-inch rectangle. Transfer dough to the prepared pan or baking sheet. Add your favorite toppings. Bake for 11 to 14 minutes or until crust is lightly browned, toppings are heated through, and cheese (if using) is melted.

176

Whole Grain Pizza Crust 🌿

PREP: 20 minutes   RISE: 2½ hours   MAKES 2 crusts (8 servings)

1¼	to 1½ cups bread flour or all-purpose flour
¾	cup whole wheat flour
¼	cup yellow cornmeal
¼	cup flaxseed meal
1	teaspoon active dry yeast
1	teaspoon kosher salt
1	cup warm water (105°F to 115°F)
	Olive oil

1 In a large bowl combine 1 cup of the bread flour, the whole wheat flour, cornmeal, flaxseed meal, yeast, and salt. Stir in the water. Turn dough out onto a lightly floured surface. Knead in enough of the remaining ¼ to ½ cup bread flour to make a moderately soft dough that is smooth and elastic (3 to 5 minutes total). Shape into a ball.

2 Place dough in a lightly greased bowl, turning once to grease surface. Cover and let rise in a warm place until double in size (2½ to 3 hours). Punch dough down. Turn out onto a lightly floured surface. Divide dough in half. Cover and let rest for 10 minutes.

PER SERVING: 144 cal., 2 g total fat (0 g sat. fat), 0 mg chol., 245 mg sodium, 27 g carb., 3 g fiber, 5 g pro.

Egg and Vegetable Salad Wraps

START TO FINISH: **30 minutes** MAKES **6 servings**

- 3   **hard-cooked eggs, chopped**
- ½   **cup chopped cucumber**
- ½   **cup chopped zucchini or yellow summer squash**
- ¼   **cup chopped red onion**
- ¼   **cup shredded carrot**
- 2   **tablespoons fat-free mayonnaise or light mayonnaise**
- 1   **tablespoon Dijon-style mustard**
- 2   **teaspoons fat-free milk**
- ½   **teaspoon snipped fresh basil or ¼ teaspoon dried basil, crushed**
-     **Dash paprika**
- 3   **10-inch multigrain, spinach, or vegetable flour tortillas**
- 3   **leaves leaf lettuce**
- 1   **large roma tomato, thinly sliced**

1 In a large bowl combine eggs, cucumber, zucchini, red onion, and carrot. For dressing, in a small bowl stir together mayonnaise, mustard, milk, basil, and paprika. Pour dressing over egg mixture; toss gently to coat.

2 Line tortillas with lettuce leaves. Top with tomato slices, slightly off center. Spoon egg mixture onto tomato slices. Fold in opposite sides of each tortilla; roll up from the bottom. Cut tortilla rolls diagonally into quarters.

PER SERVING: *161 cal., 5 g total fat (1 g sat. fat), 107 mg chol., 402 mg sodium, 21 g carb., 4 g fiber, 7 g pro.*

tip

Bored with bread? Wrap up your sandwich fixings in a tortilla, tuck them in a pita pocket, load them into a whole wheat hoagie bun, or stack them between an English muffin.

Soy Bacon and Pesto Wraps

START TO FINISH: **30 minutes** MAKES **4 servings**

1 **cup frozen shelled sweet soybeans (edamame)**

2 **tablespoons snipped fresh cilantro**

2 **tablespoons lemon juice**

2 **tablespoons water**

1 **medium fresh jalapeño chile pepper, seeded and chopped***

1 **clove garlic, halved**

4 **slices soy bacon**

4 **8-inch whole wheat or vegetable flour tortillas**

2 **cups torn mixed salad greens**

1 **cup seeded and chopped tomatoes (2 medium)**

1 Cook edamame according to package directions; drain. Rinse with cold water; drain again. In a food processor combine edamame, cilantro, lemon juice, the water, jalapeño pepper, and garlic. Cover and process until smooth. Set aside.

2 Cook bacon according to package directions. Drain on paper towels; chop bacon.

3 Spread about one-fourth of the edamame mixture on 1 edge of each tortilla. Top with salad greens, tomatoes, and bacon. Starting from the filled edge, roll up tortilla. Secure with a toothpick or partially wrap in plastic wrap or foil to hold together. Cut in half diagonally.

PER SERVING: *222 cal., 7 g total fat (1 g sat. fat), 0 mg chol., 502 mg sodium, 24 g carb., 13 g fiber, 16 g pro.*

*tip

Because chile peppers contain volatile oils that can burn your skin and eyes, avoid direct contact with them as much as possible. When working with chile peppers, wear plastic or rubber gloves. If your bare hands do touch the peppers, wash your hands and nails well with soap and warm water.

Barbecue Tempeh Wraps

PREP: 20 minutes CHILL: 1 hour MAKES 4 sandwiches

¼ cup light mayonnaise

1 tablespoon lemon juice

¼ teapoon ground black pepper

2 cups shredded cabbage with carrot (coleslaw mix)

1 small apple, cored and thinly sliced

2 tablespoons thinly sliced green onion (1)

2 teaspoons olive oil or canola oil

1 8-ounce package soy tempeh (fermented soybean cake), cut into bite-size strips

¼ cup light barbecue sauce

4 7- to 8-inch whole wheat tortillas

1 In a medium bowl stir together mayonnaise, lemon juice, and pepper. Add coleslaw mix, apple slices, and green onion; toss gently to coat. Cover and chill about 1 hour.

2 In a large nonstick skillet heat oil over medium-high heat. Add tempeh; cook for 3 to 5 minutes or until golden brown, stirring occasionally. Stir in barbecue sauce; remove from heat.

3 Stack and wrap tortillas in microwave-safe paper towels. Microwave on 100 percent power (high) about 30 seconds or until warm.

4 To serve, divide coleslaw mixture and tempeh mixture among warm tortillas. Roll up tortillas.

PER SANDWICH: *257 cal., 15 g total fat (2 g sat. fat), 5 mg chol., 500 mg sodium, 24 g carb., 9 g fiber, 16 g pro.*

White Bean and Goat Cheese Wraps

START TO FINISH: 20 minutes MAKES 6 sandwiches

1 19-ounce can cannellini beans (white kidney beans), rinsed and drained

4 ounces soft goat cheese (chèvre)

1 tablespoon snipped fresh oregano

1 tablespoon snipped fresh Italian (flat-leaf) parsley

6 8-inch whole wheat flour tortillas

6 cups fresh baby spinach

1 12-ounce jar roasted red sweet peppers, drained and thinly sliced

1 In a medium bowl slightly mash beans with a fork. Stir in cheese, oregano, and parsley.

2 Stack and wrap tortillas in microwave-safe paper towels. Microwave on 100 percent power (high) for 30 to 40 seconds or until warm.

3 Spread bean mixture on warm tortillas. Top with spinach and roasted peppers. Roll up tortillas. Cut diagonally in half.

PER SANDWICH: *248 cal., 8 g total fat (4 g sat. fat), 9 mg chol., 552 mg sodium, 31 g carb., 16 g fiber, 18 g pro.*

make it vegan

Substitute desired soy cheese for the goat cheese.

tip

Spice up your sandwich spread. Mix your favorite herb or spice into mashed avocados, mashed beans, light mayonnaise, or reduced-fat cream cheese to give your sandwich a new flavor spin.

Roasted Tofu and Veggie Pockets

PREP: 25 minutes ROAST/BAKE: 11 minutes OVEN: 450°F MAKES 6 sandwiches

Nonstick cooking spray

½ of a 16- to 18-ounce package extra-firm tub-style tofu (fresh bean curd)

1 cup thin red or yellow sweet pepper strips (1 medium)

1 cup thinly sliced zucchini (1 small)

1 medium onion, halved and thinly sliced

1 tablespoon olive oil

¼ teaspoon salt

¼ teaspoon ground black pepper

3 large whole wheat pita bread rounds, halved crosswise

2 tablespoons bottled light balsamic vinaigrette or reduced-calorie Italian salad dressing

⅓ cup shredded mozzarella-flavor soy cheese

1 Preheat oven to 450°F. Lightly coat a 15×10×1-inch baking pan with cooking spray; set aside.

2 Drain tofu; pat dry with paper towels. Cut crosswise into ¼-inch slices; cut into ½-inch strips. In a large bowl combine tofu, sweet pepper strips, zucchini, onion, oil, salt, and black pepper; toss gently to coat.

3 Spread tofu mixture evenly in the prepared baking pan. Roast for 10 to 12 minutes or until vegetables are tender, gently stirring once.

4 Fill pita pockets with tofu mixture. Drizzle filling with balsamic vinaigrette; top with cheese. Place pita pockets, filled sides up, in an ungreased 2-quart square baking dish. Bake for 1 to 2 minutes or until cheese is melted.

PER SANDWICH: *189 cal., 7 g total fat (1 g sat. fat), 0 mg chol., 433 mg sodium, 23 g carb., 4 g fiber, 9 g pro.*

Veggie Salad in a Pocket

PREP: 20 minutes CHILL: 2 to 24 hours MAKES 4 sandwiches

1 cup chopped yellow summer squash and/or zucchini

¾ cup chopped broccoli

⅔ cup seeded and chopped roma tomatoes (2 medium)

8 pitted kalamata or ripe olives, chopped

2 tablespoons snipped fresh Italian (flat-leaf) parsley or regular parsley

2 tablespoons bottled fat-free Italian salad dressing

2 6- to 7-inch whole wheat pita bread rounds, halved crosswise, or four 6- to 7-inch whole wheat flour tortillas

½ cup Spicy Navy Bean Hummus

1 In a medium bowl combine squash, broccoli, tomatoes, olives, and parsley. Drizzle with salad dressing; toss gently to coat. Cover and chill for 2 to 24 hours.

2 To assemble, spread the inside of each pita pocket or 1 side of each tortilla with 2 tablespoons of the Spicy Navy Bean Hummus. Spoon vegetable mixture into pita pockets or onto tortillas. If using tortillas, fold in half or roll up.

PER SANDWICH: *166 cal., 2 g total fat (0 g sat. fat), 0 mg chol., 599 mg sodium, 31 g carb., 6 g fiber, 7 g pro.*

Spicy Navy Bean Hummus

In a food processor combine one 15- to 19-ounce can navy or cannellini beans (white kidney beans), rinsed and drained; ¼ cup bottled fat-free Italian salad dressing; and 1 tablespoon spicy brown mustard. Cover and process until smooth. (Or mash beans with a potato masher or fork. Stir in salad dressing and mustard.) MAKES 1⅓ cups

Spinach-Mushroom Quesadillas

START TO FINISH: 30 minutes **MAKES** 4 servings

- **½ cup thinly sliced red onion**
- **2 cloves garlic, minced**
- **1 tablespoon olive oil**
- **8 ounces fresh portobello mushrooms, coarsely chopped**
- **1 9-ounce package fresh spinach**
- **½ cup shredded mozzarella cheese (2 ounces)**
- **½ cup grated reduced-fat Parmesan cheese**
- **2 tablespoons snipped fresh basil or 2 teaspoons dried basil, crushed**
- **4 7- or 8-inch whole wheat flour tortillas**
- **Olive oil nonstick cooking spray**

1 In a large skillet cook onion and garlic in hot oil over medium heat about 5 minutes or until onion is tender, stirring occasionally. Add mushrooms; cook about 5 minutes more or until mushrooms are nearly tender, stirring occasionally. Add spinach in batches, cooking and stirring just until spinach is wilted. Remove from heat. Stir in mozzarella cheese, Parmesan cheese, and basil.

2 Spoon spinach mixture onto half of each tortilla. Fold tortillas in half over filling, pressing lightly. Lightly coat both sides of each quesadilla with cooking spray.

3 Rinse and dry the same skillet; heat skillet over medium heat. Cook 2 of the quesadillas in hot skillet for 2 to 3 minutes or until light brown and cheese is melted, turning once. Transfer to a baking sheet and keep warm in a 300°F oven while cooking the remaining 2 quesadillas. Cut quesadillas in half.

PER SERVING: *293 cal., 12 g total fat (4 g sat. fat), 21 mg chol., 701 mg sodium, 29 g carb., 13 g fiber, 18 g pro.*

make it vegan

Substitute desired soy cheeses for the mozzarella and Parmesan cheeses.

tip

Mushrooms deteriorate quickly, so buy them only a day or two before you plan to use them. Store them in their package or in a paper bag for up to 2 days in the refrigerator.

Panini with Grilled Mushrooms

START TO FINISH: 25 minutes MAKES 4 sandwiches

- 3   6- to 8-ounce fresh portobello mushrooms
- 3   tablespoons olive oil
- 3   tablespoons red wine vinegar
- 6   cloves garlic, minced
- ½   teaspoon freshly ground black pepper
- ¼   teaspoon salt
- 4   slices mozzarella cheese (4 ounces)
- 4   small crusty rolls, split and toasted
- 2   cups arugula or fresh baby spinach
- 2   medium tomatoes, cut into ¼-inch slices

1 Cut off mushroom stems even with caps; discard stems. Lightly rinse mushroom caps; gently pat dry with paper towels. If desired, remove gills from undersides of caps. In a small bowl whisk together oil, vinegar, garlic, pepper, and salt. Brush both sides of mushrooms with some of the oil mixture.

2 For a charcoal grill, grill mushroom caps, stemmed sides down, on the rack of an uncovered grill directly over medium coals for 10 to 12 minutes or until tender, turning once halfway through grilling and brushing occasionally with the remaining oil mixture. (For a gas grill, preheat grill. Reduce heat to medium. Place mushroom caps on grill rack over heat. Cover and grill as above.) Cut mushrooms into ½-inch slices.

3 Place cheese slices on bottoms of rolls. Layer with mushroom slices, arugula, and tomato slices; replace tops of rolls.

PER SANDWICH: *392 cal., 18 g total fat (5 g sat. fat), 14 mg chol., 659 mg sodium, 42 g carb., 4 g fiber, 17 g pro.*

🍃 make it vegan

Substitute mozzarella-flavor soy cheese for the mozzarella cheese.

Tomato-Basil Panini

PREP: 20 minutes COOK: 2 minutes per batch MAKES 4 sandwiches

4   cups spinach

8   slices whole wheat bread;
      four 6-inch whole wheat
      hoagie buns, split; or 2 whole
      wheat pita bread rounds,
      halved crosswise and split
      horizontally

1   medium tomato, cut into 8
      slices

$\frac{1}{8}$ teaspoon salt

$\frac{1}{8}$ teaspoon ground black pepper

$\frac{1}{8}$ cup thinly sliced red onion

2   tablespoons shredded fresh
      basil

$\frac{1}{2}$ cup crumbled reduced-fat feta
      cheese (2 ounces)

      Olive oil nonstick cooking
      spray

1 Divide 2 cups of the spinach among 4 of the bread slices. Add tomato slices; sprinkle with salt and pepper. Arrange red onion and basil on top of tomato slices; sprinkle with cheese. Top with the remaining 2 cups spinach and the remaining 4 bread slices, pressing firmly.

2 Lightly coat an electric sandwich press, a covered indoor grill, a grill pan, or an extra-large nonstick skillet with cooking spray. Preheat sandwich press or indoor grill according to the manufacturer's directions or heat grill pan or skillet over medium heat.

3 Place sandwiches, in batches if necessary, in the sandwich press or indoor grill. Cover and cook for 2 to 3 minutes or until bread is toasted and cheese is melted. (If using a grill pan or skillet, place sandwiches in pan. Weight sandwiches down with a heavy skillet. Cook for 1 to 2 minutes or until bread is toasted. Turn sandwiches over, weight down, and cook for 1 to 2 minutes more or until bread is toasted and cheese is melted.)

PER SANDWICH: *174 cal., 5 g total fat (2 g sat. fat), 5 mg chol., 597 mg sodium, 27 g carb., 5 g fiber, 10 g pro.*

185

make it vegan
Substitute crumbled feta-flavor soy cheese for the feta cheese.

Panini without the Press

START TO FINISH: **30 minutes** MAKES **4 sandwiches**

8   slices sourdough bread

2   tablespoons olive oil

¼   cup mayonnaise

2   medium tomatoes, thinly sliced

1   medium zucchini, thinly sliced diagonally

1   small red onion, thinly sliced

¼   cup oil-packed dried tomatoes, drained and snipped

½   to ¾ cup fresh basil leaves

½   to ¾ cup shredded mozzarella cheese (2 to 3 ounces)

1 Brush 1 side of bread slices with oil. Spread the other side of 4 of the bread slices with mayonnaise. Layer the mayonnaise-topped bread with tomato slices, zucchini, red onion, and dried tomato. Sprinkle with basil and cheese. Top with the remaining 4 bread slices, oiled sides up.

2 Heat an extra-large skillet over medium-low heat. Place sandwiches in skillet. Weight sandwiches down with a heavy skillet. Cook until bread is lightly toasted. Turn sandwiches over, weight down, and cook until bread is lightly toasted and cheese is melted.

PER SANDWICH: *386 cal., 23 g total fat (5 g sat. fat), 13 mg chol., 526 mg sodium, 37 g carb., 3 g fiber, 11 g pro.*

Savory Vegetable Open-Face Sandwiches

START TO FINISH: **20 minutes** MAKES **4 sandwiches**

- ½ of an 8-ounce tub light cream cheese spread
- 1 tablespoon snipped fresh dill or 1 teaspoon dried dill
- ¼ teaspoon salt
- ⅛ teaspoon ground black pepper
- 2 whole wheat bagels, split and toasted, or 4 slices whole wheat bread, toasted
- ½ of a medium cucumber, thinly sliced
- ¾ cup roasted red sweet peppers, drained and cut into thin strips
- ½ of a medium onion, thinly sliced
- ⅓ of a medium avocado, seeded, peeled, and thinly sliced

  Snipped fresh dill (optional)

1 In a small bowl stir together cream cheese, 1 tablespoon snipped dill or 1 teaspoon dried dill, salt, and black pepper.

2 Spread bagels with cream cheese mixture. Top with cucumber, roasted peppers, onion, and avocado. If desired, sprinkle with additional snipped dill.

PER SANDWICH: *222 cal., 8 g total fat (3 g sat. fat), 13 mg chol., 301 mg sodium, 31 g carb., 5 g fiber, 9 g protein.*

187

Grilled Veggie-Cheese Sandwiches

START TO FINISH: 20 minutes MAKES 4 sandwiches

8   slices crusty country white or whole wheat bread

2   tablespoons butter, softened

2   tablespoons bottled ranch salad dressing

½   cup sliced roma tomatoes and/ or cucumber

4   ounces American, cheddar, provolone, or Monterey Jack cheese, thinly sliced

½   cup fresh spinach leaves

¼   cup thinly sliced red onion

1 Lightly spread 1 side of bread slices with butter. Spread the other side of bread slices with salad dressing. Top the dressing sides of 4 of the bread slices with tomato and/or cucumber slices. Layer with cheese, spinach, and red onion. Top with the remaining 4 bread slices, dressing sides down.

2 Preheat an indoor electric grill according to the manufacturer's directions or heat a large skillet over medium heat. Add sandwiches. If using a covered grill, cook sandwiches for 3 to 5 minutes or until bread is toasted and cheese is melted. If using an uncovered grill or skillet, cook sandwiches for 6 to 8 minutes or until bread is toasted and cheese is melted, turning once.

PER SANDWICH: *332 cal., 20 g total fat (10 g sat. fat), 44 mg chol., 865 mg sodium, 28 g carb., 2 g fiber, 11 g pro.*

Open-Face Veggie Burgers with Sauteed Onion

START TO FINISH: 20 minutes   MAKES 4 sandwiches

2   tablespoons olive oil

1   large sweet onion (such
       as Vidalia or Walla Walla),
       halved and thinly sliced
       (about 2 cups)

4   refrigerated or frozen grilled
       vegetable meatless burger
       patties

2   tablespoons mayonnaise

1   teaspoon yellow mustard

4   ½-inch slices ciabatta bread,
       toasted

1   cup fresh baby spinach

2   tablespoons steak sauce

1 In a large skillet heat oil over medium-high heat. Add onion; cook for 8 to 10 minutes or until very tender, stirring frequently.

2 Meanwhile, heat patties in the microwave oven according to package directions.

3 In a small bowl combine mayonnaise and mustard. Spread mixture over 1 side of bread slices. Top with spinach and patties. Stir steak sauce into cooked onion; spoon onion mixture on top of patties.

PER SANDWICH: *329 cal., 20 g total fat (3 g sat. fat), 3 mg chol., 688 mg sodium, 21 g carb., 5 g fiber, 18 g pro.*

Roasted Veggie Sandwiches

PREP: 25 minutes ROAST: 8 minutes OVEN: 450°F MAKES 4 sandwiches

1 **small zucchini, cut lengthwise into thin slices**

1 **small yellow summer squash, cut lengthwise into thin slices**

1 **medium onion, thinly sliced**

½ **cup sliced fresh mushrooms**

½ **cup thin red sweet pepper strips**

2 **tablespoons olive oil**

½ **teaspoon salt**

¼ **teaspoon ground black pepper**

2 **large pita bread rounds, halved crosswise**

4 **teaspoons bottled Italian salad dressing**

¾ **cup shredded smoked provolone or mozzarella cheese (3 ounces)**

1 Preheat oven to 450°F. In a large bowl combine zucchini, yellow squash, onion, mushrooms, sweet pepper, oil, salt, and black pepper; toss gently to coat. Spread vegetable mixture evenly in an ungreased 15×10×1-inch baking pan. Roast for 8 to 10 minutes or until vegetables are tender.

2 Fill pita pockets with roasted vegetables. Drizzle vegetables with salad dressing; top with cheese.

3 If desired, place pita pockets, filled sides up, in an ungreased 2-quart square baking dish. Bake for 2 to 3 minutes or until cheese is melted.

PER SANDWICH: *270 cal., 16 g total fat (5 g sat. fat), 15 mg chol., 669 mg sodium, 24 g carb., 2 g fiber, 10 g pro.*

Avocado Veggie Sandwiches:

Prepare as directed, except omit salad dressing. In a small bowl combine half of a seeded and peeled avocado, 1 tablespoon lime juice, and ¼ teaspoon salt. Using a fork, mash until smooth. Spread avocado mixture inside pita pockets before filling with roasted vegetables.

🌿 make it vegan
Substitute provolone- or mozzarella-flavor soy cheese for the dairy cheese.

Tomato-Edamame Grilled Cheese

PREP: 20 minutes ROAST: 15 minutes OVEN: 425°F MAKES 4 sandwiches

1 whole garlic bulb

1 teaspoon canola oil

1 12-ounce package frozen shelled sweet soybeans (edamame)

¼ cup lemon juice

¼ cup water

½ teaspoon salt

½ teaspoon ground cumin

⅓ cup snipped fresh Italian (flat-leaf) parsley

8 slices whole grain bread

1 medium tomato, cut into 8 slices

4 ounces reduced-fat Monterey Jack cheese, thinly sliced

1 Preheat oven to 425°F. Cut off the top ½ inch of the garlic bulb to expose the ends of the individual cloves. Leaving garlic bulb whole, remove any loose, papery outer layers. Place garlic bulb, cut side up, in a custard cup. Drizzle with oil. Cover with foil; roast about 15 minutes or until softened. Cool.

2 Meanwhile, cook edamame according to package directions; drain. Rinse with cold water; drain again. Squeeze pulp from 3 of the garlic cloves into a food processor. (Wrap and chill the remaining garlic for another use.)

3 Add cooked edamame, lemon juice, the water, salt, and cumin to garlic in food processor. Cover and process until smooth. Transfer to a small bowl; stir in parsley.

4 Spread 1 side of each bread slice with 2 tablespoons of the edamame mixture. (Cover and chill the remaining 1 cup mixture for another use.) Layer 4 of the bread slices with tomato and cheese slices. Top with the remaining 4 bread slices, spread sides down.

5 Heat a nonstick griddle or skillet over medium-high heat. Add sandwiches; cook until bread is toasted and cheese is melted, turning once.

PER SANDWICH: *332 cal., 12 g total fat (4 g sat. fat), 20 mg chol., 685 mg sodium, 38 g carb., 11 g fiber, 22 g pro.*

191

make it vegan

Substitute desired soy cheese for the Monterey Jack cheese.

Skillet Vegetables on Cheese Toast

START TO FINISH: 20 minutes MAKES 4 servings

- 8 ounces fresh button mushrooms, halved
- ½ of an 8-ounce package peeled fresh baby carrots, halved lengthwise
- 1 small red onion, cut into thin wedges
- 4 cloves garlic, coarsely chopped
- 2 tablespoons olive oil
- 2 tablespoons water
  Salt
  Ground black pepper
- 8 slices crusty country whole wheat bread
- 4 ounces soft goat cheese (chèvre)
  Olive oil
  Snipped fresh basil (optional)

1 Preheat broiler. In a large skillet cook mushrooms, carrots, red onion, and garlic in 2 tablespoons hot oil over medium-high heat for 2 to 3 minutes or just until vegetables start to brown. Add the water. Cook, covered, over medium heat about 5 minutes or until vegetables are crisp-tender, stirring once. Sprinkle with salt and pepper.

2 Meanwhile, for cheese toast, place bread slices on an ungreased baking sheet. Broil about 3 inches from the heat for 1 to 2 minutes or until toasted, turning once halfway through broiling. Spread bread slices with cheese. Broil for 1 to 2 minutes more or until cheese is softened.

3 To serve, spoon vegetables onto cheese toast. Drizzle with additional oil and, if desired, sprinkle with basil.

PER SERVING: 461 cal., 21 g total fat (6 g sat. fat), 13 mg chol., 596 mg sodium, 56 g carb., 8 g fiber, 15 g pro.

make it vegan
Substitute desired soy cheese for the goat cheese.

Caprese Salad Sandwiches

START TO FINISH: **30 minutes** MAKES **4 sandwiches**

1 **10-ounce loaf baguette-style French bread**

½ **cup yellow or red pear-shape tomatoes, cherry tomatoes, and/or grape tomatoes, quartered**

¼ **cup coarsely chopped cucumber**

¼ **cup thin red, yellow, or green sweet pepper strips**

1 **ounce fresh mozzarella cheese, cubed**

2 **tablespoons chopped green onion (1)**

2 **tablespoons snipped fresh basil**

1 **tablespoon red wine vinegar or cider vinegar**

1 **teaspoon olive oil**

⅛ **teaspoon ground black pepper**

¾ **cup mixed spring salad greens**

1 Cut bread crosswise into 4 portions. Cut a thin horizontal slice from the top of each portion. Using a knife, carefully remove bread from the bottom of each portion, leaving a ¼-inch shell. (Reserve center bread pieces for another use.)

2 In a small bowl combine tomatoes, cucumber, sweet pepper, cheese, green onion, basil, vinegar, oil, and black pepper.

3 Line bottoms of bread portions with salad greens. Spoon tomato mixture onto greens; replace tops of bread portions. If desired, wrap each sandwich in plastic wrap and chill for up to 2 hours before serving.

PER SANDWICH: *244 cal., 4 g total fat (2 g sat. fat), 5 mg chol., 489 mg sodium, 42 g carb., 2 g fiber, 10 g pro.*

Lemony Garbanzo Bean Sandwiches 🌿

START TO FINISH: 20 minutes MAKES 4 sandwiches

1 **15-ounce can no-salt-added garbanzo beans (chickpeas), rinsed and drained***

3 **tablespoons snipped fresh parsley**

1 **teaspoon finely shredded lemon peel**

2 **tablespoons lemon juice**

1 **tablespoon finely chopped red onion**

1 **tablespoon olive oil**

1/8 **teaspoon ground black pepper**

1/2 **of a large cucumber, peeled, quartered lengthwise, and sliced (about 1 cup)**

1/2 **cup watercress or arugula**

1/3 **cup roasted red sweet pepper strips**

1 **12-inch Italian flatbread (focaccia), quartered**

1 In a medium bowl combine drained beans, parsley, lemon peel, lemon juice, red onion, oil, and black pepper. Using a potato masher or fork, coarsely mash bean mixture. Stir in cucumber, watercress, and roasted pepper.

2 Cut each portion of flatbread in half horizontally. Fill flatbread portions with bean mixture.

PER SANDWICH: *401 cal., 8 g total fat (0 g sat. fat), 10 mg chol., 472 mg sodium, 71 g carb., 5 g fiber, 16 g pro.*

*tip
If desired, substitute 1¾ cups cooked dried garbanzo beans for the canned beans.

ELT (Egg, Lettuce, and Tomato) Sandwiches

START TO FINISH: **25 minutes** MAKES **4 sandwiches**

8 slices crusty country bread

¼ cup mayonnaise

4 slices Monterey Jack cheese with jalapeño peppers (4 ounces)

1 tablespoon butter

4 eggs

   Salt

   Ground black pepper

1 medium tomato, thinly sliced

4 leaves romaine lettuce

1 Preheat broiler. Place bread slices on an ungreased large baking sheet. Broil 4 to 6 inches from the heat for 1 to 2 minutes or until bread is lightly browned, turning once. Remove half of the bread slices and spread with mayonnaise; set aside. Top the remaining bread slices with cheese. Broil about 1 minute more or until cheese is melted.

2 In a large skillet melt butter over medium heat. Carefully break eggs into skillet. Sprinkle with salt and pepper; reduce heat to low. Cook eggs for 3 to 4 minutes or until whites are completely set and yolks start to thicken. Turn eggs; cook for 30 to 60 seconds more or to desired doneness.

3 Place eggs on the mayonnaise-topped bread slices. Top with tomato, lettuce, and the remaining bread slices, cheese sides down.

PER SANDWICH: *475 cal., 30 g total fat (11 g sat. fat), 249 mg chol., 817 mg sodium, 33 g carb., 3 g fiber, 19 g pro.*

Open-Face Egg Sandwiches

START TO FINISH: 25 minutes MAKES 4 sandwiches

- 1 cup frozen shelled sweet soybeans (edamame), thawed
- 1 small avocado, seeded and peeled
- 2 tablespoons lemon juice
- 2 cloves garlic, minced
- ¼ teaspoon salt
- ½ cup chopped red sweet pepper (1 small)
- 4 very thin slices firm-texture whole wheat bread, toasted, or 2 whole wheat pita bread rounds, split in half horizontally
- 4 hard-cooked eggs, thinly sliced

  Freshly ground black pepper

1 In a medium bowl combine edamame, avocado, lemon juice, garlic, and salt. Using a fork or potato masher, coarsely mash edamame mixture. Stir in sweet pepper.

2 Spread edamame mixture over bread slices. Top with egg slices and sprinkle with black pepper.

PER SANDWICH: *240 cal., 14 g total fat (3 g sat. fat), 212 mg chol., 293 mg sodium, 17 g carb., 6 g fiber, 14 g pro.*

tip

When ordering grilled sandwiches at restaurants, be aware that they may be made on the same grill as burgers and chicken. Tell the server that you're vegetarian and ask that your sandwich not be made next to, or in the same place, as grilled meats.

Egg Salad Sandwiches

START TO FINISH: 25 minutes   MAKES 4 sandwiches

4 hard-cooked eggs, chopped

¼ cup shredded Colby and Monterey Jack cheese (1 ounce)

2 tablespoons sweet or dill pickle relish

2 tablespoons finely chopped red sweet pepper

¼ cup mayonnaise

1½ teaspoons yellow mustard

4 croissants, split

4 leaves red-tipped leaf lettuce

Halved cherry tomatoes (optional)

1 In a medium bowl combine eggs, cheese, relish, and sweet pepper. Stir in mayonnaise and mustard. If desired, cover and chill for up to 6 hours.

2 Line bottoms of croissants with lettuce leaves. Spoon egg mixture onto lettuce; replace tops of croissants. If desired, garnish sandwiches with wooden toothpicks threaded with cherry tomato halves.

PER SANDWICH: *451 cal., 31 g total fat (12 g sat. fat), 261 mg chol., 695 mg sodium, 30 g carb., 2 g fiber, 13 g pro.*

Curried Egg Salad Sandwiches:

Prepare as directed, except stir ½ to 1 teaspoon curry powder into the egg mixture. Cover and chill for 2 to 6 hours before assembling sandwiches.

Honey-Dill Egg Salad Sandwiches:

Prepare as directed, except substitute honey mustard for the yellow mustard and stir 1 teaspoon dried dill into the egg mixture.

tip

To avoid getting that green ring around the yolk of hard-cooked eggs, cool them quickly in a bowl of ice water before storing in the refrigerator.

Summer Tomato Stack

START TO FINISH: 10 minutes MAKES 4 sandwiches

- 2 whole wheat English muffins, toasted
- 4 thin slices tomato
- 4 ounces fresh mozzarella cheese, cut into 8 slices
- 1 tablespoon snipped fresh basil
- 4 teaspoons olive oil
- ½ teaspoon salt
- ½ teaspoon cracked black pepper
- 4 grape or cherry tomatoes, halved (optional)

1. On each English muffin half, layer a tomato slice, a cheese slice, and ½ teaspoon of the basil. Repeat layers. Drizzle with oil; sprinkle with salt and pepper. If desired, top with tomato halves.

PER SANDWICH: *203 cal., 12 g total fat (4 g sat. fat), 22 mg chol., 531 mg sodium, 16 g carb., 3 g fiber, 10 g pro.*

🌿 **make it vegan**
Substitute desired soy cheese for the fresh mozzarella cheese.

198

Apple-Brie Sandwiches

START TO FINISH: 20 minutes MAKES 4 sandwiches

- 8 slices firm-texture white bread, toasted
- ⅓ cup apricot preserves
- 4 to 5 ounces Brie cheese, sliced
- 1 medium Braeburn, Gala, or Pink Lady apple, cored and sliced
- ¾ cup watercress or fresh baby spinach
- ¼ cup very thinly sliced red onion

1. Spread 1 side of bread slices with preserves. Layer 4 of the bread slices with cheese, apple, watercress, and red onion. Top with the remaining 4 bread slices, spread sides down.

PER SANDWICH: *336 cal., 11 g total fat (5 g sat. fat), 28 mg chol., 460 mg sodium, 52 g carb., 2 g fiber, 10 g pro.*

Salads

No bland iceberg with ranch dressing here! Bold
flavors and enticing ingredient combinations perk
up these hearty salads. Packed with healthful foods
such as beans, grains, nuts, cheese, fruit, herbs, and
vegetables, these fresh meals will satisfy any
appetite.

American Chopped Salad

PREP: 45 minutes COOK: 6 minutes MAKES 6 servings

- 1 cup fresh green beans, trimmed and cut into 2-inch lengths
- 8 cups chopped iceberg lettuce (1 small head)
- 2 cups grape or cherry tomatoes, halved
- 2 cups seeded and chopped cucumber (1 small)
- 1 cup frozen whole kernel corn, thawed
- 3 hard-cooked eggs, chopped
- ½ cup sliced carrot
- ½ cup shredded cheddar cheese or 2 ounces cheddar-flavor soy cheese, shredded
- ¼ cup finely chopped red onion
- ½ cup buttermilk
- ½ cup mayonnaise
- 2 tablespoons finely chopped green onion (1)
- 1 clove garlic, minced
- ⅛ teaspoon salt

 1 In a covered small saucepan cook green beans in a small amount of boiling, lightly salted water for 6 to 8 minutes or until crisp-tender; drain. Rinse in cold water until cool; drain well. Transfer to an extra-large bowl.

2 Add lettuce, tomatoes, cucumber, corn, eggs, carrot, cheese, and red onion; toss to combine.

3 For dressing, in a small bowl whisk together buttermilk and mayonnaise. Stir in green onion, garlic, and salt. Drizzle dressing over salad; toss gently to combine.

PER SERVING: *277 cal., 21 g total fat (6 g sat. fat), 123 mg chol., 283 mg sodium, 15 g carb., 3 g fiber, 9 g pro.*

Mushroom Salad with Crisp Potato Cakes

PREP: 35 minutes COOK: 30 minutes MAKES 6 servings

8   ounces russet potatoes, peeled and quartered
2   cloves garlic
½   teaspoon salt
1   egg, lightly beaten
2   tablespoons chopped green onion (1)
1   teaspoon snipped fresh dill
¼   teaspoon ground black pepper
½   cup panko (Japanese-style bread crumbs)
2   tablespoons olive oil
8   ounces fresh cremini mushrooms, quartered
1   small red onion, cut into thin wedges
1   5- to 8-ounce package mixed salad greens
2½   cups cherry tomatoes, halved
1   recipe Chive Honey Mustard Vinaigrette or ⅓ cup bottled honey-Dijon salad dressing

1 In a covered medium saucepan cook potatoes and garlic in enough boiling, lightly salted water to cover for 20 to 25 minutes or until tender; drain. Let cool slightly.

2 In a large bowl combine potato mixture, egg, green onion, dill, and pepper. Mash with a potato masher until nearly smooth. With wet hands, form the mixture into 6 patties. In a shallow dish place the panko. Coat each patty with panko.

3 In a large skillet heat oil over medium heat. Add potato patties, half at a time, and cook for 6 to 8 minutes or until golden brown, turning once halfway through cooking. Drain on paper towels.

4 Using the same skillet, add mushrooms and onion. Cook and stir for 4 to 6 minutes or until tender and light brown, adding more oil to skillet if needed.

5 On a serving platter arrange mixed greens. Top with mushroom mixture, cherry tomatoes, and potato cakes. Drizzle Chive Honey Mustard Vinaigrette over salad.

PER SERVING: *178 cal., 10 g total fat (2 g sat. fat), 35 mg chol., 370 mg sodium, 18 g carb., 3 g fiber, 5 g pro.*

Chive Honey Mustard Vinaigrette

In a screw-top jar combine 2 tablespoons olive oil, 2 tablespoons cider vinegar, 1 tablespoon snipped fresh chives, 2 teaspoons country Dijon-style mustard, 1 teaspoon honey, and ½ teaspoon salt. Cover and shake well.

Fried Green Tomato Salad

PREP: 35 minutes COOK: 4 minutes per batch MAKES 6 servings

¼ cup all-purpose flour

2 eggs, lightly beaten

1 tablespoon water

½ cup cornmeal

3 medium firm green tomatoes, cut into ½-inch slices

   Salt

   Ground black pepper

¼ cup vegetable oil

8 cups torn mixed salad greens and/or chopped romaine, iceberg, and/or Bibb lettuce

1 15- to 16-ounce can black-eyed peas, rinsed and drained

⅔ cup sliced radishes

⅓ cup chopped pecans, toasted

1 recipe Buttermilk Dressing or ⅔ cup bottled buttermilk ranch salad dressing

1 In a shallow dish place flour. In a second shallow dish whisk together eggs and the water just until combined; place cornmeal in a third shallow dish. Sprinkle tomato slices with salt and pepper. Coat each tomato slice with flour, shaking off excess. Dip into egg mixture, then coat with cornmeal.

2 In a large skillet heat oil over medium-high heat. Add tomato slices, half at a time, and cook about 4 minutes or until golden brown, turning once halfway through cooking. Drain on paper towels.

3 On a serving platter arrange salad greens. Top with fried green tomatoes, drained black-eyed peas, radishes, and pecans. Drizzle salad with Buttermilk Dressing.

PER SERVING: *322 cal., 19 g total fat (3 g sat. fat), 74 mg chol., 416 mg sodium, 30 g carb., 6 g fiber, 10 g pro.*

Buttermilk Dressing

In a small bowl combine ⅓ cup buttermilk; ¼ cup mayonnaise or salad dressing; 1 clove garlic, minced; ¼ teaspoon dry mustard; and ¼ teaspoon cracked black pepper.

Roasted Beet, Goat Cheese, and Fennel Salad

PREP: **30 minutes** ROAST: **1½ hours** COOL: **20 minutes** OVEN: **400°F** MAKES **4 servings**

1 recipe Lemon Vinaigrette
2 large beets (1 pound)
½ teaspoon salt
½ teaspoon ground black pepper
2 medium fennel bulbs
8 cups torn butterhead (Boston or Bibb) lettuce
¼ cup chopped walnuts, toasted
4 ounces crumbled goat cheese (chèvre)
2 tablespoons snipped fresh chives

1 Preheat oven to 400°F. Prepare Lemon Vinaigrette; cover and set aside.

2 Scrub beets. Wrap each beet in foil and place on a baking sheet. Roast about 1½ hours or until a knife can be easily inserted into beets. Cool about 20 minutes or until able to handle. Trim off stem and root ends of roasted beets. Peel and cut into 1-inch pieces.

3 In a medium bowl combine beets, 3 tablespoons of the Lemon Vinaigrette, ¼ teaspoon of the salt, and ¼ teaspoon of the pepper.

4 For fennel bulbs, cut off and discard stalks, including feathery leaves. Remove wilted outer layer; cut off a thin slice from bases. Wash; cut fennel lengthwise into quarters and remove the cores. Thinly slice the fennel.

5 In another medium bowl combine fennel, 3 tablespoons of the Lemon Vinaigrette, the remaining ¼ teaspoon salt, and the remaining ¼ teaspoon pepper.

6 Line individual salad plates with lettuce. Drizzle with the remaining vinaigrette. Layer with beets, walnuts, fennel, goat cheese, and chives.

PER SERVING: *394 cal., 32 g total fat (8 g sat. fat), 22 mg chol., 592 mg sodium, 20 g carb., 8 g fiber, 12 g pro.*

203

Lemon Vinaigrette

In a medium bowl whisk together ½ teaspoon finely shredded lemon peel, 3 tablespoons lemon juice, 1 tablespoon finely chopped shallot, 1½ teaspoons Dijon-style mustard, and ½ teaspoon honey. In a steady stream, slowly whisk in ⅓ cup olive oil until well combined.

tip

Beets are higher in sugar than any other vegetable. Their sweet taste really comes out when they're roasted. The red/purple color of beets comes from betacyanin, a type of phytonutrient believed to help fight cancer.

Layered Southwestern Salad with Tortilla Strips

PREP: 15 minutes BAKE: 15 minutes OVEN: 350°F MAKES 6 servings

2   6-inch corn tortillas
     Nonstick cooking spray
½   cup light sour cream
¼   cup snipped fresh cilantro
2   tablespoons fat-free milk
1   teaspoon olive oil
1   large clove garlic, minced
½   teaspoon chili powder
½   teaspoon finely shredded
     lime peel
¼   teaspoon salt
¼   teaspoon ground black pepper
6   cups torn romaine lettuce
2   cups chopped roma tomatoes
     (4 medium)
1   15-ounce can black beans,
     rinsed and drained
1   cup fresh corn kernels*
½   cup shredded reduced-fat
     cheddar cheese (2 ounces)
1   avocado, halved, seeded,
     peeled, and chopped
     Snipped fresh cilantro
     (optional)

1 Preheat oven to 350°F. Cut tortillas into ½-inch strips; place in a 15×10×1-inch baking pan. Coat tortillas lightly with cooking spray. Bake for 15 to 18 minutes or just until crisp, stirring once. Cool on a wire rack.

2 For dressing, in a small bowl whisk together sour cream, the ¼ cup cilantro, the milk, oil, garlic, chili powder, lime peel, salt, and pepper.

3 Place lettuce in a large glass serving bowl. Top with tomatoes, drained beans, corn, cheese, and avocado. Drizzle dressing over tomato mixture. Sprinkle with tortilla strips. If desired, garnish with additional snipped fresh cilantro.

PER SERVING: *227 cal., 11 g total fat (3 g sat. fat), 12 mg chol., 386 mg sodium, 29 g carb., 9 g fiber, 11 g pro.*

204

make it vegan

Substitute tofu sour cream for the dairy sour cream, soymilk for the dairy milk, and cheddar-flavor soy cheese for the cheddar cheese.

*tip

It isn't necessary to cook the corn. However, for a roasted flavor and softer texture, bake the corn with the tortilla strips. Place the strips at one end of the baking pan and the corn at the other end.

🍃 Spaghetti-Corn Relish Salad

START TO FINISH: **35 minutes**   MAKES **8 servings**

1   **14- to 16-ounce package dried multigrain, whole wheat, or regular spaghetti**

4   **fresh ears of sweet corn, husks and silks removed***

1   **small cucumber, seeded and chopped**

1   **small summer squash, chopped**

1   **small red onion, finely chopped**

1   **stalk celery, thinly sliced**

1   **large red sweet pepper, chopped**

½   **cup cider vinegar**

⅓   **cup olive oil**

1   **tablespoon sugar**

½   **teaspoon salt**

½   **teaspoon dry mustard**

½   **teaspoon celery seeds**

    Salt

1 Cook pasta according to package directions, adding corn to water with pasta during the last 3 minutes of cooking; drain. Use tongs to transfer ears of corn to cutting board; set aside. Drain pasta in colander. Rinse with cold water; drain again. Transfer to a large serving bowl.

2 Add cucumber, squash, onion, celery, and sweet pepper; stir to combine. Set aside.

3 Cool corn until able to handle. Hold corn upright. With fingers away from knife blade and cutting down the length of the corn cob, cut off corn into planks (long sections of connected kernels).

4 For dressing, in a screw-top jar combine vinegar, oil, sugar, the ½ teaspoon salt, dry mustard, and celery seeds. Cover and shake well.

5 Pour dressing over spaghetti mixture; toss to coat. Gently fold in corn planks. Season to taste with additional salt. Serve immediately. (Or cover and chill in the refrigerator for up to 24 hours.)

PER SERVING: *320 cal., 11 g total fat (1 g sat. fat), 0 mg chol., 181 mg sodium, 47 g carb., 6 g fiber, 11 g pro.*

*tip
If desired, substitute 2 cups frozen whole kernel corn for the fresh ears of sweet corn. Place corn in a large colander; drain hot pasta into colander with corn (rather than adding the corn to the pasta while it cooks). Continue as directed.

Basil-Tomato Layered Salad

PREP: 30 minutes BAKE: 3 minutes OVEN: 425°F MAKES 6 servings

1   recipe Lemon Vinaigrette

½   of an 8-ounce loaf baguette-style French bread

2   tablespoons olive oil

2   cloves garlic, minced

6   cups torn leaf lettuce or torn mixed salad greens

3   cups torn fresh basil

2   cups grape or cherry tomatoes, halved, or chopped roma tomatoes

½   cup pine nuts, toasted

2   ounces Parmesan cheese, shaved

1 Prepare Lemon Vinaigrette; set aside.

2 Preheat oven to 425°F. For breadsticks, split baguette in half horizontally. In a small bowl combine olive oil and garlic. Brush onto cut sides of baguette. Cut each bread piece lengthwise into 3 or 4 breadsticks; place on a baking sheet. Bake for 3 to 5 minutes or until lightly toasted. Transfer to a wire rack; cool.

3 In a large glass salad bowl combine lettuce and basil. Layer with tomatoes, pine nuts, and cheese. Serve with Lemon Vinaigrette and breadsticks.

PER SERVING: *449 cal., 33 g total fat (6 g sat. fat), 8 mg chol., 502 mg sodium, 30 g carb., 3 g fiber, 13 g protein.*

Lemon Vinaigrette

In a small screw-top jar combine ½ cup olive oil; 1 teaspoon finely shredded lemon peel; ⅓ cup lemon juice; 4 cloves garlic, minced; 1 teaspoon sugar; ¼ teaspoon salt; and ¼ teaspoon ground black pepper. Cover and shake well.

Asian Tofu Salad

PREP: 20 minutes   MARINATE: 30 minutes   COOK: 5 minutes   MAKES 6 servings

¼ cup reduced-sodium soy sauce

¼ cup Asian sweet chili sauce

1 tablespoon creamy peanut butter

1 clove garlic, minced

1 teaspoon grated fresh ginger

1 16- to 18-ounce package firm water-packed tofu (fresh bean curd)

1 teaspoon toasted sesame oil

1½ cups chopped, peeled jicama

1 cup seeded and thinly sliced red sweet pepper (1 medium)

1 cup coarsely shredded carrot

4 cups shredded romaine lettuce

2 tablespoons unsalted dry-roasted peanuts

2 tablespoons snipped fresh cilantro

1 For marinade, in a small bowl whisk together soy sauce, chili sauce, peanut butter, garlic, and ginger. Pat tofu dry with paper towels. Cut tofu crosswise into 12 slices. Place slices into a 2-quart rectangular baking dish. Drizzle tofu with 3 tablespoons of the marinade, turning to coat tofu. Let marinate at room temperature for 30 minutes, turning tofu occasionally. For dressing, reserve the remaining marinade; set aside.

2 In an extra-large nonstick skillet heat sesame oil over medium-high heat. Remove tofu slices from the marinade. Carefully pour marinade from baking dish into the skillet. Add tofu slices to the hot skillet. Cook tofu for 5 to 6 minutes or until light brown, turning once halfway through cooking. Remove from heat; set aside.

3 In a large bowl combine lettuce, jicama, sweet pepper, and carrot. Divide lettuce mixture among individual salad plates. Top with tofu, peanuts, and cilantro. Serve with reserved dressing.

PER SERVING: *179 cal., 7 g total fat (1 g sat. fat), 0 mg chol., 515 mg sodium, 18 g carb., 3 g fiber, 11 g pro.*

207

tip

Its knobby shape can make fresh ginger difficult to peel. To make the task easier, use a spoon to simply rub the peel off.

Asian Cobb-Style Salad 🍃

START TO FINISH: **30 minutes** MAKES **4 servings**

1 tablespoon canola oil

1 8-ounce package tempeh (fermented soybean cake), cut into bite-size strips

1½ cups snow pea pods, tips and strings removed

2 cups shredded fresh spinach

2 cups shredded napa cabbage

2 cups shredded red cabbage

3 tablespoons bias-sliced green onions

2 tablespoons canola oil

2 tablespoons rice vinegar

1 teaspoon finely snipped fresh mint

1 teaspoon honey

½ teaspoon grated fresh ginger

1 In a large skillet heat the 1 tablespoon canola oil over medium-high heat. Add tempeh. Cook for 3 to 5 minutes or until golden and edges are slightly crisp, gently stirring occasionally. Remove from heat; cool.

2 Meanwhile, cut peas diagonally in half. On a platter arrange peas, spinach, napa cabbage, red cabbage, green onions, and tempeh.

3 For dressing, in a screw-top jar combine the 2 tablespoons canola oil, the rice vinegar, mint, honey, and ginger. Cover and shake well. Drizzle dressing over salad.

PER SERVING: *243 cal., 17 g total fat (2 g sat. fat), 0 mg chol., 33 mg sodium, 14 g carb., 2 g fiber, 13 g pro.*

tip
A little goes a long way. Toss a salad with dressing instead of pouring it on top to distribute the dressing better.

Navy Bean Tabbouleh

PREP: 25 minutes STAND: 40 minutes CHILL: 4 to 24 hours MAKES 4 servings

1½ cups water

¾ cup bulgur

1 15- to 16-ounce can navy beans, rinsed and drained

¾ cup chopped red or yellow sweet pepper (1 medium)

¾ cup seeded and chopped cucumber

¼ cup thinly sliced green onions (2)

¼ cup snipped fresh basil

1 tablespoon snipped fresh oregano

3 tablespoons olive oil

1 teaspoon finely shredded lemon peel

3 tablespoons lemon juice

2 tablespoons water

¼ teaspoon salt

¼ cup pine nuts, toasted

1 In a medium saucepan bring the water to boiling; stir in bulgur. Remove from heat. Cover and let stand about 40 minutes or until tender. Drain in colander and rinse with cold water. Transfer bulgur to a large bowl.

2 Add drained beans, sweet pepper, cucumber, green onions, basil, and oregano; stir to combine.

3 For dressing, in a screw-top jar combine olive oil, lemon peel, lemon juice, the water, and the salt. Cover and shake well. Drizzle dressing over bulgur mixture; toss to coat.

4 Cover and chill for 4 to 24 hours. Just before serving stir in pine nuts.

PER SERVING: *377 cal., 17 g total fat (2 g sat. fat), 0 mg chol., 630 mg sodium, 47 g carb., 12 g fiber, 13 g pro.*

209

Roasted Tomato and Cannellini Bean Panzanella 🌿

Italian Bread Salad

PREP: **25 minutes** BAKE: **20 minutes** STAND: **10 minutes** OVEN: **400°F** MAKES **6 servings**

8 ounces crusty Italian bread, cut into 1-inch cubes

3 tablespoons olive oil

Salt

Ground black pepper

6 medium roma tomatoes, halved lengthwise

2 tablespoons red wine vinegar

1 teaspoon snipped fresh oregano or ½ teaspoon dried oregano, crushed

2 cloves garlic, minced

½ teaspoon sugar

1 15-ounce can cannellini beans (white kidney beans), rinsed and drained

1½ cups chopped, seeded cucumber (1 medium)

½ cup torn fresh basil

½ cup mozzarella- or provolone-flavor soy cheese, shredded; or dairy cheese, shredded

¼ cup thin wedges red onion

1 Preheat oven to 400°F. In a large shallow baking pan spread out bread cubes in a single layer. Drizzle with 1 tablespoon of the olive oil* and sprinkle with salt and pepper; toss to coat. Bake, uncovered, 8 minutes or until crisp and brown but soft inside. Transfer bread cubes to a large bowl. Set aside.

2 Place roma tomatoes, cut sides down, on the same baking pan. Bake, uncovered, about 12 minutes or until softened and skins begin to brown. Carefully pinch tomato skins to remove; discard.

3 For vinaigrette, in a blender or food processor combine 4 of the tomato halves, the remaining 2 tablespoons olive oil, the vinegar, oregano, garlic, and sugar. Cover and blend or process until smooth. Season to taste with salt and pepper.

4 Coarsely chop remaining tomato halves. In the large bowl with bread cubes combine the chopped tomatoes and vinaigrette. Let stand about 10 minutes or until bread cubes soften slightly and absorb vinaigrette.

5 Add drained cannellini beans, cucumber, basil, cheese, and red onion; toss to combine.

PER SERVING: *259 cal., 11 g total fat (2 g sat. fat), 0 mg chol., 641 mg sodium, 35 g carb., 6 g fiber, 11 g pro.*

*tip

If necessary, spread bread cubes into two pans and use an additional tablespoon olive oil.

Edamame Bread Salad

PREP: 30 minutes COOK: 6 minutes COOL: 20 minutes CHILL: 30 minutes to 8 hours MAKES 6 servings

¾ cup feta cheese

½ cup plain Greek yogurt or low-fat yogurt

2 tablespoons snipped fresh basil

1 small clove garlic, minced

Salt

Ground black pepper

8 cups water

½ teaspoon salt

2 12-ounce packages frozen soybeans (edamame)

1½ pounds fresh green beans, trimmed

1 recipe Balsamic Dressing

2 cups yellow and/or red cherry tomatoes, halved

12 slices crusty country bread, toasted

Fresh basil leaves (optional)

1 In a small bowl mash feta cheese and yogurt using a fork until combined. Add basil and garlic; mash until well combined. Season to taste with salt and ground black pepper. Cover and chill.

2 Meanwhile, in a large saucepan bring the water and salt to boiling. Add soybeans and green beans. Return to boiling; reduce heat. Cook, covered, for 6 to 8 minutes or until tender; drain. Transfer soybean mixture to a large bowl; cool for 20 minutes.

3 Meanwhile, prepare Balsamic Dressing. Add tomatoes to soybean mixture. Drizzle with half of the Balsamic Dressing; toss to coat. Cover and chill for at least 30 minutes or up to 8 hours.

4 To serve, spread feta mixture on bread slices; place 2 slices on each salad plate. Toss soybean mixture; mound on top of bread. Drizzle with the remaining Balsamic Dressing. If desired, garnish with additional basil leaves.

PER SERVING: *474 cal., 24 g total fat (7 g sat. fat), 27 mg chol., 679 mg sodium, 46 g carb., 10 g fiber, 22 g pro.*

Balsamic Dressing

In a blender combine ¼ cup lightly packed fresh basil leaves, ¼ cup olive oil, 2 tablespoons balsamic vinegar, and 2 tablespoons red wine vinegar. Cover and blend until smooth. Add 2 tablespoons whipping cream and blend to mix. Season to taste with salt and ground black pepper.

Southwest Black Bean Salad 🌿

START TO FINISH: **15 minutes** MAKES **4 servings**

8 cups torn mixed salad greens or romaine

2 cups no-salt-added canned black beans, rinsed and drained

2 cups bite-size red or yellow sweet pepper strips

2 cups frozen whole kernel corn, thawed

¼ cup fresh cilantro leaves

¼ cup orange juice

¼ cup cider vinegar

¼ cup canola oil

1 teaspoon ground cumin

½ teaspoon kosher or sea salt

⅛ teaspoon crushed red pepper

1 On individual serving plates arrange salad greens, drained black beans, sweet pepper strips, corn, and cilantro.

2 For dressing, in a screw-top jar combine orange juice, vinegar, oil, cumin, salt, and crushed red pepper. Cover and shake well. Drizzle dressing over the salads.

PER SERVING: *362 cal., 21 g total fat (2 g sat. fat), 0 mg chol., 395 mg sodium, 35 g carb., 12 g fiber, 16 g pro.*

tip
Toasted nuts add flavor and crunch to fruit, grain, or leafy green salads. Nuts contain heart-healthy fats and protein. Add just a tablespoon or two to reap these nutritional benefits without adding a lot of calories.

Mediterranean Beans and Greens Salad

START TO FINISH: **20 minutes** MAKES **6 servings**

8 cups torn mixed salad greens or romaine lettuce

¼ cup small fresh basil leaves

½ of a medium cucumber, thinly sliced

1 15-ounce can cannellini beans (white kidney beans), rinsed and drained

1 15-ounce can black beans, rinsed and drained

3 medium roma tomatoes, cored and cut into wedges

½ cup bottled reduced-calorie balsamic vinaigrette salad dressing

1 teaspoon finely shredded orange peel

6 slices baguette-style sourdough bread, toasted

2 ounces soft goat cheese (chèvre)

1 tablespoon snipped fresh basil

1 On a large serving platter arrange salad greens and ¼ cup basil. Arrange cucumber and the drained beans over salad greens. Top with tomato wedges.

2 For dressing, in a small bowl combine balsamic vinaigrette salad dressing and orange peel. Drizzle dressing over salad.

3 To serve, spread toasted bread with goat cheese and sprinkle with snipped basil. Serve bread with salad.

PER SERVING: *238 cal., 6 g total fat (2 g sat. fat), 4 mg chol., 809 mg sodium, 40 g carb., 9 g fiber, 15 g pro.*

tip

Toss fresh herbs with salad greens to add zip to the flavor of your salad. Try basil, cilantro, mint, dill, or Italian (flat-leaf) parsley leaves.

Greek Garbanzo Salad

PREP: 35 minutes CHILL: 4 to 24 hours MAKES 4 servings

1 15- to 16-ounce can garbanzo beans (chickpeas), rinsed and drained

2 cups chopped, seeded cucumber (1 medium)

1 cup coarsely chopped tomatoes (2 medium)

1 cup coarsely chopped green sweet pepper (1 large)

½ cup thinly sliced red onion

2 tablespoons olive oil

2 tablespoons red wine vinegar

1 tablespoon finely snipped fresh mint

1 tablespoon lemon juice

2 cloves garlic, minced

½ cup crumbled reduced-fat feta cheese (2 ounces)

   Salt

   Ground black pepper

2 cups torn mixed salad greens or romaine

1 In a large bowl combine drained garbanzo beans, cucumber, tomatoes, sweet pepper, and red onion.

2 For dressing, in a small bowl whisk together oil, red wine vinegar, mint, lemon juice, and garlic. Pour dressing over garbanzo bean mixture; toss to coat. Cover and chill for 4 to 24 hours.

3 To serve, stir feta cheese into salad. Season to taste with salt and black pepper. Serve over mixed greens.

PER SERVING: *200 cal., 10 g total fat (3 g sat. fat), 5 mg chol., 694 mg sodium, 25 g carb., 7 g fiber, 11 g pro.*

make it vegan
Substitute crumbled feta-flavor soy cheese for the feta cheese.

tip
If you love croutons, make your own by toasting cubes of a hearty wheat or multigrain bread. Purchased croutons are usually high in calories, fat, and sodium.

Greek Quinoa and Avocados

PREP: 20 minutes   COOK: 15 minutes   MAKES 4 servings

½ cup uncooked quinoa, rinsed and drained

1 cup water

2 roma tomatoes, seeded and finely chopped

½ cup shredded fresh spinach

⅓ cup finely chopped red onion

2 tablespoons lemon juice

2 tablespoons olive oil

½ teaspoon salt

2 cups fresh spinach leaves

2 ripe avocados, halved, seeded, peeled, and sliced*

⅓ cup crumbled feta cheese

1 In a small saucepan combine quinoa and the water. Bring to boiling; reduce heat. Simmer, covered, about 15 minutes or until liquid is absorbed. Place quinoa in a medium bowl.

2 Add tomatoes, shredded spinach, and onion to quinoa; stir to combine.

3 For dressing, in a small bowl whisk together lemon juice, olive oil, and salt. Drizzle dressing over quinoa mixture; toss to coat.

4 To serve, place additional spinach leaves on individual serving plates. Top with avocado slices. Spoon quinoa mixture over avocado. Sprinkle with feta cheese.

PER SERVING: *300 cal., 21 g total fat (4 g sat. fat), 11 mg chol., 456 mg sodium, 24 g carb., 7 g fiber, 7 g pro.*

***tip**
Brush avocado slices with additional lemon juice to prevent browning.

make it vegan
Substitute crumbled feta-flavor soy cheese for the feta cheese.

Quinoa Fattoush with Lemon Dressing

PREP: 40 minutes BAKE: 8 minutes OVEN: 375°F MAKES 6 servings

1½ cups water

¾ cup uncooked quinoa, rinsed and drained

2 6- to 7-inch pita bread rounds

1 15- to 16-ounce can garbanzo beans (chickpeas), rinsed and drained

1¼ cups chopped, seeded cucumber (1 medium)

1 cup chopped tomato (1 large)

¾ cup chopped yellow sweet pepper (1 medium)

¼ cup chopped red onion

2 tablespoons crumbled feta cheese

3 tablespoons lemon juice

3 tablespoons olive oil

2 teaspoons finely snipped fresh mint

1 teaspoon snipped fresh marjoram or oregano

1 clove garlic, minced

¼ teaspoon salt

¼ teaspoon ground black pepper

Additional crumbled feta cheese or garlic herb-flavored soy cheese (optional)

Lemon wedges (optional)

1 Preheat oven to 375°F. In a medium saucepan bring the water to boiling. Add quinoa; reduce heat. Simmer, covered, about 15 minutes or until tender. Drain if necessary. Spread quinoa into a shallow baking pan and let stand to cool to room temperature. Transfer cooled quinoa to a large bowl.

2 Meanwhile, halve pita rounds horizontally and tear into 1-inch pieces. Place pieces in a single layer on a baking sheet. Bake for 8 to 10 minutes or until light brown and crisp. Cool.

3 Add toasted pita pieces, drained garbanzo beans, cucumber, tomato, sweet pepper, onion, and the 2 tablespoons feta cheese to the quinoa; stir to combine.

4 For dressing, in a screw-top jar combine lemon juice, olive oil, mint, marjoram, garlic, salt, and pepper. Cover and shake well.

5 Drizzle dressing over quinoa mixture; toss to coat well. If desired, sprinkle with additional feta cheese and serve with lemon wedges.

PER SERVING: *312 cal., 10 g total fat (2 g sat. fat), 3 mg chol., 457 mg sodium, 47 g carb., 6 g fiber, 10 g pro.*

make it vegan

Substitute crumbled feta-flavor soy cheese for the feta cheese.

Israeli Couscous Salad with Tomato and Arugula

PREP: 20 minutes COOK: 17 minutes STAND: 10 minutes MAKES 6 servings

2 6.3-ounce boxes Israeli-style couscous* (2½ cups)

¼ cup olive oil

4 cups boiling water

½ teaspoon finely shredded lemon peel

3 tablespoons lemon juice

1 medium shallot, minced

1 tablespoon snipped fresh basil

2 teaspoons honey

½ teaspoon salt

¼ teaspoon ground black pepper

3 medium roma tomatoes, chopped

3 cups baby arugula

4 ounces fresh mozzarella cheese, cut into ½-inch cubes

½ cup chopped walnuts, toasted

1 In a large saucepan cook and stir couscous in 1 tablespoon of the hot oil over medium-high heat for 5 minutes or until golden brown. Carefully add the boiling water and return mixture to boiling; reduce heat. Simmer, covered, about 12 minutes or until most of the liquid is absorbed. Fluff couscous lightly with a fork. Spread couscous onto a shallow baking pan; let stand for 10 minutes to cool.

2 For dressing, in a screw-top jar combine the remaining 3 tablespoons olive oil, the lemon peel, lemon juice, shallot, basil, honey, salt, and pepper. Cover and shake well; set aside.

3 In a large bowl combine couscous, tomatoes, arugula, mozzarella cheese, and walnuts. Stir or shake dressing and drizzle over couscous mixture; stir to combine. Serve immediately. Or chill, covered, in the refrigerator for up to 6 hours.

PER SERVING: *444 cal., 20 g total fat (5 g sat. fat), 13 mg chol., 261 mg sodium, 54 g carb., 4 g fiber, 12 g pro.*

217

*tip

If you like, instead of Israeli-style couscous try 2½ cups dried orzo, ditalini, acini di pepe, or another tiny pasta shape. Brown in oil as directed, then cook in boiling salted water according to package directions. Drain and cool as directed above.

make it vegan 🌿

Substitute mozzarella-flavor soy cheese for the mozzarella cheese.

Lemon Couscous Salad with Fresh Fruit

PREP: 35 minutes STAND: 5 minutes MAKES 4 servings

1¼ cups water

¼ teaspoon salt

¾ cup whole wheat couscous or couscous

½ teaspoon finely shredded lemon peel

1 cup cubed cantaloupe

1 cup honeydew balls or cubes

½ cup fresh blueberries

½ of a medium mango, peeled and cubed

½ cup plain Greek yogurt or low-fat yogurt

1 tablespoon lemon juice

1 tablespoon honey

Dash ground cardamom or ground cinnamon

Milk (optional)

8 Bibb lettuce leaves

½ cup sliced almonds or chopped walnuts, toasted

1 In a small saucepan bring the water and salt to boiling. Stir in couscous. Cover and remove from heat. Let stand for 5 minutes. Fluff couscous lightly with a fork; stir in lemon peel. Let cool.

2 In a medium bowl combine cantaloupe, honeydew, blueberries, and mango.

3 For dressing, in a small bowl combine yogurt, lemon juice, honey, and cardamom. If necessary, stir in milk to make a salad dressing of drizzling consistency.

4 Divide lettuce leaves among individual serving plates. Spoon cooled couscous mixture onto lettuce. Top with cantaloupe mixture. Drizzle dressing over cantaloupe mixture. Sprinkle with almonds.

PER SERVING: *340 cal., 10 g total fat (2 g sat. fat), 9 mg chol., 190 mg sodium, 58 g carb., 9 g fiber, 11 g pro.*

218

🌱 make it vegan

Substitute soy yogurt for the Greek yogurt and, if using milk, substitute soymilk for the dairy milk.

Southwestern Rice and Bean Salad with Tempeh

PREP: **30 minutes** COOL: **20 minutes** MAKES **6 to 8 servings**

2 **cups water**

½ **teaspoon salt**

1 **cup uncooked long grain rice**

1 **8-ounce package tempeh (fermented soybean cake), cubed**

½ **cup salsa verde**

1 **14- to 15-ounce can black beans, rinsed and drained**

1 **cup frozen whole kernel corn, thawed**

1 **cup chopped tomato**

½ **cup chopped red onion**

¼ **cup snipped fresh cilantro**

1 **fresh jalapeño chile pepper, seeded and finely chopped***

2 **tablespoons olive oil**

2 **tablespoons lime juice**

1 **teaspoon ground cumin**

2 **ounces queso fresco or feta cheese, crumbled (½ cup)**

Lime wedges (optional)

1 In a large saucepan bring the water and salt to boiling. Add rice and return to boiling; reduce heat. Simmer, covered, about 15 minutes or until rice is tender and liquid is absorbed. Remove from heat. Let cool to room temperature. Set aside.

2 Meanwhile, in a large skillet combine tempeh and salsa. Cook, uncovered, over medium heat about 8 minutes or until tempeh is just tender and is well coated with the salsa, stirring frequently. Remove from heat. Cool tempeh mixture to room temperature. Set aside.

3 In a large bowl combine drained black beans, corn, tomato, onion, cilantro, jalapeño pepper, olive oil, lime juice, and cumin. Stir in rice and tempeh. Top with cheese. Serve immediately or cover and chill for up to 24 hours. If desired, garnish with lime wedges.

PER SERVING: *331 cal., 10 g total fat (2 g sat. fat), 0 mg chol., 506 mg sodium, 48 g carb., 5 g fiber, 17 g pro.*

*tip

Because hot chile peppers contain volatile oils that can burn your skin and eyes, avoid direct contact with chiles as much as possible. When working with chile peppers, wear plastic or rubber gloves. If your bare hands do touch the chile peppers, wash your hands and nails well with soap and warm water.

make it vegan

Substitute desired soy cheese for the queso fresco.

Wheat Berry Salad

PREP: 20 minutes COOK: 40 minutes COOL: 1 hour MAKES 4 servings

2½ cups water

1 cup uncooked wheat berries, rinsed

2 tablespoons lemon juice

2 tablespoons canola oil

1 tablespoon maple-flavored syrup

¼ teaspoon ground cinnamon

¼ teaspoon salt

¼ teaspoon ground black pepper

1 medium apple, cored, peeled, and sliced

1 large carrot, shredded

2 green onions, sliced

6 cups fresh baby spinach

¼ cup snipped dried apricots

1 In a small saucepan bring the water to boiling. Add wheat berries to boiling water. Return to boiling; reduce heat. Simmer, covered, for 40 to 50 minutes or until tender. Drain and transfer to a large bowl. Let cool for 1 hour.

2 For dressing, in a small bowl whisk together lemon juice, oil, syrup, cinnamon, salt, and pepper. Drizzle dressing over cooled wheat berries; stir to combine. Add apple, carrot, and green onions; toss to coat. Serve wheat berry mixture with baby spinach; sprinkle with dried apricots.

PER SERVING: *284 cal., 8 g total fat (1 g sat. fat), 0 mg chol., 217 mg sodium, 50 g carb., 12 g fiber, 8 g pro.*

tip

Marinate fresh vegetables in a vinaigrette, then toss them into leafy green salads or grain-based salads. The marinated veggies add flavor, nutrients, color, and crunch to most any basic salad.

Thai Bulgur Salad

PREP: 25 minutes COOK: 15 minutes MAKES 4 servings

1 cup water

½ cup bulgur

2 cups fresh or frozen shelled sweet soybeans (edamame), thawed

1 medium red sweet pepper, seeded and cut into thin bite-size strips

½ cup coarsely shredded carrot

½ cup thinly sliced red onion

2 tablespoons snipped fresh cilantro

4 cups fresh spinach leaves

1 recipe Thai Peanut Dressing

¼ cup chopped peanuts (optional)

1 In a medium saucepan bring the water to boiling; add uncooked bulgur. Return to boiling; reduce heat. Cover and simmer about 15 minutes or until bulgur is tender and most of the liquid is absorbed. Drain, if necessary. Transfer to a large bowl.

2 Add soybeans, sweet pepper, carrot, red onion, and cilantro; stir to combine.

3 On individual serving plates arrange spinach. Top with bulgur mixture. Drizzle Thai Peanut Dressing over salad. If desired, sprinkle with peanuts.

PER SERVING: *381 cal., 17 g total fat (3 g sat. fat), 0 mg chol., 420 mg sodium, 38 g carb., 12 g fiber, 25 g pro.*

Thai Peanut Dressing

In a small saucepan combine ⅓ cup water, ¼ cup creamy peanut butter, 2 tablespoons reduced-sodium soy sauce, 1 teaspoon sugar, ¼ teaspoon ground ginger, ⅛ teaspoon crushed red pepper, and 1 clove garlic, minced. Whisk constantly over medium-low heat about 3 minutes or until smooth and slightly thickened (mixture will appear curdled at first but will become smooth as it is whisked over the heat).

Greek Pasta Salad

PREP: 40 minutes CHILL: 2 to 24 hours MAKES 12 servings

12 ounces dried mostaccioli or penne (about 4 cups uncooked)

2 cups cherry tomatoes, quartered

1 medium cucumber, halved lengthwise and sliced

4 green onions, sliced

⅓ cup pitted kalamata olives, halved

½ cup olive oil

½ cup lemon juice

2 tablespoons snipped fresh basil or 2 teaspoons dried basil, crushed

2 tablespoons snipped fresh oregano or 2 teaspoons dried oregano, crushed

1 tablespoon anchovy paste (optional)

4 to 6 cloves garlic, minced

¼ teaspoon salt

¼ teaspoon ground black pepper

1 cup crumbled feta cheese (4 ounces)

Fresh oregano leaves (optional)

1 Cook pasta according to package directions; drain in a colander. Rinse with cold water; drain again. Transfer to a large bowl.

2 Add tomatoes, cucumber, green onions, and olives; stir to combine.

3 For dressing, in a screw-top jar combine the olive oil, lemon juice, basil, the 2 tablespoons oregano, anchovy paste (if using), garlic, salt, and pepper. Cover and shake well. Drizzle dressing over pasta mixture; toss to coat.

4 Cover and chill in the refrigerator for at least 2 hours or up to 24 hours. To serve, stir feta cheese into salad. If desired, garnish with additional fresh oregano leaves.

PER SERVING: *231 cal., 12 g total fat (3 g sat. fat), 8 mg chol., 200 mg sodium, 26 g carb., 2 g fiber, 6 g pro.*

222

make it vegan

Substitute crumbled feta-flavor soy cheese for the feta cheese and do not use the optional anchovy paste.

Poached Egg Salad

START TO FINISH: **20 minutes** MAKES **4 servings**

8   **eggs**

2   **medium leeks, thinly sliced**

2   **cups seedless red grapes**

2   **tablespoons olive oil**

2   **tablespoons cider vinegar**

     Salt

     Ground black pepper

4   **slices crusty bread, toasted**

1   **10-ounce package Italian mixed salad greens (romaine and radicchio)**

2   **ounces blue cheese, crumbled (½ cup)**

1 Half-fill a large skillet with water. Bring the water to boiling; reduce heat to simmering (bubbles should begin to break the surface of the water). Break 1 of the eggs into a measuring cup. Holding the lip of the cup as close to the water as possible, carefully slide egg into the simmering water. Repeat with the remaining eggs, allowing each egg an equal space in the skillet.

2 Simmer eggs, uncovered, for 3 to 5 minutes or until the whites are completely set and yolks begin to thicken but are not hard.

3 Meanwhile, in a second skillet cook leeks and grapes over medium heat in 2 tablespoons hot oil about 4 minutes or just until leeks are tender and grape skins burst. Remove from heat. Add vinegar. Sprinkle with salt and pepper.

4 To serve, on individual serving plates place toasted bread slices. With a slotted spoon remove eggs and place on top of bread. Top with greens, leek mixture, and cheese.

PER SERVING: *428 cal., 22 g total fat (7 g sat. fat), 433 mg chol., 681 mg sodium, 39 g carb., 4 g fiber, 21 g pro.*

Wild Rice Salad with Orange and Fennel 🍃

PREP: 15 minutes   COOK: 40 minutes   MAKES 2 servings

3   tablespoons uncooked wild rice, rinsed and drained
3   tablespoons uncooked regular brown rice
2   cups water
1   large orange
2   teaspoons white wine vinegar
2   teaspoons olive oil
½   teaspoon honey
¼   teaspoon ground black pepper
⅛   teaspoon salt
1   small fennel bulb
2   tablespoons snipped fresh Italian (flat-leaf) parsley

1 In a medium saucepan combine wild rice and brown rice. Stir in the water. Bring to boiling; reduce heat. Simmer, covered, about 40 minutes or until rice mixture is tender. Drain if necessary. Cool to room temperature. Transfer to a medium bowl; set aside.

2 Meanwhile, for dressing, finely shred ½ teaspoon orange peel; set aside. Peel orange. Section orange over a small bowl to catch juices; set sections aside. Add the reserved ½ teaspoon orange peel, vinegar, oil, honey, pepper, and salt to juices in bowl, whisking until combined.

3 For fennel, cut off and discard stalks, including feathery leaves. Remove wilted outer layer; cut off a thin slice from base. Wash; cut fennel lengthwise into quarters and remove the core. Thinly slice the fennel. Measure ½ cup.

4 Add orange sections, fennel, and parsley to rice mixture; stir to combine. Drizzle dressing over rice mixture; toss gently to coat.

PER SERVING: *225 cal., 5 g total fat (1 g sat. fat), 0 mg chol., 162 mg sodium, 41 g carb., 5 g fiber, 5 g pro.*

tip
Enjoy foods high in vitamin C, such as oranges and other citrus fruits, with meals to improve iron absorption.

Orange-Artichoke Salad

START TO FINISH: **25 minutes** MAKES **4 servings**

3 medium oranges

1 medium bulb fennel

1 head romaine lettuce, chopped

1 12- to 14.75-ounce jar marinated artichoke hearts, drained

¼ cup thinly sliced red onion

2 ounces Parmesan cheese

3 tablespoons olive oil

1 tablespoon white wine vinegar

1 teaspoon snipped fresh tarragon

½ teaspoon Dijon-style mustard

¼ teaspoon salt

⅛ teaspoon ground black pepper

1 Finely shred ½ teaspoon orange peel; set aside. Peel and section oranges over a large bowl to catch juices. Reserve 2 tablespoons orange juice for the dressing; reserve any remaining juice for another use.

2 For fennel, cut off and discard stalks, including feathery leaves. Remove wilted outer layer; cut off a thin slice from base. Wash; cut fennel lengthwise into quarters and remove the core. Thinly slice the fennel.

3 On a large serving platter place romaine. Top with orange sections, fennel, artichoke hearts, and red onion. Using a vegetable peeler, peel Parmesan cheese into shards. Top with Parmesan shards.

4 For dressing, in a screw-top jar combine the reserved ½ teaspoon orange peel, the reserved 2 tablespoons orange juice, olive oil, white wine vinegar, tarragon, mustard, salt, and pepper. Cover and shake well. Drizzle dressing over salad.

PER SERVING: *302 cal., 19 g total fat (4 g sat. fat), 10 mg chol., 694 mg sodium, 25 g carb., 7 g fiber, 9 g pro.*

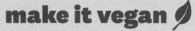

make it vegan

Substitute desired soy cheese for the Parmesan cheese.

225

Spinach, Avocado, and Orange Salad 🌿

START TO FINISH: **25 minutes** MAKES **4 servings**

1 **6-ounce package fresh baby spinach or 8 cups fresh baby spinach and/or torn mixed salad greens**

1 **cup fresh raspberries or quartered strawberries**

2 **oranges or 3 tangerines, peeled, sectioned, and cut into bite-size pieces**

2 **ripe avocados, halved, seeded, peeled, and sliced**

¼ **cup raspberry vinegar**

¼ **cup olive oil**

1 **teaspoon Dijon-style mustard**

2 **teaspoons sugar or honey**

   Freshly ground black pepper (optional)

1 On a large serving platter or individual salad plates place spinach. Arrange raspberries, orange pieces, and avocado slices over spinach.

2 For dressing, in a screw-top jar combine raspberry vinegar, olive oil, mustard, and sugar. Cover and shake well. Drizzle dressing over the spinach mixture. If desired, sprinkle with pepper.

PER SERVING: *303 cal., 27 g total fat (3 g sat. fat), 0 mg chol., 71 mg sodium, 17 g carb., 9 g fiber, 3 g pro.*

tip

Dried fruits, such as dried cranberries and raisins, are delicious in salads. Because they contribute sugar and calories, use them by the tablespoon as you would a seasoning. Or use fresh fruit instead.

Peach and Nectarine Soba Salad

START TO FINISH: **30 minutes** MAKES **4 servings**

6 ounces dried soba (buckwheat noodles) or multigrain spaghetti

2 cups frozen shelled sweet soybeans (edamame), thawed, or one 15-ounce can black beans, rinsed and drained

$2\frac{1}{4}$ cups coarsely chopped peaches or nectarines (3 medium)

1 large red sweet pepper, seeded and cut into bite-size strips

$\frac{1}{4}$ cup sliced green onions (2)

$\frac{1}{4}$ cup rice vinegar

2 tablespoons reduced-sodium soy sauce

1 tablespoon toasted sesame oil

2 teaspoons grated fresh ginger

$\frac{1}{4}$ cup sliced almonds, toasted

1 In a large saucepan cook soba according to package directions; drain in a colander. Rinse with cold water; drain again. Transfer to a large bowl.

2 Add edamame, peaches, red pepper, and green onions; toss to combine.

3 For dressing, in a small screw-top jar combine vinegar, soy sauce, sesame oil, and ginger. Cover and shake well. Drizzle dressing over soba mixture; toss to coat. Sprinkle with almonds.

PER SERVING: *368 cal., 11 g total fat (1 g sat. fat), 0 mg chol., 632 mg sodium, 55 g carb., 9 g fiber, 18 g pro.*

227

tip
Peaches and nectarines are often used interchangeably, but they are unique fruits. Peaches have a fuzzy skin; nectarines are smooth. Nectarines have twice the vitamin A and more vitamin C and potassium than peaches.

Stone Fruit Salad with Baked Goat Cheese Coins

PREP: 25 minutes BAKE: 8 minutes OVEN: 375°F MAKES 4 servings

- 4 ounces semisoft goat cheese (chèvre)
- 2 tablespoons fine dry bread crumbs
- 1 teaspoon snipped fresh rosemary
- 1 5-ounce package mesclun or torn mixed salad greens
- 2 cups sliced peaches, nectarines, apricots, and/or pitted dark sweet cherries
- 1 medium shallot, thinly sliced
- ¼ cup sliced almonds, toasted
- 2 tablespoons port vinegar, fig vinegar, or balsamic vinegar
- 2 tablespoons olive oil
- ½ teaspoon Dijon-style mustard
- 1 clove garlic, minced
- ¼ teaspoon salt
- ⅛ teaspoon ground black pepper

1 Preheat oven to 375°F. Line a baking sheet with parchment paper or greased foil; set aside.

2 For cheese coins, slice goat cheese into 8 rounds. In a shallow dish or on waxed paper combine bread crumbs and rosemary. Dip both sides of cheese rounds into crumb mixture to coat evenly. Using your fingers, press mixture gently onto rounds. Place each round onto prepared baking sheet. Bake for 6 to 8 minutes or until softened and light brown. Set aside.

3 On a serving platter arrange mesclun. Top with peaches, shallot, almonds, and cheese coins.

4 For dressing, in a screw-top jar combine vinegar, olive oil, mustard, garlic, salt, and pepper. Cover and shake well. Drizzle dressing over salad.

PER SERVING: *260 cal., 19 g total fat (7 g sat. fat), 22 mg chol., 342 mg sodium, 15 g carb., 3 g fiber, 10 g pro.*

Strawberry Spinach Salad with Roasted Asparagus

PREP: **25 minutes** ROAST: **10 minutes** OVEN: **400°F** MAKES **4 servings**

- 2 **cups strawberries, trimmed and halved**
- 2 **tablespoons white wine vinegar**
- 2 **teaspoons Dijon-style mustard**
- 1 **teaspoon honey**
- ¼ **teaspoon salt**
- ¼ **teaspoon cracked black pepper**
- ¼ **cup olive oil**
- 8 **ounces asparagus, trimmed and bias-sliced into 2-inch pieces**
- 1 **5- to 6-ounce package fresh baby spinach**
- 1 **large nectarine or peach, pitted and cut into wedges**
- ½ **cup chopped almonds, toasted**

1 Preheat oven to 400°F. For vinaigrette, in a blender combine ½ cup of the strawberries, the vinegar, mustard, honey, salt, and pepper. Cover and blend until smooth. With the motor running, add 3 tablespoons of the olive oil through the hole in the lid in a steady stream until incorporated.

2 Place asparagus in a shallow baking pan. Drizzle with the remaining 1 tablespoon olive oil. Roast, uncovered, about 10 minutes or until crisp-tender.

3 On a serving platter arrange spinach. Top with remaining strawberries, asparagus, nectarine, and almonds. Drizzle vinaigrette over salad.

PER SERVING: *254 cal., 20 g total fat (2 g sat. fat), 0 mg chol., 235 mg sodium, 17 g carb., 5 g fiber, 5 g pro.*

Salsa, Black Bean, and Mango Salad 🍃

START TO FINISH: 20 minutes   MAKES 4 servings

4   cups chopped romaine lettuce

2   cups chopped red sweet
    pepper

2   cups frozen whole kernel
    corn, thawed

1   15-ounce can black beans,
    rinsed and drained

2   mangoes, pitted, peeled, and
    sliced

½   cup cilantro-flavored salsa or
    salsa

1 On a serving platter arrange romaine lettuce. Top with red pepper, corn, drained beans, and mango slices. Spoon salsa over salad.

PER SERVING: *247 cal., 2 g total fat (0 g sat. fat), 0 mg chol., 466 mg sodium, 57 g carb., 12 g fiber, 12 g pro.*

Pear and Walnut Salad

START TO FINISH: 25 minutes   MAKES 4 servings

1   Comice pear, cored and thinly
    sliced

1   Bartlett pear, cored and thinly
    sliced

¼   cup crumbled blue cheese
    (1 ounce)

¼   cup walnuts, toasted and
    coarsely chopped

⅓   cup walnut oil or olive oil

¼   cup pear liqueur or pear
    nectar

1   tablespoon walnut Dijon-
    style mustard or Dijon-style
    mustard

    Freshly ground black pepper

1 Arrange pear slices on individual salad plates. Sprinkle with cheese and walnuts.

2 For dressing, whisk together oil, liqueur, and mustard. Season to taste with pepper. Drizzle 2 tablespoons dressing on each salad. (Store remaining dressing, covered, in the refrigerator for up to 3 days. Serve with spinach salad or cut-up fresh fruit.)

PER SERVING: *350 cal., 28 g total fat (4 g sat. fat), 6 mg chol., 209 mg sodium, 19 g carb., 3 g fiber, 3 g pro.*

tip

Fall is the peak season for pears, but most varieties are available year-round. Because each variety has a unique flavor, try using different ones in the same recipe, as this recipe does. Pears are a good source of both fiber and vitamin C.

Grilling

Fire up the grill and prepare to dig in to these mouthwatering sizzlers. Nothing's better than enjoying flame-kissed burgers, veggies, and pizza in your own backyard.

7

Black Bean Chipotle Burgers

PREP: **45 minutes** CHILL: **1 hour** GRILL: **8 minutes** MAKES **8 servings**

2 **15-ounce cans black beans, rinsed and drained**

1 **14-ounce can whole kernel corn, drained**

1 **cup finely crushed corn chips (about 2 cups)**

1 **cup cooked and cooled brown rice**

½ **cup finely chopped red onion**

½ **cup chunky salsa**

2 **to 3 teaspoons finely chopped canned chipotle peppers in adobo sauce***

1 **teaspoon ground cumin**

2 **cloves garlic, minced**

2 **tablespoons olive oil**

8 **tostada shells**

Shredded green cabbage

Chunky salsa

Thinly sliced radishes

Fresh cilantro leaves

Crumbled queso fresco (optional)

Lime wedges or avocado slices (optional)

1 For patties, in a large bowl mash half of the drained black beans with a potato masher, fork, or pastry blender until combined. Stir in the remaining black beans, the drained corn, corn chips, rice, onion, the ½ cup salsa, the chipotle peppers, cumin, and garlic.

2 Shape mixture into eight ¾-inch-thick patties. Brush both sides of patties with olive oil. Place patties on a tray; cover and chill at least 1 hour before grilling. Place patties on a grill pan.

3 For a charcoal grill, place grill pan on the rack of an uncovered grill directly over medium coals. Grill for 8 to 10 minutes or until brown, turning once halfway through grilling. (For a gas grill, preheat grill. Reduce heat to medium. Place grill pan on the rack, cover and grill as above.)

4 Meanwhile, heat tostada shells according to package directions. Serve burgers on tostada shells. Top with cabbage, additional salsa, the radishes, and cilantro. If desired, serve with cheese and lime wedges or avocado slices.

PER SERVING: *347 cal., 15 g total fat (2 g sat. fat), 0 mg chol., 699 mg sodium, 46 g carb., 11 g fiber, 14 g pro.*

*tip

Because chile peppers contain volatile oils that can burn your skin and eyes, avoid direct contact with them as much as possible. When working with chile peppers, wear plastic or rubber gloves. If your bare hands do touch the peppers, wash your hands and nails well with soap and warm water.

Black Bean Cake Burgers

PREP: 25 minutes   CHILL: 1 hour   GRILL: 9 minutes   MAKES 4 burgers

2 slices whole wheat bread, torn
¼ cup salted macadamia nuts or cashews
¼ cup loosely packed fresh cilantro leaves
2 cloves garlic
1 15-ounce can black beans, rinsed and drained
1 tablespoon hoisin sauce
¼ teaspoon salt
¼ teaspoon ground black pepper
1 egg white, lightly beaten
1 tablespoon olive oil
1 8-ounce can pineapple slices, drained
4 hamburger buns
1 recipe Lime Mayonnaise

1 For patties, place torn bread in a food processor. Cover and process until bread resembles coarse crumbs; transfer to a large bowl and set aside. Place macadamia nuts, cilantro, and garlic in food processor. Cover and process until finely chopped. Add drained beans, hoisin sauce, salt, and pepper; process with several on/off turns until beans are coarsely chopped and mixture begins to pull away from sides. Add bean mixture and egg white to bread crumbs in bowl; mix well.

2 Shape mixture into four ½-inch-thick patties. Brush both sides of patties with olive oil; place patties on a tray. Cover and chill in the refrigerator for at least 1 hour before grilling.

3 For a charcoal grill, grill patties and pineapple slices on the lightly greased rack of an uncovered grill directly over medium coals for 8 to 10 minutes or until patties are heated through (160°F) and pineapple slices are grill-marked and light brown, turning once halfway through grilling. Remove patties and pineapple slices from the grill. Lightly toast cut sides of buns for 1 to 2 minutes on grill. (For a gas grill, preheat grill. Reduce heat to medium. Place patties and pineapple slices on grill rack over heat. Cover; grill as above. Remove patties and pineapple slices from the grill and add buns; cover and grill as above.)

4 Serve bean burgers topped with Lime Mayonnaise and pineapple slices on grilled buns.

PER BURGER: *492 cal., 24 g total fat (4 g sat. fat), 5 mg chol., 872 mg sodium, 60 g carb., 9 g fiber, 15 g pro.*

Lime Mayonnaise

In a small bowl combine ¼ cup mayonnaise, ½ teaspoon finely shredded lime peel, 1 teaspoon lime juice, and 1 teaspoon snipped fresh cilantro.

tip

Root vegetables such as potatoes take a long time to fully cook on the grill. Speed up the process by boiling these vegetables for a few minutes first to partially cook them.

Cheesy Eggplant Burgers

PREP: 25 minutes GRILL: 6 minutes MAKES 6 servings

1	teaspoon garlic powder
½	teaspoon ground black pepper
⅛	teaspoon salt
½	cup chopped, seeded tomato (1 medium)
2	tablespoons olive oil
1	tablespoon snipped fresh oregano
2	teaspoons snipped fresh thyme
2	teaspoons cider vinegar
6	½-inch slices eggplant
6	¾-ounce slices smoked Gouda cheese
6	½-inch slices whole grain baguette-style French bread, toasted

1 In a small bowl combine garlic powder, pepper, and salt. In another small bowl combine half of the garlic powder mixture, the tomato, 1 tablespoon of the oil, the oregano, thyme, and vinegar. Set aside.

2 Brush both sides of the eggplant slices with the remaining 1 tablespoon oil and sprinkle with the remaining garlic powder mixture.

3 For a charcoal grill, grill eggplant slices on the rack of an uncovered grill directly over medium coals for 6 to 8 minutes or just until tender and golden brown, turning once halfway through grilling and topping with the cheese slices during the last 2 minutes of grilling. (For a gas grill, preheat grill. Reduce heat to medium. Place eggplant slices on grill rack over heat. Cover and grill as above, topping with cheese as directed.)

4 Place eggplant slices on top of toasted bread slices. Top each with tomato mixture.

PER SERVING: *201 cal., 11 g total fat (4 g sat. fat), 17 mg chol., 506 mg sodium, 19 g carb., 4 g fiber, 7 g pro.*

tip
Many vegetables shrink as they cook on the grill and end up falling through the grates. Avoid this by placing small pieces on skewers or in a grilling basket.

Portobello Burgers with Sunny Pesto Mayonnaise

PREP: 20 minutes   MARINATE: 1 hour   GRILL: 5 minutes   MAKES 4 burgers

- 4 **large portobello mushrooms, stems removed**
- ¼ **cup bottled light Italian-style vinaigrette salad dressing**
- ⅓ **cup low-fat mayonnaise or salad dressing**
- ¼ **cup salted roasted sunflower kernels (optional)**
- 2 **tablespoons pesto**
- 4 **whole grain rolls, halved and, if desired, toasted**
- 4 **slices yellow or red tomato**
- 1 **cup arugula**

1 Place mushrooms in a large resealable plastic bag set in a shallow dish. Pour Italian dressing over mushrooms. Seal bag; turn to coat mushrooms. Marinate at room temperature for 1 hour.

2 For a charcoal grill, grill mushrooms on the rack of an uncovered grill directly over medium coals for 5 to 6 minutes or until tender, turning once halfway through grilling. (For a gas grill, preheat grill. Reduce heat to medium. Place mushrooms on grill rack over heat. Cover; grill as above.)

3 Meanwhile, in a small bowl combine mayonnaise, sunflower kernels (if using), and pesto. Spread mayonnaise mixture evenly on both cut sides of whole grain rolls.

4 To serve, top each roll with a mushroom, tomato slice, and ¼ cup of arugula. Serve immediately.

PER BURGER: *339 cal., 18 g total fat (3 g sat. fat), 9 mg chol., 667 mg sodium, 36 g carb., 6 g fiber, 10 g pro.*

235

Tahini Burgers with Honey Wasabi Coleslaw

PREP: 30 minutes   GRILL: 8 minutes   STAND: 30 minutes   MAKES: 6 burgers

½   cup bulgur

1   cup boiling water

    Dash salt

1   15- to 16-ounce can pinto beans, rinsed and drained

¾   cup fine dry bread crumbs

½   cup chopped green onions (about 4)

1   medium carrot, peeled and coarsely shredded

1   egg, lightly beaten

2   tablespoons tahini

1   tablespoon soy sauce

½   teaspoon garlic powder

¼   teaspoon cayenne pepper

¼   teaspoon salt

1   tablespoon olive oil

1   recipe Honey Wasabi Coleslaw

6   whole wheat pita bread rounds, split crosswise and warmed

1 In a medium bowl combine bulgur, the boiling water, and a dash of salt. Cover bowl and allow to stand about 30 minutes or until bulgur is tender but still chewy. Drain through a fine-mesh sieve, pressing firmly to remove excess liquid. Return bulgur to bowl.

2 Add drained beans. Using a potato masher or fork, mash beans and bulgur together until thoroughly combined. Add bread crumbs, green onions, carrot, egg, tahini, soy sauce, garlic powder, cayenne pepper, and the ¼ teaspoon salt; mix well.

3 Using wet hands, shape mixture into six ¾-inch-thick patties. Brush tops and bottoms of patties with olive oil.

4 For a charcoal grill, grill patties on the rack of an uncovered grill directly over medium coals for 8 minutes, turning once halfway through grilling time. (For a gas grill, preheat grill. Reduce heat to medium. Place patties on grill rack over heat. Cover and grill as above.)

5 Serve patties topped with Honey Wasabi Coleslaw in pita bread rounds.

PER BURGER: 490 cal., 18 g total fat (3 g sat. fat), 40 mg chol., 951 mg sodium, 71 g carb., 11 g fiber, 16 g pro.

236

Honey Wasabi Coleslaw

In a large bowl combine 2½ cups finely shredded red and/or green cabbage; 2 medium carrots, peeled and shredded; ½ cup finely chopped red onion; ⅓ cup mayonnaise; 2 tablespoons rice vinegar; 2 tablespoons honey; 1½ teaspoons prepared wasabi paste; and 1 teaspoon yellow mustard. Mix well. Serve immediately while vegetables are still crisp.

tip

Tahini is an oily paste made of ground sesame seeds. It's often used to make hummus and other Middle Eastern dishes. Find it in the Asian section of the supermarket or at an Asian or Middle Eastern market.

Tandoori-Style Grilled Patties

PREP: 25 minutes   GRILL: 8 minutes   MAKES 4 servings

1   9.5-ounce package frozen meatless burger patties (such as Morningstar Farms Grillers Chick'n Veggie Patties)

2   pita bread rounds

½   cup plain 2-percent Greek yogurt or plain low-fat yogurt

1   tablespoon red wine vinegar

2   cloves garlic, minced

1   teaspoon garam masala

½   teaspoon paprika

1   cup fresh spinach leaves

1   small tomato, cut into slices

1 Grill patties according to package directions. Place pita rounds on grill rack alongside patties and grill for 3 to 4 minutes or until warm and lightly toasted, turning once halfway through grilling. Carefully split pita rounds in half horizontally.

2 For sauce, in a small bowl stir together yogurt, red wine vinegar, garlic, garam masala, and paprika.

3 To serve, place each pita half on a serving place. Top with spinach leaves, grilled patties, and tomato slices. Serve with sauce.

PER SERVING: *248 cal., 6 g total fat (1 g sat. fat), 2 mg chol., 739 mg sodium, 35 g carb., 3 g fiber, 14 g pro.*

237

tip

Leafy greens, such as romaine lettuce and radicchio, are delicious when grilled. Cut them into thick wedges, leaving the core intact, then brush with oil and grill until light brown on the edges.

Cracked Wheat Burgers with Pickled Onions and Lime Slather

PREP: 40 minutes CHILL: 1½ hours GRILL: 8 minutes MAKES 6 servings

- 1 recipe Pickled Onions
- 1 cup chopped onion (1 large)
- 2 tablespoons olive oil
- ¾ cup cracked wheat
- ¾ cup water
- 2 tablespoons soy sauce
- 1 cup rinsed and drained canned pinto beans
- ¾ cup walnuts, toasted
- ½ cup tightly packed fresh cilantro sprigs
- 3 cloves garlic, minced
- 1 teaspoon ground cumin
- ¼ teaspoon cayenne pepper
- ½ cup soft whole wheat bread crumbs
- 2 tablespoons olive oil
- 6 whole grain bagel tops, toasted (reserve bottoms for another purpose)
- 1 recipe Lime Mayonnaise

1 Prepare Pickled Onions.

2 In a medium saucepan cook ½ cup of the onion in the 2 tablespoons hot oil about 5 minutes or until onion is tender. Stir in cracked wheat and the water. Bring wheat mixture to boiling; reduce heat. Simmer, covered, about 10 minutes or until water is absorbed. Transfer wheat mixture to a medium bowl. Stir in soy sauce.

3 In a food processor combine drained pinto beans, walnuts, the remaining ½ cup onion, the cilantro, garlic, cumin, and cayenne pepper. Cover and process with several on/off turns until bean mixture is well combined. Stir bean mixture and bread crumbs into wheat mixture. Stir until combined.

4 Shape mixture into six ¾-inch-thick patties. Brush both sides of patties with the 2 tablespoons olive oil. Place patties on a tray; cover and chill for at least 1½ hours before grilling.

5 For a charcoal grill, grill patties on the rack of an uncovered grill directly over medium coals for 8 minutes, turning once halfway through grilling. (For a gas grill, preheat grill. Reduce heat to medium. Place patties on grill rack over heat. Cover; grill as above.)

6 Serve patties open-face on toasted bagel tops; top with Lime Mayonnaise. Using a slotted spoon, remove Pickled Onions from liquid; place onions on mayonnaise.

PER SERVING: *518 cal., 30 g total fat (4 g sat. fat), 5 mg chol., 765 mg sodium, 53 g carb., 8 g fiber, 14 g pro.*

Pickled Onions

In a small bowl combine half of a medium red onion, thinly sliced; 2 tablespoons lime juice; 1 tablespoon rice vinegar; ½ teaspoon salt; and ¼ teaspoon ground black pepper. Cover and chill for at least 2 hours before serving.

Lime Mayonnaise

In a small bowl combine ⅓ cup mayonnaise, ½ teaspoon finely shredded lime peel, and 1 teaspoon lime juice.

Inside-Out Veggie Burgers

PREP: **30 minutes**   CHILL: **30 minutes**   GRILL: **10 minutes**   MAKES **4 servings**

- **2   15-ounce cans garbanzo beans (chickpeas), rinsed and drained**
- **4   eggs, lightly beaten**
- **¹⁄₂   cup finely chopped red onion**
- **³⁄₄   cup finely crushed shredded wheat crackers**
- **¹⁄₄   cup snipped fresh cilantro**
- **1   tablespoon finely shredded lemon peel**
- **¹⁄₄   teaspoon salt**
- **1   tablespoon olive oil**
- **1   ripe avocado, thinly sliced**
- **1   small yellow or red tomato, sliced**
- **2   roasted red sweet peppers, drained and halved crosswise**
- **1   recipe Yogurt Sauce**

1 For patties, in a large bowl mash drained garbanzo beans, eggs, and onion together with a potato masher until a coarse paste forms. (Or place beans, eggs, and onion in a food processor; cover and process with on/off turns until a coarse paste forms. Transfer to a large bowl.) Add crackers, cilantro, lemon peel, and salt; stir until combined.

2 With wet hands, shape mixture into eight ¹⁄₂-inch-thick patties. Brush both sides of patties with olive oil. Place patties on a tray; cover and chill at least 30 minutes before grilling.

3 For a charcoal grill, grill patties on the greased rack of an uncovered grill directly over medium coals for 10 to 12 minutes or until brown, turning once halfway through grilling. (For a gas grill, preheat grill. Reduce heat to medium. Place patties on a greased grill rack. Cover and grill as above.)

4 To serve, arrange avocado slices, tomato slices, and red peppers on half of the burgers. Add Yogurt Sauce and top with remaining burgers.

PER SERVING: *366 cal., 17 g total fat (3 g sat. fat), 212 mg chol., 641 mg sodium, 41 g carb., 10 g fiber, 14 g pro.*

Yogurt Sauce
In a small bowl stir together ¹⁄₃ cup plain low-fat yogurt, 1 tablespoon snipped fresh cilantro, and 1 teaspoon lemon juice.

Veggie-Spinach Burgers

PREP: 10 minutes GRILL: 15 minutes MAKES 4 burgers

- 2 medium red onions, cut into ½-inch slices
- 4 refrigerated or frozen meatless burger patties
- ¼ cup bottled vinaigrette salad dressing
- 4 cups fresh spinach leaves
- 1 clove garlic, minced
- 1 tablespoon olive oil
- ½ cup crumbled feta cheese
- 4 hamburger buns, split and toasted

1 For a charcoal coal, grill onions on the rack of an uncovered grill directly over medium coals for 15 to 20 minutes or until tender, turning once halfway through grilling. Grill burger patties directly over the coals alongside the onions for 8 to 10 minutes or until heated through, turning halfway through grilling. Brush grilled onions with the salad dressing.

2 Meanwhile, for spinach topping, in a large skillet cook and stir the spinach and garlic in hot olive oil over medium-high heat about 30 seconds or until spinach is just wilted. Remove from heat. Stir in feta cheese.

3 To serve, place onion slices on bottoms of buns. Top with grilled burger patties, spinach mixture, and bun tops.

PER BURGER: *350 cal., 14 g total fat (4 g sat. fat), 17 mg chol., 920 mg sodium, 37 g carb., 7 g dietary fiber, 21 g protein.*

tip

For a simple, oh-so-good dessert, fire up some fruit. Try pineapple, nectarines, peaches, and/or bananas on the grill and drizzle with a little honey.

Grilled Bratwursts with Papaya Relish

PREP: **25 minutes** GRILL: **8 minutes** MAKES **4 servings**

1 **cup refrigerated papaya slices, drained**

1 **small red onion, cut into ½-inch slices**

1 **small green sweet pepper, seeded and cut into ½-inch slices**

2 **tablespoons olive oil**

4 **meatless bratwursts or hot dogs**

4 **bratwurst or hot dog buns, split**

1 **tablespoon white wine vinegar**

½ **teaspoon Jamaican jerk seasoning**

¼ **teaspoon salt**

⅛ **teaspoon ground black pepper**

1 Brush both sides of papaya, onion, and green pepper slices with olive oil.

2 For a charcoal grill, grill papaya, onion, sweet pepper, and bratwursts on the rack of an uncovered grill directly over medium coals for 8 to 10 minutes or until papaya is grill marked, bratwursts are brown and heated through, and onion and green pepper slices are crisp-tender, turning once halfway through cooking. Remove bratwursts, papaya, onion, and sweet pepper from the grill. Lightly toast cut sides of buns for 1 to 2 minutes on grill. (For a gas grill, preheat grill. Reduce heat to medium. Place papaya, red onion, sweet pepper, and bratwursts on grill rack over heat. Cover; grill as above. Remove bratwursts, papaya, onion, and sweet pepper from the grill; cover and grill as above.)

3 For relish, cut up grilled papaya, onion, and sweet pepper. Add to food processor. Cover and process with several on/off turns until chopped. In a medium bowl combine papaya mixture, vinegar, jerk seasoning, salt, and black pepper. Serve bratwursts in buns with relish.

PER SERVING: *346 cal., 16 g total fat (2 g sat. fat), 0 mg chol., 1,151 mg sodium, 34 g carb., 3 g fiber, 19 g pro.*

Grilled Veggie Sandwiches

PREP: 25 minutes GRILL: 10 minutes MAKES 4 sandwiches

- 1 small eggplant, cut crosswise into 1-inch slices
- 1 4-inch portobello mushroom, stem removed
- 1 medium yellow or green sweet pepper, seeded and halved
- 1 tablespoon olive oil
- ¼ teaspoon ground black pepper
- ⅛ teaspoon salt
- 4 5-inch whole wheat rolls, split
- 2 tablespoons light mayonnaise
- 2 cloves garlic, minced

1 Brush eggplant, mushroom, and sweet pepper with olive oil and sprinkle with black pepper and salt.

2 For a charcoal grill, grill the vegetables on the rack of an uncovered grill directly over medium coals for 10 to 12 minutes or until vegetables are just tender, turning once halfway through grilling. Add rolls, cut sides down, during last 3 minutes of grilling. (For a gas grill, preheat grill. Reduce heat to medium. Place vegetables on grill rack over heat. Cover and grill as above.) Transfer vegetables to a cutting board and cut into ½-inch slices.

3 Meanwhile, in a small bowl combine mayonnaise and garlic. Spread mayonnaise mixture over cut sides of toasted rolls. Fill rolls with grilled vegetables.

PER SANDWICH: *248 cal., 9 g total fat (1 g sat. fat), 3 mg chol., 408 mg sodium, 39 g carb., 8 g fiber, 7 g pro.*

Grilled Summer Vegetables Sandwich

START TO FINISH: **35 minutes** MAKES **4 sandwiches**

- 2 **Japanese eggplants, trimmed and halved lengthwise**
- 1 **large red onion, cut into ¼-inch slices**
- 1 **large tomato, cut into 4 slices**
- 1 **medium yellow summer squash, trimmed and cut lengthwise into 4 slices**
- 1 **tablespoon olive oil**
- ¼ **teaspoon ground black pepper**
- ⅛ **teaspoon salt**
- 2 **ounces soft goat cheese (chèvre), softened**
- 1 **tablespoon pesto**
- 8 **slices crusty whole grain bread**

1 Brush both sides of eggplant, onion, tomato, and squash slices with oil. Sprinkle with pepper and salt.

2 For a charcoal grill, grill vegetables on the rack of an uncovered grill directly over medium coals just until tender, turning once halfway through grilling. Allow 5 to 7 minutes for the squash and tomato and 7 to 9 minutes for the eggplant and onion. (For a gas grill, preheat grill. Reduce heat to medium. Add vegetables to grill rack over heat. Cover and grill as above.) Remove vegetables from grill.

3 Cut squash slices in half crosswise. In a small bowl stir together goat cheese and pesto.

4 To assemble, spread goat cheese mixture evenly onto bread slices. Top half of the bread slices with the grilled vegetables, cutting vegetables to fit as needed. Top with the remaining bread slices, spread sides down.

PER SANDWICH: *305 cal., 11 g total fat (3 g sat. fat), 8 mg chol., 383 mg sodium, 39 g carb., 11 g fiber, 14 g pro.*

Grilled Veg Sandwiches

PREP: 30 minutes GRILL: 4 minutes MAKES 4 servings

4 ciabatta rolls or other hearty
    rolls
1 lemon
2 tablespoons olive oil
1 tablespoon balsamic vinegar
3 small zucchini and/or yellow
    summer squash
1 small red onion
    Salt
    Ground black pepper
2 ounces feta cheese, crumbled
    Fresh mint leaves (optional)

1 Split rolls lengthwise. Halve and seed lemon. Lightly brush 1 tablespoon of the oil on cut sides of rolls and lemon halves; set aside.

2 In small bowl combine the remaining 1 tablespoon oil and the vinegar. Cut zucchini lengthwise into ¼-inch slices. Cut onion into ¼-inch slices. Brush zucchini and onion with some of the oil-vinegar mixture; sprinkle with salt and pepper.

3 For charcoal grill, grill zucchini, onion, and lemon on the rack of an uncovered grill directly over medium-hot coals for 4 to 6 minutes or until tender, turning halfway through grilling. Add rolls, cut sides down, during last 3 minutes of grilling. (For gas grill, heat. Reduce heat to medium-hot. Place zucchini, onion, and lemon on the rack over heat. Grill as above.)

4 Serve vegetables on rolls. Top with feta and mint. Drizzle with the remaining oil-vinegar mixture. Squeeze juice from lemon over feta.

PER SERVING: *294 cal., 11 g total fat (3 g sat. fat), 13 mg chol., 684 mg sodium, 41 g carb., 4 g fiber, 10 g protein.*

244

 **make it vegan**
Substitute crumbled feta-flavor soy cheese for the feta cheese.

Open-Face Veggie Melts

PREP: **30 minutes** GRILL: **12 minutes** MAKES **6 servings**

6 ½-inch slices eggplant

6 ½-inch slices yellow summer squash

2 ½-inch slices red onion

1 8-ounce package whole white mushrooms

1 large red sweet pepper, seeded and cut into ½-inch slices

¼ cup vegetable oil

½ teaspoon salt

¼ teaspoon ground black pepper

1 tablespoon balsamic vinegar

1½ teaspoons packed brown sugar

½ teaspoon Dijon-style mustard

1 clove garlic, finely chopped

⅛ teaspoon salt

⅛ teaspoon ground black pepper

¼ cup olive oil

1 16-ounce round loaf crusty bread, cut into six 1-inch slices

Olive oil

1 large clove garlic, peeled

8 ounces fontina cheese, shredded (2 cups)

1 In a large bowl combine eggplant, squash, red onion, mushrooms, red sweet pepper, vegetable oil, the ½ teaspoon salt and the ¼ teaspoon black pepper; toss to coat vegetables.

2 For a charcoal grill, grill eggplant, squash, and onion on the lightly greased grill rack of an uncovered grill directly over medium-hot coals for 6 to 8 minutes or until vegetables are crisp-tender, turning once halfway through grilling. (For a gas grill, preheat grill. Reduce heat to medium. Place vegetables on grill rack over heat. Cover and grill as above.) Transfer vegetables to a large bowl; keep warm.

3 Place mushrooms and sweet pepper slices in a grill basket. Place grill basket on grill rack. Grill for 6 to 8 minutes or until tender. Add to eggplant mixture.

4 For dressing, in a small bowl whisk together vinegar, brown sugar, mustard, garlic, the ⅛ teaspoon salt, and the ⅛ teaspoon black pepper. Gradually whisk in olive oil. Pour dressing over vegetable mixture, tossing to coat.

5 Brush cut sides of bread with oil. Cut garlic clove in half; rub cut sides of bread with garlic. Place bread on the grill rack. Grill for 2 to 3 minutes or until light brown, turning once halfway through grilling.

6 Divide vegetable mixture evenly among bread slices. Top each serving with cheese. Serve warm.

PER SERVING: *520 cal., 30 g total fat (9 g sat. fat), 44 mg chol., 890 mg sodium, 47 g carb., 7 g fiber, 18 g pro.*

245

make it vegan

Substitute desired soy cheese for the fontina cheese.

Pita, Cheese, and Veggie Grill

PREP: **20 minutes**   GRILL: **11 minutes**   MAKES **4 servings**

1   **8-ounce block feta cheese, quartered**

1   **medium zucchini, halved lengthwise**

1   **medium red onion, cut into ½-inch slices**

¼   **cup bottled Italian salad dressing**

   Salt

   Ground black pepper

1   **tablespoon honey**

4   **pita bread rounds**

2   **medium tomatoes, cut into wedges**

1 Drizzle feta cheese, zucchini, and onion slices with 2 tablespoons of the salad dressing. Sprinkle with salt and pepper.

2 For a charcoal grill, grill zucchini and onion on the rack of an uncovered grill directly over medium coals about 8 minutes or until vegetables are tender, turning once halfway through grilling. At the same time place a 6-inch cast-iron skillet on rack to preheat for softening the cheese. Remove vegetables. Grill pita bread and tomatoes on grill rack about 2 minutes or until bread is toasted and tomatoes are lightly charred. Place feta cheese in hot skillet; grill for 1 to 2 minutes or until softened. Remove skillet from grill. (For a gas grill, preheat grill. Reduce heat to medium. Place zucchini, onion, and skillet on grill rack over heat. Cover and grill as above.)

3 To serve, cut zucchini into chunks. Drizzle the remaining 2 tablespoons salad dressing and honey over the softened cheese, vegetables, pita bread rounds, and tomatoes.

PER SERVING: *404 cal., 17 g total fat (9 g sat. fat), 50 mg chol., 1,352 mg sodium, 48 g carb., 3 g fiber, 15 g pro.*

Falafel Gyros

PREP: 25 minutes GRILL: 10 minutes MAKES 4 servings

- 1 **15-ounce can garbanzo beans (chickpeas), rinsed and drained**
- ¼ **cup coarsely shredded carrot**
- 2 **tablespoons all-purpose flour**
- 2 **tablespoons fine dry bread crumbs**
- 2 **tablespoons snipped fresh parsley**
- 2 **tablespoons olive oil**
- 3 **cloves garlic, halved**
- 1 **teaspoon ground coriander**
- ½ **teaspoon salt**
- ½ **teaspoon ground cumin**
- ⅛ **teaspoon ground black pepper**
- 4 **pita bread rounds**
- 1 **recipe Cucumber Yogurt Sauce**
- 2 **cups shredded romaine lettuce**
  Diced tomato (optional)

1 For patties, in a food processor combine the drained beans, carrot, flour, bread crumbs, parsley, 1 tablespoon of the olive oil, the garlic, coriander, salt, cumin, and pepper. Cover and process until finely chopped and mixture holds together (should have some visible pieces of garbanzo beans and carrots). Shape mixture into four 3-inch patties, about ½ inch thick. Brush both sides of patties with the remaining 1 tablespoon olive oil. Wrap pita bread rounds in foil.

2 For a charcoal grill, grill patties and pita bread on the greased rack of an uncovered grill directly over medium coals for 10 to 12 minutes or until patties are brown and pitas are heated through, turning once halfway through grilling. (For a gas grill, preheat grill; reduce heat to medium. Place patties and pita bread on grill rack directly over heat. Cover and grill as above.)

3 Spread the Cucumber Yogurt Sauce over pita bread rounds. Top with romaine, falafels, and, if desired, diced tomato.

PER SERVING: *452 cal., 13 g total fat (2 g sat. fat), 1 mg chol., 1,126 mg sodium, 69 g carb., 8 g fiber, 15 g pro.*

Cucumber Yogurt Sauce

In a small bowl combine ⅓ cup plain low-fat yogurt; ¼ cup shredded and seeded cucumber; 2 tablespoons tahini; 2 cloves garlic, minced; and ¼ teaspoon salt. Cover and chill for at least 20 minutes.

make it vegan
Substitute soy yogurt for the dairy yogurt in the Cucumber Yogurt Sauce.

Black Bean and Mango Wraps

PREP: 20 minutes GRILL: 5 minutes MAKES 6 servings

1 20-ounce jar refrigerated mango slices, drained

1½ teaspoons Jamaican jerk seasoning

6 7- to 8-inch whole grain flour tortillas

1 15-ounce can black beans, rinsed and drained

1 11-ounce can whole kernel corn with sweet peppers, drained

¾ cup chopped, seeded tomato (1 large)

2 tablespoons snipped fresh cilantro

1 tablespoon lime juice

2 teaspoons finely chopped canned chipotle peppers in adobo sauce*

1 medium avocado, halved, seeded, peeled, and sliced

¾ cup shredded Monterey Jack cheese

1 Pat mango slices dry with paper towels. Sprinkle Jamaican jerk seasoning over both sides of mango slices; gently rub in with your fingers.

2 For a charcoal grill, grill tortillas on the greased rack of an uncovered grill directly over medium coals about 1 minute or until bottoms of tortillas have grill marks. Remove from grill and set aside.

3 Grill mango slices on the rack directly over the coals about 4 minutes or until heated through and grill-marked, turning once halfway through grilling. (For a gas grill, preheat grill. Reduce heat to medium. Place tortillas on greased grill rack over heat. Cover; grill as above. Remove tortillas from the grill and add mango; cover and grill as above.)

4 Meanwhile, in a medium bowl combine drained black beans, corn, tomato, cilantro, lime juice, and chipotle chile peppers.

5 To assemble, place tortillas, grill-mark sides down, on a flat work surface. Top each tortilla with some of the mango slices and avocado slices. Top with black bean mixture and shredded cheese. Roll up tortillas to enclose filling. Cut each in half to serve.

PER SERVING: *346 cal., 12 g total fat (4 g sat. fat), 13 mg chol., 839 mg sodium, 47 g carb., 18 g fiber, 18 g pro.*

248

*tip

Because chile peppers contain volatile oils that can burn your skin and eyes, avoid direct contact with them as much as possible. When working with chile peppers, wear plastic or rubber gloves. If your bare hands do touch the peppers, wash your hands and nails well with soap and warm water.

◊ make it vegan

Substitute soy cheese for the Monterey Jack cheese.

Portobello Wrap with White Bean-Chile Spread

PREP: 30 minutes MARINATE: 15 minutes GRILL: 6 minutes MAKES 4 servings

4 portobello mushroom caps, stems and gills removed

¼ cup bottled Italian salad dressing

1 19-ounce can white kidney beans (cannellini), drained and rinsed

2 cloves garlic, quartered

3 tablespoons olive oil

1 teaspoon chile powder

¼ teaspoon salt

2 cups baby spinach

1 tablespoon bottled Italian salad dressing

4 8-inch garlic-herb, spinach, or plain flour tortillas

4 ounces goat cheese (chèvre), crumbled or 1 cup shredded Monterey Jack cheese (4 ounces)

1 Generously brush portobello mushrooms on both sides with the ¼ cup dressing. Let stand for 15 minutes. Meanwhile, in a food processor combine drained beans, garlic, olive oil, chile powder, and salt. Cover and process until nearly smooth; set aside.

2 Toss spinach with the 1 tablespoon salad dressing; set aside.

3 For a charcoal grill, grill mushrooms on the rack of an uncovered grill directly over medium coals for 6 to 8 minutes or until mushrooms are tender and brown, turning once halfway through grilling. (For a gas grill, preheat grill. Reduce heat to medium. Place mushrooms on grill rack over heat. Cover and grill as above.)

4 Spread about one-third of the bean mixture evenly over each flour tortilla. Top with warm mushroom slices, the spinach mixture, and cheese. Roll up each tortilla around filling. Place wraps, seam sides down, on individual plates.

PER SERVING: *537 cal., 28 g total fat (8 g sat. fat), 13 mg chol., 1,158 mg sodium, 58 g carb., 10 g fiber, 23 g pro.*

249

Grilling

Asparagus Corn Tacos

PREP: 25 minutes MARINATE: 30 minutes GRILL: 4 minutes MAKES 5 to 6 servings

1 pound asparagus spears
2 tablespoons olive oil
2 tablespoons lemon juice
¼ teaspoon salt
¼ teaspoon ground black pepper
10 to 12 6-inch corn tortillas
1 recipe Italian Black-Eyed Pea Salsa
   Tomato pesto
   Shredded mozzarella cheese

1 Snap off and discard woody bases from asparagus. If desired, scrape off scales. In a large skillet cook the asparagus in a small amount of boiling water for 3 minutes. Drain well.

2 Meanwhile, for marinade, in a 2-quart rectangular baking dish stir together olive oil, lemon juice, salt, and pepper. Add drained asparagus, turning to coat. Cover and marinate at room temperature for 30 minutes. Drain asparagus, discarding marinade. Place asparagus on a grill tray or in a grill basket; set aside. Warm tortillas according to package directions; set aside.

3 For a charcoal grill, place the grill tray on the rack of an uncovered grill directly over medium heat. Grill for 3 to 5 minutes or until asparagus is tender and beginning to brown, turning once halfway through grilling.

4 Add tortillas in a single layer on the grill. Grill for 1 to 2 minutes or until heated through and grill-marked. (For a gas grill, preheat grill. Reduce heat to medium. Place the grill tray on grill rack over heat. Cover and grill as above. Remove asparagus and add tortillas. Cover and grill as above.)

5 If desired, bias-slice asparagus into shorter lengths. To assemble, place tortillas, grill-mark sides down, on a flat work surface. Top each tortilla with some of the Italian Black-Eyed Pea Salsa and asparagus. Top with tomato pesto and mozzarella cheese. Fold tortillas to enclose filling.

PER SERVING: *392 cal., 16 g total fat (4 g sat. fat), 8 mg chol., 523 mg sodium, 49 g carb., 8 g fiber, 16 g pro.*

Italian Black-Eyed Pea Salsa

In a small bowl combine one 11-ounce package refrigerated ready-to-eat black-eyed peas, ¼ cup chopped red onion, 1 tablespoon olive oil, 1 tablespoon red wine vinegar, 1 teaspoon snipped fresh thyme, ¼ teaspoon salt, and ⅛ teaspoon ground black pepper. Using a potato masher or fork, mash mixture slightly. Serve at room temperature. Store any remaining salsa, covered, in the refrigerator for up to 3 days.

Grilled Vegetable Burritos

PREP: 30 minutes GRILL: 8 minutes MAKES 4 servings

1 red sweet pepper, quartered and seeded

½ of a small eggplant, cut crosswise into ½-inch slices

1 medium zucchini, halved lengthwise

1 portobello mushroom, stem removed (about 5 ounces)

 Nonstick cooking spray

2 cloves garlic, minced

⅛ teaspoon ground black pepper

4 7- to 8-inch whole grain tortillas

1 cup shredded reduced-fat cheddar cheese

1 cup chopped fresh tomato

 pesto

1 avocado, halved, seeded, peeled, and chopped (optional)

2 tablespoons light sour cream

1 Lightly coat sweet pepper, eggplant, zucchini, and mushroom with cooking spray.

2 For a charcoal grill, grill vegetables on the rack of an uncovered grill directly over medium-hot coals for 3 minutes; turn vegetables. Grill for 3 to 5 minutes more or until vegetables are crisp-tender. (For a gas grill, preheat grill. Reduce heat to medium. Place vegetables on grill rack over heat. Cover and grill as above.) Remove vegetables from grill; cool slightly.

3 Coarsely chop vegetables. In a medium bowl toss together chopped vegetables, garlic, and black pepper. Divide vegetables among tortillas, placing vegetables just below center and to within 1 inch of the edge. Sprinkle vegetables with cheese. Fold bottom edge of each tortilla up and over filling. Fold opposite sides in over filling. Roll up from the bottom.

4 Return filled tortillas to grill rack. Grill for 1 minute; turn and grill for 1 to 2 minutes more or until tortillas are light brown. Serve with tomato, pesto, avocado, and sour cream.

PER SERVING: *293 cal., 14 g total fat (5 g sat. fat), 20 mg chol., 581 mg sodium, 25 g carb., 14 g fiber, 18 g pro.*

251

make it vegan 🌿
Substitute cheddar-flavor soy cheese for the cheddar cheese and tofu sour cream for the dairy sour cream.

Mushroom-Vegetable Fajitas 🌿

PREP: 30 minutes   GRILL: 20 minutes   MAKES 4 servings

1 small avocado, halved, seeded, and peeled
1 tablespoon lime juice
1 clove garlic, minced
½ teaspoon ground cumin
½ teaspoon dried oregano, crushed
¼ teaspoon salt
⅛ teaspoon ground black pepper
3 small fresh portobello mushrooms, stems and gills removed
2 medium red, yellow and/or green sweet peppers, halved, stemmed, and seeded
½ of a medium red onion, cut into ½-inch-thick slices
Nonstick cooking spray
4 7- to 8-inch whole wheat flour tortillas
Lime wedges (optional)

1 In a small bowl mash avocado with a potato masher or fork until nearly smooth. Stir in lime juice and garlic. Cover the surface of the avocado mixture with plastic wrap and chill in the refrigerator until ready to serve.

2 In a small bowl combine cumin, oregano, salt, and black pepper. Coat mushrooms, sweet pepper halves, and red onion slices with cooking spray. Sprinkle cumin mixture on vegetables.

3 For a charcoal grill, grill mushrooms, sweet pepper halves, and onion slices on rack of an uncovered grill directly over medium coals until vegetables are crisp-tender, turning once halfway through grilling and removing vegetables when they are done. Allow 8 to 10 minutes for the sweet peppers, 10 to 15 minutes for the mushrooms, and 15 to 20 minutes for the onion slices. (For a gas grill, preheat grill. Reduce heat to medium. Place vegetables on grill rack directly over heat. Cover and grill as above.)

4 Place tortillas on grill rack directly over medium coals. Grill for 20 to 40 seconds or until warm and tortillas are grill marked, turning once halfway through grilling. Remove from grill and cover to keep warm. Thinly slice mushrooms and sweet peppers. Coarsely chop onion slices.

5 Spread avocado mixture on the warm tortillas. Divide vegetables among the tortillas. Fold over. If desired, serve with lime wedges.

PER SERVING: *233 cal., 10 g total fat (2 g sat. fat), 0 mg chol., 475 mg sodium, 26 g carb., 15 g fiber, 11 g pro.*

252

tip
Avocados contain heart-healthy monounsaturated fat, so use them often. However, avocados are high in calories, so enjoy them in small amounts.

Veggie Fajitas with Guacamole

PREP: **30 minutes** GRILL: **20 minutes** MAKES **6 servings**

3 medium red, yellow and/or green sweet peppers, sliced

1 large onion, sliced

2 tablespoons olive oil

2 teaspoons fajita seasoning

3 cloves garlic, minced

1 8-ounce package fresh button mushrooms, halved

1 medium zucchini, halved lengthwise and cut into $\frac{1}{2}$-inch slices

6 8-inch flour tortillas

1 cup shredded Monterey Jack cheese

1 recipe Easy Guacamole

Snipped fresh cilantro (optional)

Salsa (optional)

Sour cream (optional)

1 Fold a 36×18-inch piece of heavy foil in half crosswise. Place sweet peppers and onion in the center of the foil. Drizzle with 1 tablespoon of the oil and sprinkle with 1 teaspoon of the fajita seasoning and the garlic. Bring up the opposite edges of the foil; seal with a double fold. Fold in remaining edges, leaving space for steam to build. Set aside.

2 Fold another 36×18-inch piece of heavy foil in half crosswise. Place mushrooms and zucchini in the center of the foil. Drizzle with the remaining 1 tablespoon oil and sprinkle with the remaining 1 teaspoon of the fajita seasoning. Bring up the opposite edges of the foil; seal with a double fold. Fold in remaining edges, leaving space for steam to build. Wrap tortillas in foil.

3 For a charcoal grill, grill the sweet pepper-onion packet on the rack of an uncovered grill directly over medium coals about 20 minutes or until tender, turning once halfway through grilling. Add the mushroom-zucchini packet and tortillas about halfway through grilling. Grill about 10 minutes or until mushrooms and zucchini are tender and tortillas are heated through, turning halfway through grilling. (For a gas grill, preheat grill. Reduce heat to medium. Place sweet pepper-onion packet on grill rack over heat. Cover and grill as above. Add mushroom-zucchini packet and tortillas. Cover and grill as above.)

4 Serve contents of packets with tortillas, cheese, and Easy Guacamole. If desired, top with cilantro, salsa, and sour cream.

253

PER SERVING: *346 cal., 18 g total fat (5 g sat. fat), 18 mg chol., 479 mg sodium, 37 g carb., 4 g fiber, 12 g pro.*

Easy Guacamole

In a sturdy, resealable plastic bag combine 1 ripe avocado, halved, seeded, and peeled; 1 tablespoon sour cream; 1 tablespoon snipped fresh cilantro; 2 teaspoons lime juice; and $\frac{1}{8}$ teaspoon salt. Seal bag. Knead bag with your hands to combine ingredients. Add $\frac{1}{4}$ cup diced, seeded tomato and 2 tablespoons sliced green onion to bag. Gently knead to combine.

make it vegan

Substitute desired soy cheese for the Monterey Jack cheese and tofu sour cream for the dairy sour cream in the guacamole.

Marinated Eggplant Kabobs 🌿

PREP: 25 minutes   MARINATE: 1 hour   GRILL: 10 minutes   MAKES 4 servings

3 tablespoons olive oil

3 tablespoons balsamic vinegar

2 tablespoons snipped fresh oregano

2 tablespoons Dijon-style mustard

1 teaspoon snipped fresh rosemary

4 cloves garlic, minced

½ teaspoon coarse salt

1 medium eggplant, cut into 1-inch pieces

2 medium zucchini, cut into ½-inch slices

1 large red onion, cut into wedges,* or 1 cup small red boiling onions, halved

8 green onions, cut into 4-inch pieces (optional)

2 cups hot cooked couscous

1 For marinade, in a large bowl whisk together oil, vinegar, oregano, mustard, rosemary, garlic, and salt. Add eggplant, zucchini, red onion, and, if desired, green onions; toss to coat. Cover and marinade in the refrigerator for 1 to 2 hours.

2 On eight 10-inch metal skewers alternately thread the eggplant, zucchini, red onion, and, if using, green onion, leaving ¼ inch between pieces.

3 For a charcoal grill, grill kabobs on the rack of an uncovered grill directly over medium heat for 10 to 12 minutes or until vegetables are tender and lightly brown, turning occasionally. (For a gas grill, preheat grill. Reduce heat to medium. Place kabobs on grill rack over heat. Cover; grill as above.) Serve with hot cooked couscous.

PER SERVING: *265 cal., 11 g total fat (2 g sat. fat), 0 mg chol., 402 mg sodium, 36 g carb., 8 g fiber, 6 g pro.*

*tip
To keep onion wedges from falling apart, do not trim root end.

Seitan and Pepper Kabobs

PREP: 25 minutes   MARINATE: 1 hour   GRILL: 10 minutes   MAKES 4 servings

- 2   8-ounce packages seitan wheat protein cubes (break up any large pieces)
- 1   medium green sweet pepper, seeded and cut into 1-inch pieces
- 1   medium yellow sweet pepper, seeded and cut into 1-inch pieces
- 1/3   cup balsamic vinegar
- 2   tablespoons olive oil
- 6   cloves garlic, minced
- 1   teaspoon ground black pepper
- 1   teaspoon snipped fresh rosemary or 1/4 teaspoon dried rosemary, crushed
- 1   teaspoon snipped fresh thyme or 1/4 teaspoon dried thyme, crushed
- 8   cherry tomatoes
- 1   recipe Yogurt-Dill Sauce (optional)

1 Place seitan and sweet peppers in a resealable plastic bag set in a large bowl. For marinade, in a small bowl whisk together balsamic vinegar, oil, garlic, black pepper, rosemary, and thyme. Pour marinade over seitan and sweet peppers. Seal bag; turn to coat seitan and sweet peppers. Marinate in the refrigerator for 1 to 2 hours, turning bag occasionally.

2 Drain seitan and peppers, discarding marinade. On 8 long metal skewers alternately thread seitan and sweet pepper pieces, leaving 1/4 inch between pieces.

3 For a charcoal grill, grill the kabobs on the rack of an uncovered grill directly over medium coals for 10 to 12 minutes or until sweet peppers are tender, turning occasionally to brown evenly. (For a gas grill, preheat grill. Reduce heat to medium. Place the skewers on grill rack over heat. Cover and grill as above.)

4 To serve, add a cherry tomato to the end of each skewer. If desired, serve with Yogurt-Dill Sauce.

PER SERVING: 336 cal., 11 g total fat (2 g sat. fat), 3 mg chol., 677 mg sodium, 26 g carb., 3 g fiber, 37 g pro.

Yogurt-Dill Sauce

In a small bowl stir together 1 1/3 cups plain low-fat yogurt, 2 tablespoons snipped fresh dill or 1 teaspoon dried dill, 1/4 teaspoon finely shredded lemon peel, 1/4 teaspoon ground black pepper, and 1 clove garlic, minced.

make it vegan
Substitute soy yogurt for the dairy yogurt.

Caribbean Tofu Skewers 🌿

PREP: **25 minutes** MARINATE: **8 hours** GRILL: **8 minutes** MAKES **4 servings**

1 **container refrigerated peeled and cored fresh pineapple**

1 **16- to 18-ounce package extra-firm tofu (fresh bean curd), drained and cut into 1-inch cubes**

3 **tablespoons lime juice**

1 **tablespoon olive oil**

1 **teaspoon Jamaican jerk seasoning**

¼ **teaspoon salt**

1 **clove garlic, minced**

½ **of a small red onion, cut into thin wedges**

1 **cup 1-inch pieces of red, yellow, orange, and/or green sweet pepper**

Nonstick cooking spray

1 Drain pineapple, reserving the juice. Cut pineapple into 1-inch cubes; cover and chill until needed. Place tofu in a resealable plastic bag set in a shallow dish.

2 For marinade, in a small bowl combine the reserved pineapple juice, lime juice, olive oil, jerk seasoning, salt, and garlic. Pour marinade over tofu. Seal bag; turn to coat tofu. Marinate in the refrigerator for 8 to 24 hours, turning bag occasionally. Drain tofu, reserving marinade.

3 If using wooden skewers, soak them in water for at least 30 minutes before grilling. On eight 12-inch skewers alternately thread tofu, pineapple chunks, onion wedges, and sweet pepper, leaving ¼ inch between pieces. Lightly coat assembled skewers with cooking spray.

4 For a charcoal grill, grill tofu skewers on the rack of the uncovered grill directly over medium coals about 8 minutes or until sweet peppers are crisp-tender, turning to brown tofu evenly and brushing occasionally with the reserved marinade. (For a gas grill, preheat grill. Reduce heat to medium. Place tofu skewers on grill rack over heat. Cover and grill as above.)

PER SERVING: *212 cal., 10 g total fat (1 g sat. fat), 0 mg chol., 233 mg sodium, 22 g carb., 3 g fiber, 12 g pro.*

tip
Jerk seasoning is a sweet and spicy blend of allspice, chiles, thyme, cinnamon, ginger, garlic, cloves, and green onions. You'll find it in the spice section of the supermarket.

Grilled Tofu Curry

PREP: 25 minutes MARINATE: 30 minutes GRILL: 10 minutes MAKES 4 servings

1   12- to 14-ounce package extra-firm tofu, drained
⅓   cup loosely packed fresh mint leaves
⅓   cup olive oil
¼   cup rice vinegar
2   tablespoons coarsely chopped fresh ginger
2   small jalapeño chile peppers, seeded and coarsely chopped*
3   cloves garlic
1   tablespoon sugar
2   teaspoons curry powder
1   teaspoon salt
1   teaspoon ground black pepper
1   large onion, sliced
2   cup cherry tomatoes
4   cups mesclun or mixed salad greens

1 Slice tofu crosswise into 6 slices. Cut each slice in half diagonally to make 2 triangles. Let tofu triangles drain on paper towels while preparing the marinade; set aside.

2 For marinade, in a food processor combine mint leaves, olive oil, vinegar, ginger, jalapeños, garlic, sugar, curry, ¾ teaspoon of the salt, and ¾ teaspoon of the black pepper. Cover and process until just combined.

3 Transfer tofu slices to a shallow dish; sprinkle with the remaining ¼ teaspoon salt and ¼ teaspoon pepper. Add ¼ cup of the marinade; spread to cover the tops and bottoms of each tofu triangle. Marinate at room temperature for 30 minutes.

4 Drain tofu. In a medium bowl toss onion slices with 2 tablespoons of the mint mixture. Transfer onion slices to a grill wok or tray.

5 For a charcoal grill, grill onions in grill wok on the rack of an uncovered grill directly over medium heat for 8 minutes, stirring occasionally. Add tomatoes and cook for 2 to 4 minutes more. Meanwhile, add tofu to the grill for the last 8 minutes of grilling, turning once halfway through grilling. (For a gas grill, preheat grill. Reduce heat to medium. Place grill wok on rack over heat. Cover; grill as above. Add tomatoes and tofu to grill; cover and grill as above.)

6 Serve vegetables and tofu slices over mesclun; serve with remaining mint mixture.

PER SERVING: *318 cal., 23 g total fat (3 g sat. fat), 0 mg chol., 599 mg sodium, 17 g carb., 5 g fiber, 11 g pro.*

257

*tip

Because chile peppers contain volatile oils that can burn your skin and eyes, avoid direct contact with them as much as possible. When working with chile peppers, wear plastic or rubber gloves. If your bare hands do touch the peppers, wash your hands and nails well with soap and warm water.

Mexican Tofu 🌿

PREP: 20 minutes   MARINATE: 30 minutes   GRILL: 8 minutes   MAKES 4 servings

¼ cup lime juice

1 tablespoon olive oil

1 tablespoon chili powder or 2 teaspoons adobo sauce from canned chipotle peppers in adobo sauce

4 cloves garlic, minced

¾ teaspoon ground cumin

1 16-ounce package refrigerated extra-firm water-packed tofu (fresh bean curd), well drained and cut into ½-inch slices

1 cup fresh or frozen corn kernels

¾ teaspoon kosher salt

1 cup canned pinto beans, rinsed and drained

¾ cup roasted red sweet peppers, drained and chopped

½ cup pitted ripe olives, halved

2 tablespoons snipped fresh cilantro

2 tablespoons thinly sliced green onion (1)

1 For marinade, in a shallow dish combine 2 tablespoons of the lime juice, 2 teaspoons of the olive oil, the chili powder, garlic, and ¼ teaspoon of the cumin. Add tofu slices to marinade, turning to coat tofu. Cover and marinate in the refrigerator for 30 minutes.

2 Meanwhile, in a covered small saucepan cook corn in a small amount of boiling water for 3 minutes; drain well. Set aside. In a large bowl combine the remaining 2 tablespoons lime juice, the remaining 1 teaspoon olive oil, the remaining ½ teaspoon cumin, and ¼ teaspoon of the salt. Add the drained corn, the drained beans, roasted peppers, olives, cilantro, and green onion. Set aside.

3 Remove tofu from marinade, reserving marinade. Sprinkle tofu with the remaining ½ teaspoon salt.

4 For a charcoal grill, grill tofu on the greased rack of an uncovered grill directly over medium-hot coals for 8 to 10 minutes or until light brown and heated through, turning once halfway through grilling and brushing occasionally with reserved marinade. (For a gas grill, preheat grill. Reduce heat to medium-high heat. Place tofu on greased grill rack over heat. Cover and grill as above.) Serve tofu with corn mixture.

PER SERVING: *277 cal., 12 g total fat (2 g sat. fat), 0 mg chol., 710 mg sodium, 27 g carb., 7 g fiber, 17 g pro.*

tip

Tofu is incredible grilled. Just make sure to use extra-firm tofu and press the water out. Tempeh works even better on the grill because of its firm texture. Add flavor to both tofu and tempeh by marinating them before grilling.

Grilled Marinated Tempeh

PREP: **20 minutes**   MARINATE: **4 hours**   GRILL: **8 minutes**   MAKES **4 servings**

2   8-ounce packages tempeh
½   teaspoon salt
½   teaspoon ground black pepper
¼   cup olive oil
¼   cup lime juice
¼   cup reduced-sodium soy sauce
¼   cup snipped fresh cilantro
2   teaspoons ground cumin
2   teaspoons finely chopped canned chipotle pepper in adobo sauce*
2   medium avocados, halved, seeded, peeled, and sliced
1   cup red and/or yellow cherry tomatoes
    Snipped fresh cilantro (optional)

1 Sprinkle tempeh with salt and black pepper. Place tempeh in a resealable plastic bag set in a shallow dish.

2 For marinade, in a small bowl whisk together olive oil, lime juice, soy sauce, cilantro, cumin, and chipotle pepper. Pour marinade over tempeh. Seal bag; turn to coat tempeh. Marinate in the refrigerator for 4 to 6 hours, turning bag occasionally. Remove tempeh from marinade; discard marinade.

3 For a charcoal grill, grill tempeh on the rack of an uncovered grill directly over medium coals for 8 to 10 minutes or until brown and heated through, turning once halfway through grilling. (For a gas grill, preheat grill. Reduce heat to medium. Place tempeh on grill rack over heat. Cover; grill as above.)

4 To serve, cut tempeh into 4 serving-size pieces. Top each serving with sliced avocado and tomatoes. If desired, sprinkle with cilantro.

PER SERVING: *485 cal., 36 g total fat (6 g sat. fat), 0 mg chol., 853 mg sodium, 23 g carb., 6 g fiber, 25 g pro.*

*tip

Because chile peppers contain volatile oils that can burn your skin and eyes, avoid direct contact with them as much as possible. When working with chile peppers, wear plastic or rubber gloves. If your bare hands do touch the peppers, wash your hands and nails well with soap and warm water.

Grilled Eggplant Parmesan

PREP: 25 minutes   GRILL: 10 minutes   MAKES 2 servings

4   ¾-inch slices eggplant (about 8 ounces)
¼   teaspoon salt
¼   teaspoon ground black pepper
1   tablespoon balsamic vinegar
2   teaspoons olive oil
1   teaspoon snipped fresh thyme
1   clove garlic, minced
2   tablespoons finely shredded Parmesan cheese
2   tablespoons finely shredded mozzarella cheese
1   medium roma tomato, cut into ½-inch slices
¼   cup reduced-sodium tomato pasta sauce, warmed
    Snipped fresh thyme (optional)

1 Sprinkle eggplant slices with salt and pepper. In a small bowl combine balsamic vinegar, oil, the 1 teaspoon snipped thyme, and the garlic; brush on both sides of each eggplant slice.

2 For a charcoal grill, grill eggplant slices on the rack of an uncovered grill directly over medium coals for 10 to 12 minutes or until tender, turning once halfway through grilling; add tomato slices to the grill and top eggplant slices with Parmesan and mozzarella cheeses for the last 3 minutes of grilling. (For a gas grill, preheat grill. Reduce heat to medium. Place eggplant on grill rack over heat. Cover and grill as above.)

3 To serve, top eggplant slices with tomato slices and serve with pasta sauce. If desired, top with additional snipped thyme.

PER SERVING: *153 cal., 9 g total fat (3 g sat. fat), 7 mg chol., 436 mg sodium, 13 g carb., 5 g fiber, 6 g pro.*

 **make it vegan**

Substitute desired soy cheese for the Parmesan cheese and mozzarella-flavor soy cheese for the mozzarella cheese.

Grilled Mushrooms with Red Wine Sauce

PREP: **25 minutes**   MARINATE: **2 hours**   GRILL: **8 minutes**   MAKES **4 servings**

- 4 **5- to 6-inch portobello mushrooms**
- ¼ **teaspoon salt**
- ¼ **teaspoon ground black pepper**
- ½ **cup dry red wine**
- ¼ **cup olive oil**
- 3 **tablespoons snipped fresh parsley**
- 4 **teaspoons snipped fresh oregano**
- 4 **cloves garlic, minced**
- ¼ **cup whipping cream**
- 3 **cups hot cooked egg noodles**

1 Remove stems from mushrooms; use a large spoon to scrape gills from mushrooms. Sprinkle mushrooms with salt and pepper. Place mushrooms in a large resealable plastic bag.

2 For marinade, in a small bowl combine red wine, olive oil, 2 tablespoons of the parsley, the oregano, and garlic. Pour marinade over mushrooms. Seal bag; turn to coat mushrooms. Marinate at room temperature for 2 hours, turning bag occasionally. Drain mushrooms, reserving marinade.

3 For a charcoal grill, grill mushrooms on the rack of an uncovered grill directly over medium coals for 8 to 10 minutes or until brown and tender. (For a gas grill, preheat grill. Reduce heat to medium. Place mushrooms on grill rack over heat. Cover; grill as above.)

4 Meanwhile, for cream sauce, in a small saucepan heat reserved marinade until bubbly. Stir in whipping cream; heat through. To serve, slice mushrooms and serve with cream sauce and hot cooked egg noodles. Sprinkle with the remaining 1 tablespoon parsley.

PER SERVING: *413 cal., 22 g total fat (6 g sat. fat), 55 mg chol., 171 mg sodium, 41 g carb., 4 g fiber, 10 g pro.*

Grilled California-Style Pizza

PREP: 20 minutes GRILL: 8 minutes MAKES 4 servings

- 1 tablespoon olive oil
- 1 clove garlic, minced
- ¼ teaspoon crushed red pepper
- 1 12-inch packaged prebaked pizza crust or Italian bread shell (such as Boboli brand)
- 1 cup chopped yellow or red tomato (1 large)
- ¾ cup roasted red sweet peppers, cut into thin strips
- ¼ cup thinly sliced red onion wedges
- 2 ounces semisoft goat cheese or feta cheese, crumbled or cut up
- 10 pitted kalamata olives, quartered lengthwise
- 1¼ cups shredded mozzarella cheese or shredded Italian cheese blend (5 ounces)
- 3 tablespoons snipped fresh oregano or basil

1 In a small bowl combine olive oil, garlic, and crushed red pepper; brush onto pizza crust. Top with tomato, roasted red peppers, onion, goat cheese, and olives. Sprinkle with mozzarella cheese.

2 Fold a 24×18-inch piece of heavy foil in half crosswise. Place pizza on foil, turning edges of foil up to edge of pizza.

3 For a charcoal grill, arrange medium-hot coals around outside edge of grill. Test for medium heat in center of grill. Place pizza on center of the grill rack. Cover and grill about 8 minutes or until pizza is heated through and cheese melts. (For a gas grill, preheat grill. Reduce heat to medium. Adjust for indirect cooking. Place pizza on grill rack. Grill as above.) Before serving, sprinkle with oregano.

PER SERVING: *520 cal., 24 g total fat (8 g sat. fat), 35 mg chol., 1,065 mg sodium, 56 g carb., 4 g fiber, 26 g pro.*

make it vegan

Substitute crumbled feta-flavor soy cheese for the goat cheese and mozzarella-flavor soy cheese for the mozzarella cheese.

Casseroles

Whether you're feeding a crowd or just a hungry family, nothing beats these dishes of home-baked comfort.

8

Potato-Crusted Veggie Pie

PREP: 45 minutes BAKE: 50 minutes OVEN: 350°F MAKES 6 servings

1   **14-ounce can vegetable broth**

1   **cup brown lentils, rinsed and drained**

¾   **cup water**

3   **cloves garlic, minced**

4   **medium parsnips, peeled and cut into ½-inch slices**

1   **medium red onion, cut into wedges**

1   **14.5-ounce can diced tomatoes with basil, garlic, and oregano, undrained**

2   **tablespoons tomato paste**

1   **24-ounce package refrigerated mashed potatoes**

1   **tablespoon snipped fresh thyme or ½ teaspoon dried thyme, crushed**

¼   **to ⅓ cup milk**

1½   **cups shredded Colby and Monterey Jack cheese or cheddar cheese (6 ounces)**

1 In large saucepan combine broth, lentils, the water, and garlic. Bring to boiling; reduce heat. Simmer, covered, for 20 minutes. Stir in parsnips and red onion. Return to boiling; reduce heat. Simmer, covered, for 10 to 15 minutes more or just until vegetables and lentils are tender. Remove from heat. Stir in undrained tomatoes and tomato paste.

2 Meanwhile, preheat oven to 350°F. In a medium bowl stir together mashed potatoes and thyme. Gradually stir in enough of the milk to make potatoes light and fluffy. Stir in 1 cup of the cheese.

3 Divide lentil mixture among 6 ungreased 12- to 15-ounce au gratin dishes. Spread potato mixture evenly over lentil mixture.

4 Bake, covered, for 45 to 50 minutes or until heated through. Sprinkle with the remaining ½ cup cheese. Bake, uncovered, about 5 minutes more or until cheese is melted.

PER SERVING: *432 cal., 12 g total fat (6 g sat. fat), 26 mg chol., 1,003 mg sodium, 62 g carb., 16 g fiber, 21 g pro.*

264

make it vegan

Substitute soymilk for the dairy milk and desired soy cheeses for the dairy cheeses.

tip

When buying parsnips, choose the smaller ones. They tend to have more flavor and a more tender texture. Store parsnips, unwashed, in the refrigerator for up to 3 weeks.

Lentil and Veggie Shepherd's Pie

PREP: 45 minutes   BAKE: 35 minutes   OVEN: 350°F   MAKES 8 servings

1   14-ounce can vegetable broth

1   cup brown lentils, rinsed and drained

1   cup water

3   cloves garlic, minced

4   medium carrots, cut diagonally into ½-inch slices

3   small parsnips, peeled and cut diagonally into ½-inch slices

6   white boiling onions (8 ounces), quartered, or 1 medium onion, cut into thin wedges

4   cups coarsely shredded Swiss chard or kale

1   14.5-ounce can no-salt-added diced tomatoes, undrained

2   tablespoons no-salt-added tomato paste

2   tablespoons snipped fresh basil or 2 teaspoons dried basil, crushed

1⅓   pounds potatoes (4 medium), peeled and cut up

4   cloves garlic, peeled

1   tablespoon butter

3   to 4 tablespoons fat-free milk

½   cup finely shredded Parmesan cheese (2 ounces)

1   tablespoon snipped fresh basil or ½ teaspoon dried basil, crushed

1 In a large saucepan combine broth, lentils, the water, and minced garlic. Bring to boiling; reduce heat. Simmer, covered, for 20 minutes. Add carrots, parsnips, and onions. Return to boiling; reduce heat. Simmer, covered, for 10 to 15 minutes more or just until vegetables and lentils are tender. Stir in chard; remove from heat. Stir in undrained tomatoes, tomato paste, and 2 tablespoons fresh or 2 teaspoons dried basil.

2 Meanwhile, preheat oven to 350°F. In a covered large saucepan cook potatoes and whole garlic in enough boiling, lightly salted water to cover for 20 to 25 minutes or until tender; drain. Mash with a potato masher or beat with an electric mixer on low speed. Add butter. Gradually beat in enough of the milk to make potatoes light and fluffy. Stir in cheese and 1 tablespoon fresh or ½ teaspoon dried basil.

3 Transfer lentil mixture to an ungreased 2- to 2½-quart casserole or au gratin dish. Spread potato mixture evenly over lentil mixture.

4 Bake, uncovered, about 35 minutes or until heated through.

PER SERVING: *234 cal., 3 g total fat (2 g sat. fat), 8 mg chol., 386 mg sodium, 41 g carb., 13 g fiber, 12 g pro.*

Make-Ahead Directions: Prepare as directed through Step 3. Cover dish with plastic wrap; chill for 2 to 24 hours. To serve, preheat oven to 350°F. Remove plastic wrap; cover dish with foil. Bake for 50 minutes. Bake, uncovered, for 10 to 15 minutes more or until heated through.

Cauliflower and Chickpea Gratin

PREP: 30 minutes   COOK: 15 minutes   BROIL: 1 minute   MAKES 6 servings

2	cups chopped onions (2 large)
3	tablespoons olive oil
2	14.5-ounce cans diced tomatoes, drained
1	15-ounce can garbanzo beans (chickpeas), rinsed and drained
6	cloves garlic, minced
1/4	cup snipped fresh Italian (flat-leaf) parsley
2	tablespoons capers, rinsed and drained
1	tablespoon snipped fresh oregano
1	tablespoon lemon juice
1	teaspoon snipped fresh thyme
1/2	teaspoon kosher salt
1/4	teaspoon freshly ground black pepper
1 3/4	pounds cauliflower, cut into florets
1	cup crumbled feta cheese (4 ounces)

1 Preheat broiler. In a large saucepan cook onion in hot oil over medium-high heat about 5 minutes or until tender, stirring occasionally. Stir in drained tomatoes, drained beans, and garlic. Bring to boiling; reduce heat. Simmer, covered, for 15 minutes. Stir in parsley, capers, oregano, lemon juice, thyme, salt, and pepper.

2 Meanwhile, in a covered Dutch oven cook cauliflower in a small amount of boiling water about 5 minutes or just until tender; drain.

3 Transfer hot cauliflower to an ungreased 2- to 2½-quart broilerproof baking dish. Top with hot tomato mixture; sprinkle with cheese. Broil 3 to 4 inches from the heat for 1 to 2 minutes or just until cheese starts to brown.

PER SERVING: 271 cal., 12 g total fat (4 g sat. fat), 17 mg chol., 951 mg sodium, 35 g carb., 9 g fiber, 10 g pro.

Brown Rice-Spinach Custards

PREP: 25 minutes   BAKE: 25 minutes   OVEN: 350°F   MAKES 6 servings

½   cup chopped onion (1 medium)

1   tablespoon olive oil

4   eggs, lightly beaten

¾   cup crumbled reduced-fat feta cheese (3 ounces)

½   cup low-fat cottage cheese

1   tablespoon snipped fresh dill or ½ teaspoon dried dill

½   teaspoon salt

2   10-ounce packages frozen chopped spinach, thawed and well drained

2   cups cooked brown rice

1   tablespoon lemon juice

Lemon peel strips (optional)

1 Preheat oven to 350°F. In a small skillet cook onion in hot oil over medium heat until tender, stirring occasionally. Cool slightly.

2 In a large bowl combine eggs, feta cheese, cottage cheese, dill, and salt. Stir in cooked onion, spinach, cooked brown rice, and lemon juice.

3 Place six 8- to 10-ounce ramekins or custard cups in a 15×10×1-inch baking pan. Divide rice mixture among ramekins. Bake, uncovered, for 25 to 30 minutes or until a knife inserted near centers comes out clean. If desired, garnish with lemon peel strips.

PER SERVING: *213 cal., 8 g total fat (3 g sat. fat), 146 mg chol., 648 mg sodium, 20 g carb., 4 g fiber, 14 g pro.*

Vegetable Two-Grain Casserole

PREP: 20 minutes   BAKE: 1¼ hours   STAND: 5 minutes   OVEN: 350°F   MAKES 5 servings

1   19-ounce can ready-to-serve lentil soup

1   15-ounce can black beans, rinsed and drained

1   cup small fresh mushrooms, sliced

1   cup sliced carrots (2 medium)

1   cup frozen whole kernel corn

¾   cup water

½   cup regular barley

⅓   cup bulgur

¼   cup chopped onion

½   teaspoon ground black pepper

¼   teaspoon salt

½   cup shredded reduced-fat cheddar cheese (2 ounces)

1 Preheat oven to 350°F. In an ungreased 2-quart casserole combine soup, drained beans, mushrooms, carrots, corn, the water, barley, bulgur, onion, pepper, and salt.

2 Bake, covered, about 1¼ hours or until barley and bulgur are tender, stirring twice. Stir again; sprinkle with cheese. Let stand, covered, about 5 minutes or until cheese is melted.

PER SERVING: *292 cal., 4 g total fat (2 g sat. fat), 10 mg chol., 828 mg sodium, 55 g carb., 13 g fiber, 17 g pro.*

make it vegan 🌿
Substitute cheddar-flavor soy cheese for the cheddar cheese.

Sweet Potato-Rice Casserole

PREP: 30 minutes BAKE: 30 minutes OVEN: 350°F MAKES 6 to 8 servings

2 cups water

1½ cups chopped, peeled sweet potato (1 large)

1 cup uncooked long grain white rice

½ teaspoon salt

1 15-ounce can black beans, rinsed and drained

1½ cups frozen shelled sweet soybeans (edamame), thawed

1 cup shredded Monterey Jack cheese (4 ounces)

1 8-ounce carton sour cream

1 4-ounce can diced green chile peppers, undrained

¼ cup chopped green onions (2)

2 tablespoons all-purpose flour

1 tablespoon snipped fresh sage

2 cloves garlic, minced

½ teaspoon salt

Toasted pumpkin seeds (pepitas) (optional)

1 Preheat oven to 350°F. In a medium saucepan bring the water to boiling. Stir in sweet potato, rice, and ½ teaspoon salt. Return to boiling; reduce heat. Simmer, covered, about 20 minutes or until liquid is absorbed.

2 Meanwhile, in a large bowl combine drained black beans, soybeans, ½ cup of the cheese, the sour cream, undrained chile peppers, green onion, flour, sage, garlic, and ½ teaspoon salt. Stir in cooked rice mixture.

3 Transfer mixture to an ungreased 2-quart casserole. Sprinkle with the remaining ½ cup cheese. Bake, uncovered, about 30 minutes or until heated through. If desired, sprinkle each serving with pumpkin seeds.

PER SERVING: *378 cal., 15 g total fat (8 g sat. fat), 36 mg chol., 773 mg sodium, 48 g carb., 7 g fiber, 16 g pro.*

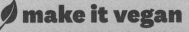

make it vegan
Substitute desired soy cheese for the Monterey Jack cheese and substitute tofu sour cream for the dairy sour cream.

Three-Bean Tamale Pie

PREP: 30 minutes BAKE: 20 minutes OVEN: 400°F MAKES 8 servings

1 cup chopped green sweet pepper

1 cup chopped onion (1 large)

3 cloves garlic, minced

1 tablespoon vegetable oil

1 15-ounce can red kidney beans, rinsed, drained, and slightly mashed

1 15-ounce can pinto beans, rinsed, drained, and slightly mashed

1 15-ounce can black beans, rinsed, drained, and slightly mashed

1 11.5-ounce can vegetable juice

1 4-ounce can diced green chile peppers, undrained

1¼ teaspoons chili powder

¾ teaspoon ground cumin

1 8.5-ounce package corn muffin mix

½ cup shredded cheddar cheese (2 ounces)

¼ cup snipped fresh cilantro or parsley

Salsa (optional)

Sour cream (optional)

1 Preheat oven to 400°F. Grease a 3-quart rectangular baking dish; set aside.

2 In a large skillet cook sweet pepper, onion, and garlic in hot oil over medium heat until tender, stirring occasionally. Stir in slightly mashed beans, vegetable juice, undrained chile peppers, chili powder, and cumin; heat through. Transfer bean mixture to the prepared baking dish.

3 Prepare corn muffin mix according to package directions. Stir in cheese and cilantro just until combined. Spoon mixture evenly over bean mixture. Bake, uncovered, for 20 to 25 minutes or until golden brown. If desired, serve with salsa and sour cream.

PER SERVING: *313 cal., 8 g total fat (3 g sat. fat), 8 mg chol., 994 mg sodium, 51 g carb., 11 g fiber, 14 g pro.*

Southern Grits Casserole

PREP: 25 minutes BAKE: 45 minutes OVEN: 350°F MAKES 8 to 10 servings

4 cups water

1 cup quick-cooking (hominy) grits

4 eggs, lightly beaten

2 cups shredded cheddar cheese (8 ounces)

½ cup milk

¼ cup sliced green onion (2)

1 or 2 fresh jalapeño chile peppers, seeded and finely chopped*

½ teaspoon garlic salt

¼ teaspoon ground white pepper

Sliced green onions (optional)

1 Preheat oven to 350°F. Grease a 2-quart casserole; set aside.

2 In a large saucepan bring the water to boiling. Gradually stir in grits. Gradually stir about 1 cup of the hot mixture into eggs. Return egg mixture to saucepan. Stir in cheese, milk, ¼ cup green onion, chopped jalapeño pepper(s), garlic salt, and white pepper. Transfer mixture to the prepared casserole.

3 Bake, uncovered, for 45 to 50 minutes or until a knife inserted near center comes out clean. If desired, sprinkle with additional green onions.

PER SERVING: *221 cal., 12 g total fat (7 g sat. fat), 137 mg chol., 281 mg sodium, 16 g carb., 1 g fiber, 12 g pro.*

*tip

Because chile peppers contain volatile oils that can burn your skin and eyes, avoid direct contact with them as much as possible. When working with chile peppers, wear plastic or rubber gloves. If your bare hands do touch the peppers, wash your hands and nails well with soap and warm water.

Tortilla and Black Bean Bake

PREP: 25 minutes BAKE: 30 minutes STAND: 10 minutes OVEN: 350°F MAKES 8 servings

2 cups chopped onions (2 large)

1 14.5-ounce can diced tomatoes, undrained

1½ cups chopped green sweet pepper (2 medium)

¾ cup picante sauce

2 teaspoons ground cumin

2 cloves garlic, minced

2 15-ounce cans black beans and/or red kidney beans, rinsed and drained

12 6-inch corn tortillas

2 cups shredded reduced-fat Monterey Jack cheese (8 ounces)

Shredded lettuce (optional)

Sliced fresh red chile pepper* (optional)

1 Preheat oven to 350°F. In a large skillet combine onions, undrained tomatoes, sweet pepper, picante sauce, cumin, and garlic. Bring to boiling; reduce heat. Simmer, uncovered, for 10 minutes. Stir in drained beans.

2 Spread one-third of the bean mixture in the bottom of an ungreased 3-quart rectangular baking dish. Top with 6 of the tortillas, overlapping as necessary; sprinkle with 1 cup of the cheese. Add another one-third of the bean mixture; top with the remaining 6 tortillas and the remaining bean mixture.

3 Bake, covered, for 30 to 35 minutes or until heated through. Sprinkle with the remaining 1 cup cheese. Let stand for 10 minutes before serving. If desired, serve on lettuce and garnish with chile pepper.

PER SERVING: 267 cal., 7 g total fat (4 g sat. fat), 20 mg chol., 971 mg sodium, 43 g carb., 10 g fiber, 15 g pro.

*tip
Because chile peppers contain volatile oils that can burn your skin and eyes, avoid direct contact with them as much as possible. When working with chile peppers, wear plastic or rubber gloves. If your bare hands do touch the peppers, wash your hands and nails well with soap and warm water.

make it vegan
Substitute desired soy cheese for the Monterey Jack cheese.

tip
Eliminate excess sodium from canned beans by rinsing beans in a colander under cold running water and draining well before using.

Three-Bean Enchiladas

PREP: 25 minutes BAKE: 25 minutes OVEN: 350°F MAKES 8 servings

16   6-inch corn tortillas
1   15-ounce can red kidney beans, rinsed and drained
1   15-ounce can pinto beans, rinsed and drained
1   15-ounce can navy beans or Great Northern beans, rinsed and drained
1   10.75-ounce can condensed cheddar cheese soup or nacho cheese soup
1   10-ounce can red or green enchilada sauce
1   8-ounce can tomato sauce
1½   cups shredded Monterey Jack cheese or cheddar cheese (6 ounces)
     Sliced pitted ripe olives (optional)
     Chopped green sweet pepper (optional)

1 Preheat oven to 350°F. Stack and wrap tortillas tightly in foil. Bake about 10 minutes or until warm.

2 Meanwhile, for filling, in a large bowl stir together drained beans and soup. Spoon about ¼ cup of the filling onto 1 edge of each warm tortilla. Starting at the filled edge, roll up tortilla. Place tortilla rolls, seam sides down, in 8 ungreased 10- to 12-ounce au gratin dishes or 2 ungreased 2-quart rectangular baking dishes.

3 For sauce, in a small bowl stir together enchilada sauce and tomato sauce. Spoon over tortilla rolls.

4 Bake, covered, about 20 minutes for the small dishes (about 30 minutes for the large dishes) or until heated through. Sprinkle with cheese. Bake, uncovered, about 5 minutes more or until cheese is melted. If desired, sprinkle with olives and sweet pepper.

PER SERVING: *360 cal., 10 g total fat (5 g sat. fat), 22 mg chol., 1,139 mg sodium, 55 g carb., 12 g fiber, 20 g pro.*

272

tip
Top off a hearty casserole with a lighter dessert. Try a bowl of fresh berries, some fruit sorbet, or a slice of cantaloupe or watermelon.

Spinach-Mushroom
Quesadillas
page 183

273

274

Grilled Veggie-
Cheese Sandwiches
page 188

Israeli Couscous Salad
with Tomato and Arugula
page 217

Stone Fruit Salad with
Baked Goat Cheese Coins

page 228

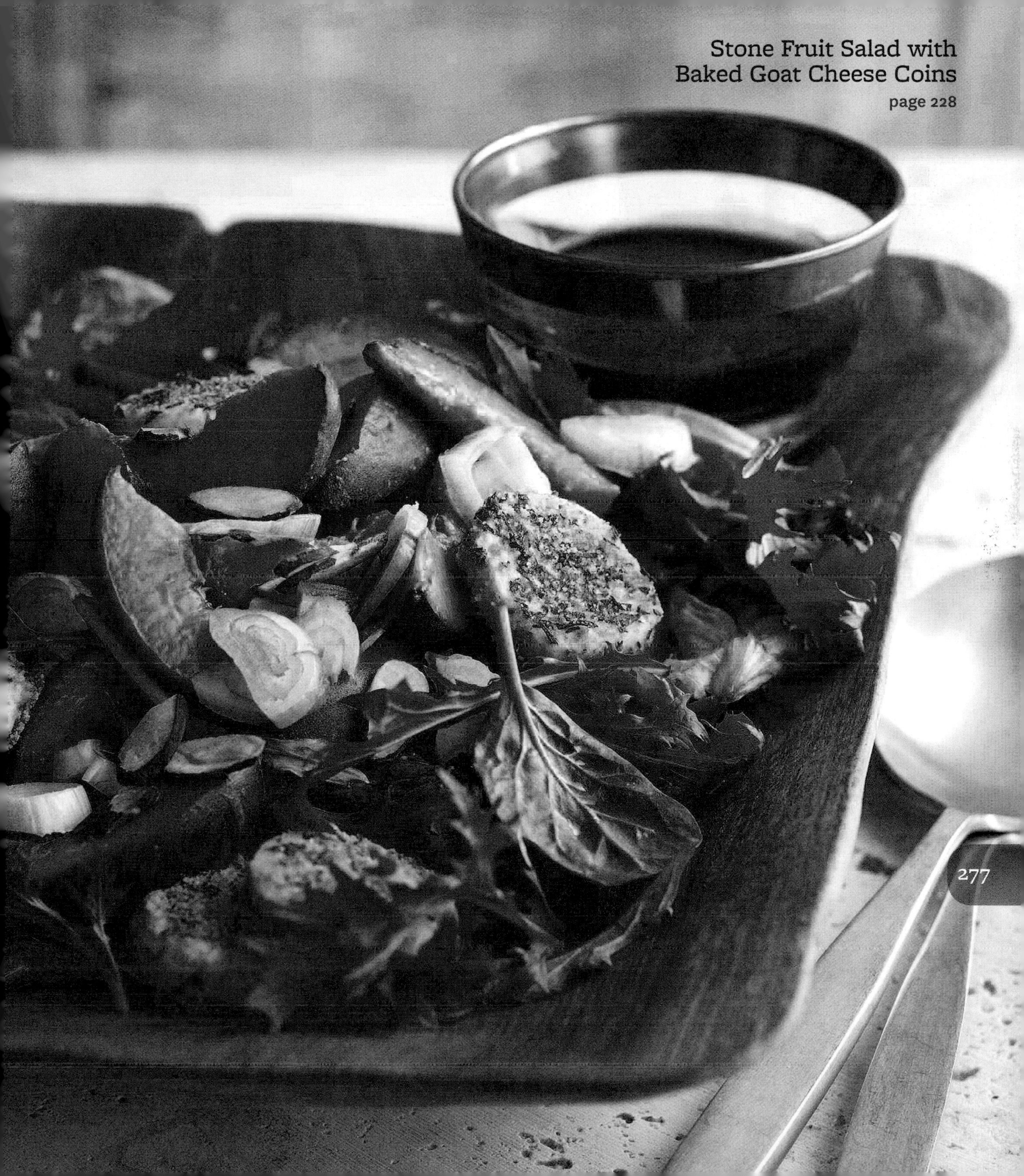

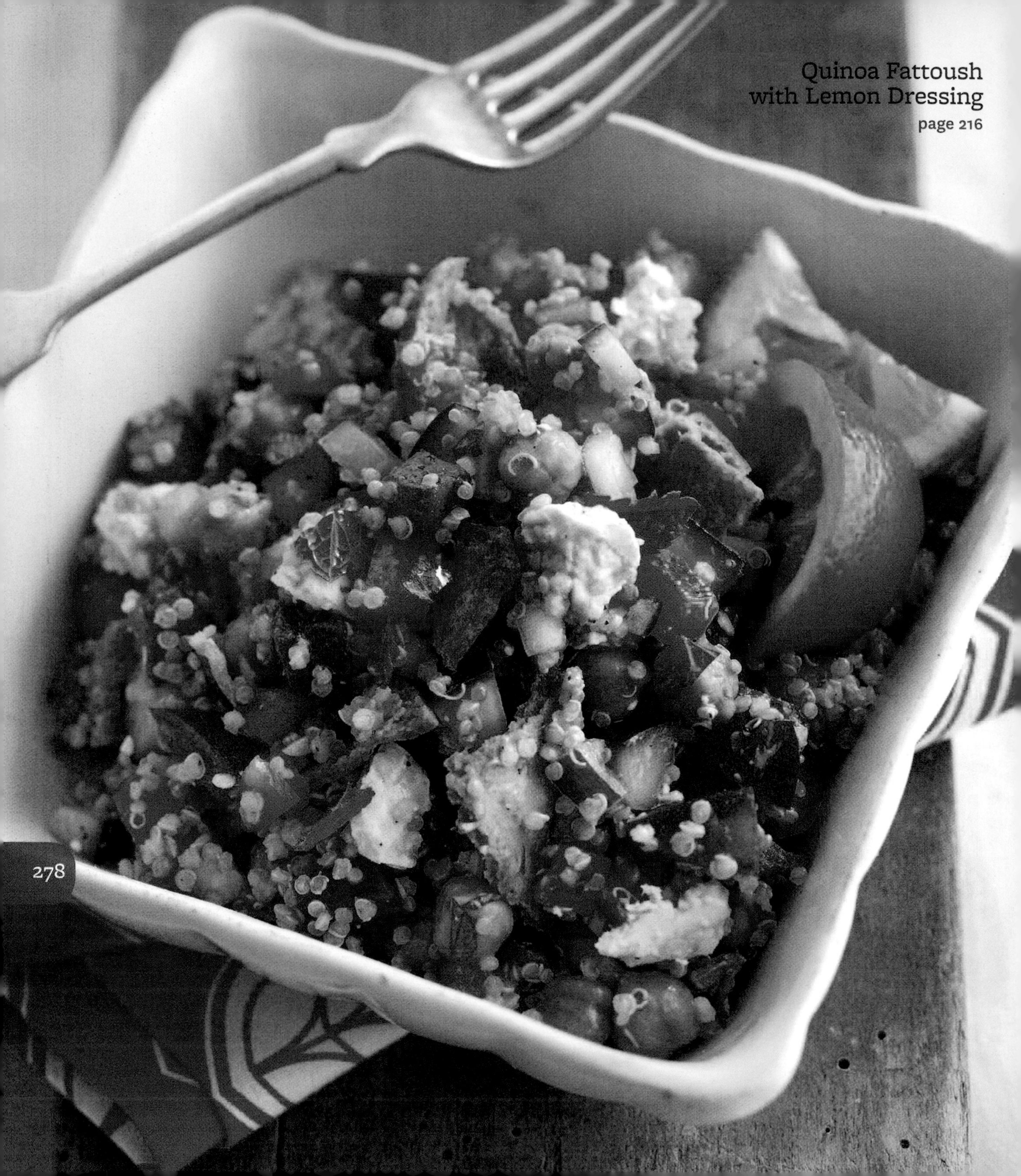

Quinoa Fattoush with Lemon Dressing

page 216

Fried Green Tomato Salad page 202

Grilled Tofu Curry page 257

Wild Rice Salad with Orange and Fennell page 224

Black Bean Chipotle Burgers page 232

Inside-Out Veggie Burgers page 239

Marinated Eggplant Kabobs page 254

Grilled Veg Sandwiches page 244

Chili Rellenos
page 292

Herbed Root Vegetable Cobbler **page 297**

284

Italian Pasta Gratin **page 307**

Zesty Vegetable Enchiladas **page 289**

Triple Pepper Nachos
page 327

Falafels
page 336

286

Portobello Curry with Green Rice page 362

287

Sage-White Bean Soup page 400

Spicy Veggie Stew page 371

Wild Rice–Mushroom Soup page 387

Roasted French Onion Soup page 377

Creamy Pumpkin Soup page 389

Wonton Soup page 380

Zesty Vegetable Enchiladas

PREP: 40 minutes BAKE: 15 minutes OVEN: 350°F MAKES 4 servings

1⅓   cups water

½   cup brown lentils, rinsed and drained

    Nonstick cooking spray

8   7- to 8-inch flour tortillas

1   cup thinly sliced carrots (2 medium)

2   small zucchini and/or yellow summer squash, quartered lengthwise and sliced (2 cups)

1   teaspoon ground cumin

1   8-ounce can tomato sauce

1   cup shredded reduced-fat Monterey Jack cheese (4 ounces)

    Dash bottled hot pepper sauce (optional)

1   14.5-ounce can Mexican-style stewed tomatoes, undrained and cut up

    Fresh cilantro sprigs (optional)

1 In a medium saucepan combine the water and lentils. Bring to boiling; reduce heat. Simmer, covered, about 30 minutes or until tender; drain.

2 Meanwhile, preheat oven to 350°F. Coat a 2-quart rectangular baking dish with cooking spray; set aside. Stack and wrap tortillas tightly in foil. Bake about 10 minutes or until warm.

3 Lightly coat a large skillet with cooking spray; heat skillet over medium heat. Add carrots; cook and stir for 2 minutes. Add zucchini and/or yellow squash and cumin; cook and stir for 2 to 3 minutes or until vegetables are crisp-tender. Remove from heat. Stir in cooked lentils, tomato sauce, ¾ cup of the cheese, and, if desired, hot pepper sauce.

4 Divide lentil mixture among warm tortillas; roll up tortillas. Arrange tortilla rolls, seam sides down, in the prepared baking dish. Sprinkle with the remaining ¼ cup cheese. Spoon undrained tomatoes over tortilla rolls.

5 Bake, uncovered, for 15 to 20 minutes or until heated through. If desired, garnish with cilantro.

PER SERVING: *450 cal., 15 g total fat (4 g sat. fat), 20 mg chol., 929 mg sodium, 57 g carb., 11 g fiber, 22 g pro.*

289

make it vegan 🌿

Substitute desired soy cheese for the Monterey Jack cheese.

tip

Cut fat in casseroles by using reduced-fat versions of cream soups, cheeses, sauces, and milk and avoiding high-fat toppers such as potato chips.

Potato Enchiladas

PREP: 40 minutes   BAKE: 35 minutes   OVEN: 350°F   MAKES 8 servings

- 2 pounds baking potatoes, peeled and quartered
- 3 tablespoons butter
- ½ teaspoon ground cumin
- ⅛ teaspoon cayenne pepper
- 4 to 6 tablespoons milk
- 1 4-ounce can diced green chile peppers, drained
- 8 7- to 8-inch flour tortillas
- 1 10.75-ounce can condensed cream of celery soup
- 1 8-ounce carton sour cream
- ¾ cup milk
- 1 cup shredded Colby and Monterey Jack cheese or taco cheese (4 ounces)
- Sliced pitted ripe olives (optional)
- Sliced green onions (optional)

1 Preheat oven to 350°F. Grease a 3-quart rectangular baking dish; set aside. In a covered medium saucepan cook potatoes in enough boiling, lightly salted water to cover for 20 to 25 minutes or until tender; drain. Mash with a potato masher or beat with an electric mixer on low speed. Add butter, cumin, and cayenne pepper. Gradually beat in enough of the 4 to 6 tablespoons milk to make potatoes light and fluffy. Stir in drained chile peppers.

2 Meanwhile, stack and wrap tortillas tightly in foil. Bake about 10 minutes or until warm.

3 Divide potato mixture evenly among warm tortillas; roll up tortillas. Place tortilla rolls, seam sides down, in the prepared baking dish. In a medium bowl stir together soup, sour cream, and ¾ cup milk. Pour soup mixture over tortilla rolls.

4 Bake, covered, for 30 minutes. Sprinkle with cheese. Bake, uncovered, for 5 to 10 minutes more or until heated through and cheese is melted. If desired, top with olives and green onions.

PER SERVING: *359 cal., 20 g total fat (11 g sat. fat), 44 mg chol., 643 mg sodium, 36 g carb., 2 g fiber, 9 g pro.*

Lasagna Ole

PREP: **35 minutes** BAKE: **30 minutes** STAND: **10 minutes** OVEN: **375°F** MAKES **6 to 8 servings**

½ cup chopped onion (1 medium)

2 tablespoons olive oil

6 cloves garlic, minced

5 cups sliced fresh mushrooms

1¼ cups sliced yellow summer squash (1 medium)

¾ cup chopped red sweet pepper (1 medium)

½ cup frozen whole kernel corn

1 6-ounce package fresh baby spinach

3 eggs

2 cups cream-style cottage cheese

1½ cups crumbled Cotija cheese or shredded mozzarella cheese (6 ounces)

½ cup fresh cilantro leaves

10 6-inch corn tortillas

1¾ cups salsa

1 Preheat oven to 375°F. Lightly grease a 2-quart baking dish; set aside. In an extra-large skillet cook onion in hot oil over medium heat about 5 minutes or until tender, stirring occasionally. Add garlic; cook and stir for 30 seconds. Add mushrooms, squash, sweet pepper, and corn. Cook and stir for 5 to 7 minutes or until mushrooms are tender and squash is crisp-tender. Stir in spinach. Cook and stir just until spinach starts to wilt. Set aside.

2 In a food processor or blender combine eggs, cottage cheese, and 1¼ cups of the Cotija cheese. Cover and process or blend until well mixed. Add cilantro. Cover and process or blend with several on/off pulses until cilantro is chopped.

3 To assemble, arrange 5 of the tortillas in the bottom of the prepared baking dish, cutting as necessary to fit. Spread with cheese mixture and vegetable mixture. Top with the remaining 5 tortillas, cutting as necessary to fit. Spread with salsa; sprinkle with the remaining ¼ cup Cotija cheese.

4 Bake, uncovered, for 30 to 40 minutes or until mixture is set. Let stand for 10 minutes before serving.

PER SERVING: *441 cal., 22 g total fat (9 g sat. fat), 152 mg chol., 1,163 mg sodium, 39 g carb., 7 g fiber, 26 g pro.*

Casseroles

Chile Rellenos

PREP: 25 minutes BAKE: 15 minutes STAND: 5 minutes OVEN: 450°F MAKES 4 servings

2 large fresh poblano chile peppers,* Anaheim chile peppers,* or green sweet peppers

1 cup shredded reduced-fat Mexican cheese blend (4 ounces)

1 to 2 fresh jalapeño chile peppers, seeded and finely chopped*

1½ cups refrigerated or frozen egg product, thawed, or 6 eggs, lightly beaten

⅓ cup milk

⅓ cup all-purpose flour

½ teaspoon baking powder

¼ teaspoon cayenne pepper

Pico de gallo, picante sauce, and/or light sour cream (optional)

1 Preheat oven to 450°F. Generously grease two 14- to 16-ounce baking dishes or four 8- to 10-ounce au gratin dishes; set aside. Halve peppers lengthwise; remove seeds and membranes. Immerse peppers into boiling water for 3 minutes; drain. Invert peppers on paper towels to drain well. Place pepper halves, cut sides up, in the prepared dishes. Top with cheese and chopped jalapeño pepper(s).

2 In a medium bowl combine egg and milk. Beat in flour, baking powder, and cayenne pepper until smooth. Pour egg mixture evenly over peppers and cheese.

3 Bake, uncovered, about 15 minutes or until a knife inserted in the egg mixture comes out clean. Let stand for 5 minutes before serving. If desired, serve with pico de gallo, picante sauce, and/or sour cream. If using the 14- to 16-ounce dishes, each dish will serve two.

PER SERVING: *206 cal., 6 g total fat (4 g sat. fat), 17 mg chol., 470 mg sodium, 17 g carb., 1 g fiber, 19 g pro.*

*tip

Because chile peppers contain volatile oils that can burn your skin and eyes, avoid direct contact with them as much as possible. When working with chile peppers, wear plastic or rubber gloves. If your bare hands do touch the peppers, wash your hands and nails well with soap and warm water.

Chiles and Cheese Individual Casseroles

PREP: 25 minutes CHILL: 2 to 24 hours BAKE: 40 minutes STAND: 10 minutes OVEN: 350°F MAKES 4 servings

2   4-ounce cans whole green chile peppers, drained

1   cup fresh asparagus cut into 1-inch pieces or frozen cut asparagus, thawed

1   small red onion, quartered and thinly sliced

1   tablespoon butter

1   cup shredded Monterey Jack cheese with jalapeño peppers or Monterey Jack cheese (4 ounces)

1   tablespoon all-purpose flour

4   eggs, lightly beaten

1¼ cups half-and-half, light cream, or milk

¼   teaspoon salt

¼   teaspoon ground black pepper

½   cup chopped tomato (1 medium)

1 Lightly grease four 12- to 16-ounce au gratin dishes; set aside. Pat chile peppers with paper towels to remove excess liquid. Make a slit along 1 side of each pepper and lay flat. Discard any seeds. Pat again with paper towels. Arrange chile peppers in a single layer in the prepared au gratin dishes, cutting as necessary to fit.

2 In a medium skillet cook asparagus and onion in hot butter over medium heat about 5 minutes or just until tender, stirring occasionally. Divide asparagus mixture among au gratin dishes. In a small bowl combine cheese and flour; toss gently to coat. Divide cheese among dishes.

3 In a medium bowl combine eggs, half-and-half, salt, and black pepper. Pour egg mixture evenly over ingredients in dishes. Cover and chill for 2 to 24 hours.

4 Preheat oven to 350°F. Place au gratin dishes in a 15x10x1-inch baking pan. Bake, uncovered, for 40 to 45 minutes or until egg mixture is set. Let stand for 10 minutes before serving. Sprinkle with tomato.

PER SERVING: *342 cal., 26 g total fat (14 g sat. fat), 272 mg chol., 578 mg sodium, 11 g carb., 1 g fiber, 18 g pro.*

293

Chilaquile Casserole

PREP: 20 minutes   BAKE: 35 minutes   STAND: 15 minutes   OVEN: 375°F   MAKES 8 servings

- 1 cup chopped onion (1 large)
- 2 cloves garlic, minced
- 1 tablespoon vegetable oil
- 12 6-inch corn tortillas, cut into 1-inch pieces
- 2 cups shredded Monterey Jack cheese (8 ounces)
- 2 4-ounce cans diced green chile peppers, undrained
- 4 eggs, lightly beaten
- 2 cups buttermilk or sour milk*
- ½ teaspoon salt
- ¼ teaspoon ground black pepper
- ⅛ teaspoon ground cumin
- ⅛ teaspoon dried oregano, crushed
- Salsa (optional)

1 Preheat oven to 375°F. In a large skillet cook onion and garlic in hot oil over medium heat until onion is tender, stirring occasionally.

2 Meanwhile, grease a 2-quart rectangular baking dish. Spread half of the tortilla pieces in the bottom of the prepared baking dish. Top with half of the cheese and 1 can of the undrained chile peppers. Sprinkle with onion mixture. Top with the remaining tortilla pieces, cheese, and chile peppers.

3 In a large bowl combine eggs, buttermilk, salt, black pepper, cumin, and oregano. Pour evenly over ingredients in dish.

4 Bake, uncovered, for 35 to 40 minutes or until center is set and edges are lightly browned. Let stand for 15 minutes before serving. If desired, top with salsa.

PER SERVING: *284 cal., 15 g total fat (7 g sat. fat), 133 mg chol., 507 mg sodium, 25 g carb., 4 g fiber, 15 g pro.*

294

*tip

To make 2 cups sour milk, place 2 tablespoons lemon juice or vinegar in a glass measuring cup. Add enough milk to make 2 cups total liquid; stir. Let stand for 5 minutes before using.

Corn and Polenta Bake

PREP: 25 minutes   BAKE: 50 minutes   OVEN: 325°F   MAKES 12 servings

2   cups fresh corn kernels
     (4 ears) or frozen whole
     kernel corn
1   cup chopped green sweet
     pepper
½   cup chopped onion
     (1 medium)
2   cloves garlic, minced
2   tablespoons vegetable oil
2   16-ounce tubes refrigerated
     cooked polenta
6   eggs, lightly beaten
1   tablespoon stone-ground
     mustard or Dijon-style
     mustard
1   teaspoon sugar
¾   teaspoon salt
¼   to ½ teaspoon coarse ground
     black pepper
1½   cups soft bread crumbs
     (2 slices)
2   tablespoons butter, melted

1 Preheat oven to 325°F. Lightly grease a 2-quart rectangular baking dish; set aside. In a large saucepan cook corn, sweet pepper, onion, and garlic in hot oil over medium heat about 5 minutes or just until tender, stirring occasionally.

2 Crumble polenta; set aside. In a large bowl combine eggs, mustard, sugar, salt, and black pepper. Stir in cooked vegetables and crumbled polenta. Transfer mixture to the prepared baking dish.

3 In a small bowl combine bread crumbs and melted butter; sprinkle over polenta mixture. Bake, uncovered, about 50 minutes or until a knife inserted near center comes out clean.

PER SERVING: *185 cal., 7 g total fat (2 g sat. fat), 111 mg chol., 551 mg sodium, 24 g carb., 3 g fiber, 7 g pro.*

Spinach Cannelloni with Fontina

PREP: 35 minutes BAKE: 25 minutes STAND: 10 minutes OVEN: 375°F MAKES 5 servings

- 1 **cup chopped fennel (1 medium)**
- 3 **cloves garlic, minced**
- 1 **tablespoon olive oil**
- 1 **6-ounce package fresh baby spinach**
- 1 **egg, lightly beaten**
- 1 **15-ounce carton ricotta cheese**
- 2/3 **cup finely shredded Parmesan cheese**
- 1/2 **teaspoon dried Italian seasoning, crushed**
- 1/2 **teaspoon finely shredded lemon peel**
- 1 **17-ounce jar marinara sauce**
- 1 **4.5- to 5-ounce package (10) ready-to-use crepes**
- 1 **10-ounce container refrigerated Alfredo pasta sauce**
- 1 **cup shredded fontina cheese (4 ounces)**

1 Preheat oven to 375°F. For filling, in an extra-large skillet cook fennel and garlic in hot oil over medium heat for 3 to 4 minutes or until tender, stirring occasionally. Add spinach; cook, covered, about 2 minutes or until wilted. Transfer spinach mixture to a sieve; press out excess liquid with the back of a large spoon. In a large bowl combine egg, ricotta cheese, Parmesan cheese, Italian seasoning, and lemon peel. Stir in spinach mixture.

2 Spread half of the marinara sauce in the bottom of an ungreased 3-quart rectangular baking dish. Spoon about 1/3 cup of the filling along the center of each crepe; roll up crepe. Arrange crepes, seam sides down, on marinara sauce in dish. Spoon the remaining marinara sauce over crepes down center of dish. Pour Alfredo sauce over crepes, spreading evenly. Sprinkle with fontina cheese.

3 Bake, uncovered, for 25 to 30 minutes or until edges are bubbly. Let stand for 10 minutes before serving.

PER SERVING: *672 cal., 47 g total fat (15 g sat. fat), 159 mg chol., 1,297 mg sodium, 36 g carb., 4 g fiber, 28 g pro.*

Herbed Root Vegetable Cobbler

PREP: 35 minutes BAKE: 1 hour 12 minutes STAND: 20 minutes OVEN: 400°F MAKES 12 servings

1 pound Yukon gold potatoes, cut into 1-inch pieces

1 pound rutabagas, peeled and cut into 1-inch pieces

4 medium carrots, cut into 1-inch pieces

2 medium parsnips, peeled and cut into 1-inch pieces

1 small red onion, cut into thin wedges

2 cloves garlic, minced

1 cup vegetable broth

1½ teaspoons dried fines herbes, herbes de Provence, or Italian seasoning, crushed

½ teaspoon salt

¼ teaspoon ground black pepper

1 4- to 5.2-ounce container semisoft cheese with garlic and herbs

1 recipe Herbed Parmesan Dumplings

1 Preheat oven to 400°F. In an ungreased 3-quart baking dish combine potatoes, rutabagas, carrots, parsnips, red onion, and garlic.

2 In a small bowl combine broth, fines herbes, salt, and pepper. Pour broth mixture over vegetables, stirring to coat. Bake, covered, about 1 hour or until vegetables are nearly tender. Stir in cheese.

3 Drop Herbed Parmesan Dumplings into 12 mounds on top of hot vegetables. Bake, uncovered, for 12 to 15 minutes more or until a toothpick inserted in centers of dumplings comes out clean. Let stand for 20 minutes before serving.

PER SERVING: *233 cal., 12 g total fat (7 g sat. fat), 53 mg chol., 497 mg sodium, 28 g carb., 3 g fiber, 6 g pro.*

Herbed Parmesan Dumplings

In a medium bowl stir together 1½ cups all-purpose flour; 2 teaspoons baking powder; 1½ teaspoons dried fines herbes, herbes de Provence, or Italian seasoning, crushed; and ½ teaspoon salt. Using a pastry blender cut in 6 tablespoons butter until mixture resembles coarse crumbs. Stir in ¼ cup finely shredded Parmesan cheese (1 ounce). In a small bowl combine 2 lightly beaten eggs and ⅓ cup milk. Add all at once to flour mixture, stirring just until moistened.

Layered Potatoes and Leeks

PREP: 35 minutes   BAKE: 35 minutes   STAND: 10 minutes   OVEN: 400°F   MAKES 4 servings

- 1 **pound potatoes (3 medium), sliced ¼ inch thick**
- 2 **tablespoons olive oil or vegetable oil**
- 3 **cups sliced fresh mushrooms (8 ounces)**
- ⅔ **cup thinly sliced leeks (2 medium)**
- 2 **cloves garlic, minced**
- ½ **teaspoon dried rosemary, crushed**
- ¼ **teaspoon salt**
- ½ **cup whipping cream**
- ¾ **cup shredded Parmesan cheese (3 ounces)**
- **Sour cream (optional)**

1 Preheat oven to 400°F. Grease a 1½-quart soufflé dish or casserole; set aside. In a covered medium saucepan cook potatoes in enough boiling, lightly salted water to cover for 3 minutes (potatoes will not be tender). Drain and cool slightly.

2 Meanwhile, in a large skillet heat 1 tablespoon of the oil over medium heat. Add mushrooms, leeks, garlic, rosemary, and salt; cook until leek is tender, stirring occasionally. Stir in cream. Bring to boiling; reduce heat. Boil gently, uncovered, about 30 seconds or until slightly thickened.

3 To assemble, arrange 1 cup of the potato slices in the bottom of the prepared soufflé dish or casserole, overlapping if necessary. Spoon one-third of the leek mixture over potatoes in dish; sprinkle with ¼ cup of the cheese. Repeat layering potatoes, leek mixture, and cheese. Top with the remaining potatoes and the remaining leek mixture; drizzle with the remaining 1 tablespoon oil.

4 Bake, uncovered, for 30 minutes. Sprinkle with the remaining ¼ cup cheese. Bake for 5 to 10 minutes more or until potatoes are tender. Cover and let stand for 10 minutes before serving. If desired, serve with sour cream.

PER SERVING: *345 cal., 24 g total fat (11 g sat. fat), 54 mg chol., 398 mg sodium, 26 g carb., 3 g fiber, 11 g pro.*

Zucchini and Eggplant Bake

PREP: 35 minutes BAKE: 20 minutes STAND: 10 minutes OVEN: 350°F MAKES 6 to 8 servings

5 cups peeled and coarsely chopped eggplant (1 medium)

4 cups thinly sliced zucchini (3 medium)

2 cups coarsely chopped red sweet peppers (3 medium)

1 cup coarsely chopped onion (1 large)

2 cloves garlic, minced

½ teaspoon salt

¼ teaspoon ground black pepper

3 tablespoons olive oil

4 eggs, lightly beaten

½ cup light mayonnaise

2 cups shredded mozzarella cheese (8 ounces)

1 cup grated Pecorino-Romano cheese (4 ounces)

12 rich round crackers, crushed (about ⅔ cup)

1 Preheat oven to 350°F. Grease a 3-quart rectangular baking dish; set aside. In an extra-large skillet cook eggplant, zucchini, sweet peppers, onion, garlic, salt, and black pepper in hot oil over medium-high heat for 10 to 15 minutes or until vegetables are tender, stirring occasionally.

2 Meanwhile, in an extra-large bowl combine eggs and mayonnaise. Stir in 1 cup of the mozzarella cheese and the Pecorino-Romano cheese. Stir in cooked vegetables. Transfer vegetable mixture to the prepared baking dish. Sprinkle with the remaining 1 cup mozzarella cheese and crushed crackers.

3 Bake, uncovered, for 20 to 25 minutes or until top is lightly browned and a knife inserted near center comes out clean. Let stand 10 minutes before serving.

PER SERVING: *440 cal., 32 g total fat (11 g sat. fat), 188 mg chol., 942 mg sodium, 21 g carb., 5 g fiber, 23 g pro.*

299

Cheesy Spaghetti Squash

PREP: 35 minutes BAKE: 35 minutes STAND: 10 minutes OVEN: 350°F MAKES 6 servings

- 1   2¼-pound spaghetti squash (1 medium)
- ¼   cup water
- 2   cups sliced fresh mushrooms
- ¾   cup chopped red or green sweet pepper (1 medium)
- ½   cup chopped onion (1 medium)
- 3   cloves garlic, minced
- 1   tablespoon olive oil
     Nonstick cooking spray
- ½   teaspoon dried Italian seasoning, crushed
- ⅛   teaspoon ground black pepper
- 1½ cups tomato-base pasta sauce
- 1   cup shredded mozzarella cheese (4 ounces)
- 2   tablespoons snipped fresh Italian (flat-leaf) parsley

1 Preheat oven to 350°F. Halve squash crosswise; remove seeds. Place squash, cut sides down, in a microwave-safe 2-quart rectangular baking dish. Add the water. Cover with vented plastic wrap. Microwave on 100 percent power (high) for 13 to 15 minutes or until squash is tender when pierced with a fork, turning dish once. Drain and cool slightly.

2 Meanwhile, in a large skillet cook mushrooms, sweet pepper, onion, and garlic in hot oil over medium heat about 5 minutes or until vegetables are tender, stirring occasionally.

3 Using 2 forks, shred and separate squash pulp into strands (you should have about 3 cups). Wipe out the same baking dish; coat with cooking spray. Spread half of the squash in the prepared baking dish. Add half of the mushroom mixture; sprinkle with Italian seasoning and black pepper. Top with half of the pasta sauce and half of the cheese. Top with the remaining squash, mushroom mixture, and pasta sauce.

4 Bake, uncovered, for 30 minutes. Sprinkle with the remaining cheese. Bake about 5 minutes more or until cheese is melted. Let stand for 10 minutes before serving. Sprinkle with parsley.

PER SERVING: *170 cal., 7 g total fat (3 g sat. fat), 12 mg chol., 350 mg sodium, 21 g carb., 2 g fiber, 8 g pro.*

300

make it vegan
Substitute mozzarella-flavor soy cheese for the mozzarella cheese.

tip
Winter squashes, such as spaghetti squash, can be difficult to cut. For safety purposes, use a long sharp knife and cut on an even surface that won't slip, such as a cutting board with rubber feet. Make your cutting board nonslip by placing a damp paper towel underneath.

Summer Squash and Chard Gratin

PREP: **35 minutes** BAKE: **30 minutes** STAND: **10 minutes** OVEN: **350°F** MAKES **6 servings**

- 2 cups chopped onions (2 large)
- 1 tablespoon olive oil
- 6 cloves garlic, minced
- 3 cups sliced fresh mushrooms (8 ounces)
- 1½ pounds zucchini and/or yellow summer squash, thinly sliced (6 cups)
- 1 pound Swiss chard, stemmed and coarsely shredded (8 cups)
- 2 eggs, lightly beaten
- 1 cup part-skim ricotta cheese
- 1 cup light or fat-free milk
- ½ cup finely shredded Parmesan cheese (2 ounces)
- 2 tablespoons snipped fresh dill
- ½ teaspoon kosher salt
- ¼ teaspoon freshly ground black pepper

1 Preheat oven to 350°F. In an extra-large skillet cook onion in hot oil over medium heat about 5 minutes or until tender, stirring occasionally. Add garlic; cook and stir for 30 to 60 seconds or until tender. Add mushrooms; cook for 5 to 8 minutes or until mushrooms are light brown and liquid is evaporated, stirring occasionally.

2 In a covered large saucepan cook zucchini and Swiss chard in a small amount of boiling, lightly salted water for 3 to 5 minutes or until crisp-tender; drain well. Stir zucchini mixture into mushroom mixture. Transfer to an ungreased 2-quart baking dish or au gratin dish; set aside.

3 In a medium bowl combine eggs, ricotta cheese, milk, Parmesan cheese, dill, salt, and pepper. Spoon mixture over zucchini mixture, spreading evenly.

4 Bake, uncovered, for 30 to 35 minutes or until set and light brown on top (center should jiggle slightly when gently shaken). Let stand for 10 minutes before serving.

PER SERVING: *225 cal., 11 g total fat (5 g sat. fat), 92 mg chol., 590 mg sodium, 19 g carb., 4 g fiber, 16 g pro.*

Tomato-Olive Bread Pudding

PREP: 25 minutes BAKE: 1 hour STAND: 15 minutes OVEN: 325°F MAKES 6 servings

8   ounces crusty country Italian bread, cut into 1-inch cubes (about 8 cups)

1   14.5-ounce can diced tomatoes with basil, garlic, and oregano, drained

1   10-ounce package frozen chopped spinach, thawed and well drained

1   cup shredded Italian cheese blend (4 ounces)

½   cup chopped onion (1 medium)

⅓   cup pitted kalamata olives, quartered

2   cloves garlic, minced

4   eggs, lightly beaten, or 1 cup refrigerated or frozen egg product, thawed

2   cups half-and-half, light cream, or milk

¼   teaspoon crushed red pepper

1 Preheat oven to 325°F. Grease a 2-quart square baking dish; set aside. In an extra-large bowl toss together bread cubes, drained tomatoes, spinach, cheese, onion, olives, and garlic. Transfer bread mixture to the prepared baking dish.

2 In a large bowl combine eggs, half-and-half, and crushed red pepper. Pour evenly over mixture in baking dish. Using the back of a large spoon, press lightly (dish will be very full).

3 Bake, uncovered, for 60 to 65 minutes or until pudding is evenly puffed and temperature in center registers 170°F on an instant-read thermometer. Let stand for 15 minutes before serving.

PER SERVING: *328 cal., 16 g total fat (8 g sat. fat), 174 mg chol., 787 mg sodium, 33 g carb., 3 g fiber, 14 g pro.*

Chilly Veggie Pizza

PREP: 25 minutes BAKE: 8 minutes CHILL: 2 to 4 hours OVEN: 375°F MAKES 6 servings

1   8-ounce package (8) refrigerated crescent rolls

1   8-ounce package cream cheese, softened

⅓   cup mayonnaise or salad dressing

2   tablespoons thinly sliced green onion (1)

½   teaspoon dried dill

½   cup shredded lettuce

⅓   cup sliced pitted ripe olives or pimiento-stuffed green olives

¼   cup chopped green and/or yellow sweet pepper

¼   cup chopped seeded cucumber

1   cup crumbled feta cheese with garlic and herbs (4 ounces)

½   cup chopped, seeded tomato (1 medium)

1 Preheat oven to 375°F. Lightly grease a 3-quart rectangular baking dish. Unroll crescent rolls. Press dough over the bottom and about ½ inch up the sides of the prepared baking dish; press dough perforations to seal. Bake for 8 to 10 minutes or until light brown. Cool.

2 Meanwhile, in a medium bowl combine cream cheese, mayonnaise, green onion, and dill. Carefully spread cream cheese mixture over cooled crust.

3 Top with lettuce, olives, sweet pepper, and cucumber. Sprinkle with feta cheese and tomato. Cover and chill for 2 to 4 hours before serving.

PER SERVING: *408 cal., 31 g total fat (14 g sat. fat), 68 mg chol., 706 mg sodium, 23 g carb., 2 g fiber, 11 g pro.*

Nutty Gorgonzola Roll-Ups

PREP: **40 minutes** BAKE: **40 minutes** OVEN: **375°F** MAKES **8 servings**

- 8   dried lasagna noodles
- 12 ounces cream cheese, softened
- 2   cups shredded Italian cheese blend (8 ounces)
- 1   cup crumbled Gorgonzola or other blue cheese (4 ounces)
- 1   cup chopped walnuts, toasted
- 2   tablespoons snipped fresh basil or 2 teaspoons dried basil, crushed
- 1   26-ounce jar tomato-basil pasta sauce
     Shredded fresh basil (optional)
     Freshly ground black pepper (optional)
- 6   cups shredded fresh spinach leaves

1 Preheat oven to 375°F. Cook lasagna noodles according to package directions; drain. Rinse with cold water; drain again. Place noodles in a single layer on a sheet of foil; set aside.

2 Meanwhile, in a large bowl combine cream cheese, Italian cheese, Gorgonzola cheese, ¾ cup of the walnuts, and the snipped or dried basil. Spread cheese mixture evenly over lasagna noodles. Roll up each noodle into a spiral.

3 Place lasagna rolls, seam sides down, in an ungreased 2-quart rectangular baking dish. Top with pasta sauce. Bake, covered, about 40 minutes or until heated through.

4 Sprinkle with the remaining ¼ cup walnuts. If desired, sprinkle with shredded basil and pepper. Serve lasagna rolls on spinach, spooning sauce in dish over rolls.

PER SERVING: *513 cal., 37 g total fat (17 g sat. fat), 77 mg chol., 813 mg sodium, 28 g carb., 4 g fiber, 21 g pro.*

Cheese 'n' Nut Stuffed Shells

PREP: 45 minutes BAKE: 45 minutes OVEN: 350°F MAKES 6 servings

24 dried jumbo shell macaroni*
2   eggs, lightly beaten
1   15-ounce carton ricotta cheese
1½ cups shredded mozzarella cheese (6 ounces)
1   cup shredded Parmesan cheese (4 ounces)
1   cup chopped walnuts
1   tablespoon snipped fresh parsley
½   teaspoon salt
¼   teaspoon ground black pepper
⅛   teaspoon ground nutmeg
1   26-ounce jar thick and chunky tomato-base pasta sauce

1 Preheat oven to 350°F. Cook pasta according to package directions; drain. Rinse with cold water; drain again.

2 Meanwhile, for filling, in a large bowl combine eggs, ricotta cheese, 1 cup of the mozzarella cheese, ¾ cup of the Parmesan cheese, the walnuts, parsley, salt, pepper, and nutmeg.

3 Spread 1 cup of the pasta sauce in the bottom of an ungreased 3-quart rectangular baking dish. Spoon 1 heaping tablespoon of the filling into each pasta shell. Arrange filled shells, filling sides up, on sauce in baking dish.

4 Spoon the remaining pasta sauce over shells. Sprinkle with the remaining ½ cup mozzarella cheese and the remaining ¼ cup Parmesan cheese. Bake, covered, about 45 minutes or until heated through.

PER SERVING: *549 cal., 32 g total fat (12 g sat. fat), 132 mg chol., 1,072 mg sodium, 36 g carb., 4 g fiber, 30 g pro.*

*tip
Cook a few extra shells to replace any that tear during cooking.

Baked Stuffed Shells

PREP: 40 minutes BAKE: 37 minutes STAND: 10 minutes OVEN: 350°F MAKES 6 servings

½ cup chopped onion (1 medium)

2 cloves garlic, minced

1 teaspoon olive oil

1 14.5-ounce can no-salt-added diced tomatoes, undrained

1 8-ounce can no-salt-added tomato sauce

1 tablespoon snipped fresh basil or ½ teaspoon dried basil, crushed

2 teaspoons snipped fresh oregano or ½ teaspoon dried oregano, crushed

¼ teaspoon salt

12 dried jumbo shell macaroni*

1 12.3-ounce package extra-firm, silken-style tofu (fresh bean curd)

¼ cup refrigerated or frozen egg product, thawed, or 1 egg, lightly beaten

½ cup finely shredded Parmesan or Romano cheese (2 ounces)

¼ teaspoon ground black pepper

½ cup shredded reduced-fat mozzarella cheese (2 ounces)

2 tablespoons shredded fresh basil (optional)

1 Preheat oven to 350°F. For sauce, in a medium saucepan cook onion and garlic in hot oil over medium heat about 3 minutes or until onion is tender, stirring occasionally. Stir in undrained tomatoes, tomato sauce, dried basil and oregano (if using), and salt. Bring to boiling; reduce heat. Simmer, uncovered, about 15 minutes or until desired consistency. Remove from heat; stir in snipped basil and oregano (if using). Set aside ¾ cup of the sauce; spread the remaining sauce in the bottom of an ungreased 2-quart rectangular baking dish.

2 Meanwhile, cook pasta according to package directions; drain. Rinse with cold water; drain again.

3 For filling, place tofu in a blender or food processor; cover and blend or process until smooth. Add egg, Parmesan cheese, and pepper; cover and blend or process just until combined. Spoon about 3 tablespoons of the filling into each pasta shell. Arrange filled shells, filling sides up, on sauce in baking dish. Spoon the reserved ¾ cup sauce over shells.

4 Bake, covered, about 35 minutes or until heated through. Sprinkle with mozzarella cheese. Bake, uncovered, about 2 minutes more or until cheese is melted. Let stand for 10 minutes before serving. If desired, sprinkle with shredded basil.

PER SERVING: *234 cal., 5 g total fat (2 g sat. fat), 10 mg chol., 357 mg sodium, 32 g carb., 3 g fiber, 14 g pro.*

*tip
Cook a few extra shells to replace any that tear during cooking.

Tofu Manicotti

PREP: 40 minutes   BAKE: 32 minutes   STAND: 10 minutes   OVEN: 350°F   MAKES 4 servings

8   dried manicotti shells
    Nonstick cooking spray
1   cup chopped fresh
    mushrooms
½   cup chopped green onions (4)
1   teaspoon dried Italian
    seasoning, crushed
1   12- to 16-ounce package
    soft tofu (fresh bean curd),
    drained
1   egg, lightly beaten
¼   cup finely shredded Parmesan
    cheese (1 ounce)
1   14.5-ounce can diced tomatoes
    with basil, garlic, and
    oregano, undrained
1   11-ounce can condensed
    tomato bisque
⅛   teaspoon ground black pepper
¾   cup shredded Italian cheese
    blend (3 ounces)

1 Cook manicotti shells according to package directions; drain. Rinse with cold water; drain again.

2 Meanwhile, preheat oven to 350°F. Coat a medium skillet with cooking spray; heat skillet over medium heat. Add mushrooms and green onions; cook until tender, stirring occasionally. Stir in Italian seasoning; set aside.

3 In a medium bowl mash tofu with a potato masher or fork. Stir in mushroom mixture, egg, and Parmesan cheese. Using a small spoon, carefully fill each cooked manicotti shell with about ¼ cup of the tofu mixture. Arrange filled shells in 4 ungreased 12- to 15-ounce au gratin dishes or 1 ungreased 3-quart rectangular baking dish.

4 In a medium bowl combine undrained tomatoes, tomato bisque, and pepper. Pour tomato mixture over filled shells.

5 Bake, uncovered, about 30 minutes or until heated through. Sprinkle with Italian cheese. Bake about 2 minutes more or until cheese is melted. Let stand for 10 minutes before serving.

PER SERVING: *411 cal., 13 g total fat (6 g sat. fat), 74 mg chol., 1,383 mg sodium, 53 g carb., 4 g fiber, 21 g pro.*

tip
Boil pasta until just tender before adding it to a casserole. Overcooked pasta will continue to cook in the oven and will get overly soft and lose its shape.

Italian Pasta Gratin

PREP: **30 minutes** BAKE: **30 minutes** STAND: **5 minutes** OVEN: **375°F** MAKES **8 servings**

- 8 **ounces dried multigrain or whole wheat penne pasta**
- 4 **cups fresh baby spinach**
- 2 **cups fresh cremini mushrooms, quartered**
- ½ **cup coarsely chopped oil-packed dried tomatoes***
- ¼ **cup chopped pitted kalamata olives**
- ½ **cup basil pesto**
- 2 **tablespoons balsamic vinegar**
- 8 **ounces fresh mozzarella cheese, cut into chunks or thinly sliced**
- ½ **cup shredded fresh basil (optional)**

1 Preheat oven to 375°F. Lightly grease four 12-ounce individual casseroles or one 1½-quart au gratin dish; set aside. In a 4-quart Dutch oven cook pasta in boiling, lightly salted water according to package directions, adding spinach and mushrooms during the last 1 minute of cooking; drain.

2 Transfer pasta mixture to an extra-large bowl. Stir in dried tomatoes and olives. Add pesto and vinegar; toss gently to coat. Transfer mixture to the prepared casseroles or au gratin dish.

3 Bake, covered, for 20 to 25 minutes or until heated through. Top with cheese. Bake, uncovered, about 10 minutes more or until cheese is melted. Let stand for 5 minutes before serving. If desired, sprinkle with basil. If using individual casseroles, each dish will serve two.

PER SERVING: *324 cal., 18 g total fat (4 g sat. fat), 25 mg chol., 438 mg sodium, 27 g carb., 3 g fiber, 15 g pro.*

*tip

If the dried tomatoes are very firm, add them to some of the hot pasta cooking water and let stand for 5 minutes. Drain well, then add to the pasta mixture as directed.

Casseroles

Tortellini-Vegetable Bake

PREP: 30 minutes BAKE: 30 minutes OVEN: 350°F MAKES 8 servings

- 2 9-ounce packages refrigerated cheese tortellini
- 1½ cups fresh sugar snap peas, trimmed and halved crosswise
- ½ cup thinly sliced carrot (1 medium)
- 1 tablespoon butter
- 1 cup sliced fresh mushrooms
- ⅓ cup vegetable broth
- 2 teaspoons all-purpose flour
- 1½ teaspoons dried oregano, crushed
- ½ teaspoon garlic salt
- ½ teaspoon ground black pepper
- 1 cup milk
- 1 8-ounce package cream cheese, cubed and softened
- 1 tablespoon lemon juice
- 1 cup quartered cherry tomatoes
- ½ cup coarsely chopped red or green sweet pepper (1 small)
- 2 tablespoons grated Parmesan cheese

1 Preheat oven to 350°F. Cook tortellini according to package directions, adding sugar snap peas and carrot during the last 1 minute of cooking; drain.

2 Meanwhile, in an extra-large skillet heat butter over medium heat. Add mushrooms; cook about 5 minutes or until mushrooms are tender, stirring occasionally. Remove from skillet.

3 In a screw-top jar combine broth, flour, oregano, garlic salt, and black pepper. Cover and shake until smooth. Add to the same skillet; add milk. Cook and stir until thickened and bubbly. Add cream cheese; cook and stir until cream cheese is smooth. Remove from heat; stir in lemon juice.

4 Stir tortellini mixture, mushrooms, tomatoes, and sweet pepper into cream cheese mixture. Transfer mixture to an ungreased 3-quart rectangular baking dish. Bake, covered, about 30 minutes or until heated through. Sprinkle with Parmesan cheese.

PER SERVING: *353 cal., 17 g total fat (9 g sat. fat), 69 mg chol., 468 mg sodium, 37 g carb., 1 g fiber, 15 g pro.*

tip

Refrigerated pastas are usually sold in the dairy case or other refrigerated sections of the grocery store. They cost more than dried pasta but take less time to cook.

Broccoli-Cauliflower Tetrazzini

PREP: 35 minutes BAKE: 15 minutes OVEN: 400°F MAKES 4 servings

8   ounces dried fettuccine or spaghetti, broken

1   16-ounce package frozen broccoli, cauliflower, and carrots

2   tablespoons butter

3   tablespoons all-purpose flour

2½ cups milk

½   cup grated Parmesan cheese

¼   teaspoon salt

¼   teaspoon ground black pepper

1   4-ounce can (drained weight) sliced mushrooms, drained

2   tablespoons grated Parmesan cheese

1 Preheat oven to 400°F. Lightly grease a 3-quart rectangular baking dish; set aside. Cook pasta according to package directions; drain. Return pasta to hot pan. Cook frozen vegetables according to package directions; drain.

2 Meanwhile, for cheese sauce, in a medium saucepan melt butter over medium heat. Stir in flour. Gradually stir in milk. Cook and stir until slightly thickened and bubbly. Cook and stir for 1 minute more. Remove from heat. Stir in ½ cup Parmesan cheese, salt, and pepper.

3 Pour ½ cup of the cheese sauce over cooked pasta; toss gently to coat. Spread pasta mixture evenly in the prepared baking dish. Top with cooked vegetables and drained mushrooms. Pour the remaining cheese sauce over mixture in dish. Sprinkle with 2 tablespoons Parmesan cheese.

4 Bake, uncovered, about 15 minutes or until heated through.

PER SERVING: *456 cal., 13 g total fat (8 g sat. fat), 38 mg chol., 602 mg sodium, 61 g carb., 5 g fiber, 21 g pro.*

Make-Ahead Directions: Prepare as directed through Step 3. Cover and chill for 2 to 24 hours. To serve, preheat oven to 400°F. Bake, covered, for 15 minutes. Bake, uncovered, for 10 to 15 minutes more or until heated through.

Vegetable Primavera Casserole

PREP: 30 minutes   BAKE: 30 minutes   STAND: 5 minutes   OVEN: 375°F   MAKES 8 servings

6   ounces dried elbow macaroni

1   16-ounce package frozen vegetable blend (any combination)

2   medium zucchini, halved lengthwise and sliced (about 2½ cups)

½   cup chopped red sweet pepper (1 small)

2   12-ounce cans evaporated milk

1   cup vegetable broth

⅓   cup all-purpose flour

1   teaspoon dried oregano, crushed

½   teaspoon salt

½   teaspoon garlic powder

½   teaspoon ground black pepper

¾   cup grated Parmesan or Romano cheese

1   medium tomato, halved lengthwise and sliced

1 Preheat oven to 375°F. Lightly grease a 3-quart rectangular baking dish; set aside. In a 4- to 5-quart Dutch oven cook macaroni in a large amount of boiling, lightly salted water for 8 minutes, adding frozen vegetables, zucchini, and sweet pepper during the last 3 minutes of cooking; drain. Return macaroni mixture to hot Dutch oven.

2 Meanwhile, in a medium saucepan whisk together evaporated milk, broth, flour, oregano, salt, garlic powder, and black pepper. Cook and stir over medium heat until thickened and bubbly. Pour over macaroni mixture, stirring to coat. Stir in ½ cup of the cheese. Transfer macaroni mixture to the prepared baking dish.

3 Bake, uncovered, for 25 minutes. Top with tomato and the remaining ¼ cup cheese. Bake about 5 minutes more or until heated through. Let stand for 5 minutes before serving.

PER SERVING: *280 cal., 9 g total fat (5 g sat. fat), 31 mg chol., 499 mg sodium, 35 g carb., 3 g fiber, 13 g pro.*

Rotini-Bean Bake

PREP: **35 minutes**   BAKE: **35 minutes**   STAND: **10 minutes**   OVEN: **375°F**   MAKES **8 servings**

12 ounces dried rotini pasta

½ cup bottled balsamic vinaigrette salad dressing

1 pound roma tomatoes, coarsely chopped

1 15-ounce can cannellini beans (white kidney beans) or garbanzo beans (chickpeas), rinsed and drained

2 cups crumbled feta cheese (8 ounces)

1 cup coarsely chopped pitted Greek black olives

½ cup seasoned fine dry bread crumbs

⅔ cup plain low-fat yogurt

¾ cup milk

⅓ cup grated Parmesan cheese

1 tablespoon all-purpose flour

1 Preheat oven to 375°F. Lightly grease a 3-quart rectangular baking dish; set aside. Cook pasta according to package directions; drain. Transfer to an extra-large bowl. Drizzle with vinaigrette dressing; toss gently to coat. Stir in tomato, drained beans, feta cheese, and olives.

2 Sprinkle ¼ cup of the bread crumbs in the bottom of the prepared baking dish. Spoon pasta mixture into dish. In a medium bowl stir together yogurt, milk, Parmesan cheese, and flour. Pour evenly over pasta mixture. Sprinkle with the remaining ¼ cup bread crumbs.

3 Bake, covered, for 25 minutes. Bake, uncovered, for 10 to 15 minutes more or until heated through and top is light brown. Let stand for 10 minutes before serving.

PER SERVING: *425 cal., 15 g total fat (6 g sat. fat), 31 mg chol., 1,045 mg sodium, 57 g carb., 6 g fiber, 19 g pro.*

Baked Pasta with Mushrooms and Spinach

PREP: 45 minutes   BAKE: 30 minutes   OVEN: 350°F   MAKES 8 servings

- 12 ounces dried cut ziti or penne pasta
- 1 15-ounce carton whole-milk ricotta cheese
- 1 egg
- 1 cup half-and-half or light cream
- 1 teaspoon sugar
- ½ teaspoon salt
- ¼ teaspoon freshly ground black pepper
- ⅛ teaspoon ground nutmeg
- ¼ cup snipped fresh thyme, parsley, basil, and/or rosemary
- ¼ cup vegetable oil
- 10 cups sliced fresh mushrooms
- ½ cup chopped onion (1 medium)
- 2 cloves garlic, minced
- 4 cups chopped fresh spinach leaves
- 2 cups shredded Swiss cheese (8 ounces)
- ½ cup shredded Parmesan cheese (2 ounces)

1 Preheat oven to 350°F. Cook pasta according to package directions; drain. Return to hot pan.

2 Meanwhile, place ricotta cheese in a food processor; cover and process until smooth. Add egg, half-and-half, sugar, salt, pepper, and nutmeg; cover and process until combined. Stir in thyme. Add ricotta mixture to cooked pasta, stirring to combine.

3 In a large skillet heat 3 tablespoons of the oil over medium-high heat. Add mushrooms; cook until mushrooms are tender and liquid is evaporated, stirring occasionally. Remove from skillet. Add the remaining 1 tablespoon oil to skillet. Add onion and garlic; cook until onion is tender, stirring occasionally. Return mushrooms to skillet. Add spinach. Cook and stir for 2 to 3 minutes or until spinach is wilted. Drain mixture well in a colander. Add mushroom mixture to pasta mixture, stirring to combine. Stir in 1 cup of the Swiss cheese.

4 Transfer mixture to an ungreased 3-quart rectangular baking dish. Bake, covered, for 20 minutes. Sprinkle with the remaining 1 cup Swiss cheese and Parmesan cheese. Bake, uncovered, for 10 to 15 minutes more or until heated through and top starts to brown.

PER SERVING: *525 cal., 28 g total fat (14 g sat. fat), 94 mg chol., 371 mg sodium, 43 g carb., 3 g fiber, 27 g pro.*

312

tip

Though it's always worth the wait, casseroles do require long baking times, which uses a lot of energy. Make the most of that energy by baking something else at the same time, such as roasted vegetables. Refrigerate or freeze the bonus dish for another meal.

Baked Ziti with Three Cheeses

PREP: 30 minutes   BAKE: 30 minutes   OVEN: 425°F   MAKES 6 servings

12   ounces dried cut ziti or penne pasta

1   14.5-ounce can fire-roasted crushed tomatoes or diced tomatoes, undrained

1   cup chopped onion (1 large)

12   cloves garlic, minced

2   tablespoons olive oil

1/2   cup dry white wine

2   cups whipping cream

1   cup shredded Parmesan cheese (4 ounces)

3/4   cup crumbled Gorgonzola or other blue cheese (3 ounces)

1/2   cup shredded fontina cheese (2 ounces)

3/4   teaspoon salt

1/4   teaspoon ground black pepper

Snipped fresh Italian (flat-leaf) parsley (optional)

1 Preheat oven to 425°F. Cook pasta according to package directions; drain. Transfer to an ungreased 3-quart rectangular baking dish. Stir in undrained tomatoes.

2 Meanwhile, in a large saucepan cook onion and garlic in hot oil over medium heat just until onion is tender, stirring occasionally. Carefully stir in wine; cook about 3 minutes or until liquid is reduced by half. Stir in cream. Bring to boiling; reduce heat. Boil gently, uncovered, about 5 minutes or until mixture is slightly thickened, stirring frequently. Remove from heat. Stir in Parmesan cheese, Gorgonzola cheese, fontina cheese, salt, and pepper.

3 Pour cheese mixture over pasta mixture. Bake, covered, for 30 to 35 minutes or until sauce is bubbly. Stir pasta to coat. If desired, sprinkle with parsley.

PER SERVING: *748 cal., 47 g total fat (27 g sat. fat), 145 mg chol., 1,088 mg sodium, 55 g carb., 3 g fiber, 23 g pro.*

313

tip

Baked ziti is a perfect dish to serve when entertaining your nonvegetarian friends. This dish is often made without meat, so guests probably won't think it's vegetarian. Add a salad and some rolls and you have a meal everyone will enjoy!

Roasted Vegetables and Spinach with Pasta

PREP: 45 minutes   BAKE: 15 minutes   OVEN: 400°F   MAKES 6 to 8 servings

- 1   1-pound eggplant, peeled and cut into 1-inch chunks (about 6 cups)
- 1   large red onion, cut into thin wedges
- 1½   cups coarsely chopped yellow and/or green sweet peppers (2 medium)
- 1   tablespoon olive oil
- ½   teaspoon salt
- 1   teaspoon olive oil
- 2   cloves garlic, minced
- ½   teaspoon dried thyme, crushed
- ¼   teaspoon fennel seeds, crushed
- ¼   teaspoon ground black pepper
- ⅛   teaspoon crushed red pepper
- 1   11-ounce can condensed tomato bisque
- 1   cup water
- 12   ounces dried cut ziti or rotini pasta (about 4 cups)
- 1   6-ounce package fresh baby spinach
- 1   cup shredded mozzarella cheese (4 ounces)

1 Preheat oven to 400°F. In an ungreased 3-quart rectangular baking dish combine eggplant, red onion, and sweet peppers. Drizzle with 1 tablespoon oil and sprinkle with salt; toss gently to coat. Roast for 30 to 35 minutes or until vegetables start to brown, stirring twice.

2 Meanwhile, in a small saucepan heat 1 teaspoon oil over medium heat. Add garlic, thyme, fennel seeds, black pepper, and crushed red pepper; cook and stir for 2 minutes. Stir in tomato bisque and the water. Bring to boiling; reduce heat. Simmer, uncovered, for 5 minutes, stirring occasionally.

3 Cook pasta according to package directions; drain. Return pasta to hot pan. Add roasted vegetables and soup mixture to cooked pasta, stirring to combine. Stir in spinach.

4 Transfer pasta mixture to the same baking dish. Sprinkle with cheese. Bake, uncovered, for 15 to 20 minutes or until heated through and cheese is melted.

PER SERVING: 382 cal., 8 g total fat (3 g sat. fat), 14 mg chol., 775 mg sodium, 63 g carb., 8 g fiber, 15 g pro.

Vegetable Pastitsio

PREP: 35 minutes BAKE: 30 minutes STAND: 5 minutes OVEN: 350°F MAKES 6 servings

8 ounces dried elbow macaroni

2 eggs, lightly beaten

¼ teaspoon salt

3 cups fresh spinach leaves, torn

3 tablespoons butter

½ cup chopped onion (1 medium)

1 clove garlic, minced

1 8-ounce can tomato sauce

1 cup frozen whole kernel corn

1 cup cubed cooked potato

¾ teaspoon dried mint, crushed

½ teaspoon dried oregano, crushed

¼ teaspoon salt

¼ teaspoon ground cinnamon

¼ teaspoon ground black pepper

¼ cup all-purpose flour

¼ teaspoon ground nutmeg

2 cups milk

1 Preheat oven to 350°F. Lightly grease a 3-quart rectangular baking dish; set aside. Cook macaroni according to package directions; drain. Rinse with cold water; drain again. In a large bowl combine eggs and ¼ teaspoon salt; stir in cooked macaroni. Transfer mixture to the prepared baking dish. Top with spinach.

2 In a large skillet heat 1 tablespoon of the butter over medium heat. Add onion and garlic; cook about 3 minutes or until onion is tender, stirring occasionally. Stir in tomato sauce, corn, potato, mint, oregano, ¼ teaspoon salt, cinnamon, and pepper; heat through. Spoon potato mixture over spinach layer.

3 In a medium saucepan heat the remaining 2 tablespoons butter over medium heat. Stir in flour and nutmeg. Gradually stir in milk. Cook and stir until thickened and bubbly. Pour over potato mixture.

4 Bake, uncovered, about 30 minutes or until heated through. Let stand for 5 minutes before serving.

PER SERVING: 343 cal., 10 g total fat (5 g sat. fat), 93 mg chol., 488 mg sodium, 51 g carb., 3 g fiber, 12 g pro.

South Indian-Style Macaroni and Cheese

PREP: 25 minutes BAKE: 25 minutes OVEN: 350°F MAKES 6 servings

- 8 ounces dried elbow, wagon wheel, or medium shell macaroni
- 2 cups frozen peas
- ½ cup soft bread crumbs
- ¼ cup grated Asiago or Parmesan cheese
- ½ teaspoon paprika
- ½ teaspoon salt
- ½ teaspoon garam masala
- ¼ teaspoon ground turmeric
- ¼ teaspoon ground black pepper
- ¼ teaspoon cayenne pepper
- 3 tablespoons butter
- 1 teaspoon garlic paste
- ½ teaspoon finely shredded fresh ginger
- 2 tablespoons all-purpose flour
- 3 cups milk
- 2 cups shredded sharp cheddar cheese (8 ounces)

1 Preheat oven to 350°F. Cook macaroni according to package directions. Place peas in a colander. Drain macaroni in colander with the peas.

2 Meanwhile, in a small bowl combine bread crumbs, Asiago cheese, and paprika; set aside. In another small bowl stir together salt, garam masala, turmeric, black pepper, and cayenne pepper.

3 In a large saucepan heat butter over medium heat. Add garlic paste and ginger; cook and stir for 1 minute. Add salt mixture; cook and stir for 2 minutes. Stir in flour. Gradually stir in milk. Cook and stir until slightly thickened and bubbly. Gradually add cheddar cheese, stirring until melted. Stir in cooked macaroni mixture.

4 Transfer mixture to an ungreased 2-quart rectangular baking dish. Sprinkle with bread crumb mixture. Bake, uncovered, for 25 to 30 minutes or until bubbly and crumbs are golden brown.

PER SERVING: *481 cal., 23 g total fat (14 g sat. fat), 70 mg chol., 652 mg sodium, 46 g carb., 4 g fiber, 23 g pro.*

Double-Cheese Mac and Cheese

PREP: 25 minutes   BAKE: 25 minutes   STAND: 10 minutes   OVEN: 350°F   MAKES 6 servings

- 12 ounces dried penne, bow tie, or rigatoni pasta
- 2 cloves garlic, minced
- 1 tablespoon butter
- 2 tablespoons all-purpose flour
- 2 cups milk
- 2 cups shredded Port du Salut or Monterey Jack cheese (8 ounces)
- 1 cup shredded American cheese (4 ounces)
- 2 tablespoons snipped fresh oregano or 1 teaspoon dried oregano, crushed
- ½ cup soft light rye or whole wheat bread crumbs
- Snipped fresh oregano (optional)

1 Preheat oven to 350°F. Cook pasta according to package directions; drain.

2 Meanwhile, in a large saucepan cook and stir garlic in hot butter over medium heat for 30 seconds. Stir in flour. Gradually stir in milk. Cook and stir until thickened and bubbly. Reduce heat. Gradually add Port du Salut cheese and American cheese, stirring until melted. Remove from heat. Stir in cooked pasta and 2 tablespoons fresh or 1 teaspoon dried oregano.

3 Transfer mixture to an ungreased 1½- to 2-quart casserole. Sprinkle with bread crumbs. Bake, uncovered, about 25 minutes or until heated through. Let stand for 10 minutes before serving. If desired, sprinkle with additional fresh oregano.

PER SERVING: 508 cal., 22 g total fat (13 g sat. fat), 80 mg chol., 613 mg sodium, 51 g carb., 2 g fiber, 25 g pro.

Greek Pasta Casserole

PREP: 25 minutes BAKE: 20 minutes STAND: 10 minutes OVEN: 375°F MAKES 6 servings

12 ounces dried rotini pasta

1 15-ounce can tomato sauce

1 10.75-ounce can condensed tomato soup

1 15-ounce can cannellini beans (white kidney beans) or garbanzo beans (chickpeas), rinsed and drained

2 cups crumbled feta cheese (8 ounces)

1 cup coarsely chopped pitted Greek black olives

½ cup seasoned fine dry bread crumbs

2 tablespoons finely shredded or grated Parmesan cheese

2 tablespoons butter, melted

1 Preheat oven to 375°F. Lightly grease a 3-quart rectangular baking dish; set aside. Cook pasta according to package directions; drain. In an extra-large bowl combine tomato sauce and soup. Stir in cooked pasta, drained beans, feta cheese, and olives. Transfer pasta mixture to the prepared baking dish.

2 In a small bowl stir together bread crumbs, Parmesan cheese, and melted butter. Sprinkle over pasta mixture.

3 Bake, uncovered, for 20 to 25 minutes or until heated through and top is lightly browned. Let stand for 10 minutes before serving.

PER SERVING: *553 cal., 19 g total fat (10 g sat. fat), 52 mg chol., 1,890 mg sodium, 74 g carb., 7 g fiber, 24 g pro.*

Dried Tomato Casserole

PREP: 25 minutes CHILL: overnight BAKE: 40 minutes STAND: 10 minutes OVEN: 350°F MAKES 12 servings

2 9-ounce packages refrigerated four-cheese ravioli

½ to 1 cup oil-packed dried tomatoes, drained and chopped

1½ cups shredded cheddar cheese (6 ounces)

1½ cups shredded Monterey Jack cheese (6 ounces)

½ cup grated Parmesan cheese

8 eggs, lightly beaten

2½ cups milk

1 to 2 tablespoons snipped fresh basil or Italian (flat-leaf) parsley

1 Grease a 3-quart rectangular or oval baking dish. Place uncooked ravioli evenly in dish. Sprinkle with dried tomato. Top with cheddar cheese, Monterey Jack cheese, and Parmesan cheese.

2 In a large bowl whisk together eggs and milk until combined. Pour over ingredients in dish. Cover and chill overnight.

3 Preheat oven to 350°F. Bake, uncovered, about 40 minutes or until top is golden brown and center is set. Let stand for 10 minutes before serving. Sprinkle with basil.

PER SERVING: *353 cal., 21 g total fat (11 g sat. fat), 213 mg chol., 490 mg sodium, 20 g carb., 1 g fiber, 21 g pro.*

tip

For added fiber and omega-3 fatty acids, stir a little ground flaxseed into a casserole.

Beans, Rice, & Grains

Beans, rice, and grains are the "meat" of the
vegetarian diet, offering many important nutrients.
Enjoy these tasty ways to use them, from
enchiladas and tostadas to stir-fries and risottos!

Pumpkin, Rice, and Bean Enchiladas

PREP: 30 minutes   BAKE: 20 minutes   OVEN: 400°F   MAKES 4 servings

Nonstick cooking spray

2 teaspoons olive oil

½ cup chopped onion

1 fresh jalapeño chile pepper, seeded and finely chopped*

1 15-ounce can pumpkin

1½ to 1¾ cups water

1 teaspoon chili powder

½ teaspoon ground cumin

¼ teaspoon salt

1 15-ounce can no-salt-added red kidney beans, rinsed and drained

1½ cups cooked brown rice

½ cup shredded reduced-fat Monterey Jack cheese with jalapeño peppers (2 ounces)

8 6-inch corn tortillas, softened**

Pico de gallo or salsa (optional)

1 Preheat oven to 400°F. Coat a 2-quart rectangular baking dish with cooking spray; set aside. In a medium saucepan heat oil over medium-high heat. Add onion and chile pepper; cook and stir until onion is tender. Stir in pumpkin, 1½ cups of the water, the chili powder, cumin, and salt. Cook and stir until heated through. If necessary, stir in enough of the additional ¼ cup water to reach desired consistency.

2 In a large bowl coarsely mash drained beans with a fork or potato masher. Stir in half of the pumpkin mixture, the cooked rice, and ¼ cup of the cheese.

3 Spoon a generous ⅓ cup bean mixture onto each tortilla. Roll up tortillas; place, seam sides down, in the prepared baking dish. Pour the remaining pumpkin mixture over tortillas.

4 Bake, covered, for 15 minutes. Sprinkle with the remaining ¼ cup cheese. Bake, uncovered, for 5 to 10 minutes more or until heated through. If desired, serve with pico de gallo.

PER SERVING: 383 cal., 7 g total fat (2 g sat. fat), 8 mg chol., 286 mg sodium, 67 g carb., 17 g fiber, 17 g pro.

*tip
Because chile peppers contain volatile oils that can burn your skin and eyes, avoid direct contact with them as much as possible. When working with chile peppers, wear plastic or rubber gloves. If your bare hands do touch the peppers, wash your hands and nails well with soap and warm water.

**tip
To soften tortillas, wrap in microwave-safe paper towels. Microwave on 100 percent power (high) for 45 to 60 seconds or until warm.

make it vegan
Substitute soy cheese for the Monterey Jack cheese with Jalapeño peppers.

Red Beans and Rice Burgers

PREP: 20 minutes COOK: 10 minutes MAKES 4 burgers

1 **15-ounce can no-salt-added red kidney beans, rinsed and drained, or 1¾ cups cooked red kidney beans**

½ **cup finely chopped onion**

¼ **cup finely chopped celery**

¼ **cup soft whole wheat bread crumbs**

2 **tablespoons snipped fresh cilantro**

1 **clove garlic, minced**

½ **teaspoon dried oregano, crushed**

½ **teaspoon ground cumin**

¼ **teaspoon salt**

¼ **teaspoon ground black pepper**

¾ **cup cooked brown rice, cooled**

4 **whole grain hamburger buns, split and toasted**

Light mayonnaise, fresh spinach leaves, tomato slices, and/or red onion slices (optional)

1 In a medium bowl coarsely mash drained beans with a fork or potato masher. Stir in onion, celery, bread crumbs, cilantro, garlic, oregano, cumin, salt, and pepper. Stir in rice.

2 Shape the bean mixture into four ½-inch-thick patties.

3 Preheat a grill pan or large skillet over medium heat. Add patties to pan or skillet. Cook for 10 to 12 minutes or until heated through, turning patties once halfway through cooking.

4 Serve burgers on toasted hamburger buns. If desired, top with light mayonnaise, spinach, tomato, and/or red onion.

PER BURGER: *253 cal., 2 g total fat (0 g sat. fat), 0 mg chol., 392 mg sodium, 48 g carb., 12 g fiber, 12 g pro.*

make it vegan
Do not use optional mayonnaise.

321

Cuban Red Beans and Rice 🌿

START TO FINISH: **35 minutes**   MAKES **4 servings**

1   **large sweet onion, cut into thin wedges**

1   **large green or red sweet pepper, seeded and chopped**

4   **cloves garlic, minced**

1   **tablespoon canola oil**

½   **cup snipped fresh cilantro**

½   **teaspoon dried oregano, crushed**

½   **teaspoon ground cumin**

¼   **teaspoon ground black pepper**

2   **15- to 16-ounce cans pinto beans and/or red kidney beans, rinsed and drained**

1   **cup vegetable broth**

¼   **cup lime juice**

1   **8.8-ounce package cooked brown rice or 2 cups cooked brown rice**

    Lime wedges and/or small hot chile peppers (optional)

1 In a large saucepan cook onion, sweet pepper, and garlic in hot oil over medium heat for 5 to 10 minutes or until onion is tender. Add ¼ cup of the cilantro, the oregano, cumin, and black pepper. Cook and stir for 1 minute more.

2 Add drained beans and broth. Bring to boiling; reduce heat. Simmer, uncovered, for 15 to 20 minutes or until liquid is thickened to desired consistency. Stir in lime juice.

3 Prepare rice according to package directions. Serve beans over rice and sprinkle with the remaining ¼ cup cilantro. If desired, serve with lime wedges and/or hot peppers.

PER SERVING: *351 cal., 6 g total fat (1 g sat. fat), 0 mg chol., 805 mg sodium, 62 g carb., 13 g fiber, 17 g pro.*

tip

Keep a stash of cooked beans and grains on hand. When cooking beans and grains, make extra. Measure the cooled, cooked beans and grains into serving-size portions and place in freezer bags. Press out air before sealing bags, label and date the bags, and freeze up to 3 months. To thaw, place frozen beans or grains in a microwave-safe bowl. Microwave, covered, on 50 percent power (medium) for 1 to 1½ minutes or until heated through, stirring once.

Tex-Mex Bean Tostadas

PREP: 15 minutes BAKE: 8 minutes OVEN: 350°F MAKES 4 servings

4 tostada shells

1 16-ounce can pinto beans, rinsed and drained

½ cup salsa*

½ teaspoon salt-free Southwest chipotle seasoning blend

½ cup shredded reduced-fat cheddar cheese (2 ounces)

1½ cups shredded iceberg lettuce

1 cup chopped tomato (1 large)

¼ cup shredded reduced-fat cheddar cheese (1 ounce) (optional)

Lime wedges (optional)

1 Preheat oven to 350°F. Place tostada shells on a baking sheet. Bake for 3 to 5 minutes or until warm.

2 Meanwhile, in a medium bowl combine drained beans, salsa, and seasoning blend. Use a potato masher or fork to coarsely mash the mixture. Divide bean mixture among the tostada shells, spreading evenly. Top with the ½ cup cheese.

3 Bake about 5 minutes or until cheese melts. Top tostadas with shredded lettuce and chopped tomato. If desired, sprinkle with the additional ¼ cup cheese and serve with lime wedges.

PER SERVING: *230 cal., 6 g total fat (3 g sat. fat), 10 mg chol., 660 mg sodium, 33 g carb., 8 g fiber, 12 g pro.*

*tip

Look for a purchased salsa with 100 mg or less sodium per serving.

make it vegan 🌿

Substitute cheddar-flavor soy cheese for the cheddar cheese.

Black Bean Cakes with Salsa

PREP: 25 minutes   COOK: 6 minutes per batch   MAKES 4 servings

1½   cups salsa
2   15-ounce cans black beans,
      rinsed and drained
1   8.5-ounce package corn
      muffin mix
1   medium fresh jalapeño
      chile pepper, seeded and
      finely chopped*
2½   teaspoons chili powder
2   tablespoons olive oil
½   cup sour cream
½   teaspoon chili powder

1 Drain ½ cup of the salsa in a colander. In a large bowl use a fork or potato masher to coarsely mash drained beans. Stir in the ½ cup drained salsa, muffin mix, half of the jalapeño chile pepper, and the 2½ teaspoons chili powder.

2 In an extra-large skillet heat 1 tablespoon of the oil over medium-high heat. For each cake, spoon ½ cup of the bean mixture into hot skillet. Use a spatula to flatten mounds into 3½-inch bean cakes. Cook about 6 minutes or until brown, turning once halfway through cooking. Remove bean cakes from skillet. Repeat with the remaining oil and bean mixture.

3 In a small bowl combine sour cream and the ½ teaspoon chili powder. Top bean cakes with the remaining 1 cup salsa, the remaining jalapeño chile pepper, and the chili-seasoned sour cream.

PER SERVING: *519 cal., 19 g total fat (4 g sat. fat), 11 mg chol., 1,553 mg sodium, 79 g carb., 12 g fiber, 20 g pro.*

*tip
Because chile peppers contain volatile oils that can burn your skin and eyes, avoid direct contact with them as much as possible. When working with chile peppers, wear plastic or rubber gloves. If your bare hands do touch the peppers, wash your hands and nails well with soap and warm water.

🌿 make it vegan
Substitute tofu sour cream for the dairy sour cream.

Black Bean Enchiladas

PREP: **30 minutes**   FREEZE: **up to 3 months**   BAKE: **45 minutes**   MAKES **6 servings**

12   **6- to 7-inch flour tortillas**

½   **cup chopped onion (1 medium)**

1   **medium fresh jalapeño or serrano chile pepper, seeded and finely chopped***

1   **teaspoon minced garlic**

1   **tablespoon olive oil or vegetable oil**

⅓   **cup sour cream**

¼   **cup mole sauce**

2   **tablespoons water**

2   **15-ounce cans black beans or pinto beans, rinsed and drained**

2   **cups shredded Monterey Jack cheese**

1   **cup sour cream**

2   **tablespoons all-purpose flour**

1   **teaspoon ground cumin**

¼   **teaspoon salt**

¾   **cup milk**

1   **recipe Mango Salsa or 1½ cups salsa**

1 Wrap 6 of the tortillas in waxed paper and microwave on 100 percent power (high) for 30 to 40 seconds or until warm. Repeat with the remaining 6 tortillas.

2 Meanwhile, for filling, in a large skillet cook onion, jalapeño pepper, and garlic in hot oil until onion is tender; remove from heat. In small bowl combine the ⅓ cup sour cream, mole sauce, and the water; add to skillet along with drained beans and 1 cup of the cheese. Spoon ⅓ cup of the bean mixture onto each tortilla near the edge; roll up. Place filled tortillas, seam sides down, in two greased 2-quart rectangular baking dishes.

3 For sauce, in medium bowl combine the 1 cup sour cream, flour, cumin, and salt; whisk in milk. Pour sauce evenly over filled tortillas. Cover with freezer wrap, label, and freeze for up to 3 months. Wrap and freeze remaining 1 cup cheese until needed.

4 To serve, thaw covered frozen casseroles and cheese overnight in refrigerator. Preheat oven to 350°F.

5 Bake, covered, for 40 minutes or until heated through. Top with remaining cheese. Bake, uncovered, about 5 minutes more or until cheese melts. Serve enchiladas with Mango Salsa.

PER SERVING: *629 cal., 33 g total fat (14 g sat. fat), 55 mg chol., 796 mg sodium, 59 g carb., 8 g, 28 g pro.*

Mango Salsa

In a small bowl combine 1½ cups drained and chopped refrigerated mango; 2 jalapeño or serrano chile peppers, seeded and finely chopped;* 2 tablespoons snipped fresh cilantro; and 1 tablespoon lemon or lime juice. Store, covered, in the refrigerator for up to 2 days.

*tip

Because chile peppers contain volatile oils that can burn your skin and eyes, avoid direct contact with them as much as possible. When working with chile peppers, wear plastic or rubber gloves. If your bare hands do touch the peppers, wash your hands and nails well with soap and warm water.

tip

To bake immediately, prepare through pouring sauce over tortillas in Step 3; omit Step 4.

Spicy Rice and Bean Cakes

PREP: 30 minutes COOK: 8 minutes per batch MAKES 4 servings

Nonstick cooking spray

1 medium red sweet pepper, seeded and finely chopped

2 cloves garlic, minced

1 15-ounce can black beans, rinsed and drained

1½ cups cooked brown rice, cooled

1 egg, lightly beaten

2 tablespoons snipped fresh cilantro

1 canned chipotle chile pepper in adobo sauce, finely chopped*

1 teaspoon adobo sauce from canned chipotle chile peppers in adobo sauce (optional)

½ teaspoon ground cumin

4 teaspoons olive oil

¼ cup light sour cream

Snipped fresh cilantro (optional)

1 Coat an unheated large nonstick skillet with cooking spray. Preheat over medium-high heat. Add sweet pepper and garlic; cook and stir until crisp-tender. Transfer sweet pepper mixture to a large bowl and cool slightly.

2 Place drained beans in a food processor;** cover and process until smooth. Transfer bean mixture to bowl with sweet pepper mixture. Stir in cooked brown rice, egg, the 2 tablespoons cilantro, the chipotle pepper, adobo sauce (if using), and cumin; mix well. With wet hands, shape mixture evenly into eight ½-inch-thick patties.

3 In the same skillet heat 2 teaspoons of the olive oil over medium heat. Add half of the bean patties. Cook for 8 to 10 minutes or until brown and heated through, carefully turning once halfway through cooking. Remove from skillet and keep warm. Repeat with the remaining 2 teaspoons oil and remaining bean patties.

4 Serve bean patties with sour cream. If desired, garnish with additional snipped cilantro.

PER SERVING: *236 cal., 8 g total fat (2 g sat. fat), 57 mg chol., 307 mg sodium, 35 g carb., 7 g fiber, 11 g pro.*

*tip

Because chile peppers contain volatile oils that can burn your skin and eyes, avoid direct contact with them as much as possible. When working with chile peppers, wear plastic or rubber gloves. If your bare hands do touch the peppers, wash your hands and nails well with soap and warm water.

**tip

If you do not have a food processor, use a potato masher to mash the beans into a nearly smooth paste.

Triple Pepper Nachos

PREP: 25 minutes BAKE: 13 minutes OVEN: 425°F MAKES 6 servings

5   7- to 8-inch whole wheat flour tortillas or 4 ounces baked tortilla chips (about 5 cups)

Nonstick cooking spray (optional)

1   15-ounce can black beans, rinsed and drained

¾   cup chunky salsa

1   cup shredded reduced-fat Colby and Monterey Jack cheese (4 ounces)

¾   cup roasted red sweet peppers, drained and cut into strips

1   pepperoncini salad pepper, seeded and cut into strips

2   to 4 tablespoons sliced pickled jalapeño chile peppers, chopped*

Thinly sliced green onions

Light sour cream (optional)

Chunky salsa (optional)

1 Preheat oven to 425°F. If using whole wheat flour tortillas, lightly coat both sides of each tortilla with cooking spray. Cut each tortilla into 6 wedges. Place wedges in a single layer on a very large ungreased baking sheet. Bake for 8 to 10 minutes or until light brown and crisp, turning once halfway through baking. Tortilla wedges will continue to crisp as they cool.

2 Meanwhile, in a medium saucepan combine drained black beans and the ¾ cup salsa; cook and stir over medium heat just until heated through.

3 On a very large ovenproof platter arrange tortilla chips 1 to 2 layers deep, overlapping slightly. Spoon bean mixture onto chips. Sprinkle cheese, roasted red peppers, pepperoncini pepper, and jalapeño peppers over bean mixture on chips.

4 Bake about 5 minutes or until cheese melts. Sprinkle with green onions. If desired, serve with sour cream and additional salsa.

PER SERVING: *201 cal., 7 g total fat (3 g sat. fat), 13 mg chol., 838 mg sodium, 24 g carb., 11 g fiber, 15 g pro.*

*tip
Because chile peppers contain volatile oils that can burn your skin and eyes, avoid direct contact with them as much as possible. When working with chile peppers, wear plastic or rubber gloves. If your bare hands do touch the peppers, wash your hands and nails well with soap and warm water.

make it vegan
Substitute desired soy cheese for the Colby and Monterey Jack cheese and substitute tofu sour cream for the optional dairy sour cream.

Baked Bean and Corn Chimichangas

PREP: 25 minutes BAKE: 10 minutes OVEN: 425°F MAKES 6 servings

Nonstick cooking spray

6 10-inch whole wheat flour or plain flour tortillas

½ cup chopped onion

1 15-ounce can black beans, rinsed and drained

1 8.75-ounce can whole kernel corn, rinsed and drained

½ cup chopped tomato

1 cup green or red salsa

¼ cup snipped fresh cilantro

¾ cup shredded reduced-fat Monterey Jack cheese

1 Preheat oven to 425°F. Coat a baking sheet with cooking spray; set aside. Wrap the tortillas in foil. Heat in the oven for 5 minutes.

2 Meanwhile, for the filling, coat an unheated large skillet with cooking spray. Preheat skillet over medium heat. Add onion; cook about 5 minutes or until tender, stirring occasionally. Add drained black beans. Use a fork or potato masher to coarsely mash beans. Stir in drained corn, tomato, and ½ cup of the salsa. Heat through. Stir in cilantro.

3 To assemble, spoon about ½ cup of the filling onto each tortilla, spooning filling just below the center. Fold bottom edge of each tortilla up and over filling. Fold opposite sides in and over filling. Roll up from the bottom. If necessary, secure rolled tortillas with wooden toothpicks. Place filled tortillas on prepared baking sheet, seam sides down. Coat top and sides of the filled tortillas with cooking spray.

4 Bake for 10 to 12 minutes or until tortillas are golden brown and crisp. To serve, sprinkle with cheese and top with the remaining ½ cup salsa.

PER SERVING: *315 cal., 11 g total fat (3 g sat. fat), 10 mg chol., 1,147 mg sodium, 47 g carb., 10 g fiber, 16 g pro.*

◊ make it vegan
Substitute soy cheese for the Monterey Jack cheese.

Spicy Black Bean Veggie Burgers

PREP: 35 minutes   CHILL: 10 minutes   COOK: 12 minutes   MAKES 6 servings

- 1 6-ounce package long grain and wild rice mix
- ¼ cup chopped onion
- ¼ cup chopped celery
- ¼ cup chopped carrot
- 1 tablespoon olive oil
- 1 15-ounce can black beans, rinsed and drained
- ½ cup frozen corn, thawed
- 2 cloves garlic, minced
- ¼ cup quick-cooking oatmeal
- 1 egg, lightly beaten
- 1 teaspoon ground cumin
- 2 teaspoons ground chili powder
- 1 teaspoon chopped chipotle chile peppers in adobo sauce*
- ¼ teaspoon salt
- ¼ teaspoon ground black pepper
    Nonstick cooking spray
- 6 hamburger buns, split and toasted, or 6 cups shredded lettuce
    Light sour cream (optional)
    Sliced avocado (optional)
    Salsa (optional)

1 Prepare rice according to package directions. Uncover and remove from heat. Cool while preparing vegetables. In a small skillet cook onion, celery, and carrot in hot olive oil over medium heat about 6 minutes or until vegetables are tender. Set aside.

2 In a large bowl place half of the drained beans and mash with a potato masher or fork until completely mashed. Add the remaining black beans, corn, garlic, oatmeal, egg, cumin, and chili powder. Mix well. Add cooled rice, cooked vegetables, chipotle pepper, salt, and black pepper.

3 Form into six ½- to ¾-inch-thick patties; place on a small baking sheet. Cover and chill about 10 minutes or until patties are firm and set up.

4 Coat a large nonstick skillet with cooking spray. Preheat over medium heat. Add patties and cook over medium heat about 12 minutes or until patties are golden brown and heated through, turning halfway through cooking.

5 Serve in burger buns or on top of shredded lettuce. If desired, top with sour cream, avocado, and/or salsa.

PER SERVING: *333 cal., 6 g total fat (1 g sat. fat), 35 mg chol., 846 mg sodium, 59 g carb., 6 g fiber, 14 g pro.*

*tip

Because chile peppers contain volatile oils that can burn your skin and eyes, avoid direct contact with them as much as possible. When working with chile peppers, wear plastic or rubber gloves. If your bare hands do touch the peppers, wash your hands and nails well with soap and warm water.

Vegetable Bowls with Spiced Yogurt-Lime Dressing

PREP: 25 minutes   MICROWAVE: 10 minutes   MAKES 4 servings

- 1 **recipe Spiced Yogurt-Lime Dressing**
- 1 **tablespoon soy sauce**
- 1 **tablespoon lime juice**
- 1 **teaspoon chili powder**
- 1 **teaspoon fresh oregano, snipped, or ½ teaspoon. dried oregano, crushed**
- 1 **teaspoon olive oil**
- 1 **pound sweet potatoes (2 to 3 medium), peeled and cut into 1-inch cubes**
- 1 **15-ounce can black beans, rinsed and drained**
- 1 **cup cherry or grape tomatoes, halved**
- 1 **medium avocado, halved, seeded, peeled, and chopped**
- 8 **large savoy cabbage leaves**
- ¼ **cup thinly sliced green onions**
  Lime wedges (optional)
  Baguette-style French bread, sliced and toasted (optional)

1 Prepare Spiced Yogurt-Lime Dressing; set aside.

2 In a small bowl stir together soy sauce, lime juice, chili powder, oregano, and olive oil; set aside. Place sweet potatoes in a medium microwave-safe bowl. Place drained beans in small microwave-safe bowl. Evenly spoon half of the soy sauce mixture onto potatoes and half onto beans; toss to coat. Cover bowls with vented plastic wrap. Microwave sweet potatoes on 100 percent power (high) about 9 minutes or until tender, stirring occasionally; set aside. Microwave beans on 100 percent power (high) 1 to 2 minutes or until heated through, stirring once.

3 Divide potatoes, beans, tomatoes, and avocado among cabbage leaves. Sprinkle with green onions. Pass Spiced Yogurt-Lime Dressing. If desired, serve with lime wedges and toasted baguette slices.

PER SERVING: *409 cal., 21 g total fat (3 g sat. fat), 2 mg chol., 896 mg sodium, 51 g carb., 14 g fiber, 13 g pro.*

Spiced Yogurt-Lime Dressing

In small bowl combine ½ cup plain low-fat yogurt, 2 tablespoons lime juice, 1 tablespoon soy sauce, 1 tablespoon chili powder, and 1 clove garlic, minced. Whisk in ¼ cup olive oil until well combined. Or serve wraps with 1 cup of bottled light ranch-style dressing with 1 tablespoon chili powder stirred in.

330

Black Bean Tostadas

START TO FINISH: **20 minutes**   MAKES **4 servings**

1 16-ounce can no-salt-added organic black beans, rinsed and drained

½ cup canned fat-free refried beans

½ teaspoon ground cumin

½ teaspoon chili powder

4 tostada shells

1 cup shredded lettuce

¾ cup diced tomato (1 large)

¼ cup shredded reduced-fat cheddar cheese

2 tablespoons fat-free sour cream

2 tablespoons snipped fresh cilantro

1 In a medium bowl use a fork or potato masher to coarsely mash together drained black beans, refried beans, cumin, and chili powder. Spread mixture over tostada shells. Sprinkle with lettuce, tomato, and cheese. Top with sour cream and sprinkle with cilantro.

PER SERVING: *218 cal., 9 g total fat (2 g sat. fat), 5 mg chol., 253 mg sodium, 22 g carb., 9 g fiber, 14 g pro.*

331

make it vegan 🍃
Substitute soy cheese for the cheddar cheese and tofu sour cream for the dairy sour cream.

Grain-Vegetable Medley

PREP: 20 minutes COOK: 10 minutes STAND: 5 minutes MAKES 4 servings

2   **cups chicken-flavor vegetable broth**

1½   **cups fresh green beans, trimmed and cut into 2-inch pieces**

⅔   **cup quick-cooking barley**

2   **tablespoons lemon juice**

1   **tablespoon olive oil**

⅛   **teaspoon salt**

⅛   **teaspoon ground black pepper**

½   **cup whole wheat couscous**

4   **cups coarsely shredded fresh spinach**

¼   **cup sliced green onions (2)**

1½   **teaspoons snipped fresh thyme or ½ teaspoon dried thyme, crushed**

   Lemon wedges (optional)

1 In a large saucepan bring broth to boiling; stir in green beans and uncooked barley. Return to boiling; reduce heat. Simmer, covered, for 10 to 12 minutes or until barley is tender.

2 Meanwhile, in a small bowl whisk together lemon juice, oil, salt, and pepper.

3 Stir uncooked couscous into barley mixture. Stir in lemon juice mixture, spinach, green onions, and thyme. Remove from heat. Cover and let stand for 5 minutes. To serve, fluff with a fork. If desired, serve with lemon wedges.

PER SERVING: *271 cal., 5 g total fat (1 g sat. fat), 0 mg chol., 451 mg sodium, 52 g carb., 11 g fiber, 10 g pro.*

Risotto with Beans and Vegetables

PREP: **20 minutes** COOK: **30 minutes** MAKES **4 servings**

- 3 **cups vegetable broth**
- 2 **cups sliced fresh mushrooms**
- ½ **cup chopped onion (1 medium)**
- 2 **cloves garlic, minced**
- 2 **tablespoons olive oil**
- 1 **cup uncooked Arborio rice**
- 1 **cup finely chopped zucchini**
- 1 **cup finely chopped carrots**
- 1 **15-ounce can cannellini beans (white kidney beans) or pinto beans, rinsed and drained**
- ½ **cup finely shredded Parmesan cheese**
- 2 **tablespoons snipped fresh Italian (flat-leaf) parsley**
  Finely shredded Parmesan cheese (optional)

1 In a medium saucepan bring broth to boiling; reduce heat and simmer until needed. Meanwhile, in a large saucepan cook mushrooms, onion, and garlic in hot oil over medium heat about 5 minutes or until onion is tender. Add rice. Cook and stir about 5 minutes more or until rice is golden brown.

2 Slowly add 1 cup of the broth to the rice mixture, stirring constantly. Continue to cook and stir until broth is absorbed. Add another ½ cup of the broth, the zucchini, and carrots to rice mixture, stirring constantly. Continue to cook and stir until broth is absorbed. Add another 1 cup broth, ½ cup at a time, stirring constantly until the broth is absorbed. (This process should take about 20 minutes.)

3 Stir the remaining ½ cup broth into rice mixture. Cook and stir until rice is slightly creamy and just tender. Stir in drained beans and the ½ cup Parmesan cheese; heat through. To serve, sprinkle with parsley and, if desired, additional Parmesan cheese.

PER SERVING: *340 cal., 11 g total fat (3 g sat. fat), 9 mg chol., 1,074 mg sodium, 53 g carb., 7 g fiber, 15 g pro.*

Garden Sliders

START TO FINISH: **30 minutes** MAKES **6 servings**

1   **15- to 16-ounce can Great Northern or cannellini beans (white kidney beans), rinsed and drained**

2   **tablespoons olive oil**

2   **cloves garlic, minced**

½   **teaspoon Italian seasoning, crushed**

     Salt

     Ground black pepper

1   **medium yellow summer squash, cut into ¼-inch slices**

24   **¼-inch slices baguette-style French bread**

2   **medium roma tomatoes, cut into ¼-inch slices**

1   **small cucumber, cut into ¼-inch slices**

     Small celery top sprigs, small tomato wedges, and/or pickle slices (optional)

1 For bean spread, in a blender or food processor combine drained beans, 1 tablespoon of the oil, the garlic, and Italian seasoning. Cover; blend or process until smooth. Season with salt and pepper.

2 To grill squash, toss squash slices with the remaining 1 tablespoon olive oil. Place in a grill basket.

3 For charcoal grill, place basket on the rack of an uncovered grill directly over medium coals. Grill about 5 minutes or just until squash is tender, turning once halfway through grilling. (For a gas grill, preheat grill. Reduce heat to medium. Place basket on grill rack over heat. Cover and grill as above.)

4 Spread 1 side of each bread slice with bean spread. Top half of the bread with tomato slices, squash, and cucumber slices. Top with remaining bread slices, spread sides down. Secure sandwiches with wooden picks. If desired, top with celery sprigs, tomato wedges, and/or pickle slices.

PER SERVING: *240 cal., 4 g total fat (0 g sat. fat), 0 mg chol., 578 mg sodium, 46 g carb., 6 g fiber, 12 g pro.*

Cannellini Bean Burgers

PREP: 25 minutes   COOK: 10 minutes   MAKES 4 burgers

1   **15- to 16-ounce can cannellini beans (white kidney beans), rinsed and drained**

¾   **cup soft whole wheat bread crumbs (1 slice)**

½   **cup chopped onion**

¼   **cup walnut pieces, toasted if desired**

2   **tablespoons coarsely snipped fresh basil or 1 teaspoon dried basil, crushed**

2   **cloves garlic, quartered**

1   **tablespoon olive oil**

4   **whole grain hamburger buns, split and toasted**

2   **tablespoons bottled light ranch salad dressing**

2   **cups fresh spinach leaves**

½   **of a medium tomato, sliced**

1 In a food processor combine drained cannellini beans, ¼ cup of the bread crumbs, the onion, walnuts, basil, and garlic. Cover and process until mixture is coarsely chopped and holds together.

2 Shape the bean mixture into four ½-inch-thick patties. Place the remaining ½ cup bread crumbs in a shallow dish. Carefully brush both sides of each patty with oil. Dip patties into bread crumbs, turning to coat.

3 Preheat a grill pan or large skillet over medium heat. Add patties to pan or skillet. Cook for 10 to 12 minutes or until heated through, turning patties once halfway through cooking. (Reduce heat to medium-low if patties brown too quickly.)

4 Spread cut sides of bun bottoms with ranch salad dressing. Top with burgers, spinach, tomato slices, and bun tops.

PER BURGER: *299 cal., 11 g total fat (1 g sat. fat), 2 mg chol., 497 mg sodium, 44 g carb., 9 g fiber, 13 g pro.*

335

Falafels

START TO FINISH: 25 minutes   MAKES 4 servings

1   15-ounce can garbanzo beans (chickpeas), rinsed and drained

¼   cup coarsely shredded carrot

2   tablespoons all-purpose flour

2   tablespoons snipped fresh parsley

1   tablespoon olive oil

3   cloves garlic, halved

1   teaspoon ground coriander

½   teaspoon ground cumin

½   teaspoon salt

⅛   teaspoon ground black pepper

2   tablespoons olive oil

½   cup mayonnaise

1   clove garlic, minced

¼   teaspoon cayenne pepper

4   pita bread rounds

1   cup fresh spinach leaves, coarsely shredded

    Coarsely shredded cucumber (optional)

1 In a food processor combine the drained beans, carrot, flour, parsley, the 1 tablespoon olive oil, halved garlic, coriander, cumin, salt, and black pepper. Cover and process until finely chopped and mixture holds together (should have some visible pieces of garbanzo beans and carrots). Shape bean mixture into four 3-inch-diameter patties.

2 In a large skillet heat the 2 tablespoons oil over medium-high heat. Add patties. Cook for 4 to 6 minutes or until brown and heated through, turning halfway through cooking.

3 Meanwhile, in a small bowl stir together mayonnaise, garlic, and cayenne pepper. Spread mixture over pita rounds. Top with spinach and falafels. If desired, top with cucumber.

PER SERVING: *607 cal., 34 g total fat (6 g sat. fat), 10 mg chol., 1,093 mg sodium, 63 g carb., 7 g fiber, 12 g pro.*

Tex-Mex Beans with Cornmeal Dumplings

START TO FINISH: **35 minutes** MAKES **5 servings**

1 cup chopped onion (1 large)

¾ cup water

1 clove garlic, minced

2 8-ounce cans no-salt-added tomato sauce

1 15-ounce can garbanzo beans (chickpeas), rinsed and drained

1 15-ounce can red kidney beans, rinsed and drained

1 4-ounce can diced green chile peppers, drained

2 teaspoons chili powder

¼ teaspoon salt

1½ teaspoons cornstarch

1 tablespoon cold water

1 recipe Cornmeal Dumplings

1 In a large skillet combine onion, the ¾ cup water, and garlic. Bring to boiling; reduce heat. Simmer, covered, about 5 minutes or until onion is tender. Stir in tomato sauce, drained beans, drained chile peppers, chili powder, and salt.

2 In a small bowl stir together cornstarch and the 1 tablespoon cold water; stir into bean mixture. Cook and stir until slightly thickened and bubbly. Reduce heat.

3 Using 2 spoons, drop Cornmeal Dumplings dough into 10 mounds on top of hot bean mixture.

4 Simmer, covered, for 10 to 12 minutes or until a toothpick inserted into the center of a dumpling comes out clean. (Do not lift cover during cooking.)

PER SERVING: *350 cal., 7 g total fat (1 g sat. fat), 0 mg chol., 803 mg sodium, 61 g carb., 12 g fiber, 15 g pro.*

Cornmeal Dumplings

In a medium bowl stir together ⅓ cup all-purpose flour, ⅓ cup yellow cornmeal, 1 teaspoon baking powder, and ¼ teaspoon salt. In a small bowl combine 1 egg white, ¼ cup fat-free milk, and 2 tablespoons vegetable oil. Add milk mixture to cornmeal mixture; stir just until combined.

Moroccan Chickpeas and Couscous 🌿

PREP: 25 minutes   STAND: 5 minutes   MAKES 6 servings

$1\frac{1}{2}$ cups water

1 cup whole wheat couscous

6 green onions, sliced

4 cloves garlic, minced

1 tablespoon olive oil

1 tablespoon grated fresh ginger

1 teaspoon ground cumin

$\frac{1}{4}$ teaspoon ground nutmeg

$\frac{1}{4}$ teaspoon ground turmeric

$\frac{1}{4}$ teaspoon ground black pepper

$\frac{1}{8}$ teaspoon salt

2 15-ounce cans chickpeas (garbanzo beans), rinsed and drained

$\frac{1}{2}$ cup pimiento-stuffed or jalapeño-stuffed green olives, coarsely chopped

$\frac{1}{2}$ cup coarsely snipped dried apricots

$\frac{1}{3}$ cup snipped fresh Italian (flat-leaf) parsley

1 In a small saucepan bring the water to boiling. Stir in couscous. Remove from heat; cover and let stand for 5 minutes.

2 In a large saucepan cook green onions and garlic in hot oil over medium heat for 3 to 5 minutes or until onions are tender, stirring occasionally. Stir in ginger, cumin, nutmeg, turmeric, pepper, and salt. Cook and stir for 1 minute. Add drained chickpeas, olives, and apricots; cook and stir until heated through.

3 Fluff couscous with a fork and stir in parsley. Top with chickpea mixture.

PER SERVING: *381 cal., 6 g total fat (1 g sat. fat), 0 mg chol., 644 mg sodium, 72 g carb., 13 g fiber, 13 g pro.*

Couscous Cakes with Salsa

PREP: 20 minutes COOK: 4 minutes per batch STAND: 20 minutes OVEN: 200°F MAKES 4 servings

½ cup whole wheat couscous

2 tablespoons whole wheat flour

¼ teaspoon baking soda

⅛ teaspoon salt

1 egg

¾ cup buttermilk or sour fat-free milk*

1 tablespoon canola oil

1 recipe Black Bean Salsa

Nonstick cooking spray

1 In a medium bowl combine uncooked couscous, whole wheat flour, baking soda, and salt. In a small bowl beat egg with a fork. Stir in buttermilk and oil. Stir buttermilk mixture into couscous mixture. Let stand for 20 minutes (batter will thicken as it stands).

2 Meanwhile, prepare Black Bean Salsa; set aside. Preheat oven to 200°F.

3 Lightly coat an unheated griddle or large nonstick skillet with cooking spray. Preheat over medium heat. For each cake, spoon 2 slightly rounded tablespoons of the couscous batter onto the hot griddle or into the skillet; quickly spread to 3½-inch cakes. Cook about 4 minutes or until brown, turning once halfway through cooking or when bottoms are lightly brown and edges are slightly dry. Remove bean cakes from griddle or skillet. Keep warm in oven while cooking remaining cakes.

4 To serve, top couscous cakes with Black Bean Salsa.

PER SERVING: *270 cal., 6 g total fat (1 g sat. fat), 55 mg chol., 639 mg sodium, 46 g carb., 8 g fiber, 13 g pro.*

Black Bean Salsa

In a medium bowl stir together ¾ cup frozen whole kernel corn, thawed; half of a 15-ounce can black beans (¾ cup), rinsed and drained; ¾ cup salsa; ½ cup chopped, peeled jicama; 1 tablespoon snipped fresh cilantro; 1 tablespoon lime juice; and ½ teaspoon ground cumin.

*tip

To make ¾ cup sour fat-free milk, place 2 teaspoons lemon juice or vinegar in a glass measuring cup. Add enough fat-free milk to make ¾ cup total liquid; stir. Let stand for 5 minutes before using.

Barley-Stuffed Peppers

PREP: 25 minutes BAKE: 22 minutes OVEN: 350°F MAKES 4 servings

1   cup sliced fresh mushrooms

1   cup water

2/3   cup quick-cooking barley

1/2   of a vegetable bouillon cube

2   large red, yellow, and/or green sweet peppers

1   egg, lightly beaten

3/4   cup chopped, seeded, and peeled tomato (1 large)

3/4   cup shredded reduced-fat mozzarella cheese

1/2   cup shredded zucchini

1/3   cup soft bread crumbs

1   tablespoon snipped fresh basil or 1/2 teaspoon dried basil, crushed

1   teaspoon snipped fresh rosemary or 1/8 teaspoon dried rosemary, crushed

1/4   teaspoon onion salt

   Several dashes bottled hot pepper sauce

1 Preheat oven to 350°F. In a medium saucepan combine mushrooms, the water, barley, and bouillon cube. Bring to boiling; reduce heat. Simmer, covered, for 12 to 15 minutes or until barley is tender; drain.

2 Meanwhile, halve sweet peppers lengthwise; remove seeds and membranes. If desired, precook sweet peppers in boiling water for 3 minutes. Place peppers, cut sides down, on paper towels to drain.

3 In a medium bowl combine egg, tomato, 1/2 cup of the cheese, the zucchini, bread crumbs, basil, rosemary, onion salt, and hot pepper sauce. Stir in cooked barley mixture. Place peppers, cut sides up, in an ungreased 2-quart rectangular baking dish. Spoon barley mixture into peppers.

4 Bake, covered, for 20 to 25 minutes or until barley mixture is heated through. Sprinkle with the remaining 1/4 cup cheese. Bake, uncovered, about 2 minutes more or until cheese melts.

PER SERVING: *231 cal., 5 g total fat (3 g sat. fat), 65 mg chol., 514 mg sodium, 33 g carb., 4 g fiber, 13 g pro.*

tip
Wild rice makes a tasty, healthful, and colorful side dish. Cut the cost of the pricey marsh grass by mixing it with brown or white rice.

Barley Risotto with Roasted Squash

PREP: 1 hour ROAST: 38 minutes OVEN: 400°F MAKES 6 servings

- 1 **pound butternut squash, peeled, halved, seeded, and cut into 1-inch pieces**
- 3 **tablespoons olive oil**
- ½ **teaspoon kosher or coarse salt**
- ¼ **teaspoon freshly ground black pepper**
  Dash ground nutmeg
- 1 **pound regular barley (2 cups), rinsed and drained**
- 6 **cups vegetable broth**
- 1 **cup finely chopped onion (1 large)**
- 1 **tablespoon minced garlic (6 cloves)**
- ½ **cup dry white wine**
- ½ **cup finely shredded Parmesan cheese**
- 1 **tablespoon snipped fresh thyme**
- 1 **teaspoon snipped fresh sage**
- 1 **tablespoon snipped fresh Italian (flat-leaf) parsley**

1 Preheat oven to 400°F. Place squash in a shallow baking pan. Drizzle 1 tablespoon of the olive oil over squash; sprinkle with salt, pepper, and nutmeg; toss to coat squash pieces. Roast about 30 minutes or until squash is tender. Set aside. In another shallow baking pan evenly spread out barley. Roast for 8 to 10 minutes or until lightly toasted. Set aside.

2 Meanwhile, in a large saucepan bring broth to boiling; reduce heat and simmer until needed.

3 In a 4-quart Dutch oven cook onion and garlic in the remaining 2 tablespoons olive oil over medium heat until onion is tender, stirring occasionally. Add toasted barley. Cook and stir for 2 minutes. Add wine, stirring constantly. Continue to cook and stir until wine is absorbed.

4 Slowly add 1 cup of the hot broth to the barley mixture, stirring constantly. Continue to cook and stir until most of the broth is absorbed. Continue adding broth, 1 cup at a time, stirring constantly until broth is nearly absorbed. When the remaining 1 cup broth has been added, cook and stir until barley mixture is slightly creamy. (This process should take about 35 minutes.) Gently fold in roasted squash, Parmesan cheese, thyme, and sage. Sprinkle with parsley.

PER SERVING: *436 cal., 10 g total fat (2 g sat. fat), 5 mg chol., 1,229 mg sodium, 72 g carb., 15 g fiber, 13 g pro.*

tip

With its hard texture and odd shape, butternut squash is difficult to cut and peel, making the precut version a popular choice even though it costs a bit more.

Southwestern Quinoa-Stuffed Acorn Squash 🌿

PREP: **25 minutes** BAKE: **60 minutes** OVEN: **350°F** MAKES **4 servings**

- 2 **small acorn squash (about 1½ pounds each)**
- 1 **cup water**
- ½ **cup uncooked quinoa, rinsed and drained**
- 1 **teaspoon ground cumin**
- ½ **teaspoon salt**
- 1 **ear fresh sweet corn, kernels cut from cob, or ½ cup frozen whole kernel corn, thawed**
- 1 **cup chopped red sweet pepper (1 medium)**
- 2 **green onions, chopped**
- 2 **medium fresh jalapeño chile peppers, seeded and minced***
- 1 **tablespoon olive oil**
- 1 **15-ounce can black beans, rinsed and drained**

1 Preheat oven to 350°F. Cut each squash in half lengthwise. Using a spoon, scoop out and discard seeds and membranes. Place squash halves, cut sides down, in a 15×10×1-inch baking pan. Bake, uncovered, for 45 to 50 minutes or until squash is just tender.

2 Meanwhile, in a medium saucepan combine the water, quinoa, cumin, and salt. Bring to boiling; reduce heat. Simmer, covered, about 15 minutes or until liquid is absorbed.

3 In a large skillet cook corn, sweet pepper, green onions, and jalapeño peppers in hot oil over medium heat about 5 minutes or until vegetables are tender, stirring occasionally.

4 Stir vegetable mixture and drained black beans into quinoa. Turn squash halves cut sides up. Spoon quinoa mixture evenly into squash halves, mounding as needed.

5 Bake, uncovered, about 15 minutes more or until heated through.

PER SERVING: *317 cal., 6 g total fat (1 g sat. fat), 0 mg chol., 572 mg sodium, 63 g carb., 12 g fiber, 13 g pro.*

*tip

Because hot chile peppers contain volatile oils that can burn your skin and eyes, avoid direct contact with chiles as much as possible. When working with chile peppers, wear plastic or rubber gloves. If your bare hands do touch the chile peppers, wash your hands and nails well with soap and warm water.

Polenta

2½   cups water
1   cup coarse-ground yellow
    cornmeal
1   cup cold water*
1   teaspoon salt

1 In a medium saucepan bring the 2½ cups water to boiling. Meanwhile, in a medium bowl stir together cornmeal, the 1 cup cold water, and the salt.

2 Slowly add cornmeal mixture to boiling water, stirring constantly. Cook and stir until mixture returns to boiling. Reduce heat to medium-low to low. Cook for 25 to 30 minutes or until mixture is very thick and tender, stirring frequently and adjusting heat as needed to maintain a slow boil. To serve, spoon soft polenta into individual serving bowls.

PER SERVING *for soft polenta and firm polenta: 85 cal., 0 g total fat (0 g sat. fat), 0 mg chol., 390 mg sodium, 18 g carb., 1 g fiber, 2 g pro.*

Firm Polenta

Prepare as above, except pour the hot soft polenta into a 9-inch pie plate, spreading into an even layer. Let stand, uncovered, for 30 minutes. Cover and chill at least 1 hour or until firm. Preheat oven to 350°F. Bake polenta, uncovered, about 25 minutes or until heated through. Let stand on a wire rack for 5 minutes. Cut into six wedges to serve. Makes 6 servings.

Fried Polenta

Prepare as above, except pour the hot soft polenta into a 7½×3½×2-inch or 8×4×2-inch loaf pan; cool. Cover and chill for at least 4 hours hours or overnight. Run a thin metal spatula around the edges of the pan. Remove polenta loaf from the pan and cut crosswise into 12 slices. In a large skillet or on a griddle heat 1 tablespoon butter over medium-high heat. Reduce heat to medium. Cook half of the polenta slices for 16 to 20 minutes or until brown and crisp, turning once halfway through cooking. Repeat with remaining polenta slices, adding 1 tablespoon butter to skillet before adding polenta slices. If desired, serve with additional butter and honey or maple-flavor syrup. Makes 6 servings.

PER SERVING: *119 cal., 4 g total fat (2 g sat. fat, 0 g trans fat), 10 mg chol., 418 mg sodium, 18 g carb., 1 g fiber, 2 g pro.*

stir-ins:

Decrease salt to ½ teaspoon and stir in ½ cup (2 ounces) shredded Parmesan, Romano, or fontina cheese after cooking.

Stir in 2 tablespoons snipped fresh basil or fresh Italian (flat-leaf) parsley or 1 teaspoon snipped fresh oregano or thyme after cooking.

Decrease salt to ½ teaspoon and stir in 2 tablespoons butter after cooking.

343

*tip
For added flavor, use chicken-flavor vegetable broth in place of the water and omit the salt.

Wheat Berry Salad with Dried Apricots

PREP: 15 minutes   COOK: 45 minutes   COOL: 1 hour   CHILL: overnight   MAKES 8 servings

3 cups water

1 cup uncooked wheat berries, rinsed and drained

⅛ teaspoon salt

1 15-ounce can garbanzo beans (chickpea), rinsed and drained

1 cup thinly sliced fresh snow peas

½ cup dried apricots, sliced

½ cup dried cranberries

¼ cup chopped green onions (2)

3 tablespoons toasted walnut oil

1 tablespoon lemon juice

½ teaspoon salt

½ teaspoon ground black pepper

1 In a medium bowl combine the water, wheat berries, and the ⅛ teaspoon salt; cover and store in the refrigerator overnight. Transfer to a medium saucepan. Bring to boiling; reduce heat. Simmer, covered, for 45 to 60 minutes or until tender. Drain; cool 1 hour.

2 In large bowl combine drained wheat berries, drained beans, snow peas, apricots, cranberries, and green onions.

3 For dressing, in a small bowl whisk together oil, lemon juice, the ½ teaspoon salt, and the pepper. Pour dressing over wheat berry mixture; stir to coat. Serve at once or cover and store in the refrigerator for up to 24 hours.

PER SERVING: *239 cal., 6 g total fat (1 g sat. fat), 0 mg chol., 342 mg sodium, 43 g carb., 7 g fiber, 6 g pro.*

tip

Wheat berries are unprocessed wheat kernels complete with the bran, germ, and endosperm. They are high in protein, fiber, and many vitamins and minerals. Find them in the health section of your supermarket.

Summer Spelt Medley

PREP: 20 minutes   COOK: 1 hour   CHILL: 1 to 24 hours   MAKES 8 servings

1½   cups uncooked spelt
1   cup chopped red sweet pepper (1 medium)
1   cup chopped, seeded cucumber
½   cup shredded carrot
¼   cup sliced green onions (2)
⅔   cup mayonnaise or salad dressing
2   tablespoons lemon juice
½   teaspoon salt
⅛   teaspoon cayenne pepper

1 In a medium saucepan combine spelt and enough water to cover by 2 inches. Bring to boiling; reduce heat. Simmer, covered, about 1 hour or until tender. Drain well and place spelt into a large bowl.

2 Add sweet pepper, cucumber, carrot, and green onions to spelt; stir to combine. In a small bowl whisk together mayonnaise, lemon juice, salt, and cayenne pepper. Add to spelt mixture; toss to coat. Cover and chill for at least 1 hour or up to 24 hours.

PER SERVING: *276 cal., 16 g total fat (3 g sat. fat), 7 mg chol., 255 mg sodium, 28 g carb., 4 g fiber, 5 g pro.*

tip

345

Whole grains spoil faster than refined grains, so store them in the refrigerator or freezer, especially if storing for longer than 6 months. Store dried beans in a cupboard or pantry at room temperature.

Tabbouleh with Edamame and Feta

PREP: 25 minutes COOK: 15 minutes MAKES: 6 servings

2½ cups water

1¼ cups bulgur

¼ cup lemon juice

3 tablespoons pesto

2 cups fresh or thawed frozen shelled sweet soybeans (edamame)

2 cups cherry tomatoes, cut up

⅓ cup crumbled reduced-fat feta cheese

⅓ cup thinly sliced green onions (2 or 3)

2 tablespoons snipped fresh parsley

¼ teaspoon ground black pepper

Fresh parsley sprigs (optional)

1 In a medium saucepan bring the water to boiling; add uncooked bulgur. Return to boiling; reduce heat. Simmer, covered, about 15 minutes or until most of the liquid is absorbed. Transfer to a large bowl.

2 In a small bowl whisk together lemon juice and pesto. Add lemon juice mixture to cooked bulgur along with soybeans, cherry tomatoes, feta cheese, green onions, the snipped parsley, and pepper. Toss gently to combine. If desired, garnish with parsley sprigs.

PER SERVING: *313 cal., 12 g total fat (1 g sat. fat), 3 mg chol., 187 mg sodium, 37 g carb., 10 g fiber, 18 g pro.*

Red Lentil Rice

PREP: **15 minutes** COOK: **30 minutes** STAND: **5 minutes** MAKES **6 servings**

1   tablespoon olive oil
½   cup chopped onion
     (1 medium)
2   cloves garlic, minced
1   teaspoon cumin
     seeds, crushed
½   teaspoon salt
⅛   teaspoon cayenne pepper
1⅓   cups uncooked basmati rice or
     long grain rice
2   14-ounce cans vegetable broth
½   cup water
1   cup frozen peas
½   cup dry red lentils, rinsed
¼   cup snipped fresh mint
1   teaspoon garam masala
1   recipe Yogurt Raita

1 In a 4-quart Dutch oven heat olive oil over medium heat. Add onion, garlic, cumin seeds, salt, and cayenne pepper. Cook and stir for 2 minutes. Add rice; cook and stir for 1 minute more. Remove from heat. Carefully add broth and water. Bring to boiling; reduce heat. Simmer, covered, for 10 minutes.

2 Stir in peas and lentils. Return to boiling; reduce heat. Simmer, covered, for 8 to 10 minutes or until lentils are just tender.

3 Remove from heat; stir in mint and garam masala. Cover and let stand for 5 minutes before serving. Serve with Yogurt Raita.

PER SERVING: *274 cal., 3 g total fat (1 g sat. fat), 2 mg chol., 815 mg sodium, 51 g carb., 4 g fiber, 10 g pro.*

Yogurt Raita

In a medium bowl combine ⅔ cup plain low-fat yogurt; ¾ cup seeded, chopped cucumber; ½ cup chopped, seeded tomato; 1 tablespoon snipped fresh mint; ⅛ teaspoon salt; and a dash ground black pepper.

make it vegan 🌿
Substitute soy yogurt for the dairy yogurt in the raita.

Lentil and Veggie Tostadas

START TO FINISH: 20 minutes MAKES 4 servings

1¾ cups water

¾ cup red lentils, rinsed
    and drained

¼ cup chopped onion

½ teaspoon salt

½ teaspoon ground cumin

1 clove garlic, minced

1 to 2 tablespoons snipped
    fresh cilantro

4 tostada shells

2 cups assorted chopped fresh
    vegetables (such as broccoli,
    tomato, zucchini, and/or
    yellow summer squash)

¾ cup shredded Monterey Jack
    cheese (3 ounces)

1 In a medium saucepan stir together the water, lentils, onion, salt, cumin, and garlic. Bring to boiling; reduce heat. Simmer, covered, for 12 to 15 minutes or until lentils are tender and most of the liquid is absorbed. Use a fork to mash the cooked lentils; stir in cilantro.

2 Spread lentil mixture on tostada shells; top with vegetables and cheese. Place tostadas on a large baking sheet. Broil 6 inches from the heat about 2 minutes or until cheese melts.

PER SERVING: *280 cal., 10 g total fat (4 g sat. fat), 19 mg chol., 427 mg sodium, 33 g carb., 7 g fiber, 15 g pro.*

make it vegan

Substitute Monterey Jack-flavor soy cheese for the Monterey Jack cheese.

tip

Lentils come in three main varieties: brown, yellow, and red. All are low in fat and high in fiber and protein, but they cook at different rates. To substitute one lentil type for another, you may need to adjust cooking times. Check the package for directions.

Hoisin Tempeh with Stir-Fry Vegetables

START TO FINISH: **25 minutes** MAKES **4 servings**

2 teaspoons canola oil

¾ teaspoon grated fresh ginger

2 cloves garlic, minced

1 8-ounce package tempeh (fermented soybean cake), cut into ½-inch pieces

4 cups sliced bok choy

1 cup julienned carrots

1 cup fresh snow peas or one 6-ounce package frozen pea pods or sugar snap peas, thawed

1 cup cremini and/or shitake mushrooms, sliced

¼ cup orange juice

3 tablespoons hoisin sauce

1½ cups hot cooked brown rice

1 Pour oil into a large wok or very large skillet; heat wok over medium-high heat. (Add more oil as necessary during cooking.) Add ginger and garlic; cook and stir about 30 seconds or until fragrant. Stir in tempeh, bok choy, and carrots. Cook and stir for 4 to 5 minutes more or until vegetables are crisp-tender. Stir in pea pods, mushrooms, orange juice, and hoisin sauce. Heat through.

2 Serve vegetable mixture over hot cooked rice.

PER SERVING: *285 cal., 10 g total fat (2 g sat. fat), 0 mg chol., 273 mg sodium, 38 g carb., 4 g fiber, 15 g pro.*

Meatless Sweet Potato Hash

START TO FINISH: **30 minutes**   MAKES **4 servings**

1   **medium onion, halved and thinly sliced**

1   **tablespoon olive oil**

1   **large sweet potato, peeled and cut into ½-inch pieces**

1   **12-ounce package refrigerated or frozen uncooked ground meat substitute (soy protein), thawed if necessary**

1   **medium zucchini, chopped**

1   **teaspoon snipped fresh rosemary or ½ teaspoon dried rosemary, crushed**

1   **tablespoon Dijon-style mustard**

1   **tablespoon fat-free milk**

2   **teaspoons honey**

Snipped fresh rosemary (optional)

1 In a very large nonstick skillet cook the onion in hot oil over medium heat for 3 minutes, stirring occasionally. Add potato pieces. Cook for 8 to 10 minutes or until potatoes are tender and brown, stirring occasionally.

2 Add ground meat substitute, zucchini, and the 1 teaspoon rosemary. Cook for 3 to 5 minutes or until zucchini is tender. In a small bowl combine mustard, milk, and honey. Stir mustard mixture into potato mixture; heat through. If desired, garnish with additional snipped rosemary.

PER SERVING: *216 cal., 7 g total fat (1 g sat. fat), 0 mg chol., 487 mg sodium, 20 g carb., 7 g fiber, 17 g pro.*

Kung Pao Mock Chicken

START TO FINISH: **20 minutes** MAKES **4 servings**

1 **10-ounce package frozen cooked breaded meatless chicken-style nuggets**

¼ **cup pineapple juice**

¼ **cup light teriyaki sauce**

1 **tablespoon Szechwan seasoning**

2 **teaspoons cornstarch**
   Nonstick cooking spray

1 **16-ounce package frozen green bean stir-fry vegetable blend**

½ **of a 16-ounce package frozen (yellow, green, and red) sweet peppers and onion stir-fry vegetables (2 cups)**

2 **tablespoons sliced almonds or coarsely chopped peanuts (toasted if desired)**

1 Prepare nuggets according to package directions. Meanwhile, in a small bowl combine pineapple juice, teriyaki sauce, Szechwan seasoning, and cornstarch. Set aside.

2 Coat an unheated large wok or very large nonstick skillet with cooking spray; heat wok over medium-high heat. Add stir-fry vegetables; cook and stir for 3 to 4 minutes or just until tender. Push vegetables from center of wok.

3 Stir teriyaki sauce mixture; add to center of wok with vegetables. Cook and stir sauce until thickened and bubbly; cook and stir for 2 minutes more, stirring to coat vegetables. Divide vegetable mixture among individual serving plates. Halve each chicken-style nugget crosswise; place halved nuggets on vegetables. Sprinkle with almonds.

PER SERVING: *266 cal., 8 g total fat (1 g sat. fat), 0 mg chol., 964 mg sodium, 32 g carb., 5 g fiber, 15 g pro.*

tip

351

Use meatless chicken-style nuggets in a variety of ways. Add them to tossed salads, wrap them in a tortilla with veggies, serve them with pasta and sauce, or just enjoy plain or with your favorite dipping sauce.

Bean-Tofu Burritos

PREP: 20 minutes STAND: 30 minutes MAKES 4 servings

½ teaspoon finely shredded lime peel

¼ cup lime juice

1 tablespoon canola oil

2 cloves garlic, minced

1 teaspoon salt-free Southwest chipotle or fiesta lime seasoning blend

⅛ teaspoon salt

1 12- to 16-ounce package firm, water-packed tofu (fresh bean curd), drained and cut into ½-inch cubes

½ cup light sour cream

1 cup canned black beans, rinsed and drained

4 8-inch whole grain or whole wheat flour tortillas

1 cup packaged shredded iceberg lettuce

1 medium yellow or red sweet pepper, seeded and cut into bite-size strips

1 In a medium bowl combine lime peel, lime juice, oil, garlic, seasoning blend, and salt. Transfer 1 tablespoon of the lime mixture to a small bowl. Add tofu to the remaining lime mixture in the medium bowl; toss to coat. Let stand for 30 minutes at room temperature, gently stirring occasionally.

2 Stir sour cream into the 1 tablespoon lime mixture in the small bowl. In another medium bowl use a fork or potato masher to coarsely mash drained beans. Stir in ¼ cup of the sour cream mixture into beans.

3 Spread bean mixture onto tortillas, leaving a 1-inch border around the edges. Use a slotted spoon to spoon tofu mixture on top of bean mixture on bottom halves of tortillas. Top tofu mixture with lettuce, sweet pepper, and the remaining sour cream mixture. Roll up tortillas. Cut into thirds to serve.

PER SERVING: *331 cal., 13 g total fat (3 g sat. fat), 8 mg chol., 589 mg sodium, 33 g carb., 15 g fiber, 22 g pro.*

352

make it vegan
Substitute tofu sour cream for the light sour cream.

🍃 Marinated Tofu with Edamame Stir-Fry

PREP: 30 minutes   MARINATE: 30 minutes   COOK: 6 minutes   MAKES 4 servings

¼   cup rice vinegar

2   tablespoons reduced-sodium soy sauce

2   tablespoons toasted sesame oil

1   tablespoon honey

1   tablespoon grated fresh ginger or 1 teaspoon ground ginger

2   cloves garlic, minced

1   16- to 18-ounce package firm or extra-firm tofu (fresh bean curd), drained and cut into 4 slices

    Nonstick cooking spray

3   cups sliced, stemmed shiitake mushrooms and/or button mushrooms

2   medium red, yellow, and/or orange sweet peppers, seeded and cut into bite-size strips

½   cup chopped red onion

4   cups coarsely shredded bok choy

1   cup frozen shelled sweet soybeans (edamame), thawed

½   teaspoon cornstarch

1   tablespoon sesame seeds, toasted

¼   teaspoon crushed red pepper (optional)

1 For marinade, in a 2-quart rectangular baking dish combine vinegar, soy sauce, 1 tablespoon of the sesame oil, the honey, ginger, and garlic. Add tofu slices, turning to coat. Marinate at room temperature for 30 minutes, turning tofu once halfway through marinating.

2 Coat an unheated nonstick grill pan with cooking spray; heat pan over medium-high heat. Transfer tofu slices to grill pan, reserving marinade in the baking dish. Cook tofu for 4 to 6 minutes or until heated through and starting to brown, turning once halfway through cooking.

3 Meanwhile, in a large nonstick skillet heat the remaining 1 tablespoon sesame oil over medium-high heat. Add mushrooms, sweet peppers, and red onion; cook and stir for 3 to 5 minutes or until crisp-tender. Add bok choy and edamame; cook and stir for 2 to 3 minutes more or until bok choy is wilted. Whisk cornstarch into the reserved marinade; add to vegetable mixture. Cook and stir until thickened and bubbly. Cook and stir for 1 minute more.

4 Divide vegetable mixture among individual serving bowls or plates. If desired, cut tofu slices in half. Place tofu on top of vegetable mixture. Sprinkle with sesame seeds and, if desired, crushed red pepper.

PER SERVING: *323 cal., 15 g total fat (1 g sat. fat), 0 mg chol., 323 mg sodium, 25 g carb., 6 g iber, 21 g pro.*

Meatless Citrus-Corn Tacos

START TO FINISH: **30 minutes** MAKES **4 servings**

½   **cup orange juice**

¼   **cup snipped fresh cilantro**

1   **teaspoon finely shredded lime peel**

2   **tablespoons lime juice**

1   **medium fresh jalapeño chile pepper, seeded and finely chopped***

3   **cloves garlic, minced**

1½   **teaspoons cornstarch**

⅛   **teaspoon salt**

⅛   **teaspoon ground black pepper**

2   **teaspoons cooking oil**

1   **medium red sweet pepper, seeded and cut into bite-size strips**

1   **12-ounce package frozen cooked and crumbled ground meat substitute (soy protein), thawed**

1   **cup frozen whole kernel corn**

8   **6-inch corn tortillas**

½   **cup light sour cream**

1 For sauce, in a small bowl combine orange juice, cilantro, lime peel, lime juice, jalapeño pepper, garlic, cornstarch, salt, and black pepper. Set aside.

2 Pour oil into a large nonstick skillet; heat skillet over medium-high heat. Add sweet pepper strips; cook and stir until crisp-tender. Remove sweet pepper strips from skillet.

3 Add ground meat substitute to skillet. Cook, stirring occasionally, for 3 to 4 minutes or until heated through. Stir in corn. Stir sauce; add to skillet. Cook and stir until thickened and bubbly. Reduce heat; cook and stir for 2 minutes more. Return sweet pepper strips to skillet; stir to combine and heat through.

4 To soften tortillas, wrap in microwave-safe paper towels. Microwave on 100 percent power (high) for 45 to 60 seconds or until warm. Divide the pepper mixture among tortillas and top with sour cream. Fold the tortillas over the filling.

PER SERVING: *361 cal., 11 g total fat (2 g sat. fat), 8 mg chol., 490 mg sodium, 47 g carb., 10 g fiber, 21 g pro.*

354

*tip

Because chile peppers contain volatile oils that can burn your skin and eyes, avoid direct contact with them as much as possible. When working with chile peppers, wear plastic or rubber gloves. If your bare hands do touch the peppers, wash your hands and nails well with soap and warm water.

Sesame-Orange Tofu

START TO FINISH: **30 minutes** MAKES **4 servings**

¼ cup finely chopped peanuts

1 tablespoon sesame seeds

1 teaspoon grated fresh ginger or ½ teaspoon ground ginger

⅛ teaspoon crushed red pepper

1 12-ounce package firm or extra-firm tub-style tofu (fresh bean curd), drained and cut into ½-inch cubes

1 tablespoon olive oil

3 cups frozen stir-fry vegetables (any combination), thawed

½ cup stir-fry sauce

2 cups hot cooked brown rice

2 green onions, thinly sliced

1 medium orange, cut into 8 wedges

1 In a large bowl combine 1 tablespoon of the peanuts, the sesame seeds, ginger, and crushed red pepper. Add tofu; gently toss to coat.

2 In a large skillet heat oil over medium heat. (If necessary, add more oil during cooking.) Add tofu mixture to skillet. Cook and gently stir until sesame seeds are toasted and tofu begins to brown.

3 Push tofu mixture to side of skillet. Add vegetables; cook and stir until heated through. Add stir-fry sauce; cook and stir gently until mixture is bubbly.

4 Serve tofu mixture over hot cooked rice. Sprinkle with the remaining 3 tablespoons peanuts and the green onions. Serve with orange wedges.

PER SERVING: *330 cal., 12 g total fat (2 g sat. fat), 1 mg chol., 854 mg sodium, 41 g carb., 6 g fiber, 16 g pro.*

355

tip

Sesame seeds, like many seeds, provide protein and calcium. Incorporate more of them into your diet by adding them to stir-fries, baked goods, and granola.

Meatless Tacos

PREP: 10 minutes **COOK:** 35 minutes **MAKES** 8 servings

- ½ cup water
- ¼ cup dry lentils, rinsed and drained
- ¼ cup chopped onion
- 8 taco shells
- 1 8-ounce can tomato sauce
- ½ of a 1.125-ounce envelope (5 teaspoons) taco seasoning mix
- 8 ounces firm or extra-firm tub-style tofu (fresh bean curd), drained and finely chopped
- 1½ cups shredded lettuce
- 1 medium tomato, chopped
- ½ cup shredded cheddar cheese
- ½ cup salsa (optional)

1 In a medium saucepan combine the water, lentils, and onion. Bring to boiling; reduce heat. Simmer, covered, for 25 to 30 minutes or until lentils are tender and liquid is absorbed.

2 Meanwhile, heat taco shells according to package directions.

3 Stir tomato sauce and taco seasoning mix into lentil mixture. Bring to boiling; reduce heat. Simmer, uncovered, for 5 minutes. Stir in tofu; heat through. Spoon lentil mixture into taco shells. Top with lettuce, tomato, and cheese. If desired, serve with salsa.

PER SERVING: *148 cal., 7 g total fat (2 g sat. fat), 7 mg chol., 460 mg sodium, 16 g carb., 3 g fiber, 7 g pro.*

Bulgur Tacos

Prepare as above, except increase water to ¾ cup and substitute ¼ cup bulgur for lentils. Simmer water, bulgur, and onion, covered, about 15 minutes or until bulgur is tender and liquid is absorbed. Makes 8 servings.

PER SERVING: *143 calories, 7 g total fat (2 g sat. fat), 7 mg chol., 460 mg sodium, 16 g carb., 2 g fiber, 6 g pro.*

Vegetable Tacos

Prepare as above, except stir 1 cup frozen whole kernel corn and ¾ cup shredded carrot into the tomato sauce mixture. Increase number of taco shells to 12. Makes 12 servings.

PER SERVING: *133 calories, 6 g total fat (2 g sat. fat), 5 mg cholesterol, 326 mg sodium, 17 g carb., 3 g fiber, 6 g pro.*

tip

When buying salad dressing, check the nutrition facts label for sodium content. Some brands and flavor varieties, such as Caesar, have far more sodium than others.

Asparagus-Leek Risotto

PREP: 20 minutes ROAST: 10 minutes COOK: 30 minutes OVEN: 450°F MAKES 4 servings

12 ounces asparagus spears

2 tablespoons olive oil

Salt

Ground black pepper

2½ cups chicken-flavored vegetable broth

½ cup white wine or chicken-flavor vegetable broth

1½ cups sliced leeks

1 cup uncooked Arborio rice or long grain rice

⅓ cup freshly grated Parmesan cheese

2 tablespoons snipped fresh parsley

½ teaspoon finely shredded lemon peel

1 tablespoon lemon juice

¼ teaspoon coarsely ground black pepper

Lemon slices (optional)

Lemon peel (optional)

1 Preheat oven to 450°F. Snap off and discard woody bases from asparagus. Place asparagus in a single layer in a shallow baking pan; brush with 1 tablespoon of the olive oil and lightly sprinkle with salt and black pepper. Roast about 10 minutes or until asparagus is crisp-tender. Cool slightly. Cut two-thirds of the asparagus into 2-inch pieces; set aside all asparagus.

2 Meanwhile, in a medium saucepan bring broth and wine to boiling; reduce heat and simmer until needed. In a large saucepan cook leeks in the remaining 1 tablespoon olive oil over medium heat about 5 minutes or until leeks are tender. Add rice. Cook and stir about 5 minutes or until rice is golden brown.

3 Slowly add 1 cup of hot broth mixture to the rice mixture, stirring constantly. Continue to cook and stir until broth mixture is absorbed. Add another ½ cup of the broth mixture, stirring constantly. Continue to cook and stir until broth mixture is absorbed. Add broth mixture, ½ cup at a time, stirring constantly until the broth mixture has been absorbed. (This process should take about 22 minutes.)

4 Stir the remaining ½ cup broth mixture into the rice mixture. Cook and stir until rice is slightly creamy and just tender. Stir in 2-inch asparagus pieces, Parmesan cheese, parsley, the ½ teaspoon lemon peel, lemon juice, and coarse black pepper. Top risotto with asparagus spears. If desired, garnish with lemon slices and additional lemon peel.

PER SERVING: *277 cal., 9 g total fat (2 g sat. fat), 6 mg chol., 605 mg sodium, 39 g carb., 3 g fiber, 8 g protein.*

Vegetable Risotto

PREP: 30 minutes COOK: 30 minutes MAKES 4 servings

7 cups chicken-flavor
vegetable broth

2 cups uncooked Arborio rice or
long grain rice

1 cup water

1 teaspoon paprika

2½ cups cubed and peeled
butternut squash (1 pound)

1¾ cups chopped and peeled
turnips or parsnips (2 small)

1½ cups coarsely chopped and
seeded red sweet peppers
(2 medium)

1 cup coarsely chopped carrots
(2 medium)

2 cups cremini mushrooms,
quartered

1¼ cups chopped zucchini
(1 medium)

½ cup sliced green onions (4)

2 tablespoons olive oil

2 teaspoons snipped
fresh thyme

1 In a large saucepan bring broth to boiling; reduce heat and simmer until needed.

2 In a 4-quart Dutch oven bring rice, the water, and paprika to boiling; reduce heat. Simmer, stirring frequently, until most of the liquid is absorbed. Add squash, turnips, sweet peppers, carrots, and 1 cup of the broth. Bring to boiling; reduce heat. Simmer and stir until most of the broth is absorbed. Continue adding 5 cups of the broth, 1 cup at a time, stirring constantly until broth is absorbed. (This process should take about 20 minutes.)

3 Add mushrooms, zucchini, green onions, and remaining 1 cup broth. Continue to cook and stir about 10 minutes more or until broth is absorbed, vegetables are tender, and rice is tender yet slightly firm in the center.

4 Remove from heat; stir in olive oil. Sprinkle with thyme. Serve half of the risotto. Reserve the remaining risotto to make Veggie Risotto Cakes. Store risotto in an airtight container in the refrigerator for up to 3 days.

PER SERVING: *495 cal., 8 g total fat (1 g sat. fat), 0 mg chol., 1,238 mg sodium, 98 g carb., 7 g fiber, 12 g pro.*

Veggie Risotto Cakes with Horseradish Sour Cream

PREP: 30 minutes   COOK: 16 minutes   OVEN: 300°F   MAKES 6 to 8 servings

½   recipe Vegetable Risotto (see recipe, page 360)

½   cup grated Parmesan cheese

2   tablespoons snipped fresh Italian (flat-leaf) parsley

1   cup all-purpose flour

2   eggs, lightly beaten

1   cup fine dry bread crumbs

6   tablespoons olive oil

1   recipe Horseradish Sour Cream

    Snipped fresh Italian (flat-leaf) parsley

1 Preheat oven to 300°F. In a large bowl stir together the Vegetable Risotto, the grated Parmesan cheese, and the 2 tablespoons parsley. Form the risotto mixture into twelve to fourteen ¾-inch-thick patties.

2 Place flour, eggs, and bread crumbs in 3 separate shallow dishes. Coat each patty with flour, tapping off excess. Coat in the egg, letting excess drip off, then dip in the bread crumbs to coat. Transfer to a sheet of waxed paper. Repeat with remaining patties.

3 In a very large skillet heat 3 tablespoons of the olive oil over medium heat. Add 6 to 7 of the risotto patties in a single layer, frying on 1 side about 4 minutes or until golden brown. Turn carefully; fry about 4 minutes more or until second side is golden brown. Drain on paper towels. Repeat with remaining patties. Keep risotto cakes warm in a oven.

4 Serve with Horseradish Sour Cream. Sprinkle with additional snipped Italian parsley.

PER SERVING: *562 cal., 28 g total fat (8 g sat. fat), 96 mg chol., 915 mg sodium, 64 g carb., 4 g fiber, 14 g pro.*

Horseradish Sour Cream

In a small bowl stir together one 8-ounce carton sour cream, 2 tablespoons prepared horseradish, and 2 teaspoons Dijon-style mustard. Cover and chill until ready to use. Makes about 1 cup.

Spinach-Pea Risotto

PREP: 10 minutes COOK: 30 minutes MAKES 6 servings

2 cloves garlic, minced

2 tablespoons olive oil

1 cup uncooked Arborio rice

½ cup thinly sliced carrot

2 14-ounce cans vegetable broth (3½ cups)

2 cups fresh spinach leaves, coarsely chopped

1 cup frozen baby or regular peas

2 ounces Parmigiano-Reggiano cheese, shredded

⅓ cup thinly sliced green onions (2 or 3)

¼ cup thin wedges fresh radishes

2 teaspoons snipped fresh tarragon

Parmigiano-Reggiano cheese (optional)

1 In a large saucepan cook and stir garlic in hot oil over medium heat for 30 seconds. Add rice. Cook and stir about 5 minutes more or until rice is golden brown. Remove from heat. Stir in carrot.

2 Meanwhile, in a medium saucepan bring broth to boiling; reduce heat and simmer until needed.

3 Slowly add 1 cup of hot broth to the rice mixture, stirring constantly. Continue to cook and stir over medium heat until broth is absorbed. Add another ½ cup broth, stirring frequently until broth is absorbed. Continue to cook and stir until broth mixture is absorbed. Add broth, ½ cup at a time, stirring constantly until the broth mixture has been absorbed. (This process should take about 22 minutes.)

4 Stir the remaining broth into the rice mixture. Cook and stir until rice is slightly creamy and just tender.

5 Stir in spinach, peas, the shredded Parmigiano-Reggiano cheese, green onions, radishes, and tarragon; heat through. If desired, top with additional Parmigiano-Reggiano cheese cut into shards with a vegetable peeler. Serve immediately.

PER SERVING: 191 cal., 7 g total fat (2 g sat. fat), 7 mg chol., 723 mg sodium, 25 g carb., 2 g fiber, 7 g pro.

Veggie-Stuffed Portobello Mushrooms

PREP: 25 minutes   BAKE: 17 minutes   OVEN: 425°F   MAKES 4 servings

1 small yellow sweet pepper, seeded and cut into bite-size strips

1 small red onion, chopped

1 medium zucchini, coarsely shredded

1 carrot, coarsely shredded

1 stalk celery, thinly sliced

2 cloves garlic, minced

2 to 3 tablespoons olive oil

1 tablespoon snipped fresh basil

1 tablespoon lemon juice

¼ teaspoon salt

¼ teaspoon ground black pepper

1 5-ounce package fresh baby spinach

½ cup fine dry bread crumbs

½ cup finely shredded Parmesan cheese

4 4- to 5-inch portobello mushroom caps, stems removed

4 slices provolone cheese

1 Preheat oven to 425°F. Line a 15×10×1-inch baking pan with foil. In a large skillet cook and stir sweet pepper, onion, zucchini, carrot, celery, and garlic in hot oil over medium-high heat for 4 minutes. Stir in basil, lemon juice, salt, and black pepper.

2 Top sweet pepper mixture with spinach. Cook, covered, about 2 minutes more or until spinach is wilted. Remove from heat. Stir crumbs and half of the Parmesan cheese into spinach mixture; set aside.

3 If desired, remove gills from mushrooms. Arrange mushrooms, stemmed sides up, on prepared pan. Top each with slice of provolone cheese. Divide spinach mixture among mushroom caps. Bake for 15 minutes (mushrooms will water out slightly). Top with the remaining Parmesan cheese. Bake about 2 minutes more or until heated through.

PER SERVING: *296 cal., 17 g total fat (7 g sat. fat), 25 mg chol., 617 mg sodium, 24 g carb., 4 g fiber, 14 g pro.*

361

Portobello Curry with Green Rice

PREP: 30 minutes COOK: 15 minutes MAKES 4 servings

2 cups water

1 cup uncooked basmati rice or long grain rice

½ teaspoon salt

1 cup unsweetened coconut milk

½ cup snipped fresh cilantro

4 teaspoons grated fresh ginger

2 cloves garlic, minced

1 tablespoon lime juice

1 pound portobello mushrooms, cut into ½-inch slices

2 tablespoons canola oil

½ cup sliced green onions (4)

2 teaspoons Madras (spicy) curry powder or curry powder

⅛ teaspoon crushed red pepper

1 cup cherry tomatoes, halved or quartered

   Salt

   Ground black pepper

2 tablespoons coarsely chopped cashews or peanuts

1 In a medium saucepan combine the water, rice, and salt. Bring to boiling; reduce heat. Simmer, covered, for 15 to 20 minutes or until rice is tender and liquid is absorbed.

2 Meanwhile, in blender or food processor combine ½ cup of the coconut milk, the cilantro, 1 teaspoon of the ginger, half of the minced garlic, and the lime juice. Cover; blend or process until nearly smooth. Stir coconut milk mixture into rice. Cover; keep warm.

3 In large skillet cook mushrooms in hot oil over medium heat for 5 minutes, stirring occasionally. Add green onions, curry powder, red pepper, the remaining 3 teaspoons ginger, and the remaining minced garlic. Cook and stir for 1 minute more. Stir in tomatoes and the remaining ½ cup coconut milk; heat through. Season to taste with salt and pepper.

4 To serve, divide rice mixture among individual plates. Top with mushroom mixture and sprinkle with cashews.

PER SERVING: *438 cal., 24 g total fat (14 g sat. fat), 0 mg chol., 465 mg sodium, 51 g carb., 6 g fiber, 9 g pro.*

Spaghetti Squash with Chunky Tomato Sauce

PREP: 25 minutes COOK: 15 minutes MAKES 4 servings

1 tablespoon olive oil

1 cup coarsely chopped zucchini

2/3 cup chopped onion

1/2 cup shredded carrot

2 cloves garlic, minced

1 14.5-ounce can diced tomatoes, undrained

1 8-ounce can tomato sauce

2 tablespoons tomato paste

2 teaspoons dried Italian seasoning, crushed

1/8 teaspoon ground black pepper

4 cups cooked spaghetti squash*

1/4 cup shredded Parmesan cheese (2 ounces)

Small fresh basil leaves (optional)

1 For sauce, in a large saucepan heat oil over medium heat. Add zucchini, onion, carrot, and garlic; cook until tender, stirring occasionally. Add undrained diced tomatoes, tomato sauce, tomato paste, Italian seasoning, and pepper. Bring to boiling; reduce heat. Simmer, uncovered, for 15 minutes, stirring occasionally.

2 Serve sauce over spaghetti squash. Sprinkle with Parmesan cheese. If desired, garnish with basil leaves.

PER SERVING: *154 cal., 6 g total fat (1 g sat. fat), 4 mg chol., 610 mg sodium, 23 g carb., 3 g fiber, 5 g pro.*

*tip

To cook spaghetti squash, cut a 3-pound spaghetti squash in half lengthwise; remove seeds and strings. Place one half, cut side down, in a microwave-safe baking dish. Using a fork, prick the skin all over. Microwave on 100 percent power (high) for 6 to 7 minutes or until tender when pierced with a fork; carefully remove from baking dish. Repeat with the other half. (Or preheat oven to 350°F. Place both halves, cut sides down, in a shallow baking pan and bake for 30 to 40 minutes or until tender.) Cool slightly; using 2 forks, shred and separate the squash pulp into strands. Makes about 4 cups.

make it vegan

Substitute desired soy cheese for the Parmesan cheese.

tip

If you're in a rush, use a purchased pasta sauce instead of making your own. Look for brands with little to no added sugar.

Spicy Vegetable Fried Rice

START TO FINISH: **30 minutes** MAKES **4 servings**

- 4 **eggs**
- 2 **tablespoons water**
  Nonstick cooking spray
- 1 **tablespoon olive oil**
- 1 **tablespoon finely chopped fresh ginger**
- 2 **cloves garlic, minced**
- 2 **cups chopped Chinese cabbage**
- 1 **cup coarsely shredded carrot**
- 1 **cup fresh pea pods, trimmed**
- 2 **cups cooked brown rice, chilled**
- ⅓ **cup sliced green onions (2 or 3)**
- 2 **tablespoons reduced-sodium soy sauce**
- 1 **to 2 teaspoons Sriracha chile sauce**
- 2 **tablespoons snipped fresh cilantro**
  Lime slices or wedges

1 In a small bowl whisk together eggs and the water. Coat an unheated large nonstick skillet with cooking spray. Preheat skillet over medium heat. Pour in egg mixture. Cook, without stirring, until mixture begins to set on the bottom and around edges. With a spatula or large spoon, lift and fold the partially cooked eggs so that the uncooked portion flows underneath. Continue cooking over medium heat for 2 to 3 minutes or until egg mixture is cooked through, but is still glossy and moist, keeping eggs in large pieces. Carefully transfer eggs to a medium bowl; set aside.

2 In the same skillet heat oil over medium-high heat. Add ginger and garlic; cook and stir for 30 seconds. Add cabbage, carrot, and pea pods; cook and stir for 2 minutes. Stir in cooked eggs, brown rice, green onions, soy sauce, and chile sauce; cook and stir for 2 to 3 minutes more or until heated through. Sprinkle with cilantro. Serve with lime slices.

PER SERVING: *250 cal., 9 g total fat (2 g sat. fat), 212 mg chol., 367 mg sodium, 31 g carb., 4 g fiber, 11 g pro.*

Stuffed Zucchini with Black Beans, Corn, and Poblano Pepper

PREP: 30 minutes BAKE: 20 minutes OVEN: 400°F MAKES 2 servings

2 medium zucchini (about 8 ounces each)

1 teaspoon olive oil

1 fresh poblano chile pepper, seeded and finely chopped*

¼ cup finely chopped onion

2 cloves garlic, minced

½ cup fresh or frozen corn kernels

⅓ cup chopped tomato

⅓ cup canned no-salt-added black beans, rinsed and drained

½ cup shredded reduced-fat Monterey Jack cheese (2 ounces)

2 tablespoons snipped fresh cilantro

1 Preheat oven to 400°F. Trim ends of zucchini; cut each zucchini in half lengthwise. Using a melon baller or a small measuring spoon, scoop out and discard pulp, leaving ¼-inch shells. Place zucchini shells, cut sides up, in a shallow baking pan.

2 In a large nonstick skillet heat oil over medium heat. Add chile pepper and onion. Cook about 6 minutes or until tender, stirring occasionally. Add garlic; cook and stir for 1 minute. Stir in corn, tomato, and drained black beans. Cook about 2 minutes or until heated through, stirring occasionally. Remove from heat. Stir in ¼ cup of the cheese and the cilantro.

3 Using a small spoon, spoon bean mixture evenly into zucchini halves, packing filling lightly and mounding as needed. Sprinkle with the remaining ¼ cup cheese. Bake, uncovered, about 20 minutes or until zucchini is tender.

PER SERVING: *243 cal., 9 g total fat (4 g sat. fat), 20 mg chol., 274 mg sodium, 31 g carb., 6 g fiber, 15 g pro.*

*tip

Because chile peppers contain volatile oils that can burn your skin and eyes, avoid direct contact with them as much as possible. When working with chile peppers, wear plastic or rubber gloves. If your bare hands do touch the peppers, wash your hands and nails well with soap and warm water.

make it vegan

Substitute desired soy cheese for the Monterey Jack cheese.

Potato, Zucchini, and Carrot Pancakes

PREP: 30 minutes COOK: 8 minutes per batch BAKE: 10 minutes OVEN: 425°F MAKES: 4 servings

Nonstick cooking spray

1¼ cups shredded zucchini (1 medium)

4 cups shredded, peeled baking potatoes (about 1½ pounds)

1 cup shredded carrot (1 large)

¼ cup all-purpose flour

5 large eggs

2 teaspoons snipped fresh thyme or ½ teaspoon dried thyme, crushed

½ teaspoon salt

¼ teaspoon ground black pepper

1 tablespoon canola oil

1 recipe Spring Greens Salad

Mixed peppercorns, crushed (optional)

1 Preheat oven to 425°F. Lightly coat 2 small baking sheets with cooking spray; set aside.

2 Drain zucchini in a colander; press to squeeze out excess liquid. In a large bowl combine zucchini, potatoes, carrot, flour, 1 of the eggs, thyme, salt, and pepper.

3 In an extra-large nonstick skillet heat half of the oil over medium heat. To make a pancake, spoon about a 1-cup portion of the potato mixture into skillet; evenly press and round edges with back of spatula to form a pancake. Cook 2 pancakes at a time, 4 to 5 minutes each side or until golden brown, turning once halfway through cooking. Transfer pancakes to prepared baking sheets. Repeat with remaining oil and potato mixture.

4 With the back of a wooden spoon or a ¼-cup measure gently press each pancake, slightly off-center, to make a 3-inch-diameter depression, deep enough to hold an egg. Pour 1 egg into each pancake nest. Place pancakes with eggs in oven, being careful not to tilt baking sheets. Bake, uncovered, 10 to 12 minutes or until eggs are cooked through. Transfer pancakes to individual serving plates. Serve with Spring Greens Salad. If desired, sprinkle with crushed peppercorns.

PER SERVING: *362 cal., 20 g total fat (4 g sat. fat), 264 mg chol., 599 mg sodium, 34 g carb., 4 g fiber, 13 g pro.*

Spring Greens Salad

In a large bowl combine 3 cups watercress and 1 small carrot, peeled and cut lengthwise into thin ribbons. For dressing, in a small bowl combine 2 teaspoons white wine vinegar, 1 teaspoon Dijon-style mustard, ¼ teaspoon salt, and ⅛ teaspoon ground black pepper. Gradually whisk in 3 tablespoons olive oil. Toss dressing with watercress mixture.

Zucchini Cakes with Mushroom Ragout

START TO FINISH: **25 minutes**   OVEN: **400°F**   MAKES **4 servings**

Nonstick cooking spray

½ of a medium zucchini, shredded (1 cup)

1 8.5-ounce package corn muffin mix

1 cup shredded cheddar cheese (4 ounces)

¼ cup milk

1 egg, lightly beaten

¼ teaspoon cayenne pepper

1 tablespoon olive oil

12 ounces assorted mushrooms, quartered (4½ cups)

Salt

Ground black pepper

1 cup drained roasted red sweet peppers

1 Preheat oven to 400°F. Lightly coat twelve 2½-inch muffin cups with cooking spray; set aside.

2 In a medium bowl combine zucchini, muffin mix, cheese, milk, egg, and cayenne pepper; spoon evenly into prepared muffin cups. Bake for 11 to 14 minutes or until golden brown.

3 Meanwhile, in a large skillet heat olive oil over medium-high heat. Add mushrooms; cook for 3 to 4 minutes or until tender, stirring occasionally. Season to taste with salt and black pepper.

4 For sauce, place roasted peppers in a blender or food processor. Cover; blend or process until nearly smooth.

5 Arrange 3 cakes on each plate with some of the mushrooms and pepper sauce.

PER SERVING: *443 cal., 21 g total fat (7 g sat. fat), 84 mg chol., 701 mg sodium, 49 g carb., 2 g fiber, 16 g pro.*

367

tip

If you're keeping an eye on carbohydrates, make quinoa your go-to grain. It's lower in carbohydrates than most grains and it is a complete protein.

Zucchini-Carrot Burgers

START TO FINISH: 25 minutes MAKES 2 servings

- 2 tablespoons refrigerated or frozen egg product, thawed
- 1½ teaspoons olive oil
- ½ teaspoon dried oregano, crushed
- ½ cup crushed stone-ground wheat crackers (about 11)
- ½ cup finely shredded zucchini
- ½ cup finely shredded carrot
- 2 tablespoons chopped green onion
- ¼ cup plain low-fat yogurt
- 1 small clove garlic, minced
- ¼ teaspoon finely shredded lemon peel
- 1 large whole wheat pita bread round, halved crosswise
- ½ cup shredded leaf lettuce
- ½ of a small tomato, thinly sliced
- ¼ of a small cucumber, thinly sliced

1 In a medium bowl combine egg product, ½ teaspoon of the oil, and the oregano. Add the crushed crackers, zucchini, carrot, and green onion; mix well. Form the vegetable mixture into two 3½-inch round patties.

2 In a medium nonstick skillet heat the remaining 1 teaspoon oil over medium heat. Add patties to skillet. Cook for 5 to 7 minutes or until patties are golden brown, turning once halfway through cooking.

3 Meanwhile, for sauce, in a small bowl combine the yogurt, garlic, and lemon peel.

4 To serve, fill each pita bread half with a patty. Add the lettuce, tomato, cucumber, and sauce.

PER SERVING: *253 cal., 8 g total fat (2 g sat. fat), 2 mg chol., 364 mg sodium, 38 g carb., 5 g fiber, 9 g pro.*

Soups & Stews

Cozy up with a steamy bowl of one of these classic comfort foods. Whether you're craving creamy, chunky, full of veggies, or low-cal, you'll find something worth ladling and savoring.

10

Vegetable Broth 🌿

PREP: **40 minutes** COOK: **2 hours** MAKES **13 cups**

16   cups water

8   medium carrots, cut up

6   stalks celery, cut up

2   large sweet onions, unpeeled and quartered

2   large tomatoes, quartered

8   ounces fresh cremini mushrooms

6   cloves garlic, unpeeled and halved

3   4-inch sprigs fresh thyme

3   4-inch sprigs fresh rosemary

2   teaspoons salt

½   teaspoon ground black pepper

1 In an 8- to 10-quart Dutch oven combine the water, carrots, celery, onions, tomatoes, mushrooms, garlic, thyme, rosemary, salt, and pepper. Bring to boiling; reduce heat. Simmer, covered, for 1 hour, stirring occasionally.

2 Uncover. Simmer for 1 hour more. Cool slightly. Set a fine-mesh wire sieve in a large heatproof bowl; carefully pour broth mixture into the sieve. Discard vegetable mixture.

3 Place broth in storage containers. Cover and chill in the refrigerator for up to 3 days or freeze for up to 6 months.

PER 1 CUP: *3 cal., 0 g total fat (0 g sat. fat), 0 mg chol., 370 mg sodium, 0 g carb., 0 g fiber, 0 g pro.*

Corn Stock:

Prepare as above, except substitute 12 corn cobs (corn kernels removed) for the tomatoes and 2 large sprigs fresh parsley for the rosemary. Omit the carrots, celery, and mushrooms. Continue as directed. Makes 11 cups.

Spicy Veggie Stew

START TO FINISH: **40 minutes** MAKES **4 servings**

- 2 tablespoons olive oil
- 3 large red, yellow, and/or green sweet peppers, seeded and chopped
- 2 cups cubed eggplant (half of a small)
- 1 large onion, sliced
- 2 stalks celery, sliced
- 2 cloves garlic, minced
- 3 large ripe tomatoes, chopped
- ¼ to ½ cup tomato juice*
- 1 15-ounce can garbanzo beans (chickpeas), rinsed and drained
- 2 teaspoons snipped fresh thyme or 1 teaspoon dried thyme, crushed
- ½ teaspoon crushed red pepper
- ¼ teaspoon salt
- ¼ teaspoon ground black pepper
- 4 ounces feta cheese, crumbled (optional)
- Snipped fresh thyme (optional)

1 In an extra-large skillet heat oil over medium heat. Add sweet peppers, eggplant, onion, and celery. Cook for 10 to 15 minutes or until tender, stirring occasionally. Add garlic; cook and stir for 1 minute more.

2 Add tomatoes, tomato juice, drained garbanzo beans, snipped dried thyme (if using), and crushed red pepper to skillet. Cook, covered, for 5 to 10 minutes or until heated through, stirring occasionally. Stir in the 2 teaspoons snipped fresh thyme (if using), salt, and black pepper.

3 If desired, sprinkle each serving with feta cheese and additional snipped fresh thyme.

PER SERVING: *232 cal., 9 g total fat (1 g sat. fat), 0 mg chol., 579 mg sodium, 34 g carb., 10 g fiber, 11 g pro.*

*tip

You may need to adjust the amount of tomato juice based on the juiciness of the fresh tomatoes.

make it vegan

Do not use the optional feta cheese, or substitute feta-flavor soy cheese.

Vegetable Soup with Cornmeal Croutons

PREP: 20 minutes   BAKE: 12 minutes   COOK: 15 minutes   MAKES 6 to 8 servings

- ½ cup sliced leek or chopped onion
- 1 tablespoon olive oil or vegetable oil
- 1 8-ounce package fresh mushrooms, quartered
- 1 large yellow or red sweet pepper, seeded and coarsely chopped
- 4 cloves garlic, minced
- 3 cups water
- 1 28-ounce can Italian-style tomatoes, undrained and cut up
- 1 15- to 19-ounce can cannellini beans (white kidney beans), rinsed and drained
- ½ teaspoon salt
- ¼ teaspoon ground black pepper
- 4 cups baby spinach leaves
- 1 recipe Cornmeal Croutons

1 In a large saucepan cook leek in hot oil over medium heat until tender, stirring occasionally. Add mushrooms, sweet pepper, and garlic; cook for 5 minutes more, stirring occasionally.

2 Add water, undrained cut-up tomatoes, drained beans, salt, and black pepper. Bring to boiling; reduce heat. Simmer, uncovered, for 5 minutes. Stir in spinach. Serve with Cornmeal Croutons.

PER SERVING: *333 cal., 11 g total fat (2 g sat. fat), 42 mg chol., 928 mg sodium, 50 g carb., 6 g fiber, 15 g pro.*

Cornmeal Croutons

Preheat oven to 350°F. Grease a very large baking sheet or 2 large baking sheets; set aside. In a medium bowl lightly beat 1 egg. Add one 8.5-ounce package corn muffin mix, ⅔ cup finely shredded Romano or Parmesan cheese, and 2 tablespoons milk. Drop into small mounds by scant teaspoonfuls onto prepared baking sheet(s). Lightly sprinkle with freshly ground black pepper and, if desired, coarse sea salt. Bake for 12 to 14 minutes or until golden. Remove from baking sheet; cool completely on a wire rack.

tip

Leeks can be tricky to prepare. To clean a leek, cut a big slice from the base or root end and cut off the dark green leaves. Then cut the leek into pieces, place in a colander, and rinse well between the layers until all the dirt is removed.

Tomato-Barley Soup with Garden Vegetables

PREP: 15 minutes   COOK: 18 minutes   MAKES 4 servings

1	14-ounce can vegetable broth
1¾	cups water
¾	cup quick-cooking barley
¾	cup thinly sliced carrots*
1	teaspoon dried thyme, crushed
⅛	teaspoon ground black pepper
1	19-ounce can ready-to-serve tomato-basil soup
2	cups coarsely chopped* zucchini and/or yellow summer squash
1	cup frozen cut green beans

1 In a large saucepan combine vegetable broth, the water, barley, carrots, thyme, and pepper. Bring to boiling; reduce heat. Simmer, covered, for 10 minutes, stirring occasionally.

2 Stir in tomato-basil soup, zucchini, and green beans. Return to boiling; reduce heat. Simmer, covered, for 8 to 10 minutes more or until vegetables and barley are tender, stirring occasionally.

PER SERVING: *243 cal., 3 g total fat (0 g sat. fat), 0 mg chol., 988 mg sodium, 49 g carb., 9 g fiber, 7 g pro.*

*tip

You can substitute one 16-ounce package of your favorite frozen vegetable blend for the carrots, zucchini, and green beans, adding it with the tomato-basil soup.

tip

Using canned soup in a homemade soup or stew can act as a seasoning when you don't have a lot of herbs and spices on hand. Choose a flavorful canned soup, such as the tomato-basil soup used in this recipe. Look for a low-sodium soup; you can add a sprinkle of salt before serving if the soup or stew tastes flat.

Tomato-Basil Soup

PREP: 30 minutes   COOK: 40 minutes   MAKES 4 servings

- 3½   **pounds ripe tomatoes**
- 2   **tablespoons butter or margarine**
- 2   **cloves garlic, minced**
- 1   **cup finely chopped onion (1 large)**
- 1½   **cups loosely packed fresh basil leaves**
- 1½   **teaspoons sea salt or kosher salt**
- ¼   **teaspoon ground black pepper**
- 1½   **cups finely shredded Gruyère or Emmentaler cheese (6 ounces)**
- ½   **cup whipping cream**
- 1   **tablespoon Armagnac or cognac (optional)**

1 Set aside 1 tomato. To peel remaining tomatoes, dip in boiling water for 30 seconds or until skins start to split. Dip in cold water. When cool enough to handle, remove skins and core tomatoes. Coarsely chop; set aside.

2 In a large saucepan melt butter over medium heat. Add the garlic and cook for 30 seconds. Add onion; cook and stir for 4 to 5 minutes or until tender. Add the chopped tomatoes. Bring to boiling; reduce heat. Simmer, covered, for 30 minutes, stirring occasionally. Remove from heat; cool slightly.

3 In a food processor add half of the tomato mixture. Cover and process until almost smooth. Repeat with remaining tomato mixture. Return all of the soup to the saucepan.

4 Finely chop basil; reserve ¼ cup. Stir the remaining basil, the salt, and pepper into tomato mixture. Heat through. Add cheese, cream, and, if desired, Armagnac. Heat and stir just until cheese melts (do not boil).

5 Chop the reserved tomato; combine with the reserved ¼ cup basil. Sprinkle each serving with chopped tomato and basil.

PER SERVING: *453 cal., 34 g total fat (20 g sat. fat), 111 mg chol., 841 mg sodium, 21 g carb., 6 g fiber, 20 g pro.*

Homemade Hearty Tomato Soup

START TO FINISH: **40 minutes**   MAKES **4 servings**

2 tablespoons olive oil

1 cup coarsely chopped onion
(1 large)

2 tablespoons chopped shallot
(1 medium)

2 cloves garlic, minced

2 14.5-ounce cans no-salt-added
diced tomatoes, undrained

1 14-ounce can vegetable broth

½ cup coarsely chopped carrot
(1 medium)

½ cup coarsely chopped celery
(1 stalk)

2 tablespoons snipped
fresh basil

1 tablespoon lemon juice

1 teaspoon sugar

⅛ teaspoon cayenne pepper
Finely shredded fresh basil
(optional)

1 In a large saucepan heat oil over medium heat. Add onion, shallot, and garlic; cook about 5 minutes or until onion is tender, stirring frequently. Add 1 can of undrained tomatoes, the broth, carrot, celery, snipped basil, lemon juice, sugar, and cayenne pepper. Bring to boiling; reduce heat. Simmer, covered, for 20 to 25 minutes or until vegetables are very tender. Remove from heat; cool slightly.

2 In a food processor or blender add half of the tomato mixture. Cover and process or blend until almost smooth. Repeat with the remaining tomato mixture. Return all of the soup to the saucepan.

3 Stir in the remaining can of undrained tomatoes. Cook, uncovered, over low heat about 10 minutes or until heated through, stirring frequently.

4 If desired, garnish each serving with shredded basil.

PER SERVING: *141 cal., 7 g total fat (1 g sat. fat), 0 mg chol., 491 mg sodium, 19 g carb., 5 g fiber, 3 g pro.*

tip

Change your soup to fit the season. A chilled gazpacho is wonderful on a hot summer day, and light asparagus soup is perfect in the spring.

Roasted Leek and Carrot Soup 🌿

PREP: **20 minutes** ROAST: **30 minutes** COOK: **5 minutes** OVEN: **425°F** MAKES **4 servings**

8	**medium carrots, cut into 1-inch pieces**
4	**leeks, coarsely cut up**
2	**tablespoons olive oil**
1/2	**teaspoon fennel seeds**
2	**14-ounce cans vegetable broth**
1/4	**teaspoon salt**
1/4	**teaspoon ground black pepper**
1	**teaspoon lemon juice**

1 Preheat oven to 425°F. In a 15×10×1-inch baking pan combine carrots and leeks. Drizzle with olive oil; toss to coat. Roast, uncovered, about 30 minutes or until tender, stirring once.

2 Meanwhile, in a small skillet toast fennel seeds over medium heat for 1 to 2 minutes or until toasted and aromatic. Use a spice grinder or a mortar and pestle to grind seeds.

3 In a large saucepan combine roasted vegetables, ground fennel, broth, salt, and pepper. Bring to boiling. Remove from heat; cool slightly.

4 In a blender or food processor add half of the vegetable mixture. Cover and blend or process until almost smooth. Repeat with remaining vegetable mixture. Return all of the soup to the saucepan. Stir in lemon juice. Heat through.

PER SERVING: *180 cal., 7 g total fat (1 g sat. fat), 0 mg chol., 1,136 mg sodium, 27 g carb., 5 g fiber, 3 g pro.*

tip

Dress up a simple soup with a flavorful garnish. Add a spoonful of pesto, a sprig of fresh herbs, a sprinkle of cheese, or a little fresh salsa.

Roasted French Onion Soup

PREP: **20 minutes** ROAST: **45 minutes** COOK: **20 minutes** BROIL: **3 minutes** OVEN: **375°F** MAKES **4 servings**

2 **large sweet onions (such as Vidalia or Walla Walla), sliced**

2 **cloves garlic, minced**

1 **tablespoon olive oil**

1 **tablespoon butter, melted**

¼ **teaspoon salt**

¼ **teaspoon ground black pepper**

4 **cups beef-flavor vegetable broth**

1 **tablespoon dry sherry (optional)**

1 **teaspoon Worcestershire sauce**

4 **slices French bread, toasted**

4 **ounces Gruyère cheese, shredded (1 cup)**

Gruyère cheese, shredded (optional)

1 Preheat oven to 375°F. In a 13×9×2-inch baking pan combine onions and garlic. Drizzle with oil and melted butter; toss gently to coat. Sprinkle with salt and pepper. Roast, uncovered, for 45 to 50 minutes or until very tender and light brown, stirring occasionally.

2 Remove pan from oven. Carefully add 1 cup of the broth to the pan, stirring to remove any brown bits from the bottom of the pan. Transfer onion mixture to a large saucepan. Add the remaining 3 cups broth, sherry (if using), and Worcestershire sauce. Bring to boiling; reduce heat. Simmer, covered, for 20 minutes.

3 Preheat broiler. On a foil-lined baking sheet arrange bread slices. Sprinkle bread with the 4 ounces shredded cheese. Broil about 4 inches from the heat for 3 to 4 minutes or until cheese melts and turns light brown.

4 Serve soup topped with bread slices and, if desired, sprinkle with additional shredded cheese.

PER SERVING: *349 cal., 16 g total fat (8 g sat. fat), 39 mg chol., 1,171 mg sodium, 38 g carb., 3 g fiber, 15 g pro.*

make it vegan

Substitute olive oil for the 1 tablespoon butter and substitute desired soy cheese for the Gruyère cheese.

Hot and Sour Soup

PREP: 25 minutes STAND: 20 minutes COOK: 15 minutes MAKES 4 servings

- 1   16-to 18-ounce package extra-firm tofu (fresh bean curd), drained and cut into $\frac{1}{2}$-inch cubes
- 1   tablespoon soy sauce
- 1   tablespoon toasted sesame oil
- 1   cup boiling water
- $\frac{1}{2}$ cup dried wood ear mushrooms, chopped ($\frac{3}{4}$ ounce)
- 2   14-ounce cans vegetable broth
- 1   8-ounce can sliced bamboo shoots, drained
- $\frac{1}{4}$ cup finely shredded carrot
- $\frac{1}{4}$ cup rice vinegar or white vinegar
- 2   tablespoons soy sauce
- 1   teaspoon sugar
- 1   teaspoon grated fresh ginger
- 1   teaspoon chili oil
- $\frac{1}{4}$ teaspoon ground white pepper
- 1   tablespoon cornstarch
- 1   tablespoon cold water
- 1   beaten egg
- 2   tablespoons thinly sliced green onion (1)

1 In a medium bowl gently stir together tofu cubes, the 1 tablespoon soy sauce, and the sesame oil; set aside. In a small bowl pour the boiling water over dried mushrooms. Let stand 20 minutes; drain.

2 In a large saucepan combine broth, mushrooms, bamboo shoots, carrot, vinegar, the 2 tablespoons soy sauce, the sugar, ginger, chili oil, and white pepper. Bring to boiling; reduce heat. Simmer, covered, for 2 minutes. Add tofu mixture. Simmer, covered, for 1 minute more.

3 In a small bowl stir together cornstarch and the water. Slowly stir into soup mixture. Cook and stir until slightly thickened and bubbly. Cook and stir 2 minutes more.

4 Slowly pour the egg into the soup in a steady stream while stirring 2 or 3 times to create egg shreds. Remove saucepan from heat. Stir in green onion.

PER SERVING: *180 cal., 8 g total fat (1 g sat. fat), 53 mg chol., 1,754 mg sodium, 13 g carb., 3 g fiber, 12 g pro.*

Tahini Miso Soup

START TO FINISH: **30 minutes** MAKES **6 servings**

1 tablespoon sesame oil

¾ cup sliced green onions (12)

1 tablespoon grated
fresh ginger

2 cloves garlic, minced

4 cups water

¼ teaspoon ground black pepper

4 ounces dried soba noodles,
broken into 1- to 2-inch pieces

½ cup hot water

⅓ cup miso paste

2 tablespoons tahini

1 12.3-ounce package firm tofu
(fresh bean curd), drained
and cut into ½-inch cubes

1 tablespoon shredded nori or
wakame (seaweed)

1 In a large saucepan heat sesame oil over medium heat. Add green onions, ginger, and garlic. Cook and stir for 2 minutes. Add the 4 cups water and pepper. Bring to boiling. Add soba noodles. Return to boiling; reduce heat. Simmer, uncovered, for 5 minutes.

2 In a small bowl whisk together the ½ cup hot water, miso, and tahini. Stir into soup. Add tofu and seaweed. Simmer, uncovered, for 1 to 2 minutes more or until heated through.

PER SERVING: *202 cal., 8 g total fat (1 g sat. fat), 0 mg chol., 728 mg sodium, 22 g carb., 3 g fiber, 11 g pro.*

tip

Don't overdo it. Vegetables can easily be overcooked in a soup or stew, especially when you're not following a recipe. Keep an eye on the simmering mixture and periodically check vegetable tenderness.

Wonton Soup

START TO FINISH: **40 minutes** MAKES **4 servings**

¼ cup shredded carrot

¼ cup finely chopped red
sweet pepper

¼ cup finely chopped
fresh mushrooms

¼ cup sliced green onions (2)

2 tablespoons finely chopped
dry-roasted peanuts

2 tablespoons snipped
fresh cilantro

1 tablespoon soy sauce

⅛ teaspoon cayenne pepper

20 wonton wrappers

2 quarts water (8 cups)

4 cups chicken-flavored
vegetable broth

6 green onions, cut into
thin slivers

1 1-inch piece peeled
fresh ginger

2 teaspoons toasted sesame oil

1 For filling, in a medium bowl combine carrot, sweet pepper, mushrooms, sliced green onions, peanuts, cilantro, soy sauce, and cayenne pepper.

2 Top each wonton wrapper with 1 rounded teaspoon of filling. Fold the lower corner of the wonton over the filling and tuck the point under the wonton's filling. Roll the wonton up slightly to cover the filling, leaving about 1 inch of skin unrolled at the top corner. Moisten a side corner. Grasp corners; overlap them over the filling, attaching moistened corner to other corner and pinching slightly to seal. Set aside.

3 In a 4- to 5-quart Dutch oven bring the water to boiling. With a spoon, add wontons, 1 at a time, to the boiling water. Return to boiling; reduce heat. Simmer, uncovered, for 5 minutes. Gently drain; rinse with cool water.

4 Meanwhile, in a large saucepan combine broth, slivered green onions, and ginger. Bring to boiling; reduce heat. Simmer, uncovered, about 2 minutes or until green onions are crisp-tender. Remove ginger; discard. Carefully add wontons. Stir in sesame oil. Heat through.

PER SERVING: *197 cal., 6 g total fat (1 g sat. fat), 4 mg chol., 1,164 mg sodium, 30 g carb., 2 g fiber, 7 g pro.*

Edamame Soup with Feta Croutons

START TO FINISH: **30 minutes** MAKES **6 servings**

¾ cup chopped sweet onion (such as Vidalia or Walla Walla)

4 teaspoons canola oil

1 cup thinly sliced carrots (2 medium)

2 cloves garlic, minced

2 14-ounce cans reduced-sodium vegetable broth

1 12-ounce package frozen shelled sweet soybeans (edamame)

1½ teaspoons snipped fresh thyme

1 egg white

1 tablespoon water

½ cup panko (Japanese-style bread crumbs)

4 ounces reduced-fat feta cheese, cut into ¾-inch cubes

Fresh thyme leaves (optional)

1 In a large saucepan cook onion in 2 teaspoons of the hot oil over medium heat about 5 minutes or until tender, stirring occasionally. Add carrots and garlic; cook and stir for 1 minute more. Add broth and edamame. Bring to boiling; reduce heat. Simmer, uncovered, about 5 minutes or until edamame and carrots are tender. Stir in thyme.

2 Meanwhile, for feta croutons, in a small bowl beat egg white and the water with a fork until frothy. Place bread crumbs in another small bowl. Dip feta cubes, 1 at a time, into egg white to coat. Allow excess egg white mixture to drip off; coat feta cubes with bread crumbs.

3 In a large skillet heat the remaining 2 teaspoons oil over medium-high heat. Add feta cubes. Cook for 2 to 3 minutes or until brown but not softened, turning carefully to brown all sides of cubes. Drain feta croutons on paper towels.

4 Top each serving with feta croutons and, if desired, thyme leaves.

PER SERVING: *193 cal., 9 g total fat (2 g sat. fat), 6 mg chol., 621 mg sodium, 15 g carb., 4 g fiber, 14 g pro.*

Apple and Sweet Potato Soup

PREP: 25 minutes ROAST: 20 minutes OVEN: 400°F MAKES 4 servings

3   medium sweet potatoes, peeled and cut into wedges (about 1½ pounds)

2   medium Granny Smith apples, peeled, cored, and cut into wedges

1   medium onion, cut into wedges

1   clove garlic, halved

1   tablespoon olive oil

1   tablespoon butter, melted

1   teaspoon ground cumin

½   teaspoon paprika

¼   teaspoon ground cinnamon

¼   teaspoon salt

¼   teaspoon ground black pepper

2   14-ounce cans vegetable broth

1 Preheat oven to 400°F. On a shallow roasting pan combine sweet potatoes, apples, onion, and garlic. Drizzle with olive oil and melted butter. Sprinkle with cumin, paprika, cinnamon, salt, and pepper; toss to coat. Roast, uncovered, for 20 to 25 minutes or until vegetables and fruit are very tender. Remove from oven; cool slightly.

2 In a blender or food processor add half of the sweet potato mixture and half of the broth. Cover and blend or process until almost smooth. Transfer mixture to a large saucepan. Repeat with the remaining sweet potato mixture and broth. Heat through.

PER SERVING: *215 cal., 7 g total fat (2 g sat. fat), 8 mg chol., 1,000 mg sodium, 38 g carb., 6 g fiber, 2 g pro.*

make it vegan

Substitute an additional tablespoon of olive oil for the tablespoon of butter.

Hot African Stew

START TO FINISH: **40 minutes** MAKES **6 servings**

1 tablespoon canola oil

1 large onion, sliced

1 large red sweet pepper, seeded and chopped

1/2 teaspoon crushed red pepper

3 1/2 cups beef-flavor vegetable broth

1 cup chopped unsalted peanuts

6 tiny new potatoes, cut into 1-inch pieces

1 medium sweet potato, peeled and cut into 1-inch pieces

1 19-ounce can fava beans, rinsed and drained

1 14 1/2-ounce can diced tomatoes, undrained

Light sour cream (optional)

Snipped fresh chives (optional)

1 In a large saucepan heat oil over medium heat. Add onion and sweet pepper; cook until golden and tender, stirring occasionally. Stir in crushed red pepper; cook for 1 minute. Add broth and peanuts.

2 Bring to boiling. Add new potatoes and sweet potato. Return to boiling; reduce heat. Simmer, covered, about 25 minutes or until potatoes are tender, stirring occasionally. Stir in drained beans and undrained tomatoes; heat through.

3 If desired, top each serving with sour cream and chives.

PER SERVING: *297 cal., 15 g total fat (2 g sat. fat), 0 mg chol., 817 mg sodium, 31 g carb., 11 g fiber, 13 g pro.*

make it vegan

If serving with sour cream, substitute tofu sour cream for the dairy sour cream.

tip

Peanuts may seem like an odd ingredient in a stew, but they are traditional in this classic African stew. Full of protein, monounsaturated fats, and antioxidants, peanuts make a great addition to other vegetarian soups and stews as well.

383

Split Pea Soup

PREP: 20 minutes   COOK: 1 hour 20 minutes   MAKES 4 servings

2   cups vegetable broth
     or chicken-flavor
     vegetable broth

2   cups water

1   cup dry split peas, rinsed
     and drained

1/4 teaspoon dried
     marjoram, crushed

1/8 teaspoon ground black pepper

1   bay leaf

1   9-ounce package frozen
     vegetable Italian-style
     sausage (such as Morningstar
     Farms), thawed slightly,
     halved lengthwise, and sliced
     into half-moon pieces

2   medium carrots, halved
     lengthwise and sliced (1 cup)

1/2 cup chopped celery (1 stalk)

1/2 cup chopped onion

2   cloves garlic, minced

1 In a large saucepan combine broth, the water, split peas, marjoram, pepper, and bay leaf. Bring to boiling; reduce heat. Simmer, covered, for 1 hour, stirring occasionally.

2 Stir in vegetable sausage, carrots, celery, onion, and garlic. Return to boiling; reduce heat. Simmer, covered, for 20 to 30 minutes more or until vegetables are tender. Discard bay leaf.

PER SERVING: *314 cal., 5 g total fat (1 g sat. fat), 0 mg chol., 1,176 mg sodium, 42 g carb., 15 g fiber, 24 g pro.*

tip

Miso, a fermented soybean paste, can add rich flavor to soups and stews, not to mention protein and B vitamins. Add a teaspoon to the recipe to start and gradually add more to taste.

Corn-Chile Chowder

PREP: 20 minutes   ROAST: 15 minutes   COOK: 25 minutes   OVEN: 450°F   MAKES 6 to 8 servings

Nonstick cooking spray

1   15.25-ounce can whole kernel corn, drained

½   cup chopped onion (1 medium)

½   cup chopped fresh Anaheim* or poblano chile pepper* or green sweet pepper

½   cup chopped red sweet pepper

3   cloves garlic, minced

2   tablespoons cooking oil

3   large potatoes, cut into ½-inch cubes (about 1¼ pounds)

3   cups water or vegetable broth

1   8.5-ounce can baby lima beans, drained

1   4-ounce can diced green chiles, undrained

2   cups half-and-half or light cream

1   14.75-ounce can cream-style corn

⅔   cup sliced baby zucchini (about 4) or 1 small zucchini, halved lengthwise and sliced

1 Preheat oven to 450°F. To roast corn, lightly coat a 15×10×1-inch baking pan with cooking spray. Spread the drained corn in the prepared pan. Roast, uncovered, about 15 minutes or until corn is golden brown, stirring occasionally.

2 Meanwhile, in a large saucepan cook and stir the onion, peppers, and garlic in the hot oil over medium-high heat about 5 minutes or until onion is tender. Stir in potatoes, the water, drained beans, and undrained chiles. Stir in roasted corn. Bring to boiling; reduce heat. Simmer, uncovered, for 15 minutes, stirring occasionally.

3 Stir in half-and-half, cream-style corn, and zucchini. Cook and stir about 5 minutes more or until heated through (do not boil).

PER SERVING: *371 cal., 15 g total fat (7 g sat. fat), 30 mg chol., 518 mg sodium, 55 g carb., 6 g fiber, 10 g pro.*

*tip

Because chile peppers contain volatile oils that can burn your skin and eyes, avoid direct contact with them as much as possible. When working with chile peppers, wear plastic or rubber gloves. If your bare hands do touch the peppers, wash your hands and nails well with soap and warm water.

385

Curried Butternut Squash Soup

START TO FINISH: 50 minutes MAKES 4 servings

- ½ cup chopped onion, chopped (1 medium)
- 3 tablespoons butter
- 2 teaspoons red curry powder or curry powder
- 2 teaspoons grated fresh ginger
- ½ teaspoon salt
- 1 14-ounce can vegetable broth
- 1¼ cups water
- 1½ pounds butternut squash, peeled, seeded, and cut into 1-inch cubes (4 cups)
- 1 14-ounce can unsweetened coconut milk
- ½ cup half-and-half or light cream
- ⅓ cup chopped fresh cilantro
  Fresh chopped cilantro (optional)

1 In a large saucepan cook onion in hot butter over medium heat about 10 minutes or until tender. Stir in curry powder, ginger, and salt. Cook for 30 seconds more.

2 Stir in vegetable broth and water; bring to boiling. Add squash. Return to boiling; reduce heat. Simmer, covered, about 40 minutes or until squash is tender. Remove from heat; cool slightly.

3 In a blender or food processor add half of the squash mixture. Cover and blend or process until almost smooth. Repeat with remaining squash mixture. Return all of the soup to saucepan.

4 Stir in coconut milk, half-and-half, and chopped cilantro. Heat through. If desired, garnish with additional fresh cilantro.

PER SERVING: *428 cal., 36 g total fat (29 g sat. fat), 34 mg chol., 780 mg sodium, 28 g carb., 6 g fiber, 5 g pro.*

Wild Rice–Mushroom Soup

PREP: 15 minutes   COOK: 55 minutes   STAND: 20 minutes   MAKES 4 servings

- ½ cup chopped dried wild mushroom blend (³⁄₄ ounce)
- 4 cups chicken-flavored vegetable broth
- ½ cup uncooked wild rice, rinsed and drained
- ½ cup textured vegetable protein
- ½ cup thinly sliced green onions (4)
- ¼ cup dried cranberries
- 1 cup milk
- 2 tablespoons all-purpose flour
- 1 teaspoon snipped fresh thyme
- ¼ teaspoon ground black pepper
- 1 tablespoon dry sherry (optional)

1 In a small bowl cover mushrooms with 1 cup boiling water. Let stand 20 minutes; drain.

2 Meanwhile, in a medium saucepan combine the broth and wild rice. Bring to boiling; reduce heat. Simmer, covered, for 40 minutes. Stir in vegetable protein, green onions, cranberries, and mushrooms. Cook about 10 minutes more or until rice is tender.

3 In a small bowl combine milk, flour, thyme, and pepper. Stir into rice mixture. Cook and stir until thickened and bubbly. Cook and stir for 1 minute more. If desired, stir in sherry; heat through.

PER SERVING: *215 cal., 2 g total fat (1 g sat. fat), 5 mg chol., 700 mg sodium, 38 g carb., 5 g fiber, 13 g pro.*

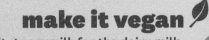

make it vegan

Substitute soymilk for the dairy milk.

387

Pumpkin Soup with Spiced Croutons

START TO FINISH: 30 minutes MAKES 4 servings

1   cup sliced carrots (2 medium)
2   tablespoons butter
½   cup finely chopped onion (1 medium)
½   cup finely chopped celery (1 stalk)
1   clove garlic, minced
4   cups chicken-flavor vegetable broth
2   15-ounce cans pumpkin
½   cup half-and-half or light cream
½   cup water
3   tablespoons maple syrup
1   teaspoon pumpkin pie spice
    Salt
    Ground black pepper
1   recipe Spiced Croutons
    Celery leaves (optional)

1 In a large saucepan cook carrots in hot butter over medium heat for 2 minutes. Add onion, celery, and garlic. Cook for 8 to 10 minutes more or until vegetables are tender.

2 Stir in broth, pumpkin, half-and-half, the water, maple syrup, and pumpkin pie spice. Heat through. Season to taste with salt and pepper.

3 To serve, top with Spiced Croutons and, if desired, celery leaves.

PER SERVING: 398 cal., 18 g total fat (10 g sat. fat), 42 mg chol., 1,208 mg sodium, 57 g carb., 9 g fiber, 8 g pro.

Spiced Croutons

In a large bowl combine 3 cups 1-inch bread cubes with 2 teaspoons pumpkin pie spice; toss to coat. In a large skillet cook bread cubes in 2 tablespoons hot butter about 8 minutes or until toasted, turning occasionally.

Creamy Pumpkin Soup

START TO FINISH: **30 minutes** MAKES **4 servings**

1 teaspoon canola oil

2/3 cup sliced leeks (2 medium)

3 1/2 cups chicken-flavor vegetable broth

1 15-ounce can pumpkin

2 teaspoons snipped fresh thyme or 1 teaspoon dried thyme, crushed

1/4 teaspoon ground black pepper

1 8-ounce carton light sour cream

Fresh thyme sprigs (optional)

1 In a large saucepan heat oil over medium-high heat. Add leeks. Cook and stir about 3 minutes or until tender. Stir in broth, pumpkin, dried thyme (if using), and pepper. Bring to boiling; reduce heat. Simmer, covered, for 20 minutes. Remove from heat; cool slightly. Stir in fresh snipped thyme (if using).

2 In a blender or food processor add half of the pumpkin mixture. Cover and blend or process until almost smooth. Repeat with remaining pumpkin mixture. Return all of the soup to saucepan; heat through. Stir in half of the sour cream.

3 Swirl remaining sour cream into each serving. If desired, garnish with thyme sprigs.

PER SERVING: *146 cal., 8 g total fat (4 g sat. fat), 20 mg chol., 635 mg sodium, 17 g carb., 3 g fiber, 4 g pro.*

make it vegan

Substitute tofu sour cream for the dairy sour cream.

389

Roasted Root Vegetable Soup

PREP: 30 minutes   BAKE: 35 minutes   OVEN: 425°F   MAKES 4 servings

2   medium carrots, peeled and cut into 1-inch pieces

1   medium sweet potato, peeled and cut into 1-inch cubes

1   medium parsnip, peeled and cut into 1-inch pieces

½   of a medium red onion, cut into thin wedges

3   cloves garlic, thinly sliced

1   tablespoon olive oil

1   teaspoon dried thyme, crushed

⅛   teaspoon ground black pepper

3   cups fat-free milk

1   cup vegetable broth

¼   cup all-purpose flour

1 Preheat oven to 425°F. In a 13×9×2-inch baking pan combine carrots, sweet potato, parsnip, red onion, and garlic. Drizzle with oil; sprinkle with half of the thyme and all of the pepper. Toss to coat.

2 Cover with foil. Bake for 20 minutes. Remove foil; stir vegetables. Bake, uncovered, for 15 to 20 minutes more or until vegetables are tender.

3 Meanwhile, in a large saucepan, whisk together milk, broth, flour, and the remaining thyme until smooth. Cook and stir over medium heat until thickened and bubbly. Add roasted vegetables. Cook and stir about 1 minute more or until heated through.

PER SERVING: *191 cal., 4 g total fat (1 g sat. fat), 4 mg chol., 354 mg sodium, 31 g carb., 3 g fiber, 8 g pro.*

Broccoli-Potato Soup with Greens

START TO FINISH: **20 minutes** MAKES **4 servings**

2 **medium round red potatoes, chopped**

1¾ **cups chicken-flavor vegetable broth**

3 **cups small broccoli florets**

2 **cups milk**

2 **cups smoked Gouda cheese, shredded (8 ounces)**

3 **tablespoons all-purpose flour**
Freshly ground black pepper

2 **cups torn winter greens (such as curly endive, chicory, romaine, escarole, or spinach)**

Smoked Gouda cheese, shredded (optional)

1 In a large saucepan combine potatoes and broth. Bring to boiling; reduce heat. Simmer, covered, for 8 minutes. Slightly mash potatoes with potato masher or a fork. Add broccoli and milk; bring just to simmering.

2 In a medium bowl combine cheese and flour; toss to coat. Gradually add to soup, stirring until cheese melts. Season to taste with pepper. Divide among individual shallow serving bowls. Top with greens and, if desired, additional cheese.

PER SERVING: *334 cal., 17 g total fat (11 g sat. fat), 55 mg chol., 1,254 mg sodium, 30 g carb., 4 g fiber, 19 g pro.*

Bean-Potato Chowder

START TO FINISH: **20 minutes** MAKES **4 servings**

1   20-ounce package refrigerated diced potatoes with onions

1   14-ounce can vegetable broth

3   cups milk

1   cup shredded Swiss cheese (4 ounces)

⅓   cup all-purpose flour

1   teaspoon dried Italian seasoning, crushed

1   15-ounce can navy beans, rinsed and drained

1 In a large saucepan combine potatoes and broth. Bring to boiling; reduce heat. Simmer, covered, for 4 minutes. Add milk; bring just to simmering.

2 In a medium bowl combine cheese, flour, and Italian seasoning; toss gently to coat. Gradually add cheese mixture to potato mixture, stirring until cheese melts. Cook and stir over medium heat until thickened and bubbly. Stir in drained beans; cook and stir for 1 minute more.

PER SERVING: *494 cal., 12 g total fat (7 g sat. fat), 40 mg chol., 1,344 mg sodium, 70 g carb., 9 g fiber, 25 g pro.*

tip

Transform a side-dish soup into a hearty main dish by adding grains. However, uncooked rice or pasta will absorb a lot of broth and could make the soup thicker than desired. Keep liquid levels the same by adding cooked grains to the liquid.

Creamy Potato Soup

START TO FINISH: **45 minutes** MAKES **8 servings**

- 2 **cups thinly sliced onions or leeks**
- 1 **tablespoon olive oil**
- 2 **cups milk**
- 3 **tablespoons all-purpose flour**
- 1 **pound Yukon gold potatoes, peeled and sliced**
- 4 **cups chicken-flavored vegetable broth**
- 8 **ounces Swiss-style cheese such as Gruyère or baby Swiss, shredded**
- **Salt**
- **Ground black pepper**
- **Snipped fresh herbs (such as basil, oregano, thyme, rosemary)**
- 2 **ounces baby Swiss cheese, thinly sliced (optional)**

1 In a large saucepan cook onions in hot oil over medium heat for 5 to 10 minutes or until tender. In a small bowl whisk together milk and flour; add to onions. Cook and stir for 5 minutes.

2 Add potatoes and broth. Bring to boiling; reduce heat. Simmer, covered, about 20 minutes or until potatoes are tender. Remove from heat; cool slightly.

3 In a blender add half of the potato mixture. Cover and blend until almost smooth. Repeat with the remaining potato mixture. Return all of the soup to saucepan; heat through on medium heat. Gradually add the shredded cheese, stirring until cheese melts. Season to taste with salt and pepper.

4 To serve, sprinkle each serving with fresh herbs. If desired, garnish with sliced cheese.

PER SERVING: *220 cal., 11 g total fat (6 g sat. fat), 31 mg chol., 491 mg sodium, 19 g carb., 1 g fiber, 12 g pro.*

393

Loaded Baked Potato Soup

START TO FINISH: **35 minutes** MAKES **6 servings**

2   medium baking potatoes
    (1 pound), scrubbed and cut
    into 1-inch pieces
¼   cup butter
⅓   cup all-purpose flour
½   teaspoon salt
¼   teaspoon ground black pepper
5   cups milk
1   8-ounce container sour cream
4   ounces smoked cheddar
    cheese, shredded (1 cup)
¼   cup snipped fresh chives

1 In a covered medium saucepan cook potatoes in enough boiling, lightly salted water to cover for 15 to 17 minutes or until tender; drain.

2 Meanwhile, in a large saucepan melt butter over medium heat. Stir in flour, salt, and pepper. Add milk all at once. Cook and stir until slightly thickened and bubbly. Cook and stir for 1 minute more. Add potatoes. Mash potatoes slightly against the side of the pan with the back of a fork or use a potato masher to slightly mash potatoes.

3 For garnishes, set aside ¼ cup of the sour cream, ¼ cup of the cheese, and 2 tablespoons chives. In a small bowl stir together the remaining sour cream and ½ cup of the hot soup, gradually stirring in another ½ cup soup. Return sour cream mixture to saucepan. Stir in the remaining ¾ cup cheese and 2 tablespoons chives. Cook and stir over low heat until cheese melts; heat through (do not boil).

4 Serve soup topped with reserved sour cream, cheese, and chives.

PER SERVING: *383 cal., 24 g total fat (15 g sat. fat), 71 mg chol., 660 mg sodium, 30 g carb., 2 g fiber, 13 g pro.*

New England Chowder

START TO FINISH: **45 minutes** MAKES **4 servings**

1 cup chopped onion (1 large)

½ cup chopped celery (2 stalks)

2 cloves garlic, minced

2 tablespoons butter

3 cups chopped round red potatoes (about 1 pound)

2 cups vegetable broth

1 teaspoon Worcestershire sauce

½ teaspoon salt

⅛ teaspoon ground black pepper

2 cups plain soymilk

1 cup tofu sour cream

2 tablespoons all-purpose flour

1 tablespoon snipped fresh thyme and/or savory

Fresh thyme and/or savory sprigs (optional)

1 In a large saucepan cook onion, celery, and garlic in hot butter over medium heat about 5 minutes or until softened but not tender. Stir in the potatoes, broth, Worcestershire sauce, salt, and pepper. Bring to boiling; reduce heat. Simmer, covered, for 15 to 20 minutes or until potatoes are tender. With the back of a fork, mash potatoes slightly against the side of the pan or use a potato masher to slightly mash potatoes.

2 In a small bowl stir together soymilk, tofu sour cream, flour, and snipped thyme; add to potato mixture. Cook and stir until slightly thickened and bubbly. Cook and stir 1 minute more.

3 If desired, garnish with additional fresh thyme sprigs.

PER SERVING: *385 cal., 22 g total fat (14 g sat. fat), 15 mg chol., 1,234 mg sodium, 50 g carb., 3 g fiber, 8 g protein.*

make it vegan

Substitute oil for the butter.

Beer and Cheese Soup

START TO FINISH: 25 minutes   MAKES 4 servings

- 12 green onions (1 bunch)
- 3 tablespoons olive oil
- 2 cups refrigerated shredded hash brown potatoes
- ¾ cup roasted red sweet peppers, drained
- ¾ cup pale lager or nonalcoholic beer
- 2 cups milk
- 8 ounces American cheese, shredded
- ¼ teaspoon paprika

1 Slice green onions, separating white portions from green tops. Set aside green tops. In a large saucepan heat 2 tablespoons of the oil over medium heat. Add the white portions of the onions. Cook and stir under tender.

2 In a blender combine cooked onions, 1 cup of the potatoes, peppers, and beer. Cover and blend until almost smooth. Return to saucepan. Bring to boiling; reduce heat. Simmer, uncovered, for 5 minutes.

3 Add milk and cheese to onion mixture. Cook and stir over medium heat until cheese melts and soup is heated through (do not boil).

4 In a small skillet cook the remaining 1 cup potatoes in the remaining 1 tablespoon hot oil over medium-high heat about 8 minutes or until golden, stirring occasionally. Drain potatoes on paper towels; sprinkle with paprika.

5 To serve, top soup with potatoes and green tops. If desired, sprinkle with additional paprika.

PER SERVING: *467 cal., 30 g total fat (14 g sat. fat), 63 mg chol., 1,096 mg sodium, 28 g carb., 2 g fiber, 19 g pro.*

Cauliflower Cheese Soup

START TO FINISH: **30 minutes** MAKES **6 servings**

1 cup chopped green onions (8)

1 tablespoon olive oil

5 cups chicken-flavor vegetable broth

5 cups small cauliflower florets (1 pound)

¼ cup all-purpose flour

1 cup shredded cheddar cheese (4 ounces)

1 cup shredded American cheese (4 ounces)

1 tablespoon snipped fresh chervil or parsley

¼ teaspoon salt

¼ teaspoon ground nutmeg

¼ teaspoon cracked black pepper

1 In a large saucepan cook green onions in hot oil about 2 minutes or until tender. Carefully add 4 cups of the broth. Bring to boiling. Add cauliflower. Return to boiling; reduce heat. Simmer, uncovered, for 6 to 8 minutes or until cauliflower is just tender.

2 In a small bowl whisk together flour and the remaining 1 cup chicken broth. Stir into saucepan. Cook and stir until slightly thickened and bubbly. Cook and stir for 2 minutes more.

3 Remove from heat. Gradually add cheddar cheese and American cheese, stirring until cheese melts. Stir in chervil, salt, nutmeg, and pepper.

PER SERVING: *223 cal., 15 g total fat (8 g sat. fat), 38 mg chol., 1,080 mg sodium, 12 g carb., 3 g fiber, 12 g pro.*

Tuscan Bean Soup

START TO FINISH: **20 minutes**   MAKES **4 servings**

1 **cup packaged peeled baby carrots, coarsely chopped**

⅓ **cup chopped onion (1 small)**

3 **tablespoons olive oil**

1 **32-ounce box vegetable broth**

2 **15-ounce cans cannellini beans (white kidney beans), rinsed and drained**

2 **to 3 teaspoons dried Italian seasoning, crushed**

1 **5-ounce package baby spinach**

Freshly cracked black pepper

Soft cracker bread (lavosh) (optional)

1 In a large saucepan cook and stir carrots and onion in 1 tablespoon of the hot olive oil over medium-high heat for 3 minutes. Add broth, drained beans, and Italian seasoning. Bring to boiling; reduce heat. Simmer, uncovered, for 8 minutes, stirring occasionally. Slightly mash beans with potato masher or fork.

2 Meanwhile, in a large skillet heat the remaining 2 tablespoons oil over medium-high heat. Add spinach; toss with tongs for 1 to 2 minutes or just until wilted. Remove from heat.

3 To serve, top soup with spinach and sprinkle with pepper. Serve with cracker bread.

PER SERVING: *254 cal., 11 g total fat (1 g sat. fat), 0 mg chol., 1,269 mg sodium, 38 g carb., 12 g fiber, 14 g pro.*

Red Bean Stew

2   teaspoons canola oil

1   cup chopped onion (1 large)

3   cloves garlic, minced

1   14-ounce can vegetable broth

2   tablespoons tomato paste

1   teaspoon snipped fresh oregano or ¼ teaspoon dried oregano, crushed

1   teaspoon adobo sauce from canned chipotle peppers in adobo sauce or ½ teaspoon adobo seasoning*

1   15- to 16-ounce can red kidney beans, rinsed and drained

1   tablespoon snipped fresh cilantro

2   cups hot cooked brown rice

Lime wedges (optional)

1 In a large saucepan heat oil over medium heat. Add onion and garlic; cook and stir for 4 to 5 minutes or until onion is tender. Add broth, tomato paste, dried oregano (if using), and adobo sauce. Stir in drained beans. Mash mixture slightly with a potato masher or with the back of a wooden spoon.

2 Bring to boiling; reduce heat. Simmer, uncovered, for 5 minutes, stirring occasionally. Stir in cilantro and fresh oregano (if using).

3 Serve stew with rice and, if desired, garnish with lime wedges.

PER SERVING: *246 cal., 4 g total fat (0 g sat. fat), 0 mg chol., 641 mg sodium, 48 g carb., 9 g fiber, 11 g pro.*

*tip
Look for adobo seasoning at a market that specializes in Hispanic foods.

tip
Vegetarian diets sometimes lack iron, an important nutrient mostly found in meat products. Kidney beans offer a meatless iron source. One cup of the beans contains almost 30% of the recommended daily amount of iron.

Sage-White Bean Soup 🍃

START TO FINISH: **40 minutes** MAKES **6 servings**

1 tablespoon olive oil

½ cup chopped onion
(1 medium)

2 tablespoons garlic, minced
(12 cloves)

3½ cups chicken-flavor
vegetable broth

3 15-ounce cans Great Northern
beans, rinsed and drained

2 tablespoons snipped fresh
sage or 2 teaspoons dried
sage, crushed

¼ teaspoon ground black pepper
Fresh sage leaves (optional)

1 recipe Sage French Bread
Toasts (optional)

1 In a large saucepan heat oil over medium heat. Add onion and garlic. Cook and stir about 5 minutes or until onion is tender. Stir in broth, drained beans, dried sage (if using), and the pepper. Bring to boiling; reduce heat. Simmer, covered, for 20 minutes.

2 Stir in snipped fresh sage (if using). Remove from heat. Mash bean mixture slightly with a potato masher or with the back of a wooden spoon. If desired, garnish each serving with a fresh sage leaf and serve Sage French Bread Toasts.

PER SERVING: *164 cal., 3 g total fat (0 g sat. fat), 0 mg chol., 723 mg sodium, 33 g carb., 10 g fiber, 13 g pro.*

Sage French Bread Toasts

Preheat oven to 425°F. Lightly coat both sides of eight ½-inch slices whole grain baguette-style French bread with olive oil nonstick cooking spray. Sprinkle all sides of bread slices with 1 tablespoon snipped fresh sage or 1 teaspoon dried sage, crushed. Arrange slices on an ungreased baking sheet. Bake for 5 to 7 minutes or until light brown and crisp, turning once halfway through baking.

Super-Bean Vegetarian Chili

START TO FINISH: **30 minutes** MAKES **2 servings**

1 14.5-ounce can no-salt-added diced tomatoes, undrained

1 cup water

1 cup chopped onion (1 large)

1 cup canned organic, no-salt-added black beans, rinsed and drained

¾ cup canned black-eyed peas, rinsed and drained

¼ cup no-salt-added tomato paste

1 tablespoon chili powder

¼ teaspoon ground cumin

¼ cup shredded reduced-fat cheddar cheese (optional)

In a medium saucepan combine undrained tomatoes, the water, onion, drained beans, drained black-eyed peas, tomato paste, chili powder, and cumin. Bring to boiling; reduce heat. Simmer, covered, for 10 minutes.

2 To serve, sprinkle each serving with cheese (if desired).

PER SERVING: *273 cal., 1 g total fat (0 g sat. fat), 0 mg chol., 437 mg sodium, 56 g carb., 16 g fiber, 14 g pro.*

make it vegan
Do not use the optional cheddar cheese.

401

Metric Information
The charts on this page provide a guide for converting measurements from the U.S. customary system, which is used throughout this book, to the metric system.

PRODUCT DIFFERENCES
Most of the ingredients called for in the recipes in this book are available in most countries. However, some are known by different names. Here are some common American ingredients and their possible counterparts:

- All-purpose flour is enriched, bleached, or unbleached white household flour. When self-rising flour is used in place of all-purpose flour in a recipe that calls for leavening, omit the leavening agent (baking soda or baking powder) and salt.
- Baking soda is bicarbonate of soda.
- Cornstarch is cornflour.
- Golden raisins are sultanas.
- Light-colored corn syrup is golden syrup.
- Powdered sugar is icing sugar.
- Sugar (white) is granulated, fine granulated, or castor sugar.
- Vanilla or vanilla extract is vanilla essence.

VOLUME AND WEIGHT
The United States traditionally uses cup measures for liquid and solid ingredients. The chart below shows the approximate imperial and metric equivalents. If you are accustomed to weighing solid ingredients, the following approximate equivalents will be helpful.

- 1 cup butter, castor sugar, or rice = 8 ounces = $\frac{1}{2}$ pound = 250 grams
- 1 cup flour = 4 ounces = $\frac{1}{4}$ pound = 125 grams
- 1 cup icing sugar = 5 ounces = 150 grams

Canadian and U.S. volume for a cup measure is 8 fluid ounces (237 ml), but the standard metric equivalent is 250 ml.

1 British imperial cup is 10 fluid ounces.

In Australia, 1 tablespoon equals 20 ml, and there are 4 teaspoons in the Australian tablespoon.

Spoon measures are used for smaller amounts of ingredients. Although the size of the tablespoon varies slightly in different countries, for practical purposes and for recipes in this book, a straight substitution is all that's necessary. Measurements made using cups or spoons always should be level unless stated otherwise.

COMMON WEIGHT RANGE REPLACEMENTS

Imperial / U.S.	Metric
$\frac{1}{2}$ ounce	15 g
1 ounce	25 g or 30 g
4 ounces ($\frac{1}{4}$ pound)	11 5 g or 125 g
8 ounces ($\frac{1}{2}$ pound)	225 g or 250 g
16 ounces (1 pound)	450 g or 500 g
1$\frac{1}{4}$ pounds	625 g
1$\frac{1}{2}$ pounds	750 g
2 pounds or 2$\frac{1}{4}$ pounds	1,000 g or 1 Kg

OVEN TEMPERATURE EQUIVALENTS

Fahrenheit Setting	Celsius Setting*	Gas Setting
300°F	150°C	Gas Mark 2 (very low)
325°F	160°C	Gas Mark 3 (low)
350°F	180°C	Gas Mark 4 (moderate)
375°F	190°C	Gas Mark 5 (moderate)
400°F	200°C	Gas Mark 6 (hot)
425°F	220°C	Gas Mark 7 (hot)
450°F	230°C	Gas Mark 8 (very hot)
475°F	240°C	Gas Mark 9 (very hot)
500°F	260°C	Gas Mark 10 (extremely hot)
Broil	Broil	Grill

Electric and gas ovens may be calibrated using celsius. However, for an electric oven, increase celsius setting 10 to 20 degrees when cooking above 160°C. For convection or forced air ovens (gas or electric), lower the temperature setting 25°F/10°C when cooking at all heat levels.

BAKING PAN SIZES

Imperial / U.S.	Metric
9x1$\frac{1}{2}$-inch round cake pan	22- or 23x4-cm (1.5 L)
9x1$\frac{1}{2}$-inch pie plate	22- or 23x4-cm (1 L)
8x8x2-inch square cake pan	20x5-cm (2 L)
9x9x2-inch square cake pan	22- or 23x4.5-cm (2.5 L)
11x7x1$\frac{1}{2}$-inch baking pan	28x17x4-cm (2 L)
2-quart rectangular baking pan	30x19x4.5-cm (3 L)
13x9x2-inch baking pan	34x22x4.5-cm (3.5 L)
15x10x1-inch jelly roll pan	40x25x2-cm
9x5x3-inch loaf pan	23x13x8-cm (2 L)
2-quart casserole	2 L

U.S. / STANDARD METRIC EQUIVALENTS

$\frac{1}{8}$ teaspoon = 0.5 ml	
$\frac{1}{4}$ teaspoon = 1 ml	
$\frac{1}{2}$ teaspoon = 2 ml	
1 teaspoon = 5 ml	
1 tablespoon = 15 ml	
2 tablespoons = 25 ml	
$\frac{1}{4}$ cup = 2 fluid ounces = 50 ml	
$\frac{1}{3}$ cup = 3 fluid ounces = 75 ml	
$\frac{1}{2}$ cup = 4 fluid ounces = 125 ml	
$\frac{2}{3}$ cup = 5 fluid ounces = 150 ml	
$\frac{3}{4}$ cup = 6 fluid ounces = 175 ml	
1 cup = 8 fluid ounces = 250 ml	
2 cups = 1 pint = 500 ml	
1 quart = 1 litre	

Index

Note: Page references in *italics* refer to photographs.

A

All-Wrapped-Up Salad, 87, 137
Almonds
    Curried Couscous with Vegetables, 65
    Everything Breakfast Bars, 32
    Lemon Couscous Salad with Fresh
        Fruit, 218
    Oatmeal with Fruit and Nuts, 38, 130
    Strawberry Spinach Salad with
        Roasted Asparagus, 229
American Chopped Salad, 200
Apples
    Apple and Sweet Potato Soup, 382
    Apple-Brie Sandwiches, 198
    Butternut Squash Phyllo Strudel, 85,
        137
    Cheddar-Apple Bundles, 86
    Mixed-Grain Muesli, 40
    Oatmeal with Fruit and Nuts, 38, 130
    Peanut Butter Breakfast Bars, 33
    Pumpkin-Apple Quick Oatmeal, 39
Apricots
    Apricot-Pear Syrup, 29
    Moroccan Chickpeas and Couscous,
        338
    Stone Fruit Salad with Baked Goat
        Cheese Coins, 228, *277*
    Wheat Berry Salad with Dried
        Apricots, 344
Artichokes
    Artichoke-Basil Lasagna, 160
    Garlic-Artichoke Pasta, 68
    Mediterranean Pepper and Artichoke
        Pizza, 170
    Orange-Artichoke Salad, 225
    Oven Omelets with Artichokes and
        Spinach, 17
    Savory Stuffed Portobellos, 84

Arugula
    Israeli Couscous Salad with Tomato
        and Arugula, 217, *276*
    Olive and Arugula Flatbread Pizza
        Salad, *144,* 175
Asian Cobb-Style Salad, 208
Asian Noodle Bowl, 94
Asian Tofu Salad, 207
Asparagus
    Asparagus Corn Tacos, 250
    Asparagus-Leek Risotto, 357
    Asparagus-Mushroom Primavera, 127,
        142
    Asparagus Pesto Pasta, 126
    Chiles and Cheese Individual
        Casseroles, 293
    Fennel and Asparagus Pie, 20
    Garden-Special Primavera, 128
    Linguine with Gorgonzola Sauce, 98
    Mushroom, Asparagus, and Tofu
        Quiches, 19, 132
    Ramen Noodles with Vegetables, 93
    Strawberry Spinach Salad with
        Roasted Asparagus, 229
    Summer Fresh Quesadillas, 83
    Tomato, Spinach, and Feta Strata, 21
Avocados
    All-Wrapped-Up Salad, 87, 137
    Avocado Veggie Sandwiches, 190
    Black Bean and Corn Quesadillas, 82,
        137
    Black Bean and Mango Wraps, 248
    Easy Guacamole, 253
    Greek Quinoa and Avocados, 215
    Grilled Marinated Tempeh, 259
    Inside-Out Veggie Burgers, 239, *280*
    Layered Southwestern Salad with
        Tortilla Strips, 204
    Mushroom-Vegetable Fajitas, 252, *281*
    Open-Face Egg Sandwiches, 196

    Savory Vegetable Open-Face
        Sandwiches, 187
    Spinach, Avocado, and Orange Salad,
        226
    Vegetable Bowls with Spiced Yogurt-
        Lime Dressing, 330

B

Bacon, Soy, and Pesto Wraps, 178
Baked Pasta with Mushrooms and
    Spinach, 312
Baked Stuffed Shells, 305
Baked Ziti with Three Cheeses, 313
Balsamic Dressing, 211
Bananas
    Banana-Oat Breakfast Cookies, 34
    Grilled Peanut Butter, Banana, and
        Berry Sandwiches, 36
    Peanut Butter–Berry Smoothies,
        42, *129*
Barbecue Tempeh Wraps, 179, *274*
Barley
    about, 7
    Barley Risotto with Roasted Squash,
        341
    Barley-Stuffed Peppers, *133,* 340
    Corn and Grain Gratin, 61
    Grain-Vegetable Medley, 332
    Greek Beans and Barley, 44
    Mixed-Grain Muesli, 40
    Multigrain Pilaf, 67, *134*
    Mushroom-Barley Soup, 54
    Tomato-Barley Soup with Garden
        Vegetables, 373
    Vegetable Two-Grain Casserole, 267
Bars
    Double Pumpkin Bars, 31
    Everything Breakfast Bars, 32
    Peanut Butter Breakfast Bars, 33

Basic Crepes, 26
Basil
    Artichoke-Basil Lasagna, 160
    Basil-Tomato Layered Salad, 206
    Fresh-Herb Pasta Primavera, 145
    Fusilli with Garlic Pesto and Pecorino
        Romano, 125, *139*
    Herbed Cheese Pizza, 164
    Linguine in Fresh Tomato Sauce with
        Garlic-Basil Toast, 121
    Mushroom and Herb Pizza, 24, *132*
    Panini without the Press, 186
    Ravioli with Spinach Pesto, 107
    Spaghetti with Fresh Pesto, 113
    Spaghetti with Roasted Tomatoes and
        Pine Nuts, 152
    Tomato-Basil Panini, 185
    Tomato-Basil Soup, 374
    Tricolor Tomato Ravioli, 119
Beans. *See also* Black beans; Chickpeas;
    Edamame; Green beans; White beans
    Bean and Cheese Burritos, 81
    Bean-Potato Chowder, 392
    Bean-Tofu Burritos, 352
    Chili Beans and Potatoes, 48
    Chili Bean-Stuffed Peppers, 52
    Chili-Style Vegetable Pasta, 72
    Chipotle-Bean Enchiladas, 80
    cooking instructions, 9
    Corn-Chile Chowder, 385
    Cracked Wheat Burgers with Pickled
        Onions and Lime Slather, 238
    Cuban Red Beans and Rice, 322
    dried, buying, 8
    dried, cooking, 9
    Fried Green Tomato Salad, 202, *279*
    Hot African Stew, 383
    Italian Beans with Pesto, 73
    Italian Black-Eyed Pea Salsa, 250
    Mexican Burritos or Tacos, 47
    Mexican Tofu, 258
    Pumpkin, Rice, and Bean Enchiladas,
        320
    Red Bean Lasagna, 161
    Red Beans and Rice Burgers, 321
    Red Beans Creole, 49, *136*
    Red Bean Stew, 399
    Spicy Bean Tostadas, 82
    Super-Bean Vegetarian Chili, 401
    Sweet Potato Tamale Pie, 46
    Tahini Burgers with Honey Wasabi
        Coleslaw, 236

Tex-Mex Beans with Cornmeal
    Dumplings, 337
Tex-Mex Bean Tostadas, 323
Three-Bean Enchiladas, 272
Three-Bean Tamale Pie, 269
types of, 8
Vegetable Curry, 75
Beer and Cheese Soup, 396
Beets
    Roasted Beet, Goat Cheese, and Fennel
        Salad, 203
    Saucy Mushroom Borscht, 103
Berries
    Banana-Oat Breakfast Cookies, 34
    Berry-Peach Breakfast Smoothies, 41
    Blueberry-Oat Bran Pancakes, 30
    Blueberry-Oat Scones with Flaxseeds,
        35, *131*
    Everything Breakfast Bars, 32
    Grilled Peanut Butter, Banana, and
        Berry Sandwiches, 36
    Peanut Butter–Berry Smoothies,
        42, *129*
    Power Smoothies, 42, *129*
    Smoky Berry Topper, 92
    Spinach, Avocado, and Orange Salad,
        226
    Strawberry Spinach Salad with
        Roasted Asparagus, 229
Black beans
    Bean-Tofu Burritos, 352
    Black Bean and Corn Chimichangas,
        328
    Black Bean and Corn Quesadillas, 82,
        137
    Black Bean and Mango Wraps, 248
    Black Bean Cake Burgers, 233
    Black Bean Cakes with Salsa, 324
    Black Bean Chipotle Burgers, 232, *280*
    Black Bean Enchiladas, 325
    Black Bean Lasagna, 157
    Black Bean Salsa, 339
    Black Bean Tostadas, 331
    cooking instructions, 9
    Huevos Rancheros Breakfast Nachos,
        23
    Layered Southwestern Salad with
        Tortilla Strips, 204
    Mediterranean Beans and Greens
        Salad, 213
    Salsa, Bean, and Cheese Pizza, 172
    Salsa, Black Bean, and Mango Salad,
        230

Southwest Black Bean Pizza, 171
Southwest Black Bean Salad, 212
Southwestern Quinoa-Stuffed Acorn
    Squash, 342
Southwestern Rice and Bean Salad
    with Tempeh, 219
Spicy Black Bean Veggie Burgers, 329
Spicy Rice and Bean Cakes, 326
Stuffed Peppers, 77
Stuffed Zucchini with Black Beans,
    Corn, and Poblano Pepper, 365
Super-Bean Vegetarian Chili, 401
Super Breakfast Burritos, 25
Sweet-and-Sour Cabbage Rolls, 53
Sweet Potato-Rice Casserole, 268
Taco-Style Black Beans and Hominy, 47
Three-Bean Tamale Pie, 269
Tortilla and Black Bean Bake, 271
Tortilla Lasagna, 79
Triple Pepper Nachos, *285*, 327
Vegetable Bowls with Spiced Yogurt-
    Lime Dressing, 330
Vegetable Two-Grain Casserole, 267
Vegetarian Feijoada Brazilian Rice and
    Black Beans, 45
Vegetarian Gumbo, 50
Black-eyed peas
    cooking instructions, 9
    Fried Green Tomato Salad, 202, *279*
    Italian Black-Eyed Pea Salsa, 250
    Super-Bean Vegetarian Chili, 401
Blueberries
    Blueberry-Oat Bran Pancakes, 30
    Blueberry-Oat Scones with Flaxseeds,
        35, *131*
    Power Smoothies, 42, *129*
    Smoky Berry Topper, 92
Bratwursts, Grilled, with Papaya Relish,
    241
Bread pudding
    Mock Cheese Soufflé, 18
    Tomato, Spinach, and Feta Strata, 21
    Tomato-Olive Bread Pudding, *282*, 302
Breads. *See also* Tortillas
    Blueberry-Oat Scones with Flaxseeds,
        35, *131*
    Cornmeal Croutons, 372
    Sage French Bread Toasts, 400
    Spiced Croutons, 388
Bread salads
    Edamame Bread Salad, 211
    Roasted Tomato and Cannellini Bean
        Panzanella, 210

Breakfast Pita Pizza, 28
Broccoli
    Broccoli-Cauliflower Tetrazzini, 309
    Broccoli Lasagna, 156
    Broccoli-Potato Soup with Greens, 391
    Garden Vegetables Lasagna, 159
    Mac and Cheese Spaghetti, 153
    Pasta with Broccoli and Asiago, 104
    Saucepan Macaroni and Cheese, *140*,
        149
    Soba-Vegetable Toss, 147
    Spicy Pasta and Broccoli, 102
    Tomato-Broccoli Frittata, 15
    Veggie Salad in a Pocket, 182
    Winter Garden Pasta, 115
Broccoli Rabe and Penne, 118
Broth, Vegetable, 370
Brown Rice-Spinach Custards, 267
Bruschetta Burgers, 90
Buckwheat, about, 7
Bulgur
    about, 7
    Bulgur Tacos, 356
    Italian Beans with Pesto, 73
    Navy Bean Tabbouleh, 209
    Tabbouleh with Edamame and Feta,
        346
    Tahini Burgers with Honey Wasabi
        Coleslaw, 236
    Thai Bulgur Salad, 221
    Vegetable Two-Grain Casserole, 267
Burgers
    Black Bean Cake Burgers, 233
    Black Bean Chipotle Burgers, 232, *280*
    Bruschetta Burgers, 90
    Cannellini Bean Burgers, *274, 335*
    Cheesy Eggplant Burgers, 234
    Cracked Wheat Burgers with Pickled
        Onions and Lime Slather, 238
    Double Mushroom Burgers with Onion
        Spread, 91
    Inside-Out Veggie Burgers, 239, *280*
    Open-Face Veggie Burgers with
        Sautéed Onion, 189
    Portobello Burgers with Sunny Pesto
        Mayonnaise, 235
    Red Beans and Rice Burgers, 321
    Spicy Black Bean Veggie Burgers, 329
    Tahini Burgers with Honey Wasabi
        Coleslaw, 236
    Tandoori-Style Grilled Patties, 237
    Veggie-Spinach Burgers, 240

    You Choose Veggie Burgers, 92, *138*
    Zucchini-Carrot Burgers, 368
Burritos
    Bean and Cheese Burritos, 81
    Bean-Tofu Burritos, 352
    Mexican Burritos or Tacos, 47
    Super Breakfast Burritos, 25
Buttermilk Dressing, 202
Butternut Squash Lasagna, *143*, 155
Butternut Squash Phyllo Strudel, 85, *137*

C

Cabbage. *See also* Bok choy
    Asian Cobb-Style Salad, 208
    Barbecue Tempeh Wraps, 179, *274*
    Honey Wasabi Coleslaw, 236
    Spicy Vegetable Fried Rice, 364
    Sweet-and-Sour Cabbage Rolls, 53
Camembert Pizzas with Focaccia Crusts,
    173, *274*
Cannellini Bean Burgers, *274, 335*
Caper and Eggplant Tomato Sauce, 151
Caprese Salad Sandwiches, 193
Caribbean Tofu Skewers, 256
Carrots
    Gingered Carrot Soup, 55
    Herbed Root Vegetable Cobbler, *284,*
        297
    Hoisin Tempeh with Stir-Fry
        Vegetables, 349
    Mile-High Meatless Lasagna Pie, 154
    Potato, Zucchini, and Carrot Pancakes,
        366
    Ramen Noodles with Vegetables, 93
    Roasted Leek and Carrot Soup, 376
    Skillet Vegetables on Cheese Toast, 192
    Spicy Vegetable Fried Rice, 364
    Veggie-Stuffed Pasta Shells, 150
    Zucchini-Carrot Burgers, 368
Cashew-Vegetable Stir-Fry, 75
Cauliflower
    Broccoli-Cauliflower Tetrazzini, 309
    Cauliflower and Chickpea Gratin, 266
    Cauliflower Cheese Soup, 397
Cha-Cha Corn Chowder, 59
Cheese
    Apple-Brie Sandwiches, 198
    Artichoke-Basil Lasagna, 160
    Avocado Veggie Sandwiches, 190
    Baked Pasta with Mushrooms and
        Spinach, 312
    Baked Ziti with Three Cheeses, 313

Beer and Cheese Soup, 396
Black Bean and Corn Quesadillas, 82,
    137
Black Bean Lasagna, 157
Broccoli-Potato Soup with Greens, 391
Camembert Pizzas with Focaccia
    Crusts, 173, *274*
Cauliflower Cheese Soup, 397
Cheddar Cheese, 12, 18, 28, 71, 81, 86, 87,
    140, 149, 153, 156, 251, 270, 316, 318,
    394, 397
Cheese Manicotti with Roasted Pepper
    Sauce, 162
Cheese 'n' Nut Stuffed Shells, 304
Cheesy Eggplant Burgers, 234
Chile Rellenos, *283, 292*
Chipotle-Bean Enchiladas, 80
Creamy Potato Soup, 393
Double-Cheese Mac and Cheese, 317
Feta Cheese, 13, 21, 89, 96, 101, *140*, 185,
    211, 222, 246, 266, 267, 302, 311, 318,
    346, 381
Fresh Tomato Pizzas with Three
    Cheeses, 166
Fusilli with Garlic Pesto and Pecorino
    Romano, 125, *139*
Garden Vegetables Lasagna, 159
Grilled Veggie-Cheese Sandwiches,
    188, *275*
Herbed Cheese Pizza, 164
Herbed Frittata with Edamame, 14, *132*
Huevos Rancheros Breakfast Nachos,
    23
Lasagna Ole, 291
Linguine with Gorgonzola Sauce, 98
Mediterranean Pepper and Artichoke
    Pizza, 170
Mile-High Meatless Lasagna Pie, 154
Mixed-Mushroom Pizza, 165
Monetary Jack Cheese, 46, 79, 99, 157,
    172, 191, 271, 272, 293, 294, 318, 325,
    328, 348
Mozzarella Cheese, 20, 24, 37, 83, 90,
    132, 158, 159, 161, 162, 164, 166, 167,
    170, 173, 183, 184, 186, 198, 262, *273*,
    284, 300, 304, 307
Nutty Gorgonzola Roll-Ups, 303
Open-Face Veggie Melts, 245
Parmesan Cheese, 123, *143*, 145, 155, 183,
    260, *273*, 297, 298, 304, 313, 318
Pasta with Broccoli and Asiago, 104
Potato-Crusted Veggie Pie, 264

Cheese (*continued*)
Red Bean Lasagna, 161
Roasted Beet, Goat Cheese, and Fennel
Salad, 203
Roasted French Onion Soup, *288*, 377
Roasted Veggie Sandwiches, 190
Skillet Vegetables on Cheese Toast, 192
Smoked Provolone Pizza, 164
Southwest Black Bean Pizza, 171
soy cheese, about, 10
Spinach and Feta Casserole, 89, *140*
Spinach Cannelloni with Fontina, 296
Stone Fruit Salad with Baked Goat
Cheese Coins, 228, *277*
Summer Squash and Chard Gratin, 301
Super Breakfast Burritos, 25
Tofu Manicotti, *281*, 306
Tomato-Basil Soup, 374
Two-Cheese Macaroni Bake, 101
Vegetable Casserole, 51
Vegetable Flatbreads with Goat Cheese,
174
Vegetable Lasagna, 158
White Bean and Goat Cheese Wraps,
180
Cheesy Eggplant Burgers, 234
Cheesy Multigrain Spaghetti with Tofu, 71
Cheesy Red Pepper Pizza, 173
Cheesy Spaghetti Squash, 300
Chickpeas
Cauliflower and Chickpea Gratin, 266
Chili-Style Vegetable Pasta, 72
cooking instructions, 9
Falafel Gyros, 247
Falafels, *286*, 336
Greek Garbanzo Salad, 214
Inside-Out Veggie Burgers, 239, *280*
Lemony Garbanzo Bean Sandwiches,
194
Moroccan Chickpeas and Couscous, 338
Quinoa Fattoush with Lemon Dressing,
216, *278*
Spicy Veggie Stew, *287*, 371
Spicy Winter Squash Stew, 58
Tex-Mex Beans with Cornmeal
Dumplings, 337
Vegetable Casserole, 51
Wheat Berry Salad with Dried
Apricots, 344
Chilaquile Casserole, 294
Chile peppers
Cha-Cha Corn Chowder, 59
Chilaquile Casserole, 294

Chile Rellenos, *283*, 292
Chiles and Cheese Individual
Casseroles, 293
Chipotle-Bean Enchiladas, 80
Corn-Chile Chowder, 385
Double Pepper Topper, 92
Huevos Rancheros, 22
Poblano-Tofu Scramble, 27
Stuffed Zucchini with Black Beans,
Corn, and Poblano Pepper, 365
Super Breakfast Burritos, 25
Tex-Mex Beans with Cornmeal
Dumplings, 337
Chili, Super-Bean Vegetarian, 401
Chili Beans and Potatoes, 48
Chili Bean-Stuffed Peppers, 52
Chili-Style Vegetable Pasta, 72
Chilly Veggie Pizza, 302
Chimichangas, Black Bean and Corn, 328
Chipotle-Bean Enchiladas, 80
Chive Honey Mustard Vinaigrette, 201
Chocolate
Everything Breakfast Bars, 32
Grilled Peanut Butter, Banana, and
Berry Sandwiches, 36
Chowder
Bean-Potato Chowder, 392
Cha-Cha Corn Chowder, 59
Corn-Chile Chowder, 385
New England Chowder, 395
Cookies and bars
Banana-Oat Breakfast Cookies, 34
Double Pumpkin Bars, 31
Everything Breakfast Bars, 32
Peanut Butter Breakfast Bars, 33
Corn. *See also* Hominy
Asparagus Corn Tacos, 250
Black Bean and Corn Chimichangas,
328
Black Bean and Corn Quesadillas, 82,
137
Black Bean and Mango Wraps, 248
Black Bean Chipotle Burgers, 232, *280*
Black Bean Salsa, 339
Cha-Cha Corn Chowder, 59
Chili Beans and Potatoes, 48
Corn and Grain Gratin, 61
Corn and Polenta Bake, 295
Corn-Chile Chowder, 385
Corn Stock, 370
Layered Southwestern Salad with
Tortilla Strips, 204
Meatless Citrus-Corn Tacos, 354

Mexican Tofu, 258
Salsa, Black Bean, and Mango Salad, 230
Southwest Black Bean Salad, 212
Southwestern Corn Spoonbread, 60
Spaghetti-Corn Relish Salad, 205
Stuffed Peppers, 77
Stuffed Zucchini with Black Beans,
Corn, and Poblano Pepper, 365
Super Breakfast Burritos, 25
Tortilla Lasagna, 79
Vegetable Tacos, 356
Cornmeal (and corn muffin mix). *See also*
Polenta
Black Bean Cakes with Salsa, 324
Cornmeal Croutons, 372
Cornmeal Dumplings, 337
Southwestern Corn Spoonbread, 60
Three-Bean Tamale Pie, 269
Zucchini Cakes with Mushroom
Ragout, 367
Couscous
Couscous Cakes with Salsa, 339
Couscous-Stuffed Peppers, 78
Curried Couscous with Vegetables, 65
Grain-Vegetable Medley, 332
Israeli Couscous Salad with Tomato
and Arugula, 217, *276*
Lemon Couscous Salad with Fresh
Fruit, 218
Moroccan Chickpeas and Couscous, 338
Cracked wheat
about, 7
Cracked Wheat Burgers with Pickled
Onions and Lime Slather, 238
Mixed-Grain Muesli, 40
Cranberries
Banana-Oat Breakfast Cookies, 34
Everything Breakfast Bars, 32
Creamy Potato Soup, 393
Creamy Pumpkin Soup, *288*, 389
Crepes
Basic Crepes, 26
Spinach Cannelloni with Fontina, 296
Croutons
Cornmeal, 372
Spiced Croutons, 388
Cuban Red Beans and Rice, 322
Cucumbers
Cucumber Yogurt Sauce, 247
Greek Garbanzo Salad, 214
Lemony Garbanzo Bean Sandwiches, 194
Savory Vegetable Open-Face
Sandwiches, 187

Udon with Tofu, 148
Yogurt Raita, 347

D

Dates
Double Pumpkin Bars, 31
Oatmeal with Fruit and Nuts, 38, 130
Dips and spreads
Double Pepper Topper, 92
Easy Guacamole, 253
Lime Mayonnaise, 233, 238
Smoky Berry Topper, 92
Spicy Navy Bean Hummus, 182
Ultra Ketchup Topper, 92
Double-Cheese Mac and Cheese, 317
Double Mushroom Burgers with Onion
Spread, 91
Double Pepper Topper, 92
Double Pumpkin Bars, 31
Dried Tomato Casserole, 318
Drinks. See Smoothies
Dumplings
Cornmeal Dumplings, 337
Herbed Parmesan Dumplings, 297

E

Easy Guacamole, 253
Edamame
about, 8
Edamame Bread Salad, 211
Edamame Soup with Feta Croutons, 381
guide to, 10
Herbed Frittata with Edamame, 14, 132
Marinated Tofu with Edamame Stir-
Fry, 353
Multigrain Pilaf, 67, 134
Open-Face Egg Sandwiches, 196
Peach and Nectarine Soba Salad, 227
Soy Bacon and Pesto Wraps, 178
Sweet Beans and Pasta, 100
Sweet Potato-Rice Casserole, 268
Tabbouleh with Edamame and Feta, 346
Thai Bulgur Salad, 221
Thai-Style Vegetable Rice, 64
Tomato-Edamame Grilled Cheese, 191
Eggplant
Cheesy Eggplant Burgers, 234
Eggplant and Caper Tomato Sauce, 151
Grilled Eggplant Parmesan, 260
Grilled Summer Vegetables Sandwich,
243
Grilled Vegetable Burritos, 251

Grilled Vegetable Pizzas, 167
Grilled Veggie Sandwiches, 242
Lentil "Moussaka," 62
Marinated Eggplant Kabobs, 254, 280
Open-Face Veggie Melts, 245
Ratatouille with Lentils, 63
Roasted Vegetables and Spinach with
Pasta, 314
Spicy Veggie Stew, 287, 371
Zucchini and Eggplant Bake, 299
Eggs
Cheddar and Zucchini Frittata, 12
Curried Egg Salad Sandwiches, 197
Egg and Vegetable Salad Wraps, 177
Egg Salad Sandwiches, 197
ELT (Egg, Lettuce, and Tomato)
Sandwiches, 195
Herbed Frittata with Edamame, 14, 132
Honey-Dill Egg Salad Sandwiches, 197
Huevos Rancheros, 22
Huevos Rancheros Breakfast Nachos, 23
Mediterranean Frittata, 13
Mushroom and Herb Pizza, 24, 132
Mushroom-Olive Frittata, 16
Open-Face Egg Sandwiches, 196
Oven Omelets with Artichokes and
Spinach, 17
Poached Egg Salad, 223
Spicy Vegetable Fried Rice, 364
Super Breakfast Burritos, 25
Tomato-Broccoli Frittata, 15
Enchiladas
Black Bean Enchiladas, 325
Chipotle-Bean Enchiladas, 80
Potato Enchiladas, 290
Pumpkin, Rice, and Bean Enchiladas, 320
Three-Bean Enchiladas, 272
Zesty Vegetable Enchiladas, 284, 289
Everything Breakfast Bars, 32

F

Fajitas
Mushroom-Vegetable Fajitas, 252, 281
Veggie Fajitas with Guacamole, 253
Falafel Gyros, 247
Falafels, 286, 336
Farfalle with Mushrooms and Spinach, 124
Fennel
Fennel and Asparagus Pie, 20
Orange-Artichoke Salad, 225
Roasted Beet, Goat Cheese, and Fennel
Salad, 203

Wild Rice Salad with Orange and
Fennel, 224, 279
Fettuccine Alfredo, 123
Firm Polenta, 343
Flaxseeds, Blueberry-Oat Scones with,
35, 131
Fluffy Oat Bran Pancakes, 30
Fresh-Herb Pasta Primavera, 145
Fresh Tomato Pizzas with Three Cheeses,
166
Fried Green Tomato Salad, 202, 279
Fried Polenta, 343
Frittatas
Cheddar and Zucchini Frittata, 12
Herbed Frittata with Edamame, 14, 132
Mediterranean Frittata, 13
Mushroom-Olive Frittata, 16
Tomato-Broccoli Frittata, 15
Fruit. See also Berries; specific fruits
Lemon Couscous Salad with Fresh
Fruit, 218
Stone Fruit Salad with Baked Goat
Cheese Coins, 228, 277
Fusilli with Garlic Pesto and Pecorino
Romano, 125, 139

G

Garbanzo beans. See Chickpeas
Gardener's Pie, 87
Garden Sliders, 334
Garden-Special Primavera, 128
Garden Vegetables Lasagna, 159
Garlic
Fusilli with Garlic Pesto and Pecorino
Romano, 125, 139
Garlic-Artichoke Pasta, 68
Linguine in Fresh Tomato Sauce with
Garlic-Basil Toast, 121
Gingered Carrot Soup, 55
Ginger-Soy Sauce, 148
Grains. See also Barley; Bulgur; Cornmeal;
Couscous; Oats; Quinoa; Rice; Wheat
berries
Cracked Wheat Burgers with Pickled
Onions and Lime Slather, 238
Grain-Vegetable Medley, 332
guide to, 7
Mixed-Grain Muesli, 40
Southern Grits Casserole, 270
Summer Spelt Medley, 345
Greek Beans and Barley, 44
Greek Garbanzo Salad, 214

Greek Pasta Casserole, 318
Greek Pasta Salad, 222
Greek Quinoa and Avocados, 215
Greek-Style Pizza, 169
Green beans
    Edamame Bread Salad, 211
    Garden-Special Primavera, 128
    Grain-Vegetable Medley, 332
    Greek Beans and Barley, 44
    Kung Pao Mock Chicken, 351
    Pasta with Green Beans and Dried
        Tomatoes, 117
    Ravioli in Browned Butter Sauce, 106
    Spaghetti with Fresh Pesto, 113
    Tomato-Barley Soup with Garden
        Vegetables, 373
Greens. *See also* Cabbage; Lettuce;
    Spinach
    Broccoli-Potato Soup with Greens, 391
    Fried Green Tomato Salad, 202, *279*
    Israeli Couscous Salad with Tomato
        and Arugula, 217, *276*
    Lentil and Veggie Shepherd's Pie, 265
    Mediterranean Beans and Greens
        Salad, 213
    Mushroom-Olive Frittata, 16
    Mushroom Salad with Crisp Potato
        Cakes, 201
    Olive and Arugula Flatbread Pizza
        Salad, *144*, 175
    Pasta with Swiss Chard, 146
    Poached Egg Salad, 223
    Savory Bean and Kale Soup, 56
    Southwest Black Bean Salad, 212
    Spring Greens Salad, 366
    Stone Fruit Salad with Baked Goat
        Cheese Coins, 228, *277*
    Summer Squash and Chard Gratin, 301
    Vegetarian Feijoada Brazilian Rice and
        Black Beans, 45
Grilled Bratwursts with Papaya Relish, 241
Grilled California-Style Pizza, 262
Grilled Eggplant Parmesan, 260
Grilled Marinated Tempeh, 259
Grilled Mushrooms with Red Wine Sauce,
    261
Grilled Peanut Butter, Banana, and Berry
    Sandwiches, 36
Grilled Summer Vegetables Sandwich, 243
Grilled Tofu Curry, 257, *279*
Grilled Vegetable Burritos, 251
Grilled Vegetable Pizzas, 167

Grilled Veggie-Cheese Sandwiches, 188,
    275
Grilled Veggie Sandwiches, 242
Grilled Veg Sandwiches, 244, *281*
Grits Casserole, Southern, 270
Guacamole, Easy, 253
Gumbo, Vegetarian, 50

H

Herbs. *See also specific herbs*
    Herbed Cheese Pizza, 164
    Herbed Frittata with Edamame, 14, *132*
    Herbed Parmesan Dumplings, 297
    Herbed Root Vegetable Cobbler, *284*,
        297
Hoisin Tempeh with Stir-Fry Vegetables,
    349
Homemade Hearty Tomato Soup, 375
Honey-Dill Egg Salad Sandwiches, 197
Honey Wasabi Coleslaw, 236
Horseradish Sour Cream, 359
Hot African Stew, 383
Hot and Sour Soup, 378
Hot Tossed Vegetable Ravioli, 110
Huevos Rancheros, 22
Huevos Rancheros Breakfast Nachos, 23
Hummus, Spicy Navy Bean, 182

I

Inside-Out Veggie Burgers, 239, *280*
Israeli Couscous Salad with Tomato and
    Arugula, 217, *276*
Italian Beans with Pesto, 73
Italian Black-Eyed Pea Salsa, 250
Italian Pasta Gratin, *284*, 307

K

Kale
    Savory Bean and Kale Soup, 56
    Vegetarian Feijoada Brazilian Rice and
        Black Beans, 45
Ketchup Topper, Ultra, 92
Kung Pao Mock Chicken, 351

L

Lasagna
    Artichoke-Basil Lasagna, 160
    Black Bean Lasagna, 157
    Broccoli Lasagna, 156
    Butternut Squash Lasagna, *143*, 155
    Garden Vegetables Lasagna, 159
    Lasagna Ole, 291

Mile-High Meatless Lasagna Pie, 154
    Red Bean Lasagna, 161
    Tortilla Lasagna, 79
    Vegetable Lasagna, 158
Layered Potatoes and Leeks, 298
Layered Southwestern Salad with Tortilla
    Strips, 204
Leeks
    Asparagus-Leek Risotto, 357
    Layered Potatoes and Leeks, 298
    Roasted Leek and Carrot Soup, 376
Legumes. *See also* Beans; Lentils
    dry, cooking, 9
    guide to, 8
    Split Pea Soup, 384
Lemons
    Lemon Couscous Salad with Fresh
        Fruit, 218
    Lemon Vinaigrette, 203, 206
    Lemony Garbanzo Bean Sandwiches,
        194
Lentils
    buying, 8
    cooking instructions, 9
    Curried Lentil Soup, 57, *133*
    Lentil and Veggie Shepherd's Pie, 265
    Lentil and Veggie Tostadas, 348
    Lentil "Moussaka," 62
    Meatless Tacos, 356
    Pasta with Lentil Sauce, 70, *135*
    Potato-Crusted Veggie Pie, 264
    Ratatouille with Lentils, 63
    Red Lentil Rice, 347
    serving ideas, 8
    Vegetable Tacos, 356
    Zesty Vegetable Enchiladas, *284*, 289
Lettuce
    All-Wrapped-Up Salad, 87, *137*
    American Chopped Salad, 200
    Basil-Tomato Layered Salad, 206
    Black Bean Tostadas, 331
    ELT (Egg, Lettuce, and Tomato)
        Sandwiches, 195
    Layered Southwestern Salad with
        Tortilla Strips, 204
    Orange-Artichoke Salad, 225
    Roasted Beet, Goat Cheese, and Fennel
        Salad, 203
    Salsa, Black Bean, and Mango Salad,
        230
    Spicy Bean Tostadas, 82
    Tex-Mex Bean Tostadas, 323

Lime Mayonnaise, 233, 238
Linguine in Fresh Tomato Sauce with Garlic-Basil Toast, 121
Linguine with Gorgonzola Sauce, 98
Loaded Baked Potato Soup, 394

M

Mac and Cheese Spaghetti, 153
Mangoes
  Black Bean and Mango Wraps, 248
  Mango Salsa, 325
  Salsa, Black Bean, and Mango Salad, 230
Marinated Eggplant Kabobs, 254, 280
Marinated Tofu with Edamame Stir-Fry, 353
Meatless burger patties
  Bruschetta Burgers, 90
  Double Mushroom Burgers with Onion Spread, 91
  Open-Face Veggie Burgers with Sautéed Onion, 189
  Tandoori-Style Grilled Patties, 237
  Veggie-Spinach Burgers, 240
  You Choose Veggie Burgers, 92, 138
Meatless Citrus-Corn Tacos, 354
Meatless Sweet Potato Hash, 350
Meatless Tacos, 356
Mediterranean Beans and Greens Salad, 213
Mediterranean Frittata, 13
Mediterranean Pepper and Artichoke Pizza, 170
Mexican Burritos or Tacos, 47
Mexican Tofu, 258
Mile-High Meatless Lasagna Pie, 154
Miso
  guide to, 10
  Tahini Miso Soup, 379
Mixed-Grain Muesli, 40
Mixed-Mushroom Pizza, 165
Mock Cheese Soufflé, 18
Moroccan Chickpeas and Couscous, 338
Muesli, Mixed-Grain, 40
Multigrain Pilaf, 67, 134
Mushrooms
  Asparagus-Mushroom Primavera, 127, 142
  Baked Pasta with Mushrooms and Spinach, 312
  Breakfast Pita Pizza, 28
  Double Mushroom Burgers with Onion Spread, 91

Farfalle with Mushrooms and Spinach, 124
Grilled Mushrooms with Red Wine Sauce, 261
Grilled Veggie Sandwiches, 242
Italian Pasta Gratin, 284, 307
Lasagna Ole, 291
Layered Potatoes and Leeks, 298
Marinated Tofu with Edamame Stir-Fry, 353
Mile-High Meatless Lasagna Pie, 154
Mixed-Mushroom Pizza, 165
Mushroom, Asparagus, and Tofu Quiches, 19, 132
Mushroom and Herb Pizza, 24, 132
Mushroom-Barley Soup, 54
Mushroom-Olive Frittata, 16
Mushroom Salad with Crisp Potato Cakes, 201
Mushroom-Vegetable Fajitas, 252, 281
Open-Face Veggie Melts, 245
Panini with Grilled Mushrooms, 184
Portobello Burgers with Sunny Pesto Mayonnaise, 235
Portobello Curry with Green Rice, 287, 362
Portobello Wrap with White Bean-Chile Spread, 249
Saucy Mushroom Borscht, 103
Savory Stuffed Portobellos, 84
Skillet Vegetables on Cheese Toast, 192
Slow Cooker Risotto, 66, 133
Smoky Mushroom Stroganoff, 122
Spinach-Mushroom Quesadillas, 183, 273
Thai-Style Veggie Pizza, 168
Tomato and Cheese Ravioli, 109
Tortillas Filled with Mushrooms, Spinach, and Fresh Mozzarella, 37
Vegetable Lasagna, 158
Veggie Fajitas with Guacamole, 253
Veggie-Stuffed Portobello Mushrooms, 361
Wild Rice-Mushroom Soup, 288, 387
Zucchini Cakes with Mushroom Ragout, 367

N

Nachos
  Huevos Rancheros Breakfast Nachos, 23
  Triple Pepper Nachos, 285, 327
Navy Bean Tabbouleh, 209

Nectarines
  Peach and Nectarine Soba Salad, 227
  Stone Fruit Salad with Baked Goat Cheese Coins, 228, 277
  Strawberry Spinach Salad with Roasted Asparagus, 229
New England Chowder, 395
Noodles
  Asian Noodle Bowl, 94
  Noodle Big Bowls with Spinach and Tofu, 105
  Nutty Gorgonzola Roll-Ups, 303
  Peach and Nectarine Soba Salad, 227
  Ramen Noodles with Vegetables, 93
  Saucy Mushroom Borscht, 103
  Smoky Mushroom Stroganoff, 122
  Soba-Vegetable Toss, 147
  Tahini Miso Soup, 379
  Udon with Tofu, 148
Nuts. See also Almonds; Peanuts; Walnuts
  Cashew-Vegetable Stir-Fry, 75
  Nutty Gorgonzola Roll-Ups, 303
  Spaghetti with Roasted Tomatoes and Pine Nuts, 152

O

Oat bran
  Blueberry-Oat Bran Pancakes, 30
  Fluffy Oat Bran Pancakes, 30
Oats
  about, 7
  Banana-Oat Breakfast Cookies, 34
  Blueberry-Oat Bran Pancakes, 30
  Blueberry-Oat Scones with Flaxseeds, 35, 131
  Double Pumpkin Bars, 31
  Fluffy Oat Bran Pancakes, 30
  Mixed-Grain Muesli, 40
  Oatmeal with Fruit and Nuts, 38, 130
  Peanut Butter Breakfast Bars, 33
  Pumpkin-Apple Quick Oatmeal, 39
  Spiced Irish Oatmeal, 41
Olives
  Chilly Veggie Pizza, 302
  Eggplant and Caper Tomato Sauce, 151
  Greek Pasta Casserole, 318
  Greek Pasta Salad, 222
  Greek-Style Pizza, 169
  Grilled California-Style Pizza, 262
  Linguine in Fresh Tomato Sauce with Garlic-Basil Toast, 121
  Mediterranean Frittata, 13

Olives (*continued*)
Moroccan Chickpeas and Couscous, 338
Mushroom-Olive Frittata, 16
Olive and Arugula Flatbread Pizza
Salad, *144, 175*
Rotini-Bean Bake, 311
Tomato-Olive Bread Pudding, *282, 302*
Omelets, Oven, with Artichokes and
Spinach, 17
Onions
Open-Face Veggie Burgers with
Sautéed Onion, 189
Pickled Onions, 238
Roasted French Onion Soup, *288, 377*
Open-Face Egg Sandwiches, 196
Open-Face Veggie Burgers with Sautéed
Onion, 189
Open-Face Veggie Melts, 245
Oranges
Orange-Artichoke Salad, 225
Sesame-Orange Tofu, 355
Spinach, Avocado, and Orange Salad,
226
Wild Rice Salad with Orange and
Fennel, 224, *279*

P

Pancakes. *See also* Crepes
Blueberry-Oat Bran Pancakes, 30
Fluffy Oat Bran Pancakes, 30
Pear-Ginger Pancakes, 29
Potato, Zucchini, and Carrot Pancakes,
366
Panini with Grilled Mushrooms, 184
Panini without the Press, 186
Papaya Relish, Grilled Bratwursts with,
241
Pasta. *See also* Couscous; Lasagna;
Noodles; Ravioli; Spaghetti; Tortellini
Asparagus-Mushroom Primavera, 127,
142
Asparagus Pesto Pasta, 126
Baked Pasta with Mushrooms and
Spinach, 312
Baked Stuffed Shells, 305
Baked Ziti with Three Cheeses, 313
Broccoli-Cauliflower Tetrazzini, 309
Broccoli Rabe and Penne, 118
Cheese Manicotti with Roasted Pepper
Sauce, 162
Cheese 'n' Nut Stuffed Shells, 304
Chili-Style Vegetable Pasta, 72

Double-Cheese Mac and Cheese, 317
Farfalle with Mushrooms and Spinach,
124
Fettuccine Alfredo, 123
Fresh-Herb Pasta Primavera, 145
Fusilli with Garlic Pesto and Pecorino
Romano, 125, *139*
Garden-Special Primavera, 128
Garlic-Artichoke Pasta, 68
Greek Pasta Casserole, 318
Greek Pasta Salad, 222
Italian Pasta Gratin, *284, 307*
Linguine in Fresh Tomato Sauce with
Garlic-Basil Toast, 121
Linguine with Gorgonzola Sauce, 98
Pasta with Broccoli and Asiago, 104
Pasta with Green Beans and Dried
Tomatoes, 117
Pasta with Lentil Sauce, 70, *135*
Pasta with Pepper-Cheese Sauce, 99
Pasta with Swiss Chard, 146
Penne with Walnuts and Peppers, 116
Pesto Beans and Pasta, 69
Roasted Vegetables and Spinach with
Pasta, 314
Rotini-Bean Bake, 311
Saucepan Macaroni and Cheese, *140,
149*
South Indian-Style Macaroni and
Cheese, 316
Spicy Pasta and Broccoli, 102
Sweet Beans and Pasta, 100
Tofu Manicotti, *281, 306*
Two-Cheese Macaroni Bake, 101
Vegetable Pastitsio, 315
Vegetable Primavera Casserole, 310
Veggie-Stuffed Pasta Shells, 150
Peaches
Berry-Peach Breakfast Smoothies, 41
Peach and Nectarine Soba Salad, 227
Stone Fruit Salad with Baked Goat
Cheese Coins, 228, *277*
Strawberry Spinach Salad with
Roasted Asparagus, 229
Peanut butter
Banana-Oat Breakfast Cookies, 34
Grilled Peanut Butter, Banana, and
Berry Sandwiches, 36
Peanut Butter-Berry Smoothies,
42, *129*
Peanut Butter Breakfast Bars, 33
Peanut Butter-Pear Sandwiches, 36
Thai Peanut Dressing, 221

Peanuts
Asian Noodle Bowl, 94
Hot African Stew, 383
Sesame-Orange Tofu, 355
Thai-Style Veggie Pizza, 168
Pears
Apricot-Pear Syrup, 29
Peanut Butter-Pear Sandwiches, 36
Pear and Walnut Salad, 230
Pear-Ginger Pancakes, 29
Peas
Asian Cobb-Style Salad, 208
Asparagus Pesto Pasta, 126
Hoisin Tempeh with Stir-Fry
Vegetables, 349
Red Lentil Rice, 347
South Indian-Style Macaroni and
Cheese, 316
Spicy Vegetable Fried Rice, 364
Spinach-Pea Risotto, 360
Thai-Style Veggie Pizza, 168
Tortellini and Peas, 95
Tortellini-Vegetable Bake, 308
Wheat Berry Salad with Dried
Apricots, 344
Penne with Walnuts and Peppers, 116
Peppers. *See also* Chile peppers
Barley-Stuffed Peppers, *133, 340*
Breakfast Pita Pizza, 28
Cheese Manicotti with Roasted Pepper
Sauce, 162
Cheesy Red Pepper Pizza, 173
Chili Bean-Stuffed Peppers, 52
Couscous-Stuffed Peppers, 78
Double Pepper Topper, 92
Greek-Style Pizza, 169
Grilled California-Style Pizza, 262
Inside-Out Veggie Burgers, 239, *280*
Kung Pao Mock Chicken, 351
Marinated Tofu with Edamame Stir-
Fry, 353
Mediterranean Frittata, 13
Mediterranean Pepper and Artichoke
Pizza, 170
Mushroom-Vegetable Fajitas, 252, *281*
Pasta with Green Beans and Dried
Tomatoes, 117
Pasta with Pepper-Cheese Sauce, 99
Penne with Walnuts and Peppers, 116
Ravioli with Sweet Peppers, 120, *141*
Rice and Sweet Pepper Bowl, 76
Roasted Tofu and Veggie Pockets, 181

Roasted Vegetables and Spinach with Pasta, 314
Savory Vegetable Open-Face Sandwiches, 187
Seitan and Pepper Kabobs, 255
Soba-Vegetable Toss, 147
Southwest Black Bean Salad, 212
Spicy Veggie Stew, 287, 371
Stuffed Peppers, 77
Tortellini Alfredo with Roasted Peppers, 97
Triple Pepper Nachos, 285, 327
Vegetarian Gumbo, 50
Veggie Fajitas with Guacamole, 253
White Bean and Goat Cheese Wraps, 180
Pesto
Asparagus Pesto Pasta, 126
Fusilli with Garlic Pesto and Pecorino Romano, 125, 139
Italian Beans with Pesto, 73
Pesto Beans and Pasta, 69
Ravioli with Spinach Pesto, 107
Soy Bacon and Pesto Wraps, 178
Spaghetti with Fresh Pesto, 113
Phyllo Strudel, Butternut Squash, 85, 137
Pickled Onions, 238
Pies
Fennel and Asparagus Pie, 20
Gardener's Pie, 87
Lentil and Veggie Shepherd's Pie, 265
Mile-High Meatless Lasagna Pie, 154
Potato-Crusted Veggie Pie, 264
Sweet Potato Tamale Pie, 46
Three-Bean Tamale Pie, 269
Pineapple
Black Bean Cake Burgers, 233
Caribbean Tofu Skewers, 256
Pine Nuts and Roasted Tomatoes, Spaghetti with, 152
Pita, Cheese, and Veggie Grill, 246
Pizza
Breakfast Pita Pizza, 28
Camembert Pizzas with Focaccia Crusts, 173, 274
Cheesy Red Pepper Pizza, 173
Chilly Veggie Pizza, 302
Fresh Tomato Pizzas with Three Cheeses, 166
Greek-Style Pizza, 169
Grilled California-Style Pizza, 262
Grilled Vegetable Pizzas, 167
Herbed Cheese Pizza, 164

Mediterranean Pepper and Artichoke Pizza, 170
Mixed-Mushroom Pizza, 165
Mushroom and Herb Pizza, 24, 132
Olive and Arugula Flatbread Pizza Salad, 144, 175
Salsa, Bean, and Cheese Pizza, 172
Smoked Provolone Pizza, 164
Southwest Black Bean Pizza, 171
Thai-Style Veggie Pizza, 168
Vegetable Flatbreads with Goat Cheese, 174
Pizza dough
Pizza Dough, 169
Thin Pizza Crust, 176
Whole Grain Pizza Crust, 176
Poached Egg Salad, 223
Poblano-Tofu Scramble, 27
Polenta
Corn and Polenta Bake, 295
Firm Polenta, 343
Fried Polenta, 343
Polenta, 88, 343
Roasted Vegetables with Polenta, 88
Sweet Potato Tamale Pie, 46
Vegetable Casserole, 51
Portobello Burgers with Sunny Pesto Mayonnaise, 235
Portobello Curry with Green Rice, 287, 362
Portobello Wrap with White Bean-Chile Spread, 249
Potatoes. See also Sweet potatoes
Bean-Potato Chowder, 392
Beer and Cheese Soup, 396
Broccoli-Potato Soup with Greens, 391
Chili Beans and Potatoes, 48
Creamy Potato Soup, 393
Gardener's Pie, 87
Herbed Root Vegetable Cobbler, 284, 297
Hot African Stew, 383
Layered Potatoes and Leeks, 298
Lentil and Veggie Shepherd's Pie, 265
Lentil "Moussaka," 62
Loaded Baked Potato Soup, 394
Mushroom Salad with Crisp Potato Cakes, 201
New England Chowder, 395
Potato, Zucchini, and Carrot Pancakes, 366
Potato-Crusted Veggie Pie, 264
Potato Enchiladas, 290

Power Smoothies, 42, 129
Protein, 5, 6
Pumpkin
Creamy Pumpkin Soup, 288, 389
Double Pumpkin Bars, 31
Pumpkin, Rice, and Bean Enchiladas, 320
Pumpkin-Apple Quick Oatmeal, 39
Pumpkin Soup with Spiced Croutons, 388

Q
Quesadillas
Black Bean and Corn Quesadillas, 82, 137
Spinach-Mushroom Quesadillas, 183, 273
Summer Fresh Quesadillas, 83
Quiches, Mushroom, Asparagus, and Tofu, 19, 132
Quinoa
about, 7
Greek Quinoa and Avocados, 215
Quinoa Fattoush with Lemon Dressing, 216, 278
Southwestern Quinoa-Stuffed Acorn Squash, 342
Spicy Winter Squash Stew, 58

R
Raisins
Curried Couscous with Vegetables, 65
Sweet-and-Sour Cabbage Rolls, 53
Ramen Noodles with Vegetables, 93
Raspberries
Smoky Berry Topper, 92
Spinach, Avocado, and Orange Salad, 226
Ratatouille with Lentils, 63
Ravioli
Dried Tomato Casserole, 318
Hot Tossed Vegetable Ravioli, 110
Ravioli in Browned Butter Sauce, 106
Ravioli Skillet, 108
Ravioli with Spinach Pesto, 107
Ravioli with Sweet Peppers, 120, 141
Tomato and Cheese Ravioli, 109
Tricolor Tomato Ravioli, 119
Red Beans and Rice Burgers, 321
Red Beans Creole, 49, 136
Red Bean Stew, 399
Red Lentil Rice, 347

Rice
    Arborio, about, 7
    Asparagus-Leek Risotto, 357
    Black Bean Chipotle Burgers, 232, *280*
    Brown Rice-Spinach Custards, 267
    Chili Bean-Stuffed Peppers, 52
    converted, about, 7
    Cuban Red Beans and Rice, 322
    Multigrain Pilaf, 67, 134
    Portobello Curry with Green Rice, *287*, 362
    Pumpkin, Rice, and Bean Enchiladas, 320
    Red Beans and Rice Burgers, 321
    Red Beans Creole, 49, *136*
    Red Lentil Rice, 347
    Rice and Sweet Pepper Bowl, 76
    Risotto with Beans and Vegetables, 333
    Savory Stuffed Portobellos, 84
    Slow Cooker Risotto, 66, *133*
    Southwestern Rice and Bean Salad with Tempeh, 219
    Spicy Black Bean Veggie Burgers, 329
    Spicy Rice and Bean Cakes, 326
    Spicy Vegetable Fried Rice, 364
    Spinach-Pea Risotto, 360
    Stuffed Peppers, 77
    Sweet-and-Sour Cabbage Rolls, 53
    Sweet Potato-Rice Casserole, 268
    Thai-Style Vegetable Rice, 64
    Tortilla Lasagna, 79
    Vegetable Risotto, 358
    Vegetarian Feijoada Brazilian Rice and Black Beans, 45
    Veggie Risotto Cakes with Horseradish Sour Cream, 359
    white, types of, 7
    wild rice, about, 7
    Wild Rice-Mushroom Soup, *288*, 387
    Wild Rice Salad with Orange and Fennel, 224, *279*
Risotto
    Asparagus-Leek Risotto, 357
    Barley Risotto with Roasted Squash, 341
    Risotto with Beans and Vegetables, 333
    Slow Cooker Risotto, 66, *133*
    Spinach-Pea Risotto, 360
    Vegetable Risotto, 358
    Veggie Risotto Cakes with Horseradish Sour Cream, 359
Roasted French Onion Soup, *288*, 377
Roasted Leek and Carrot Soup, 376

Roasted Root Vegetable Soup, 390
Roasted Tofu and Veggie Pockets, 181
Roasted Tomato and Cannellini Bean Panzanella, 210
Roasted Vegetables and Spinach with Pasta, 314
Roasted Vegetables with Polenta, 88
Roasted Veggie Sandwiches, 190
Rotini-Bean Bake, 311

S
Sage French Bread Toasts, 400
Sage-White Bean Soup, *287*, 400
Salad dressings
    Balsamic Dressing, 211
    Buttermilk Dressing, 202
    Chive Honey Mustard Vinaigrette, 201
    Lemon Vinaigrette, 203, 206
    Thai Peanut Dressing, 221
Salads
    American Chopped Salad, 200
    Asian Cobb-Style Salad, 208
    Asian Tofu Salad, 207
    Basil-Tomato Layered Salad, 206
    Edamame Bread Salad, 211
    Fried Green Tomato Salad, 202, *279*
    Greek Garbanzo Salad, 214
    Greek Pasta Salad, 222
    Greek Quinoa and Avocados, 215
    Israeli Couscous Salad with Tomato and Arugula, 217, *276*
    Layered Southwestern Salad with Tortilla Strips, 204
    Lemon Couscous Salad with Fresh Fruit, 218
    Mediterranean Beans and Greens Salad, 213
    Mushroom Salad with Crisp Potato Cakes, 201
    Navy Bean Tabbouleh, 209
    Orange-Artichoke Salad, 225
    Peach and Nectarine Soba Salad, 227
    Pear and Walnut Salad, 230
    Poached Egg Salad, 223
    Quinoa Fattoush with Lemon Dressing, 216, *278*
    Roasted Beet, Goat Cheese, and Fennel Salad, 203
    Roasted Tomato and Cannellini Bean Panzanella, 210
    Salsa, Black Bean, and Mango Salad, 230

Southwest Black Bean Salad, 212
Southwestern Rice and Bean Salad with Tempeh, 219
Spaghetti-Corn Relish Salad, 205
Spinach, Avocado, and Orange Salad, 226
Spring Greens Salad, 366
Stone Fruit Salad with Baked Goat Cheese Coins, 228, *277*
Strawberry Spinach Salad with Roasted Asparagus, 229
Thai Bulgur Salad, 221
Wheat Berry Salad, 220
Wheat Berry Salad with Dried Apricots, 344
Wild Rice Salad with Orange and Fennel, 224, *279*
Salsa, Bean, and Cheese Pizza, 172
Salsa, Black Bean, and Mango Salad, 230
Salsas
    Black Bean Salsa, 339
    Italian Black-Eyed Pea Salsa, 250
    Mango Salsa, 325
Sandwiches. *See also* Burgers; Wraps
    Apple-Brie Sandwiches, 198
    Avocado Veggie Sandwiches, 190
    Caprese Salad Sandwiches, 193
    Curried Egg Salad Sandwiches, 197
    Egg Salad Sandwiches, 197
    ELT (Egg, Lettuce, and Tomato) Sandwiches, 195
    Falafel Gyros, 247
    Garden Sliders, 334
    Grilled Bratwursts with Papaya Relish, 241
    Grilled Peanut Butter, Banana, and Berry Sandwiches, 36
    Grilled Summer Vegetables Sandwich, 243
    Grilled Veggie-Cheese Sandwiches, 188, *275*
    Grilled Veggie Sandwiches, 242
    Grilled Veg Sandwiches, 244, *281*
    Honey-Dill Egg Salad Sandwiches, 197
    Lemony Garbanzo Bean Sandwiches, 194
    Open-Face Egg Sandwiches, 196
    Open-Face Veggie Melts, 245
    Panini with Grilled Mushrooms, 184
    Panini without the Press, 186
    Peanut Butter–Pear Sandwiches, 36
    Pita, Cheese, and Veggie Grill, 246

Roasted Tofu and Veggie Pockets, 181
Roasted Veggie Sandwiches, 190
Savory Vegetable Open-Face
    Sandwiches, 187
Skillet Vegetables on Cheese Toast, 192
Spinach-Mushroom Quesadillas, 183,
    273
Summer Tomato Stack, 198
Tomato-Basil Panini, 185
Tomato-Edamame Grilled Cheese, 191
Veggie Salad in a Pocket, 182
Saucepan Macaroni and Cheese, 140, 149
Sauces. See also Salsas
    Cucumber Yogurt Sauce, 247
    Eggplant and Caper Tomato Sauce, 151
    Ginger-Soy Sauce, 148
    Horseradish Sour Cream, 359
    Spiced Yogurt-Lime Dressing, 330
    Yogurt-Dill Sauce, 255
    Yogurt Sauce, 239
Saucy Mushroom Borscht, 103
Sausages. See Bratwursts
Savory Bean and Kale Soup, 56
Savory Stuffed Portobellos, 84
Savory Vegetable Open-Face Sandwiches,
    187
Scones, Blueberry-Oat, with Flaxseeds,
    35, 131
Seitan and Pepper Kabobs, 255
Sesame-Orange Tofu, 355
Skillet Vegetables on Cheese Toast, 192
Slow Cooker Risotto, 66, 133
Smoked Provolone Pizza, 164
Smoky Berry Topper, 92
Smoky Mushroom Stroganoff, 122
Smoothies
    Berry-Peach Breakfast Smoothies, 41
    Peanut Butter–Berry Smoothies,
        42, 129
    Power Smoothies, 42, 129
Soba-Vegetable Toss, 147
Soufflé, Mock Cheese, 18
Soups. See also Stews
    Apple and Sweet Potato Soup, 382
    Bean-Potato Chowder, 392
    Beer and Cheese Soup, 396
    Broccoli-Potato Soup with Greens, 391
    Cauliflower Cheese Soup, 397
    Cha-Cha Corn Chowder, 59
    Corn-Chile Chowder, 385
    Creamy Potato Soup, 393
    Creamy Pumpkin Soup, 288, 389

Curried Butternut Squash Soup, 386
Curried Lentil Soup, 57, 133
Edamame Soup with Feta Croutons,
    381
Gingered Carrot Soup, 55
Homemade Hearty Tomato Soup, 375
Hot and Sour Soup, 378
Loaded Baked Potato Soup, 394
Mushroom-Barley Soup, 54
New England Chowder, 395
Pumpkin Soup with Spiced Croutons,
    388
Roasted French Onion Soup, 288, 377
Roasted Leek and Carrot Soup, 376
Roasted Root Vegetable Soup, 390
Sage-White Bean Soup, 287, 400
Split Pea Soup, 384
Tahini Miso Soup, 379
Tomato-Barley Soup with Garden
    Vegetables, 373
Tomato-Basil Soup, 374
Tuscan Bean Soup, 398
Vegetable Broth, 370
Vegetable Soup with Cornmeal
    Croutons, 372
Wild Rice-Mushroom Soup, 288, 387
Wonton Soup, 288, 380
Southern Grits Casserole, 270
South Indian-Style Macaroni and Cheese,
    316
Southwest Black Bean Pizza, 171
Southwest Black Bean Salad, 212
Southwestern Corn Spoonbread, 60
Southwestern Quinoa-Stuffed Acorn
    Squash, 342
Southwestern Rice and Bean Salad with
    Tempeh, 219
Soy-based products. See also Meatless
    burger patties; Soybeans; Tempeh;
    Tofu
    about, 8
    guide to, 10
    Kung Pao Mock Chicken, 351
    Meatless Citrus-Corn Tacos, 354
    Meatless Sweet Potato Hash, 350
    Mexican Burritos or Tacos, 47
    Soy Bacon and Pesto Wraps, 178
    Split Pea Soup, 384
    Tahini Miso Soup, 379
Soybeans. See also Edamame
    about, 8
    cooking instructions, 9

Soymilk, guide to, 10
Spaghetti
    Cheesy Multigrain Spaghetti with
        Tofu, 71
    Eggplant and Caper Tomato Sauce, 151
    Mac and Cheese Spaghetti, 153
    Spaghetti-Corn Relish Salad, 205
    Spaghetti with Fresh Marinara, 112
    Spaghetti with Fresh Pesto, 113
    Spaghetti with Roasted Tomatoes and
        Pine Nuts, 152
    Spaghetti with Two-Tomato Toss, 114
    Winter Garden Pasta, 115
Spaghetti Squash with Chunky Tomato
    Sauce, 363
Spelt
    about, 7
    Summer Spelt Medley, 345
Spiced Croutons, 388
Spiced Irish Oatmeal, 41
Spiced Yogurt-Lime Dressing, 330
Spicy Bean Tostadas, 82
Spicy Black Bean Veggie Burgers, 329
Spicy Pasta and Broccoli, 102
Spicy Rice and Bean Cakes, 326
Spicy Vegetable Fried Rice, 364
Spicy Veggie Stew, 287, 371
Spicy Winter Squash Stew, 58
Spinach
    Asian Cobb-Style Salad, 208
    Baked Pasta with Mushrooms and
        Spinach, 312
    Brown Rice-Spinach Custards, 267
    Farfalle with Mushrooms and Spinach,
        124
    Grain-Vegetable Medley, 332
    Greek Quinoa and Avocados, 215
    Italian Pasta Gratin, 284, 307
    Mile-High Meatless Lasagna Pie, 154
    Noodle Big Bowls with Spinach and
        Tofu, 105
    Nutty Gorgonzola Roll-Ups, 303
    Oven Omelets with Artichokes and
        Spinach, 17
    Ravioli with Spinach Pesto, 107
    Red Bean Lasagna, 161
    Roasted Vegetables and Spinach with
        Pasta, 314
    Spaghetti with Roasted Tomatoes and
        Pine Nuts, 152
    Spinach, Avocado, and Orange Salad,
        226

Index

Spinach (continued)
    Spinach and Feta Casserole, 89, 140
    Spinach Cannelloni with Fontina, 296
    Spinach-Mushroom Quesadillas, 183,
      273
    Spinach-Pea Risotto, 360
    Spinach Tortellini with Beans and Feta,
      96, 140
    Strawberry Spinach Salad with
      Roasted Asparagus, 229
    Thai Bulgur Salad, 221
    Tomato, Spinach, and Feta Strata, 21
    Tortillas Filled with Mushrooms,
      Spinach, and Fresh Mozzarella, 37
    Tricolor Tomato Ravioli, 119
    Tuscan Bean Soup, 398
    Vegetable Lasagna, 158
    Vegetable Pastitsio, 315
    Veggie-Spinach Burgers, 240
    Veggie-Stuffed Pasta Shells, 150
    Wheat Berry Salad, 220
    White Bean and Goat Cheese Wraps,
      180
Split peas
    cooking instructions, 9
    Split Pea Soup, 384
Spoonbread, Southwestern Corn, 60
Spreads. See Dips and spreads
Spring Greens Salad, 366
Squash. See also Pumpkin; Zucchini
    Avocado Veggie Sandwiches, 190
    Barley Risotto with Roasted Squash,
      341
    Butternut Squash Lasagna, 143, 155
    Butternut Squash Phyllo Strudel, 85,
      137
    Cheesy Spaghetti Squash, 300
    Curried Butternut Squash Soup, 386
    Curried Couscous with Vegetables, 65
    Garden Vegetables Lasagna, 159
    Greek Beans and Barley, 44
    Grilled Summer Vegetables Sandwich,
      243
    Lasagna Ole, 291
    Open-Face Veggie Melts, 245
    Ratatouille with Lentils, 63
    Ravioli Skillet, 108
    Ravioli with Spinach Pesto, 107
    Roasted Veggie Sandwiches, 190
    Southwestern Quinoa-Stuffed Acorn
      Squash, 342

Spaghetti Squash with Chunky
    Tomato Sauce, 363
Spicy Winter Squash Stew, 58
Summer Squash and Chard Gratin, 301
Vegetable Risotto, 358
Veggie Salad in a Pocket, 182
Stews
    Hot African Stew, 383
    Red Bean Stew, 399
    Spicy Veggie Stew, 287, 371
    Spicy Winter Squash Stew, 58
    Super-Bean Vegetarian Chili, 401
Stock, Corn, 370
Stone Fruit Salad with Baked Goat Cheese
    Coins, 228, 277
Strawberries
    Grilled Peanut Butter, Banana, and
      Berry Sandwiches, 36
    Peanut Butter–Berry Smoothies,
      42, 129
    Spinach, Avocado, and Orange Salad,
      226
    Strawberry Spinach Salad with
      Roasted Asparagus, 229
Strudel, Butternut Squash Phyllo, 85, 137
Stuffed Peppers, 77
Stuffed Zucchini with Black Beans, Corn,
    and Poblano Pepper, 365
Summer Fresh Quesadillas, 83
Summer Spelt Medley, 345
Summer Squash and Chard Gratin, 301
Summer Tomato Stack, 198
Super-Bean Vegetarian Chili, 401
Super Breakfast Burritos, 25
Sweet-and-Sour Cabbage Rolls, 53
Sweet Beans and Pasta, 100
Sweet potatoes
    Apple and Sweet Potato Soup, 382
    Curried Lentil Soup, 57, 133
    Hot African Stew, 383
    Meatless Sweet Potato Hash, 350
    Sweet Potato-Rice Casserole, 268
    Sweet Potato Tamale Pie, 46
    Thai-Style Vegetable Rice, 64
    Vegetable Bowls with Spiced Yogurt-
      Lime Dressing, 330
Swiss chard
    Lentil and Veggie Shepherd's Pie, 265
    Mushroom-Olive Frittata, 16
    Pasta with Swiss Chard, 146
    Summer Squash and Chard Gratin, 301
Syrup, Apricot-Pear, 29

T

Tabbouleh, Navy Bean, 209
Tabbouleh with Edamame and Feta, 346
Tacos
    Asparagus Corn Tacos, 250
    Bulgur Tacos, 356
    Meatless Citrus-Corn Tacos, 354
    Meatless Tacos, 356
    Mexican Burritos or Tacos, 47
    Vegetable Tacos, 356
Taco-Style Black Beans and Hominy, 47
Tahini Burgers with Honey Wasabi
    Coleslaw, 236
Tahini Miso Soup, 379
Tandoori-Style Grilled Patties, 237
Tempeh
    Asian Cobb-Style Salad, 208
    Barbecue Tempeh Wraps, 179, 274
    Grilled Marinated Tempeh, 259
    guide to, 10
    Hoisin Tempeh with Stir-Fry
      Vegetables, 349
    Southwestern Rice and Bean Salad
      with Tempeh, 219
    Vegetarian Feijoada Brazilian Rice and
      Black Beans, 45
Tex-Mex Beans with Cornmeal
    Dumplings, 337
Tex-Mex Bean Tostadas, 323
Thai Bulgur Salad, 221
Thai Peanut Dressing, 221
Thai-Style Vegetable Rice, 64
Thai-Style Veggie Pizza, 168
Thin Pizza Crust, 176
Three-Bean Enchiladas, 272
Three-Bean Tamale Pie, 269
Tofu
    Asian Tofu Salad, 207
    Baked Stuffed Shells, 305
    Bean-Tofu Burritos, 352
    Breakfast Pita Pizza, 28
    Bulgur Tacos, 356
    Caribbean Tofu Skewers, 256
    Cheesy Multigrain Spaghetti with
      Tofu, 71
    Grilled Tofu Curry, 257, 279
    guide to, 10
    Hot and Sour Soup, 378
    Marinated Tofu with Edamame Stir-
      Fry, 353
    Meatless Tacos, 356
    Mexican Tofu, 258

Mushroom, Asparagus, and Tofu Quiches, 19, 132
Noodle Big Bowls with Spinach and Tofu, 105
Poblano-Tofu Scramble, 27
Roasted Tofu and Veggie Pockets, 181
Sesame-Orange Tofu, 355
Tahini Miso Soup, 379
Tofu Manicotti, 281, 306
Udon with Tofu, 148
Vegetable Tacos, 356
Tomatoes
  Basil-Tomato Layered Salad, 206
  Bruschetta Burgers, 90
  Camembert Pizzas with Focaccia Crusts, 173, 274
  Caprese Salad Sandwiches, 193
  Cheesy Multigrain Spaghetti with Tofu, 71
  Dried Tomato Casserole, 318
  Eggplant and Caper Tomato Sauce, 151
  ELT (Egg, Lettuce, and Tomato) Sandwiches, 195
  Fresh Tomato Pizzas with Three Cheeses, 166
  Fried Green Tomato Salad, 202, 279
  Garlic-Artichoke Pasta, 68
  Greek Pasta Salad, 222
  Grilled Vegetable Pizzas, 167
  Homemade Hearty Tomato Soup, 375
  Huevos Rancheros, 22
  Israeli Couscous Salad with Tomato and Arugula, 217, 276
  Linguine in Fresh Tomato Sauce with Garlic-Basil Toast, 121
  Panini without the Press, 186
  Pasta with Green Beans and Dried Tomatoes, 117
  Pasta with Lentil Sauce, 70, 135
  Roasted Tomato and Cannellini Bean Panzanella, 210
  Spaghetti Squash with Chunky Tomato Sauce, 363
  Spaghetti with Fresh Marinara, 112
  Spaghetti with Roasted Tomatoes and Pine Nuts, 152
  Spaghetti with Two-Tomato Toss, 114
  Summer Fresh Quesadillas, 83
  Summer Tomato Stack, 198
  Tomato, Spinach, and Feta Strata, 21
  Tomato and Cheese Ravioli, 109

Tomato-Barley Soup with Garden Vegetables, 373
Tomato-Basil Panini, 185
Tomato-Basil Soup, 374
Tomato-Broccoli Frittata, 15
Tomato-Edamame Grilled Cheese, 191
Tomato-Olive Bread Pudding, 282, 302
Tricolor Tomato Ravioli, 119
Vegetarian Gumbo, 50
White Beans with Dried Tomatoes, 50
Tortellini
  Spinach Tortellini with Beans and Feta, 96, 140
  Tortellini Alfredo with Roasted Peppers, 97
  Tortellini and Peas, 95
  Tortellini-Vegetable Bake, 308
Tortillas. See also Burritos; Enchiladas; Tacos; Wraps
  Black Bean and Corn Chimichangas, 328
  Black Bean and Corn Quesadillas, 82, 137
  Black Bean Tostadas, 331
  Chilaquile Casserole, 294
  Huevos Rancheros, 22
  Huevos Rancheros Breakfast Nachos, 23
  Lasagna Ole, 291
  Layered Southwestern Salad with Tortilla Strips, 204
  Lentil and Veggie Tostadas, 348
  Mushroom-Vegetable Fajitas, 252, 281
  Salsa, Bean, and Cheese Pizza, 172
  Spicy Bean Tostadas, 82
  Spinach-Mushroom Quesadillas, 183, 273
  Summer Fresh Quesadillas, 83
  Taco-Style Black Beans and Hominy, 47
  Tex-Mex Bean Tostadas, 323
  Tortilla and Black Bean Bake, 271
  Tortilla Lasagna, 79
  Tortillas Filled with Mushrooms, Spinach, and Fresh Mozzarella, 37
  Triple Pepper Nachos, 285, 327
  Veggie Fajitas with Guacamole, 253
Tostadas
  Black Bean Tostadas, 331
  Lentil and Veggie Tostadas, 348
  Spicy Bean Tostadas, 82
  Tex-Mex Bean Tostadas, 323
Tricolor Tomato Ravioli, 119
Triple Pepper Nachos, 285, 327

Tuscan Bean Soup, 398
Two-Cheese Macaroni Bake, 101

U
Udon with Tofu, 148
Ultra Ketchup Topper, 92

V
Vegetables. See also specific vegetables
  American Chopped Salad, 200
  Cashew-Vegetable Stir-Fry, 75
  Chilly Veggie Pizza, 302
  Corn Stock, 370
  Egg and Vegetable Salad Wraps, 177
  Fresh-Herb Pasta Primavera, 145
  Gardener's Pie, 87
  Garden Sliders, 334
  Garden-Special Primavera, 128
  Garden Vegetables Lasagna, 159
  Grilled Veggie-Cheese Sandwiches, 188, 275
  Herbed Root Vegetable Cobbler, 284, 297
  Hoisin Tempeh with Stir-Fry Vegetables, 349
  Hot Tossed Vegetable Ravioli, 110
  Lentil and Veggie Shepherd's Pie, 265
  Lentil and Veggie Tostadas, 348
  Potato-Crusted Veggie Pie, 264
  Risotto with Beans and Vegetables, 333
  Roasted Root Vegetable Soup, 390
  Roasted Vegetables with Polenta, 88
  Sesame-Orange Tofu, 355
  Spicy Vegetable Fried Rice, 364
  Vegetable Bowls with Spiced Yogurt-Lime Dressing, 330
  Vegetable Broth, 370
  Vegetable Casserole, 51
  Vegetable Curry, 75
  Vegetable Flatbreads with Goat Cheese, 174
  Vegetable Lasagna, 158
  Vegetable Pastitsio, 315
  Vegetable Primavera Casserole, 310
  Vegetable Risotto, 358
  Vegetable Soup with Cornmeal Croutons, 372
  Vegetable Tacos, 356
  Vegetable Two-Grain Casserole, 267
  Veggie Salad in a Pocket, 182
  Veggie-Stuffed Pasta Shells, 150
  Veggie-Stuffed Portobello Mushrooms, 361

415

Vegetarian diet
  easing into meatless diet, 4
  health benefits, 4
  healthy diet choices, 6
  ideas for flavorful meals, 4
  nutritional considerations, 5
  protein sources, 5, 6
  types of vegetarians, 6
Vegetarian Feijoada Brazilian Rice and
    Black Beans, 45
Vegetarian Gumbo, 50
Veggie Fajitas with Guacamole, 253
Veggie Risotto Cakes with Horseradish
    Sour Cream, 359
Veggie Salad in a Pocket, 182
Veggie-Spinach Burgers, 240
Veggie-Stuffed Pasta Shells, 150
Veggie-Stuffed Portobello Mushrooms,
    361

W

Walnuts
  Butternut Squash Phyllo Strudel, 85,
    137
  Camembert Pizzas with Focaccia
    Crusts, 173, 274
  Cheese 'n' Nut Stuffed Shells, 304
  Cracked Wheat Burgers with Pickled
    Onions and Lime Slather, 238
  Israeli Couscous Salad with Tomato
    and Arugula, 217, 276
  Nutty Gorgonzola Roll-Ups, 303
  Pear and Walnut Salad, 230
  Penne with Walnuts and Peppers,
    116
Wheat berries
  about, 7
  Corn and Grain Gratin, 61
  Multigrain Pilaf, 67, 134
  Slow Cooker Risotto, 66, 133
  Wheat Berry Salad, 220
  Wheat Berry Salad with Dried
    Apricots, 344

White beans
  Bean-Potato Chowder, 392
  Cannellini Bean Burgers, 274, 335
  cooking instructions, 9
  Garden Sliders, 334
  Greek Pasta Casserole, 318
  Mediterranean Beans and Greens
    Salad, 213
  Navy Bean Tabbouleh, 209
  Pesto Beans and Pasta, 69
  Portobello Wrap with White Bean-
    Chile Spread, 249
  Ravioli Skillet, 108
  Risotto with Beans and Vegetables,
    333
  Roasted Tomato and Cannellini Bean
    Panzanella, 210
  Rotini-Bean Bake, 311
  Sage-White Bean Soup, 287, 400
  Savory Bean and Kale Soup, 56
  Spaghetti with Roasted Tomatoes and
    Pine Nuts, 152
  Spicy Navy Bean Hummus, 182
  Spinach Tortellini with Beans and Feta,
    96, 140
  Three-Bean Enchiladas, 272
  Tuscan Bean Soup, 398
  Vegetable Casserole, 51
  Vegetable Soup with Cornmeal
    Croutons, 372
  White Bean and Goat Cheese Wraps,
    180
  White Beans with Dried Tomatoes, 50
  Winter Garden Pasta, 115
Whole Grain Pizza Crust, 176
Wild rice
  about, 7
  Multigrain Pilaf, 67, 134
  Wild Rice-Mushroom Soup, 288, 387
  Wild Rice Salad with Orange and
    Fennel, 224, 279
Winter Garden Pasta, 115
Wonton Soup, 288, 380

Wraps
  All-Wrapped-Up Salad, 87, 137
  Barbecue Tempeh Wraps, 179, 274
  Black Bean and Mango Wraps, 248
  Egg and Vegetable Salad Wraps, 177
  Portobello Wrap with White Bean-
    Chile Spread, 249
  Soy Bacon and Pesto Wraps, 178
  White Bean and Goat Cheese Wraps, 180

Y

You Choose Veggie Burgers, 92, 138

Z

Zesty Vegetable Enchiladas, 284, 289
Zucchini
  Avocado Veggie Sandwiches, 190
  Cheddar and Zucchini Frittata, 12
  Corn-Chile Chowder, 385
  Garden Vegetables Lasagna, 159
  Greek Beans and Barley, 44
  Grilled Vegetable Burritos, 251
  Grilled Veg Sandwiches, 244, 281
  Marinated Eggplant Kabobs, 254, 280
  Mile-High Meatless Lasagna Pie, 154
  Panini without the Press, 186
  Pita, Cheese, and Veggie Grill, 246
  Potato, Zucchini, and Carrot Pancakes,
    366
  Ravioli Skillet, 108
  Roasted Tofu and Veggie Pockets, 181
  Roasted Veggie Sandwiches, 190
  Stuffed Zucchini with Black Beans,
    Corn, and Poblano Pepper, 365
  Tomato-Barley Soup with Garden
    Vegetables, 373
  Vegetable Lasagna, 158
  Veggie-Stuffed Pasta Shells, 150
  Zesty Vegetable Enchiladas, 284, 289
  Zucchini and Eggplant Bake, 299
  Zucchini Cakes with Mushroom
    Ragout, 367
  Zucchini-Carrot Burgers, 368